God's Forever Family

God's Forever Family

The Jesus People Movement in America

LARRY ESKRIDGE

OXFORD
UNIVERSITY PRESS

OXFORD
UNIVERSITY PRESS

Oxford University Press is a department of the University of Oxford. It furthers
the University's objective of excellence in research, scholarship, and education
by publishing worldwide. Oxford is a registered trade mark of Oxford University
Press in the UK and certain other countries.

Published in the United States of America by Oxford University Press
198 Madison Avenue, New York, NY 10016, United States of America.

© Oxford University Press 2013

First issued as an Oxford University Press paperback, 2018

Library of Congress Cataloging-in-Publication Data
Eskridge, Larry, 1954–
God's forever family : the Jesus people movement in America / Larry Eskridge.
pages cm
ISBN 978–0–19–532645–1 (cloth : alk. paper); 978–0–19–088135–1 (paper : alk. paper)
1. Jesus People—United States.   2. United States—Church history—20th century.   I. Title.
BV3773.E85 2013
277.3'082—dc23
2012043309

For Dave Eddy

Contents

Acknowledgments

TRYING TO DOCUMENT and interpret a sprawling, grassroots religious movement while trying to hold a day job is not recommended as a route to a serene and well-ordered life. But thankfully there have been any number of people whose knowledge, advice, criticism, competence, wisdom, friendship, and sense of humor have made the journey possible, and enjoyable.

Many thanks to Cynthia Read, executive editor at Oxford University Press, for her help—and patience—with this project. Andrew Attaway's editorial talents and eye for strategic chopping and pruning were key in the late stages of the project. Lisbeth Redfield and Marcela Maxfield were both kind and helpful in the process of bringing the manuscript and assorted details in order along the way. Sravanthi Sridharan and Anthony Alexander capably shepherded the final preparations on the manuscript.

I noted that I have been holding down an actual job while researching and writing this book. That position with the Institute for the Study of American Evangelicals (ISAE) at Wheaton College has been a blessing in every conceivable way. I extend thanks to the people at Wheaton College and especially my ISAE colleagues. Special nods go to student workers like Mary Noll Venables, Blake Killingsworth, Zack Thompson, Noah Blan, Amber Thomas, and Eric Brandt, who were a joy to be around and helped out with an occasional Jesus People–related chore. ISAE assistants Carmin Ballou, Jennifer House Farmer, and Katri Brewer Delac were coworkers and friends and lent a hand with computer issues and compiling lists. Director Edith Blumhofer and Institute cofounder and longtime advisor Mark Noll—besides being excellent scholars—proved themselves even better colleagues and friends.

The genesis of this book came more years ago than I care to admit as the result of my participation in George Marsden's Notre Dame graduate seminar on Fundamentalism and Evangelicalism. There, under George's learned eye (and with his hospitality and that of his wife, Lucie, whose fantastic dinners took the sting out of my weekly 250-mile round-trip between Wheaton and South Bend), I put together my first foray into the world of the Jesus People, an examination of Billy Graham's relationship to the Jesus generation. Eventually, I ended up working with David Bebbington as a doctoral student in history at the University of Stirling in Scotland. David's cool, Cambridge-trained, British academic's approach was the perfect counterpoint to my flighty, pop-culture-attuned, American ways. I always appreciated not only his knowledge and genuine interest in my progress but also his friendship and the hospitality he and his wife, Eileen, manifested on my several sojourns in Stirling.

Of course, the assistance of staff at various libraries and archives was essential. The research librarians at the University of California at Irvine, the University of Washington, Judson College (in Elgin, Illinois), and Regent University in Virginia Beach were a big help, particularly in the latter two cases, where my use of ancient technology (turntables and reel-to-reel tape players!) complicated research. Thanks also to Paula Marolis and Dori Ryen at the Campus Crusade for Christ Archives in Orlando and the secretaries at the *Jesus* film offices then located in San Clemente, California, for their assistance. Nancy Gower from the Archives at the Hubbard Library at Fuller Theological Seminary was a big help in chasing down files and photographs, both when I was there and at a distance. Particular thanks, however, are reserved for resource people at Wheaton College, such as Ferne Weimer, the former head of the Billy Graham Center Library (thanks for the study room!), and the immensely knowledgeable staff at the Billy Graham Center Archives who have helped me over the years, including Paul Ericksen, the late Jan Nasgowitz, Bob Shuster, and Wayne Weber.

In doing the outside-the-library spadework, I am indebted to any number of people who lent, copied, provided access to, or outright gave me Jesus People materials that they had in their personal possession. Many thanks, therefore, to Achim Bühl, Dave Bunker, Janet Cameron, David Di Sabatino, Ron Enroth, Chuck Fromm, Eric Haley, Mark Hollingsworth, David Hoyt, Mike Johnson, Karl Kahler, Bill Lowery, Lowell Lytle, John and Mary Ann MacDonald, Phil Mahlow, Duane Pederson, Eric Pement, Kent Philpott, Joan Pritchard, Ron Rendleman, Charlie Rizzo, Rick Sacks, Tim Smith, Hugh Steven, Bob Sperlazzo, and Gary Sweeten. It is no exaggeration to say that without their help, *God's Forever Family* would never have seen the light of day.

While finding material is one thing, making sense of it, once found, is quite another. I've been enriched by interaction—formal and informal—with a number of people who not only graciously listened to me babble about the Jesus People or read chapter drafts but also helped refine my thinking and sometimes backed me away from errors and wrongheaded assumptions. This numerous, mostly academic, subset includes John D'Elia, Darren Dochuk, Bruce Douville, Chuck

Fromm, Michael Hamilton, the late Sarah Hammond, Barry Hankins, Mike Hertenstein, Mark Hutchinson, Rick Kennedy, Tommy Kidd, Tim Larsen, Kathryn Long, Jim Mathiesen, Brett McCracken, Timothy Miller, Colin Nicolson, the late Tim Phillips, Mark Rogers, William Romanowski, Preston Shires, David Stowe, Andy Tooley, and John Wigger. Thanks also to the University of Stirling's Emma MacLeod and John Wolffe from the Open University for their helpful comments and recommendations as members of my dissertation committee. Readers' reports of my dissertation by two anonymous scholars commissioned by Oxford University Press to evaluate it for possible publication were full of insight and pointed out several ways in which a potential book could be improved. I must particularly note hours of conversation with David Di Sabatino, whose near-encyclopedic command of the sources and knowledge of the Jesus movement rescued me from many an intractable dead end. The fact that we shared a goofy sense of humor made the chats a lot more fun. The feedback I received from these people was invaluable; naturally, any errors of omission or commission in the final product are mine, and mine alone.

I am also grateful to the more than 800 people who took the time to fill out the much too long online survey that David Di Sabatino and I cooked up. In retrospect, I am more than mildly surprised at the depth of the answers and the anecdotes so many people had the patience and goodwill to pass along. Special thanks to webmaster David Hollandsworth for making the whole thing a cyber reality.

It has also been a privilege to sit down and talk with dozens and dozens of members of the Jesus generation. With very few exceptions, they cheerfully responded to letters, e-mails, phone calls, and badgering about contacts and materials. Whether meeting face-to-face or simply over the telephone, I was inevitably treated with kindness and warmth as I took—what was, I'm afraid—advantage of their willingness to give hours of their time to remember those days decades ago and share their feelings and insights. I am especially appreciative of Steve and Sandi Heefner, John Higgins, David Hoyt, Bill Lowery, the late John MacDonald, Connie Bremer-Murray, the late Jim Palosaari, Fr. Duane Pederson, Kent Philpott, Ron Rendleman, the late Martin "Moishe" Rosen, Rick and Megan Sacks, and Ted and Elizabeth Wise. I know that there are a dozen histories of groups and segments within the Jesus movement that need to be written and that there will be points of my interpretation and analysis with which my interviewees might disagree, but at bottom, I hope they can see that I tried to get their story right. Finally, I am thankful for those friends and family who worked at keeping my head on straight. The folks at Pleasant Hill Community Church helped me along the pilgrim way, even while helping me keep my hand to this particular plow by routinely asking, "How's that book coming along?" Thanks to the extended Eskridge and Thompson families for oceans of good times and warm memories. My son Ian, daughter-in-law Janelle, and young grandson, Colt, have been a source of great joy for "Paw." Sons Zack and Matt have literally grown up during the period when this book was in the making and made every minute better along the way.

Finally, none of this would have happened without the support, help, and love of my best friend, Joni. Wife, mother, big-time IT specialist, singer, skilled amateur photographer, and Ol'-Mose-the-coonhound-walker, you are the glue that has kept everything together. I hit the marriage lottery in winning thy lovely hand: Thank you for everything.

God's Forever Family

Introduction

Remembering the Jesus Generation

BY THE SUMMER OF 1971, a battered American public had been through the social, cultural, and political wringer, enduring a series of revolutions in the space of a few short years. There had been the civil rights revolution, complete with racist resistance and frustration-driven urban riots across the country; dark murmurings of political revolution as anarchy reigned on the nation's college campuses over the Vietnam War and the draft; the advent of the Pill and the sexual revolution; the spread of LSD and the psychedelic revolution; and the countercultural flower power of the hippie revolution. To make matters worse, all of these seismic changes had directly involved the attitudes, concerns, and evolution of America's huge, up-and-coming Baby Boomer generation. As the June 21 issue of *Time* hit the nation's newsstands, the readers of the country's premier weekly newsmagazine might have been forgiven had they not wanted to hear tell of yet another revolution—particularly one involving the nation's youth.

But the revolution the June 21 issue touted bespoke anything but the rejection of old-fashioned values and morality that so many Americans feared. On the cover of the magazine was the familiar, deep-eyed visage of Jesus Christ—albeit drawn psychedelic-style and in Day-Glo colors. The hippiefied cover portrait highlighted the issue's lead story on what the banner headline proclaimed "The Jesus Revolution," a remarkable upsurge in a traditional, evangelical Christianity with a hippie twist that was increasingly making itself visible across the country.

"Fresh-faced, wide-eyed young girls and earnest young men," the *Time* reporters gushed, "badger businessmen and shoppers on Hollywood Boulevard, near the Lincoln Memorial, in Dallas, in Detroit and in Wichita, 'witnessing' for Christ with breathless exhortations. Christian coffeehouses have opened in many cities...a strip joint has been converted to a 'Christian nightclub' in San Antonio. Communal 'Christian houses' are multiplying like loaves and fishes...Bibles abound." Color photos of beach baptisms in California; hippies in hands-raised Pentecostal bliss; gum-smacking, bubble-blowing worshippers at a New Jersey "Jesus Rally"; a circle of praying athletes in the middle of a football field; and a band of happy commune dwellers in upstate New York accompanied the eight-page story. But to these seasoned reporters used to covering the plethora of new social and cultural trends and movements that the previous decade had unleashed on American society, this "Jesus Revolution" was different than anything they had encountered. "There is an uncommon morning freshness to this movement, a buoyant atmosphere of hope and love along with the usual rebel zeal," commented the writers; "...their love seems more sincere than a slogan, deeper than the fast-fading sentiments of the flower children: what startles the outsider is the extraordinary sense of joy that they are able to communicate." The writers were taken aback at the Jesus People's "total belief in an awesome, supernatural Jesus Christ, not just a marvelous man who lived 2,000 years ago but a living God who is both Saviour and Judge....Their lives revolve around the necessity for an intense personal relationship with that Jesus and...[they] act as if divine intervention guides their every movement and can be counted on to solve every problem."[1]

Of course, by the time a public figure, celebrity, trend, or movement reached the cover of a magazine like *Time*, it was almost always near the peak of its stature or cultural vitality. In the case of the Jesus People, *Time* was certifying the status of a religious movement that had already attracted considerable attention in the religious and secular media. Eventually, the movement would be tabbed as one of the top ten news stories of 1971.[2]

The Jesus movement blossomed from seemingly insignificant beginnings, its first embryonic embodiment in San Francisco's Haight-Ashbury during 1967's famed Summer of Love. While the Bay Area was the movement's first identifiable Jesus People outpost, similar manifestations of a hippieized Christianity popped up in the next two years—in Oregon, Seattle, Spokane, Fort Lauderdale, Detroit, Milwaukee, upstate New York, seemingly anywhere that the counterculture and evangelical Christianity might rub shoulders.

But it was in sunny Southern California that the interaction between these apparently polar opposite cultural entities really took off beginning in 1968, as evangelical pastors and youth workers like Arthur Blessitt at His Place on Sunset Strip, David Berg's Lighthouse Club in Huntington Beach, Don Williams and his Hollywood Presbyterian Church–sponsored Salt Company coffeehouse, Tony and Susan Alamo's Alamo Foundation in Los Angeles, and, especially, Chuck Smith's "Little Country Church"—Calvary Chapel—in suburban Costa Mesa began to reach hundreds and then thousands of Los Angeles area youth.

By mid-1969, a full-blown Jesus People scene had taken root in the region running roughly from Santa Barbara down to San Diego and from Long Beach out to Riverside and San Bernardino. Communal Jesus Houses with names like 1st Corinthians House and Mansion Messiah housed converts from the drug culture, and scores of coffeehouses such as the Fire Escape in Stanton and the Lost Coin in San Diego hosted Bible studies and guitar-strumming Christian singers. A bevy of new Jesus music bands with names like Agape, Mustard Seed Faith, and the J.C. Power Outlet set up shop in parks, gymnasiums, and churches to seek out the lost and encourage the faithful. "Underground" Jesus papers like Duane Pederson's *Hollywood Free Paper* served as evangelistic tracts and foldable, portable bulletin boards for various Jesus People hangouts and events. Promoting their causes, opinions, and enthusiasms much like their secular peers in the counterculture and New Left—but with a supercharged gospel-fueled intensity—the Jesus People produced posters, bumper stickers, buttons, and jewelry to announce their presence.

The presence of this new Jesus People scene in densely populated and culturally influential Southern California served to galvanize, connect, and promote the nascent Jesus movement. By late 1970, Jesus freaks were in evidence in Ontario and Texas and in such unhip places as Boise, Idaho, and Waterloo, Iowa. Jesus was beginning to pop up at every turn in youth culture, as attested by a sudden upsurge in religiously tinged pop music and the controversial release of the rock opera *Jesus Christ Superstar*. So when Billy Graham encountered hundreds of "One Way"-signifying (a raised index finger pointing heavenward) Jesus People at the Rose Bowl Parade on New Year's Day 1971 and talked to reporters about it afterward, the nation's press was ready to take the story and run with it.

Over the next several months, stories on the Jesus People appeared in *Life* magazine and the *Wall Street Journal*, in the nation's newspapers and in local newscasts. Religious leaders, celebrities, and politicians shared their overwhelmingly favorable opinions on the movement.

By mid-June 1971, as *Time*'s cover story attested the movement's arrival, journalists, pastors, and actual participants in the movement were in the midst of a mad rush to get books into print to capitalize on the Jesus People's sudden celebrity. By the end of 1972, nearly fifty books had been published on, about, by, or somehow connected to the Jesus People.[3] To salve the curiosity of academic-minded observers of the American religious and cultural scene, a few scholars—mostly social scientists—tried their hand at describing and understanding the nascent Jesus movement.[4] But the most books were written by evangelical observers who were not only interested in reporting on the Jesus movement but also eager to promote the Jesus People as evidence of a generational movement to Christ, if not as the portent of a sweeping national revival. Here again Billy Graham proved most influential. In his best-selling book *The Jesus Generation*, Graham wrote that he was "convinced that the 'Jesus revolution'" was making a "profound impact on the youth of America" and that he even saw signs of its "spreading to other countries." Although he felt that it represented "a minority" of American young people, he was persuaded that it was "growing rapidly." Indeed, he felt "it may be the answer to the prayers of millions of Christians who have been praying for spiritual awakening."[5] But Graham seemed reticent when compared with others' enthusiasm for what was happening. Two excited Southern Baptist observers provided a typically excited assessment of the movement:

> The movement—for lack of a better word—is raging across the nation like a wind-driven brush fire, jumping any obstacle to break out—almost by spontaneous combustion—in dozens of places, in dozens of forms....This is revival spirit unprogrammed, with no mission board strategies, no super-evangelists at the head.[6]

However, by the latter part of 1972, it is safe to say that very few people outside the bounds of the movement itself—or the larger realm of evangelicalism—were paying much attention to the Jesus People. Curiosity and fashion are fickle things, and by the fall of 1972, it was apparent that the public's curiosity had been sated; stories about the Jesus movement had dwindled significantly. There had been a brief and notable upsurge in late June during Campus Crusade for Christ's "EXPLO '72" conference in Dallas, which attracted 85,000 young people for a week of seminars, rallies, and evangelizing and a crowd of nearly 200,000 for a daylong, conference-closing "Jesus Music Festival." "Godstock," as the press dubbed it, once again landed the Jesus People on the front page and gave them a slot on the evening news. But after the well-behaved, Jesus-cheering young people cleared out of Dallas, it was apparent that the media considered the Jesus Freaks to be yesterday's news. Except for a tiny trickle of stories in evangelical magazines and a few late-to-the-market (mostly academic) books, the buzz over the Jesus People dried up during late 1972 and early 1973. By the fall of 1973, the evangelical monthly *Eternity* printed an article by Ronald Enroth that told the magazine's readers that, despite the lack of media coverage, the Jesus People were, actually, still around and thriving.[7]

The Jesus People, in fact, did soldier on long after the media and academic spotlight had turned elsewhere. Indeed, the vast burst of publicity in 1971 had helped spread the movement across the country. Independent of the organized church, thousands of young people formed communes, fellowships, and coffeehouses; created their own Jesus Rock bands; and printed their own street papers to hand out on evangelistic forays. And the pastors and youth workers, whom sociologist Robert Ellwood described as leaping "with alacrity" in their desire to reap a harvest of young souls by adapting the music, terminology, jargon, and accoutrements of the Jesus People, spread the movement into every nook and cranny of the United States.[8]

Eventually, however, the movement did peter out. By the late 1970s, many of its older, longtime members had moved on to school, marriage, jobs, families, and local church life. New musical styles and youth cultures arose that rejected the countercultural model from which the Jesus People emerged, and the movement—almost without exception—withered away. I witnessed much of this rise and fall firsthand as a high school senior and young adult living in the far northwest suburbs of Chicago in the 1970s. I—along with many of my peers—was influenced by the Jesus movement. My coming of age included attending Jesus rallies and concerts, going to coffeehouses, reading Jesus papers from across the United States, and flashing the One Way symbol at passing cars bedecked with Jesus stickers. At one point, I was even a twenty-one-year-old elder at a coffeehouse in my hometown of Round Lake, Illinois.

As the movement faded away in the late 1970s, I, along with my old Jesus People friends, moved on with our lives, with most being absorbed into the larger evangelical subculture, which by that time increasingly impinged on the national consciousness by dint of its massive media presence and its growing consternation over the nation's cultural and political drift. Eventually, I moved into the academic professions and in the late 1980s joined the staff of the Institute for the Study of American Evangelicals (ISAE) at Wheaton College—Billy Graham's alma mater—in Wheaton, Illinois. There, as I helped implement conferences and study projects, I was inevitably asked about possible research interests. When I mentioned—among several possibilities—a desire to revisit the impact of the Jesus People movement from a critical distance, I was usually met with a look of glazed indifference: "There wasn't really much there," commented one historian; "it was just an ephemeral moment—a fad, don't you think?"

I thought not. Looking back on all the articles and books about the Jesus People movement that I had seen in my high school days, the photos of hundreds of young people gathered on California beaches for mass baptism services, the TV specials on the J-E-S-U-S–cheering crowds at the Cotton Bowl at EXPLO '72, and the extensive network of Jesus People groups, churches, coffeehouses, newspapers, and traveling Jesus Music artists in the Midwest in the early and mid-1970s, I believed that a significant religious movement had occurred. To my mind, the germ of the historical question had been set: what to make of this collision between old-time evangelical religion and 1960s American counterculture? Did the fact that it lasted as a coherent movement for only about a decade mean that the Jesus People were not much more than a faddish, ephemeral blip on the American religious landscape? Or was it representative of larger changes in American culture and religion that exerted a genuine, lasting influence on the shape of American evangelicalism?

All too often, we are tempted to dismiss or look down on the religious enthusiasms of youth culture as little more than a religious equivalent of the hula hoop or bellbottom pants.[9] I suspect that the "youth factor" may be a key ingredient in why the Jesus People were so quickly forgotten. University of Massachusetts literature professor Nick Bromell, in a thoughtful book on the formative nature of 1960s rock culture, *Tomorrow Never Knows: Rock and Psychedelics in the 1960s*, perceives the problems with this mind-set toward youthful enthusiasms in writing about the international uber-phenomenon that was Beatlemania:

> An extraordinary, indeed in the twentieth-century United States a singular phenomenon, it has never been taken seriously by historians of the '60s or of rock 'n' roll. The tendency has always been to be embarrassed by Beatlemania. Documentaries consistently present this moment in the Beatles' career with an awe that is also a sneer. While marveling that the four moptops could exert such orphic force, they pointedly condescend to the young teenagers, almost all of them girls, who pursued and panted, screamed and wept and fainted whenever the Beatles came within reach.[10]

Bromell notes, however, that to overlook Beatlemania is to absolutely miss what was going on during this period. "Those who were young at the time," he writes, "will remember that Beatlemania was an essential precondition of the Beatles phenomenon" and all that followed. It was, he admits, "a ridiculous spectacle," yet a force that existed despite "what other people thought" and—importantly—had "power to convert others to the Beatles cult." Moreover, Bromell argues that the teenage girls of 1963–1964 "created Beatlemania...Beatlemania was a creation, not a Pavlovian reaction...they seized and made a world, taking power and space away from the control of adults." Ultimately, he contends, it was those selfsame teenagers, "surrendered absolutely to their passions," who were the driving force that "demolished so much of the rigid, sexless self-control" that typified 1950s American society.[11]

Similarly, for those interested in the dynamics of American religion, the recent and contemporary trajectory of the larger evangelical movement, and the overarching evolution of American culture, to overlook the ecstatic religious fervor and bold, evangelistic enthusiasm of the Jesus People would be to miss a major part of the American evangelical Zeitgeist of the period between 1966 and 1976.

It is well past time for a reexamination of the Jesus movement's genesis, development, and lasting impact. Nearly all of the popular and scholarly examinations of the movement were written amid the publicity boom that surrounded the Jesus People during 1971 and 1972, and much of it was centered on the movement in California. To bring to light the postpublicity and non-Californian aspect of the movement, this book grapples with four major sources that have been largely untapped to this point: the prolific written sources produced by the Jesus People in the years following 1971, including the dozens of Jesus People street papers from all across the country; the contemporary coverage of the movement and perceptions of its larger cultural (and pop culture) impact; retrospective interviews with a number of figures associated with the movement—including many from outside California—who provide insight into the long-term spread, development, and disappearance of the Jesus People;[12] and the written responses to a survey of participants in the movement put together by Jesus People historian and film documentarian David Di Sabatino and myself, hosted on the Internet from late 1997 to April 2004. I compiled the results and pulled them together in 2004 (see Appendix) for my doctoral dissertation, which constitutes the roots of this book. The survey was hardly scientific in its methodology, but it did pull in responses from more than 800 individuals. It is, to date, the largest attempt to gauge the scope, nature, involvement, and memories of the Jesus freaks themselves in this far-flung, decentralized, nationwide movement.

This study argues that the Jesus People movement is one of the most significant American religious phenomena of the postwar period. Much ink has been expended, both journalistically and academically, observing and explaining the dramatic resurgence and activism of evangelical Christians in the United States since the 1970s. However, there has been little attempt to explain the important role the Jesus People played in this evangelical renaissance. This book contends that we cannot begin to understand the resurgence of evangelicalism during the late twentieth and early twenty-first centuries without taking into account the crucial way in which the Jesus People movement shaped the development and direction of the larger American evangelical subculture.

The Jesus People movement was the culmination of a trend that had begun as far back as the 1920s and 1930s and produced the Youth for Christ movement during World War II. The desire to incorporate the countercultural Jesus People themselves and the acceptance (often grudging) of their taste for hippie fashions, music, and ambience sent the message that it was all right for evangelical kids to occupy their own cultural space distinct from that of their older evangelical brethren. In fact, the Jesus People movement marked the first time that American evangelical youth received a go-ahead to replicate the larger youth culture, albeit with proper evangelical respect for moral probity. This strategy of accommodation has since become a part of the evangelical landscape both in the United States and, increasingly, in other areas of the globe where American evangelical styles are influential.

Closely related to the matter of youth culture was the manner in which the Jesus People impacted the evangelical relationship to popular culture as a whole. The enthusiasm they showed for buttons, bumper stickers, Bible covers,

posters, crosses, and other "Jesus Junque" was but one aspect of the Jesus
People's friendliness toward popular culture. Part and parcel of the Baby Boom
television-immersed generation, the Jesus People moved and breathed within the
surrounding culture like fish in water. As a matter of course, they incorporated
their pop culture sensibilities into their religious lives, in the process constituting
the leading edge of what has proven to be a mortal blow to traditional evangelical
abstention from "worldly entertainments."

This pop culture–friendly aspect of the Jesus People movement had
tremendous implications for the role of music within the evangelical subculture.
First, the Jesus People's enthusiasm for pop and rock music-based idioms brought
forth Jesus Rock and, in so doing, marked the beginnings of what would eventually become the Contemporary Christian Music (CCM) industry, which has
become a major component of American evangelicalism's mass media and bookstore infrastructure, as well as a significant aspect of everyday life and devotion,
spawning radio station formats, summer festivals, Web sites, and the like.

But the emergence of CCM is just part of the larger musical impact of the
Jesus People movement. The Jesus People's taste for simple, folk-based melodies
and scriptural passages in their corporate worship has had a profound impact on
the worship of American evangelical congregations. The minstrels of the Jesus
People movement were major architects of what has become known as praise
and worship music. The object of scorn for many traditionalists and church
music professionals, the popularity of this music has, in turn, became the focus
of the infamous "worship wars," which have embroiled thousands of American
Protestant congregations since the 1980s.[13]

The rise of these new styles of evangelical music, easily accessible to anyone familiar with the larger popular culture, bespeaks another way in which
the Jesus People movement has impacted American evangelicalism: the rise
of the seeker-sensitive megachurch. Two of the prototypes for the megachurch
model—the original Calvary Chapel in Costa Mesa, California, and Willow
Creek Community Church in South Barrington, Illinois—both trace their roots
(albeit very differently) to the days of the Jesus People movement. Both have
become influential models and planters of similarly styled churches. The casual,
come-as-you-are informality and attachment to up-tempo contemporary music
and pop culture that are the staple of this dynamic new ecclesiastical form flow
directly from the Jesus People movement.

Yet the largest impact of the Jesus Revolution was greater than the sum of its parts.
Tens of thousands of youth from outside evangelical ranks found the Jesus movement to be a congenial entry point into the larger American evangelical subculture.
More important, millions of evangelical youth were able to negotiate a truce between
the demands of their own religious heritage and the allure of secular youth culture.

Indeed, the much-discussed resurgence of evangelicalism that became apparent by the 1980s probably could not have occurred, had the movement not taken place.

In his epic *A Religious History of the American People*—published during the very height of the Jesus Movement in 1972—historian Sydney Ahlstrom diligently tucked the Jesus People into a long, last-minute, discursive footnote near the end of the book in a chapter titled "The Turbulent Sixties." Amid his recounting of the sensationalism, radicalism, and strife of that period, he cast the Jesus People as something of a breath of youthful fresh air for both those in their generation and their older contemporaries in evangelical churches. But Ahlstrom, seasoned historian that he was, knew that it was folly to attempt to forecast their ultimate historical impact:

> ...their long-term significance cannot be known. Whether they should be considered in a footnote (as here) is a question which only the future will answer. To grim, tormented times they brought the blessings of joy and love; but there is no apparent reason for seeing them as an exception to the larger generalizations attempted in this chapter. Yet surprises are the stuff of history.[14]

The purpose of this book is to show that the Jesus People—strangely forgotten in public memory and neglected and largely dismissed by scholars of recent American culture and religion—did indeed turn out to be one of those fascinating surprises that are the stuff of history.

I

"Jesus Knocked Me off My Metaphysical Ass"

THE FIRST "JESUS FREAKS" IN SAN FRANCISCO

IN EARLY JULY 1961, more than 10,000 evangelical teenagers and several hundred adult workers from across the United States and Canada descended on the old Billy Sunday campgrounds in Winona Lake, Indiana, for Youth for Christ's (YFC) seventeenth annual convention. For two weeks, the delegates maintained a hectic regimen of early morning devotions ("quiet time"), swimming, Bible studies, baseball, prayer meetings, and barbecues in the heat and humidity of the Midwestern summer. In the evenings, the campers assembled to hear various youth evangelists, take in YFC's talent contests, and cheer on the finals of the YFC Bible Quiz, which pitted the very best teams from around North America in a furious competition combining Bible memorization and knowledge with game show theatrics. After the meeting, many of the kids headed over to the Eskimo Inn, the air-conditioned game room and soda shop, for ice cream and conversation or perhaps a game of Ping-Pong.[1]

Out of the thousands of gathered youth at Winona Lake that summer, if there was one teenager who was the star, it had to be TAMI. A slim, stylishly dressed, attractive blond with her hair in the de rigueur ponytail, TAMI's movements during the meeting were an event ready to happen. She made her grand entrance like a parade queen, perched on the back of a white convertible and greeted by a crowd of her peers. Later, she met YFC President Ted W. Engstrom in front of the assembled delegates and then had center stage all to herself as she shared her testimony of how she had come to follow Christ. TAMI, the daughter of another YFC executive was, of course, a living, walking YFC public relations campaign that borrowed from secular ad strategies and teen magazines' attempts to create an "everyteen" to hawk their wares. "Teens Are Most Important" (TAMI) was YFC's attempt to create a symbolic "every YFCer"—someone who "typifies everything a Christian teenager should be" for the 1960s, YFC's self-proclaimed "decade of destiny."[2]

In many ways, the idyllic, early-1960s, middle-class evangelical world of TAMI and the YFC convention mirrored culturewide perceptions of the state of American youth. Going into the 1960s, there was little indication of the cultural turmoil that would swarm around a sizable segment of the Baby Boom generation later in the decade. In fact, if the experts were to be believed, the rising generation of adults-to-be appeared to fit in quite nicely with their elders' values and expectations. That was certainly the thrust of a late-1961 survey of American youth by pollsters George Gallup and Evan Hill, published—appropriately enough—in the ultimate journalistic symbol of wholesome consensus, the *Saturday Evening Post*. Their research indicated that American teenagers were happy with their world, if not downright complacent. "The typical American youth shows few symptoms of frustration," they wrote, "and is most unlikely to rebel or involve himself in crusades of any kind."[3] In fact, the typical youth demonstrated "little spirit of adventure"; most simply wanted "a little ranch house, an inexpensive new car, a job with a large company, and a chance to watch TV each evening after the smiling children are asleep in bed."[4] What concerns there were, according to Gallup and Hill, centered on the Cold War and the effectiveness of educational and religious efforts. Even so, the pollsters concluded that American youth appeared very favorably inclined toward religion and tended toward the traditional at that: more than 75% firmly believed in God, and nearly two-thirds believed that the Bible was "completely true."[5]

Gallup and Hill's findings were very similar to those put forth in a 1962 article by Harvard sociologist Talcott Parsons. "The general orientation," he said of American teenagers, appeared to be "an eagerness...to accept higher orders of respectability" and a "readiness to work within the system."[6] Two years later, he found the situation to be much the same. Indeed, he believed that youth were generally becoming more conservative and, perhaps most important, seemed more amenable to adult control.[7] Parsons's sentiments were echoed in a statement by one university administrator who opined in the early 1960s that "employers will love this generation....They are going to be easy to handle."[8]

In retrospect, early '60s cultural observers like Parsons and the Gallup organization were just as wrong as that college administrator—Clark Kerr, chancellor and president of the University of California at Berkeley—in most of their observations about the direction of American youth. Fueled by an expanding roster of cultural, social, and political crises, a growing segment of young people began to express their dissatisfaction with the system and with American values. The resultant counterculture would shake the foundations of American life.

The counterculture had its origins in the antiestablishment, hedonistic attitudes of the '50s Beat movement. Fed up with what they perceived as the sterile conformity and consumerism of postwar middle-class life, a sizable number of American youth began to drop out of the rat race of school and career to seek fulfillment through personal and communal relationships, drugs, sex, music, and esoteric spirituality. With a history of bohemian and Beat-friendly neighborhoods, San Francisco, particularly its Haight-Ashbury district, became the first major out-post of this developing counterculture in late 1966 and during 1967's famous Summer of Love. Surprisingly, within the initial flowering of San Francisco's hippie community, an evangelical Christian strain of the counterculture—what would come to be known as the Jesus People movement—first appeared in the persons of a converted bohemian couple from Sausalito with an ofttimes difficult relationship with a square Baptist pastor.

Pastor MacDonald, Meet the Wises

John MacDonald was a native of Stockton, California, and a classmate of Billy Graham's at fundamentalist Wheaton College in Illinois (class of '43). Following degrees at Westminster Theological Seminary in Philadelphia and the American Baptist seminary in Berkeley, California, MacDonald pastored several churches in Northern California. In 1960, he was chosen as the pastor of the First Baptist Church of Mill Valley, California, a moderate-sized church of about 200.[9] The community was "arty," as MacDonald described it, and "close to some of the other high-toned residential communities" in wealthy Marin County, just north of San Francisco across the Golden Gate Bridge (figure 1.1).[10]

Sometime in late 1964, Elizabeth "Liz" Wise began to attend the church. Raised in Auburn, California (about thirty miles east of Sacramento), in a pious family that attended the First Baptist Church of Auburn, she had undergone a religious conversion at the age of eleven at a Bible conference at the Mount Hermon campgrounds near Santa Cruz. Pastor MacDonald and his conservative congregation welcomed the quiet young woman, oblivious to the fact that she often attended services while coming down from the previous night's acid trip. As months passed, she continued to come back, and she asked the people at the church to pray for her husband, Warren "Ted" Wise.[11]

As it turned out, Ted and Elizabeth Wise were part of the vanguard of Beat-sympathetic free spirits that predated the 1967 Summer of Love in the Bay area.[12] Ted Wise was a native of Lakeport, California, a small community on the shores of Clear Lake, about seventy miles north of San Francisco. When he was a child, his family had moved to Auburn, where he nourished an interest in art and literature until joining the Navy in the mid-1950s. While serving aboard a Navy tender in the Pacific Fleet, he learned how to work with canvas and began learning the sail-making trade; on shore leave in Japan, he experimented with marijuana and heroin. Even as a child, Wise had been fascinated by the idea of drug use; he cherished a magazine photo of a Mexican peasant with an array of mind-bending mushrooms. As a teenager, he was captivated by the 1955 Frank Sinatra film *The Man with the Golden Arm*, which he remembered made heroin addiction look

FIGURE 1.1 John MacDonald (r.), Pastor of First Baptist Church, Mill Valley, CA, and family ca. 1960.

Courtesy of Mary Ann MacDonald.

attractive: "All you had to do was roll around in agony a bit...the worst thing that could happen to me would be to meet Kim Novak."[13]

Upon returning home to Auburn, Wise enrolled at Sierra College. While he continued to nurse his interest in the "jazz musician's smoking preference," he met Elizabeth, a young woman who, like Ted, was interested in art and poetry. At Sierra, they were devotees of an English professor with connections to the Beat scene in San Francisco. The allure of the exciting artistic and literary scene there prompted Elizabeth to move to San Francisco in the summer of 1959 in hopes of starting a career in modeling; Ted followed her shortly thereafter and enrolled in the California College of Arts and Crafts in Oakland. Once in town, they quickly moved into a Beat commune on O'Farrell Street in the city's North Beach bohemian enclave. "Our basic identity," Wise recalled, "was as beatniks." Life in the commune proved a constant source of new ideas and fascinating discussions, as artists, academics, and literary figures such as Allen Ginsberg and Lawrence Ferlinghetti turned up regularly at dinnertime.[14]

In 1961, the couple married, and a daughter was born. To make ends meet for his new family, Ted found work in the boatyards, eventually landing at Sutter Sail in the "boho-friendly" village of Sausalito, and the Wises relocated across the bay. Throughout this period, drug use loomed large in the Wises' lives. Marijuana was the foundational drug of choice (George Hunter—leader of the legendary San Francisco band the Charlatans—was one of Ted's primary connections for pot), but mushrooms of all sorts, mescaline/peyote ("it was amazing"), and amphetamines were all on the menu. But the imagination of many of the people in Wise's circle was fired by what they were hearing about the wonders of LSD, and Wise was no exception. After a failed attempt to secure some of the new mystery drug from "Chemical Buddha" (British philosopher turned Bay Area Zen Buddhist maven, Alan Watts), in late 1964, Wise and friends finally scored a batch of prime black-market LSD that came straight from the labs of Swiss pharmaceutical manufacturer Sandoz. His first trip was an epiphany: "We tried it, and it was a phenomenal experience," Wise recalled. LSD use became routine; often he would go to work high on acid. "Small doses were very interesting," he remembered, noting that after the initial score, supply was not a problem: "We had a lot of it."[15]

By 1965, Ted Wise's life seemed to be shaping up just to his liking. From his job, he made connections with the owners of racing boats and yachts and spent much of his time on weekends as a crew member for his bosses' customers. Plying a craft he loved, hanging out with interesting people, and using drugs—everything in life seemed to be coming up roses. All in all, he lived what he later claimed "on the outside looked like the coolest life one could have," with a mix of friends that included "beats to yachtsman [sic], jazz musicians, artists and poets...America's Cup captains...Yogis, Buddhists, Anarchists, [and] Communists."[16]

The internal reality, however, was apparently less than cool. Wise was regularly working long hours, going out carousing with friends, and sleeping with a succession of girlfriends, while Liz stayed at home with a family that soon included two children.[17] Knowledge of Ted's philandering caused increasingly rancorous relations within the marriage—later, Wise even admitted to plotting to murder Liz.[18] Mercifully, on one of his frequent LSD trips, he began to be troubled by insights into his own character or, more precisely, his lack thereof. He became increasingly convinced that, at bottom, Ted Wise was a self-centered liar, cheat, and thief; as he put it: "I went into the palace looking for the prince on the throne but discovered only the rat in the basement."[19]

Ted, whose exposure to Christianity thus far had been a couple of visits to church with his grandmother and a few mandatory chapel services in the Navy, was antagonistic when his wife began to attend services at First Baptist in Mill Valley, but he noted, "She came back from church just glowing." Eventually, he decided to read the New Testament: "I didn't want to be hypocritical about it; I was always putting it down but [had] never actually read it."[20] What he found, however, surpassed his mild expectations of finding a new role model in Jesus Christ. "I just got fascinated by Jesus," Wise recalled. As he read, he was particularly impressed by Christ's claims to divinity and Paul's assertions that all people had a need to respond individually to his invitation to be born again. Convinced that Jesus was God, Wise later described his experience as a Paul-like conversion: "While on my way to my own Damascus...I found it necessary to cry out to God to save my life in every sense of the word. Jesus knocked me off my metaphysical ass. I could choose Him or literally suffer a fate worse than death."[21]

Having embraced Christianity, Wise felt his next step was something of a heavenly legal requirement—making a public acknowledgment of his belief in Jesus. One Saturday night in early 1965, he and Liz took a healthy hit of LSD and traveled to Berkeley to visit an old friend, Danny Sands. At the party, they found a house full of pot-smoking people plundering a major score Sands had just brought north from Mexico. Isolated in the midst of the mellow, marijuana-imbibing crowd, Wise began announcing that "Jesus is my Lord," much to his fellow partiers' discomfort and befuddlement. Leaving the party, Wise, who had driven before while on LSD, experienced a nightmare of a ride back across the Bay Bridge. "It seemed like the bridge was going straight up," Wise remembered years later. Even more disconcerting, he claimed, "it seemed like I was out of the car, somewhere else, [but] conscious of myself still driving the car." Hearing demonic voices urging him to "Flee!" he prayed and was rationalizing his past behavior when he claimed he heard an audible angelic voice telling him that excuse making was inappropriate when speaking to God: his best option would be to "Shut up!" Eventually, the Wises returned home, and Ted believed that God had rescued him—and had audibly ordered him to attend church the next morning.[22]

Come Sunday morning, the more distressing effects of the trip had worn off, but at another level things had gotten worse; he now felt that in addition to having a Sabbath requirement to head over to First Baptist in Mill Valley, the Lord was telling him to say something—the same thing, in fact—to everyone he met that day: "He is back!" Unable to argue himself out of the conviction that God was really talking to him, he and Liz drove to church. At the prescribed "invitation" closing, Ted got up from his seat, walked forward to the front of the church, and made his declaration that "Jesus is Lord." One of his friends later recalled Wise's description of what happened next:

> They were all upset.... This was not in the program. The pastor, John MacDonald, was completely surprised and decided to shake my hand. And I said, "He is back." And John said, "That's nice." Then I talked to the elders and told them that "He is back." They stood there and looked at me strangely.... Not a word.... The next weird thing that happened after that I told the whole [story of the last two days] to John MacDonald, verbatim, because he wanted to know how I became a Christian. He didn't know what to do about it. Like "Wait a minute, is this thing real or not," because he knew I was high. God would [have been] hard-pressed to find a time [when] I wasn't high. I had already read that we are saved in the midst of our sins. It was fine with me that he caught me high and not fornicating. I was in serious trouble with some serious circumstances, and God answered my prayers to a greater degree than I had anticipated.[23]

Although the Mill Valley Baptists were just as befuddled and discomfited by Wise as the partygoers in Berkeley had been the night before, the Sunday morning commitment was not the one-off response to an acid trip gone bad. In the months that followed, Wise shed his extracurricular lady friends, met regularly for personal Bible study with MacDonald, and kept on getting high ("no 'thou shall nots' about that"). After completing the prescribed course of instruction for baptism, Ted Wise, the drug-taking beatnik, had become, as he later said, a "dues-paying, meeting-going, praying-out-loud member" of the First Baptist Church.[24]

As Wise set out on this new personal course, he began to tell his friends of his faith and invite them to church. Many thought he had lost his mind, but others were intrigued by the new peace that had descended on the Wise household. As a result, some of them—much to the surprise or horror of many in the staid congregation—began accepting Wise's invitation to visit the Mill Valley Baptists.[25] While the congregation extended an official welcome to the visitors, many within Pastor MacDonald's tradition-minded flock were having difficulty adjusting to his growing ministry among Marin County's free spirits—the presence of Ted Wise often proved to be a difficult exercise in cross-cultural Christian brotherhood. Much of the conflict stemmed from Wise's readiness to ask questions that skirted assumptions and Sunday school pieties held unquestioningly by many of his new evangelical brethren. Writing in 1970, MacDonald described Wise's hyperparticipation at Bible studies and in Sunday school classes:

> Ted was not simply one to ask questions and be satisfied with any answer. If he didn't understand a statement, he could not drop the matter.... We were made aware of his utter newness in things biblical and, perhaps more to the point, in current evangelical vocabulary.... From the beginning, Ted's questions were mixed with opinions. He brought with him, out of...psychedelphia [sic] many assumptions about reality. A curt dismissal of some Old Testament passage might be his impulse at the moment. More often it was a dogmatic statement of what a given passage must mean. Very frequently it was a proclamation of pure idealism.[26]

For the veteran saints of First Baptist, the give-and-take between Wise and MacDonald and other church members often proved to be little less than "an interruption—even an exasperation.... [Ted's] combination of persistence and sharpness was...capable of rankling other sensitive souls" in the church. MacDonald observed that the whole process often left many in his congregation feeling "that the sacred had been profaned."[27] One particularly awkward moment came one Sunday morning when Wise brought a friend with him who had served six months in prison for some minor offense. During the course of his sermon MacDonald began excoriating people who had landed in jail, opining that they deserved the punishment they received. At about that point, Wise recalled, the guest, whose "experience had not been that God had been running the jails," stood up and told MacDonald, "Brother, you're full of shit!" and walked out.[28]

Between such incidents and Wise's interaction with the pastor, MacDonald later estimated that perhaps as many as half of his original congregation eventually left the church because of the hip newcomers who eventually made their way to First Baptist.[29] But while MacDonald was sensitive to his members' frustrations and was often irritated by Wise's outspoken ways and criticisms of the ingrained tradition of business as usual, he realized that there was something there that he could not easily dismiss:

> His idealism stemmed in part from his old hippie outlook, and in part from the fact that the Bible was new to him. What he read, he accepted at face value and he offered no resistance....Most refreshing was his readiness to do whatever he understood God to be requiring of him. Having no buildup of rationalizing Scripture to where it could not get a response, he frequently came up with valid insights which the rest of us would miss.[30]

Moreover, he also realized that the irritation factor was cutting both ways: Wise and his friends had trouble understanding how longtime, self-professed Christians could read the Bible and be unmoved by Christ's teachings or so thoroughly miss the point of a Scripture passage. "He couldn't understand why others didn't get the message," MacDonald wrote. "Continually I found myself pleading with him to be more patient, and at the same time, realistic."[31]

For his part, Wise found MacDonald and the straight, suburban, middle-class folks at First Baptist every bit as frustrating as they found him. Reminiscing years later, Wise recalled thinking that "these church folks were not at all like the people I had read about in the Book of Acts." Particularly perplexing were the economic dynamics he saw at play in First Baptist. Wise remembered: "They didn't live together or share much of anything, they didn't hold everything in common or give to each as any had in need. They had a tough time coughing up the salary for their one pastor."[32]

Although the Wises genuinely liked MacDonald and the various church folk they met, they could see no reason to sever connections with their friends in the bohemian, fast-developing-into-hippie, scene in San Francisco. And in that regard, the couple soon found an outlet for a hipper take on the Christian faith while keeping their attachment to MacDonald's church. Within the Wises' immediate circle, three other couples began to be particularly influenced by their enthusiasm for the Bible and Christianity and, by late 1966, had begun to form the nucleus of a Bay Area group of bohemian evangelical Christians.

A Small Circle of Friends

Jim and Judy Doop (pronounced "Dopp") had first run into Ted and Liz at a neighborhood party and had been intrigued at the way the hip Wise made his newfound Christian "trip" sound relevant and exciting. A native of Des Moines, Iowa, Jim Doop had served a stint in the Marines (primarily as a trombonist in the Marine Corps Band) and was attending Grandview College in Des Moines when he met Judy Marshall, a girl from an upper-class Presbyterian family who once had harbored a desire to become a missionary. Married after a three-month whirlwind courtship in 1959, they headed out to California in 1961 and ended up in Berkeley, where Jim worked for Mills Women's College. Hoping to pursue his dream of becoming a stand-up comedian in the mold of Lenny Bruce, Jim began working in clubs and strip joints on the weekend as "Jimmy Sand" and picked up a fairly solid weekday job as a full-time factory sales rep for the Philip Morris Tobacco Company. On the personal side, the Doops' life was a bizarre mix of middle-American respectability and California bohemian hip. Regular attendees at a local Lutheran church—despite the fact that Jim was fairly doubtful about there even being a God—and social hosts for the North Carolina delegation during the 1964 Republican convention (Jim Doop was an admirer of Barry Goldwater), they indulged their wild side with a steady stream of cocktails and were early members of Berkeley's Sexual Freedom League.[33]

This bifurcated lifestyle began to grate on their marriage. "[We were] torn in two directions, free but not free," remembered Judy Doop Marshall.[34] As a result, they found themselves more than open to both the allure of the Bay Area drug scene and a desire for spiritual truth. Both of those paths intersected in their new friends, the Wises. Jim Doop looked to Ted Wise as something of a father figure, respecting both his biblically infused wisdom and his knowledge of drugs—the latter admiration won by dint of Wise's tales of his own numerous excursions on acid. After experimenting with LSD a couple of times, Doop dropped by Wise's house one evening in October 1966 to visit and smoke some joints. During their conversation, he reported mixed results with his first encounters with acid—his first trip had been exhilarating, but his second had been depressing. Doop remembered years later that Wise then leaned close to him and shared his own revelatory insight about "the Rat that lives in the cellar of our soul." Oddly affected by the marijuana, Doop lay down on the floor and began to contemplate Wise's words with Bob Dylan's recently released album *Blonde on Blonde* playing in the background. While he lay there, he began to meditate on his spiritual condition and came to a profound realization:

> I finally got it. I was the rat. And it was my soul that was repenting. I thought to myself, "Maybe there is a God." I hadn't considered that possibility in a number of years, when suddenly a peace came over me, my breathing became easier. My chest became lighter. And I said, letting out

a long sigh, "Oh, Father, forgive me." Immediately the entire weight that
was on my chest was gone, and the rush of relief from my heart was one of
exultation.... My eyes were closed and there was a bright light in front of
me. I felt such happiness. I had never known anything like this before....

I understood in an instant that God is my Father and I am His child.... The
joy, the peace and love that I had on my heart for God and others was just
incredible. Never had I realized anything comparable before....[35]

In the days and weeks that followed, Doop's appetite for the Bible was insatiable.
"My mind was being blown away by the Bible's brilliance, by its simplicity," he
recalled; "the words of Jesus just enlarged my love for God and for mankind.... I
felt so cool that I [started telling] my friends I was dropping LSD, smoking marijuana and that Jesus Christ was my Lord.... I had turned on, tuned in, and Christ
was leading me out."[36] The new spiritual Jim Doop proved very popular in his
own household. When he finally sat down with Judy and explained the changes
that had come over him, she was ecstatic. Happily, she told him that she, too, had
been moving back toward God and that this was an answer to her prayers.[37]

As the Doops embarked on their new odyssey with Jesus, their close friends the
Heefners were experiencing their own existential and marital crises. A childhood
friend of Jim Doop's, Steve Heefner had regularly attended Sunday school and
church camps while growing up in Des Moines and had even taken in a late '50s Oral
Roberts campaign in the area. He had gone on to attend Drake University, where he
graduated with a degree in journalism. While at Drake, he met and married Sandi
Buckberg, a Chicago-born sociology major from a Catholic background.[38]

Blessed with a rich, sonorous voice, Steve had begun working part-time while
in college as a radio announcer at a local Des Moines station and, following graduation, snared a job as a disc jockey at KIOA. Over the next few years, Heefner
worked his way up the radio market ladder, hopscotching to jobs in Madison,
Wisconsin; Peoria, Illinois; and Milwaukee, where he became "Steve O'Shea"
because his program director at WOKY insisted on having Irish names for all his
djs. On New Year's Day 1965, O'Shea started a job at KNBR, the NBC affiliate in
San Francisco. The next year, he landed the six to nine evening slot at the city's
major pop station, KFRC ("The Big 610"), where he also hosted *Perspective*, a weekend talk show that featured interviews with people like celebrity media witch Sybil
Leek, Church of Satan founder Anton LaVey, author and Merry Prankster leader
Ken Kesey, and LSD gurus Timothy Leary and Richard Alpert (later Ram Dass).[39]

Heefner/O'Shea's status as a rock dj—he emceed the Rolling Stones' 1966
concert at the Cow Palace—made him a genuine celebrity in the Bay Area, and he
frequently hobnobbed with the musicians in the developing San Francisco music
scene. He knew the guys in the Grateful Dead and Quicksilver Messenger Service
well, danced with Joan Baez at an after-concert party, sat with the Stones' Brian Jones

at the Monterey Pop Festival, and was particularly good friends with Janis Joplin, a nine-time guest on his *Perspectives* show. When Jimi Hendrix came to town to play the Fillmore West, they hung out, and Hendrix sat in the studio answering the station's song request line. The Heefners were living the mid-'60s California, rock 'n' roll good life—replete with a "$20,000 salary" for his disc jockeying, a new Ford Mustang, a green 1960 Jaguar sports coupe, and a tony "$28,000 home in Mill Valley."[40]

Despite the flirtation with fame and fortune, Steve Heefner was a pretty miserable man. He was becoming increasingly fed up with the internal politics in major-market rock radio, and his marriage was not going well. He had a girlfriend on the side, and his wife knew about her—no recipe for household peace. As he searched around for some sort of answer to his personal sense of emptiness and dissatisfaction, his acquaintance with Ted Wise became a deeper friendship. Sandi Heefner had first met the "very interesting, artsy-looking" Liz Wise at a local Welcome Wagon type of event when the Heefners moved into Marin County. Becoming social friends at first (the Heefner holiday party where the Doops first met the Wises was also the Heefners' introduction to the Wises as a couple), he found Wise's Scripture-filled conversation increasingly more intriguing—so much so that for the first edition of his *Perspectives* show on KFRC, his roundtable guests were rock promoter Bill Graham of Fillmore West fame; Grace Slick, the lead singer of the Jefferson Airplane; and Ted Wise. Wise proved to be the ideal evangelist for someone in Heefner's shoes—mired in a chaotic personal life, drawn to the freedom and honesty of the emerging hip scene, and yet impressed with the message of Christianity. In addition to marijuana-mellowed conversations with Wise, Heefner attended several Bible studies at his house.[41]

Against that background, a strange incident on Saturday, October 31, in the downtown financial district had a profound impact on his perception of what was going on around him. Ken Kesey was the guest on *Perspectives* that day, talking about his "Acid Test Graduation" party that would be held that night at the Winterland Ball Room. After the interview, one of the guys in Kesey's Merry Pranksters group furtively pulled "O'Shea" off to the side. Heefner asked the Prankster what this whole thing was really all about; he bent down and in a whisper told him: "Jesus Christ, man. And he's gathering his church in this period and a lot of people are going to be coming to the Lord…that's what's happening, man." With this cryptic revelation added to the things on his mind, Heefner went to Wise to ask him to shepherd his first acid trip. As a favor to his friend ("I thought if [he] was going to take LSD it was better that [he] took it with me," Wise recalled), he agreed to accompany him on his inaugural experience with psychedelics. Shortly thereafter, Heefner took his first acid trip in the company of Ted Wise. Afterward, he recalled that it was immediately after coming off acid that he had seen the light: "All I know is that when I took LSD I was a seeker, and when I woke up the next morning I was a Christian!" This was not your grandmother's Sawdust Trail.[42]

Dan and Sandy Sands were the last couple in the Wises' circle to sign on board with Christianity, but Danny Sands had known Ted and Liz Wise since their days at Sierra College. The son of an ex-Marine, Sands had been raised in Costa Mesa in Orange County and entered the Navy after high school, where he was transferred from a gunnery crew to a desk job after telling his commanding officer that he really was quite uncomfortable with war. After being discharged, he followed an attraction to the Northern California Beat scene—stoked by readings of Alan Ginsberg's *Howl!* and Lawrence Ferlinghetti's *Coney Island of the Mind*—and ended up in Auburn at Sierra College. His love of literature ingratiated the reticent, soft-spoken man to Wise (who introduced Sands to marijuana), and the pair became close friends after a Jack Kerouac–inspired cross-country trip to Miami. But Wise did not share Sands's bent toward radical politics: "He thought the communists were conservative, he was so far left," Wise remembered; "he was an anarchist and serious about it."[43]

After moving to the Bay Area in 1961, Sands met a student at San Jose State named Sandra "Sandy" Palmer, a Washington state native who had grown up in Cloverdale, California. The two of them were involved in a ban-the-bomb activist commune called Acts for Peace. They eventually married and left the commune; by the time the Wises had embraced Christianity, the Sandses had two children, and Danny was living in an old ramshackle house in a mostly black Berkeley neighborhood, working as a painter, and stealing car parts and hustling drugs on the side.[44]

By the time Ted Wise had converted to Christianity, he was beginning to see Sands as a major drag on his life: "I wanted him out of my life; I was tired of [his] direction, his morality, everything." Still, the friendship hung on, with Wise trying to evangelize Sands, and Sands trying to get Wise to reconsider his new faith. But during a long, late-night conversation in early 1967—fueled by some speed (amphetamines) provided by one of Wise's coworkers at the sail shop—Sands finally came to the realization that he was ready to claim "Jesus as his Lord and Savior." Sands's wife was initially less than thrilled but came around shortly and became, as she noted years later, "totally into it!"[45] A nucleus of hip, Bible-fixated, evangelically inclined Christians had been formed and was ready to start spreading their beliefs among their friends and contacts in the emerging counterculture—the first manifestation of what would eventually become known as the Jesus People movement.

Holding All Things in Common—Christian Communal Living?

Like Timothy Leary, Allen Ginsberg, the Grateful Dead, the Diggers, Hells Angels, and 20,000 or so other old Beats, young rebels, and free spirits, Ted and Elizabeth Wise—members of the First Baptist Church of Mill Valley—were in attendance at the famous gathering of the tribes that took place at the Human Be-In at San

Francisco's Golden Gate Park on January 14, 1967. Amid all the hip revelers arrayed in their face paint and colorful costumes, the Wises had their own little tribe, a party of eight adults and a herd of children camped out on an old silken spinnaker, picnicking and enjoying the day's speeches, music, and general good-time vibes. They avoided the acid that was making the rounds that day but freely partook of the marijuana joints that were circulating in the crowd. Jim Doop looked back on that day many years later and remembered that it was like nothing he had ever experienced:

> There was a wonderful feeling of love with all these people. I had never been in such a positive atmosphere with people like this in my life. Nobody scowled at anybody. Everyone just smiled at each other, and greeted one another. I had never felt love from strangers before.[46]

But for most of the adults in the Wise tribe that day, the Human Be-In portended an even deeper reality than the heady mixture of cultural ferment and Aquarian optimism that fueled the rest of the throng. Doop recalled that as he sat in the sunshine and listened to the music of the Grateful Dead, there could be only one metaphor that got at what he was feeling: "I expected Christ to return at any moment. I couldn't believe that it could get any better than this." By the time the Jefferson Airplane had started their set, Doop remembered, "I thought I was pretty close to heaven. I just didn't know that it was available to experience anything so spiritually high....I was so grateful to God for allowing me to be a part of this phenomenon."[47]

By this time, the Wises and their hip, born-again friends were well on their way to forming a Christian commune. Their enthusiasm was fueled by a number of factors. First was the increasingly ubiquitous experimentation with communal living within the developing counterculture. Second were their own readings of verses 44 and 45 of chapter 2 in the Acts of the Apostles describing the early days of the Church in Jerusalem: "And all that believed were together, and had all things common; and sold their possessions and goods, and parted them to all men, as every man had need."[48] If the Bible said it, that was good enough reason to experience it. A statement made years later by Ted Wise got at the operating assumption that was beginning to drive much of their thought as they read this passage: "[we] agreed on one thing: that we ought to live out the Book of Acts like a script."[49]

Within the group's inner dynamic, Dan Sands led the charge for communal living, fueled by his readings of the New Testament, his experience in the Acts of Peace community, and a course on communal living he had just taken at a free college in Berkeley. Most of the rest of the group was also bullish on the idea; Ted Wise was more reticent about the endeavor but, given the moment, was willing to go along with the rest of the group. But the most determinedly resistant to the setup was Sandi Heefner. She had pretty much written off her Catholic upbringing and, while positive about the new spiritual direction of her husband and the others, was taking a lot of the God-talk she had been hearing with a grain of salt. Moreover, her first exposure to the Sands's ruffled brand of housekeeping (at a potluck dinner during which combining households was a major topic of conversation) only steeled her resolve to protect her family's lifestyle.[50]

In March 1967, Sands, newly inspired by Jesus' challenge to the rich young ruler in the Gospels of Mark and Matthew, sold, or put into storage, most of his belongings. Packing up an old 1954 Dodge station wagon for an extended camping trip, he loaded up his wife and daughters and set off roaming the state of California. Although part of his mission was evangelistic, a major component of it was his conviction that if God meant for them to have a Christian commune, some prime spot—or some chance meeting—would show up during his sojourn on the road. Several properties did come to their attention, but no immediate possibilities turned up.[51]

Within several weeks after the Sandses set off on the road, the drive toward communal living was given a practical boost from the forces of economic reality. In April 1967, Steve and Sandi Heefner decided to walk away from a rent-to-buy arrangement they had on their Mill Valley house and moved in with their longtime friends, the Doops. At about the same time, Ted Wise was fired from his sail-making job. The root of the problem was his conversion. One source of friction was a foreman who had previously been his closest friend in the shop; alienated from his mother's Pentecostalism, he had reacted extremely negatively to Wise's newfound Christianity. Another bone of contention was Wise's decision to resign his membership at a prestigious yacht club—a membership he had obtained through his employer's influence. Wise reasoned that his new Christian loyalties didn't leave him enough time and money to belong to a yacht club. He sent a letter of resignation explaining his new priorities and asking to be removed from membership. Unfortunately for Wise, the letter left the members of the club feeling that he thought they were a bunch of heathens. Confronted by his embarrassed boss, Wise claimed that they reached a mutual parting of the ways.[52]

As the story of his firing was translated to MacDonald, however, it seemed like persecution for the gospel's sake.[53] Sympathetic to Wise's plight, the church stepped in with some financial help and tried to find him another job—until MacDonald had a chat with Wise's former boss. According to MacDonald, he maintained that Wise had been fired because of all the time he was devoting to evangelizing coworkers, deliverymen, and customers and claimed that he had "exercised much patience...bending over backward" to accommodate his sailmaker's religious enthusiasm. Nonetheless, the minister was told that Wise had become "so aggressively argumentative" that not only was his own work being disrupted but also the whole shop was being affected. Wise's case was not helped in MacDonald's eyes by the fact that he wanted a similar job in the boatyards to the one that he had been fired from and was "unwilling to take just any job"—an attitude that did not quite line up with the Protestant work ethic that reigned in the church. To make the situation all the more tense, MacDonald lamented that "prospective employers we knew couldn't overlook [Wise's] even modified hippie appearance." As a result, Baptist benevolence for the Wise household began to dry up.[54]

Around this same time, Dan Sands and his family had wandered back into the Bay Area, camping near San Anselmo. Running on financial empty, they were, like the Wises, looking for a way to stretch their resources. Viewing the current situation, it became obvious to their minds that the Lord had graciously opened the door to Christian communal living; the Sandses moved in with the Wises, sharing their apartment. Scraping to make ends meet, they limped on through small gifts and occasional chip-in money from their non-Christian hippie friends—some of whom would crash at the Wise-Sands apartment for the odd night or two.[55]

The four couples continued to discuss the possibility of joining their two mini-communes in a larger effort but found the Heefners to be a logistical obstacle to the endeavor. Steve was out of sorts because he was down to hosting his weekend *Perspectives* talk show on KFRC, having just been relieved of his weeknight disc jockey duties because the station management had tired of his inclination to talk about his spiritual journey and interject biblical banter in between playing songs by the Beatles and Jefferson Airplane.[56] Understandably, this new reality added to the stress in their marriage, which—despite the fact that Steve had jettisoned his girlfriend upon his new spiritual commitment—was still on shaky ground, to say the least. Everything came to a head on a mid-May weekend camping getaway with their son and the Doops' daughter. Arguing non-stop all the way down to Monterey, the trip turned into an exercise in icy marital silence. One night she grabbed her sleeping bag and staked out a spot by herself on the beach. Over the next few hours, she wrestled with her situation, her life, and the constant witness about Jesus that her husband and their friends had been laying on her. At that point, she "gave in to the Lord" and felt an immediate sense of peace and elation.[57] But there was more. Recalling the experience years later, she said that while she was lying there, she noticed something strange up in the night sky:

> When I looked up in the sky there was a huge figure-eight made out of stars.... I'm not into flights of fancy. I rubbed my eyes and looked away and did all the things they do in the movies and kept looking and peeking up—and there it was as strong and as bright as ever. Anyway it was an "eight" and I knew what it meant—that I would be the eighth person [in the communal group].... From that point on, I couldn't stop talking about Jesus Christ.[58]

Coming home all smiles from their camping trip, the Heefners enthusiastically decided to plunge ahead with their spiritual commitment. Soon thereafter, KFRC's major rock 'n' roll competitor in the Bay Area, KYA, offered Steve O'Shea a new job as the disc jockey in the afternoon drive slot. With the Heefners fully on board and with the expectation that Steve's relatively lucrative salary would cover the group's basic expenses, the four couples decided that the current situation was about as good a time as any to give living in Christian community a whirl. The first step was unloading the things that were anchoring them down. Jim Doop gave notice at Philip Morris, effective in early June, and put his house on the market for a quick sale. The slicker cars in the group—Heefner's 1960 Jaguar and Doop's 1965 Ford Crown Victoria—were sold to add to the group's collective treasury. They also hunted for a place big enough—and cheap enough—to accommodate eight adults and seven children. This quest proved to be more of a problem than they anticipated: It seemed that many of the solid citizens of Marin County were not particularly eager to rent their properties to a hippie-looking commune, Christian or not.[59]

When the deadline arrived for the Doops and Heefners to be out of their house, the group had still been unable to turn up anything that would suit their collective needs. As a stopgap measure, the two families found a house located at the Tam Junction on Highway One, just south of Mill Valley. Closer to the Wise-Sands apartment, it was now easier for the families to spend time together and pursue their Kingdom Gospel work. That summer, some of the women helped out with First Baptist's vacation Bible school. The men, meanwhile, decided to start heading down to the Haight. Up until this time, they had been going informally to the burgeoning hippie district to hang out, see friends, and talk to people about Christ. But the more they talked, the more they felt the need to do something more organized. Steve Heefner remembers that Wise announced he and Sands were going to the Haight with some food to hand out and "talk to the people about the Lord."[60]

Jim Doop later looked back and pinpointed that day as Monday, June 19; he and Heefner drove across the Golden Gate Bridge to meet Wise and Sands in the Drog Store eatery at the corner of Haight and Masonic. The agenda called for Heefner to eventually leave to do his shift at the radio station and then meet them early in the evening, either in the Haight or over in Golden Gate Park, where they might talk to small groups of people on Hippie Hill. Over the next few weeks, the expedition became a routine, with the men going to the Haight on the weekdays, and various combinations of the married couples heading back into the hippie district on the weekends.[61] The first indigenous attempt of counterculturally friendly bohemian Christians to evangelize the hippies had been launched. But the Establishment evangelical church was close behind; aware of this new mission field and the small group of hip evangelists, it was attempting to back their efforts and create a larger, more organized outreach into the counterculture.

Reaching Out to the Hippies

Parallel to the move to communal living during the spring of 1967, the gulf between Wise and his friends and the conservative mind-set of the people at

First Baptist had also come to a head (figure 1.2). The main point of contention
was the plight of the thousands of young seekers who were expected to pour into
San Francisco in the weeks and months ahead. Wise became acutely aware of
this through his many friendly contacts in the Haight, which included several
members of the Diggers, a local artist-anarchist group. The Diggers had just been
ordered to evacuate their Free Store on Page Street because of the San Francisco
city health department's attempt to crack down on the Haight. With an order to
vacate the premises, the group's food distribution and housing programs were
in danger of being eradicated at a time when the hippie district's population was
growing day by day. Distressed by the Diggers' predicament and the ongoing reality of thousands of young people flooding into the city with little prospect for
food and shelter, Wise felt this was the perfect opportunity for Christians to show
their love and concern. "I told John that all of these people were going to come,"
he remembered in an interview years later, "and they were going to be needy and
that they were going to need food...there was a great opportunity here if we had
a way to feed people." So Wise approached MacDonald with a modest proposal to
work full-time trying to reach the hippies, starting by getting the church to lend its
facilities to the Diggers (figure 1.2).[62]

MacDonald now found himself impaled on the tripartite horns of an ethical,
evangelistic, and pragmatic dilemma: How might he actually address the physical
and spiritual situation, avoid alienating his erstwhile bohemian acolyte, and yet
manage to somehow hang onto his congregation? Knowing that Wise's scheme
had zero chance with his deacon board, the pastor hemmed and hawed about
insurance liabilities and Mill Valley's being across the Golden Gate Bridge from

FIGURE 1.2 On the streets of the Haight, fall 1967: left to right, Ted Wise, Steve
Heefner, unidentified, Jim Doop, unidentified.

Courtesy of Karl Kahler.

San Francisco. Wise was more than a little annoyed by his rationalizations but was satisfied when MacDonald offered him a chance to air his concerns to the people at First Baptist. It turned out that the pastor had to attend a special meeting and gave Ted a shot at running the "mid-week Sabbath," the church's Wednesday-night prayer meeting and Bible study. MacDonald figured that Wise could give his testimony, lead the group in prayer, and thereby begin to raise the church's consciousness about what was going on in the area. Wise had other ideas, however, and decided to turn the prayer meeting into a thumbnail seminar on contemporary youth and the appeal of exotic new religions. For audiovisual aids, he brought in several copies of the *Oracle* and the *Berkeley Barb*, as well as a record player to play Bob Dylan songs that bespoke the contemporary philosophical and/or spiritual quest. Jim Doop reminisced years later about how the evening went:

> I took a seat and a few people asked where Reverend MacDonald was, and looked suspiciously at Ted's setup....The majority of these people were older than middle aged. Very conservative....I looked around the room and the expressions of the faces were anywhere from "shook" to "What am I doing here?" to "No Expression." It was the latter that most concerned me. Ted tried to explain why hippies turned to these other religions after they took LSD, and that he felt it was urgent that the Christian Church get involved immediately. Ted told them the children of Mill Valley were already involved, and that unless the church was willing to give them up to foreign gods, the church better get involved soon....When he finished, no one said a thing. People just got up....Ted wasn't disappointed....He said the whole thing was worth doing just to see the expressions on some of the people's faces.[63]

In the following days, MacDonald got an earful from his members about Wise's prayer meeting stint. For his part, Wise was surprised when a very upset MacDonald took him to task for free-styling the prayer meeting and exposing the church's more cloistered saints to the lurid details of the hippie life and—most shockingly—his use of Bob Dylan. Wise could not understand MacDonald's reaction; after all, he reasoned, the theme of his presentation constituted the core of their interaction over the previous two years.[64] Matters became worse when, with a sense of resignation, Wise observed that it was obvious that MacDonald and the people of First Baptist simply did not care about the hippies and were not willing to help them. By this point, MacDonald claimed, he had come to the realization that his credibility as a Christian—to say nothing of all of his work with the Wises, Sandses, and Ted's other friends—was on the line. He maintained that he truly did want to do something to help the kids and agreed to accompany Wise on a tour of the Haight the very next day.[65]

Going to the hippie district the next afternoon, the Baptist pastor was moved by what he saw as they walked along. Sauntering along the streets and ducking into hippie businesses, MacDonald became more and more aware of what was actually going on (in Wise's words, "This was his first understanding that he was square") and of the very real physical needs of the runaways choking the sidewalks. At bottom, he began to see the Haight as every bit as much a cross-cultural evangelistic field as any tribal group overseas. The hippie enclave deserved the attention of the institutional church but it—and he—was utterly unequipped to pull it off:

> Ted and I strolled the streets and entered several establishments together. I noted the ease with which he related to the citizens there—and the estrangement with respect to myself. By dress and appearance, he belonged. Clearly I did not. He readily stopped for a few words or to give some money to someone in need. Obviously, he had remarkable rapport.[66]

MacDonald was conflicted. He felt "Ted was too far" from what he "considered to be a mature believer" with the proper understanding "of Christian living," yet he believed "God seemed to be saying to me, 'Here is a breakthrough tailored for Haight-Ashbury...I've provided all this—you must trust Me for the rest.'" So, when they got back to Mill Valley, MacDonald began to contact various leaders in Bay Area evangelical circles that he felt were less hidebound by tradition and might be open to taking a chance on an unorthodox outreach in the Haight. Rather quickly, he drew together a mixed group of mostly Baptist pastors, laymen, and officials who were interested in the project, including the pastor of San Francisco's First Baptist Church, fellow Wheaton alumnus John Streater; Ed Plowman of Park Presidio Baptist; William Mansdoerfer, executive director of Family Radio (a growing chain of evangelical FM stations); evangelical attorney George Hardisty; and Jack Karman, the veteran operator of a Bay Area rescue mission. They met with Wise and his friends in the basement of the First Baptist Church of San Francisco and, satisfied with what they heard and convinced that the city's evangelical churches were utterly clueless on how to reach the hippie population, decided to formally band together. They dubbed their new nonprofit group Evangelical Concerns, Inc., printed some literature, and began to seek funds to establish a ministry center in the Haight that would provide some food for indigent hippies and support the Bay Area evangelicals' "missionary to the hippies, Ted Wise."[67]

2

Jesus Comes to Haight-Ashbury

BY LATE SUMMER 1967, Evangelical Concerns had leased a storefront in the Armenian Hall on Page Street as a base to begin the evangelization of Haight-Ashbury. A little more than a block north of the intersection of Haight and Ashbury streets and a block south of Golden Gate Park's hippie magnet, the Panhandle, the Living Room (as it was generally labeled in the press) or The Mission (as its staff tended to call it) became a reality as the Summer of Love began to fade.[1] In the storefront window hung two of Ted Wise's paintings—an oxbow with Jesus' words from Matthew 11:30, "For my yoke is easy, and my burden is light," painted in script and a psychedelic-looking painting quoting Jesus' words from the cross: "Father, forgive them; for they know not what they do." Inside, other Scripture verses and artwork hung on the walls, exuding a comfortably hippie vibe. The room itself was roughly twenty by forty and contained a large table, a white wicker couch, and a motley assemblage of chairs that could accommodate perhaps thirty wandering souls who might come in off the street at any one time. In addition to a cramped back room, there was a single, frequently used toilet and a small kitchen alcove with an old refrigerator and some hot plates. From the limited funds available from Evangelical Concerns, occasional gifts from a few local churches and businessmen, and the gleanings of Wise and friends' wives (the "Kitchen Sweats," as they called themselves) from local grocers' out-of-date foods, the Mission was able to feed its members and offer a cup of coffee, day-old doughnuts, or a bowl of hot soup to the neighborhood's wandering youth.[2]

By the time The Mission/Living Room hit its stride, the ethos of the Haight was already in the midst of a precipitous decline. For all its colorful eccentricity and idealistic hopes, the hippie reality of the Summer of Love in Haight-Ashbury had devolved into a mixture of overcrowding, hunger, filth, bad drug trips, crime, and predatory personal behavior. The streets of San Francisco's do-your-own-thing hippie ethos often turned into an every man for himself struggle for existence. This jarring reality ultimately proved fatal to the countercultural dream, even as it provided a powerful impetus to the nascent Jesus People movement.

Sheer overcrowding was one source of misery in the Haight. An estimated 75,000 young people made their way to San Francisco in 1967—many more than the hip infrastructure and the city's overburdened social services could handle. Every night, thousands of near-penniless young people crashed in whatever hovel they could afford or find, and many slept outside in the cold damp of the city night.[3]

Along with the lack of housing came a shortage of food. Eager hands snatched up free sandwiches, bread, and doughnuts distributed by various groups, straight and hip. Eventually the need proved so great that the overwhelmed Diggers closed down a daily late afternoon soup giveaway in the Panhandle.[4] By mid-summer 1967, the *Oracle* advised young people intent on coming to San Francisco that they might as well forgo the flowers for their hair if they were not also going to bring a sleeping bag, clothes, food, and money.[5]

The free and easy hippie celebration of sexuality also manifested itself in all sorts of unforeseen "bummers." Venereal diseases were rampant in the Haight, and hippies seeking treatment for syphilis, gonorrhea, and herpes combined with drug overdoses to overwhelm the Free Clinic and the city's health department.[6] Even more troubling was the generally degrading effect life in the Haight had on the young runaway girls who came to the Bay area. As one young teenage girl named Alice told early Jesus People figure David Hoyt, "Girls didn't have any trouble finding a place to spend the night" if they were willing to pay the right price.[7] Others turned to full-fledged prostitution to feed themselves and their drug habits. Sexual violence toward women was also a grim reality. As early as April 1967, one hippie broadside lamented the situation: "Rape is as common as bullshit on Haight Street." In general, by midsummer 1967, women in the Haight were at risk for all sorts of emotional and physical violence from their male counterparts.[8]

While these discomforts and hardships were daunting enough, the hippies' fervent belief in the spiritual and personal blessings of drug use was responsible for perhaps the largest share of trouble. Besides growing harassment from the police, overdoses, bad trips, and the hyperaggressiveness associated with speed were a constant of life in the Haight. These problems multiplied as overcrowding grew and the drug supply's safety and quality were increasingly compromised. A closely related problem was a dramatic increase in assaults and robbery (rip-offs) in the hippie district as a new attempt to control its hitherto free-and-easy drug trade overwhelmed the Golden Rule ethos of the counterculture. As one author described it, "The flower movement was like a valley of thousands of plump white rabbits surrounded by wounded coyotes." When two popular hippie drug dealers were found brutally murdered in separate incidents late that summer, it became clear to many that the bloom was off the hippie rose.[9]

Amid this chaos, the Page Street Living Room mission proved to be a haven for wandering young people for close to two years. Borrowing a page from the long-established routines of skid row missions, they attracted kids with a chance to rest and traded food for a chance to expose their clientele to the gospel. At the Mission, the bare minimum of that translated to quietly eating one's soup while listening to one of the staff read from the American Bible Society's new translation of the New Testament, *Good News for Modern Man*. Steve Heefner remembered that their attempts to get kids into the mission for this program were pretty straightforward: "We were right up front; we'd say 'Hey, we got soup here, we got soup and New Testament. You sit down and you eat the soup, you have to listen to the New Testament.'" At times, he recalled the hippies complained. "They might go in the direction of 'That's un-American, that's not right, that's so uncool.' And we said, 'Well, that's the way it is. And here, we got doughnuts, too.'" More often than not, their pitch proved successful.[10]

Inside, casual conversations "were always steered toward talking about Jesus." The vast majority of those who came politely listened and left, but sometimes they engaged the staff in philosophical discussions about religion. Surely, most appreciated a place to sit down for a while, a cup of coffee or a meal, and, on rare occasions—in violation of the group's lease—a place to sleep for the night.[11]

But not everyone appreciated the arrival of a hip version of evangelical Christianity in the Haight. It was not unusual for some drop-ins to stir up aggressive theological and philosophical arguments. Proving to be more of a nuisance were the neighborhood troublemakers who regularly included the Page Street Mission on their rounds. One creepy drifter who came in for handouts was an ex-con named Charles Manson. For a while, he was a regular, often spooking many of the other Haight denizens. Mickey Stevens, an aspiring guitar player, remembers that he "let Charlie Manson jam on [his] electric in there, occasionally." But eventually he quit, claiming that after Manson had been playing, "it seemed like [his] guitar was demon possessed. Seriously!"[12] Ted Wise recalled one peculiar incident in which Manson sat staring at him while "playing" an acoustic guitar: "He was plucking things on it and trying to 'talk' to me with it." Jim Doop recalled another instance when Manson was proclaiming that he was God, to which Wise responded with a guffaw, saying, "If you're God, I am truly disappointed." Steve Heefner recalled him as being "highly disruptive" but noted with some satisfaction that he always "had soup and had to sit there and listen to the Word." Eventually, Manson realized that his games did not seem to impress any of the mission's regulars, and he stopped coming.[13]

Perhaps the biggest thorn in the side of the hippie Christians was "Tall Tom," a lanky Southern, drug-addled, fiddle-playing hippie reputed to have been a grad of M.I.T. and a Rhodes Scholar, who was in the habit of arguing with the staff, spewing profanities, and making innuendos about Jesus' sexual orientation. One time after a shouting match with Steve Heefner, he walked outside, picked up a brick he found lying on the sidewalk, and threw it against the plate glass window. It bounced off. Irritated, the young man picked up the brick again and hurled it at the window—only to have it bounce off a second time. After repeating the process a few more times, he stalked off, mumbling to himself. Heefner recalled turning to Wise and asking in disbelief: "Did you see that?" Wise replied that he had, to which Heefner exclaimed, "I'm glad you were here to see it, too!"[14]

Although no records were kept of how many contacts or converts the Living Room mission made, it seems clear that they were achieving a fair amount of success in their work. Jim Doop was quoted in an article in the *Oakland Tribune* in mid-1968 claiming that "some weeks we have the blessed experience of helping as many as 20 people make definite decisions to come clean and be followers of Christ."[15] Years later, Steve Heefner estimated that he had personally witnessed to "something like 2,000 kids on the street" during those days. Even a conservative estimate made by one of the group in an early 1990s interview would have meant contact with close to 20,000 people.[16] Whatever the exact number, it was clear that the people at the Page Street Mission interacted with thousands of young people, persuading a number of them to make a Christian commitment in the process.

Sometimes these contacts stuck around and became involved with the mission. One of them was Rick Sacks, a young hippie from a wealthy Jewish family in Boston. A troubled adolescence had led him to drop out of high school, followed by a short, miserable stint in the Army. He eventually headed to the West Coast and ended up in San Francisco, where the combination of drugs and the spiritual quest fired his nineteen-year-old imagination. Attracted by the various religious trips floating around the Haight, he became an enthusiast for a simple brown rice diet and spent his days rapping about philosophy and religion while earning his keep selling drugs suitable for the hippie seeker—acid, peyote, mescaline, and grass. Sacks actually underwent a conversion experience one night after stumbling into a one-off storefront meeting, perhaps run by gospel mission evangelist Jack Karman. "It was like a bright light shining on my life," Sacks said. "Not the white light of acid which shows you how naked you are—but the soft enveloping light of the love of Jesus."[17]

But despite Sacks's born-again experience, the straitlaced, coat-and-tie fundamentalist vibe at the meeting held no allure. Enthralled with the Bible, he wandered back and forth between Big Sur and the Haight, soaking up spiritual insights but feeling isolated from the hippie religious ethos with which he had once been so comfortable. It was then that he came across the Mission, where he saw an active, open Christian spirituality that he could embrace. "They were all ready to submit to the truth," Sacks recalled of Wise and friends' approach to Jesus' teachings and the Scriptures. "It wasn't just talking about it, it was doing it. [If the Bible said] 'give my coat as well'—here's my coat—there wasn't any question about it."

Sacks soon became an integral member of the group, evolving into something of a caretaker for the mission, often occupying the back room in the Page Street storefront.[18]

Lonnie Frisbee, another of the Living Room's early disciples, would play a key role in the growth of the early Jesus Movement outside the Bay Area. A seventeen-year-old from Costa Mesa down in Orange County, Frisbee had been born with a clubfoot and reared in an evangelical home troubled by divorce, and as a child, he was reportedly sexually abused by a friend of the family. As a teenager, he demonstrated an artistic bent and attained minor teenage eminence as one of the regular dancers on L.A. dj Lloyd Thaxton's afternoon TV show, *Shebang*. Slight of build, long-haired, bearded, and often dressed in leather with small pouches hanging from his belt, he looked like a little teenage Jesus. When the guys from the Living Room bumped into Frisbee in the fall of 1967, they found him holding forth on a street corner, waving a Bible and preaching about Jesus, flying saucers, and Christ consciousness. Taking him in hand, they took him for some coffee to discuss his beliefs and eventually brought him to the group house, where he informed them that he had just had his own personal theophany.[19] Just a few weeks before, he had been wandering nude—on acid—in the vicinity of Tahquitz Falls near Palm Springs, where he claimed he was confronted by Jesus:

> ...he explained to me that he was the only way to know God. I accepted him and he said "I am going to send you to the people." Then he gave me a vision of thousands of people and they were wandering around in a maze of darkness with no direction or purpose for their lives. He showed me that there was a light on me that he was placing on my life.... I was going to bear the Word of the Lord.[20]

Wise and the others perceived from Frisbee's fragmented testimony that the boy "had a Christian background" (he had gone forward in an altar call at eight) but that "his head was bent out of shape" by drugs.[21] Rescuing him from a bad living arrangement in the Haight, the group accepted Frisbee, and, after studying the Bible with the others, he eventually moved toward more orthodox views.[22] With the addition of converts like Frisbee and Sacks, the Page Street Mission increasingly functioned as a new evangelical Christian community within the larger Bay Area hippie scene.

Into the Haight—Kent the Preacher Meets David the Krishna

Although the support of conservative Protestant straights in the form of Evangelical Concerns helped to underwrite the efforts of the bohemian believers at the Living

Room, a more informal parallel attempt to evangelize the Haight had also been undertaken through the initiative of twenty-five-year-old seminarian Kent Philpott. Philpott had grown up in Oregon and Southern California, where he had some contact with the Beat element as a teen in the Los Angeles area. Following an early marriage, a stint in the Air Force, and a psychology degree from Sacramento State, Philpott was converted at a Baptist church and soon thereafter enrolled at the Southern Baptists' Golden Gate Seminary in Mill Valley.[23] In October 1966, while still a student, he accepted a part-time position as the pastor at a small church in Byron, California, sixty miles from Mill Valley in rural Contra Costa County.[24]

Despite having struck a course for a traditional career in the ministry, Philpott's curiosity was piqued by the coverage of what was going on in Haight-Ashbury. One night in April 1967, after hearing Scott McKenzie's recently released song, "San Francisco (Be Sure to Wear Flowers in Your Hair)," on the radio, Philpott journeyed into the Haight. Although the major influx of young seekers and runaways was yet to come that summer, what he saw proved unsettling:

> My first night in the Haight really shocked me. A scene I'll never forget was an old homosexual walking down Haight Street with his arm around a little boy about eleven years of age. The little kid I could see was loaded out of his mind. Also, that night I sat next to a guy my age who was a dope dealer. He told me that his life was ruined and that he was trapped in the dope scene. As I drove home that night, I knew my Lord had shown me these things for a reason.... The next night I was back in the Haight.[25]

Coming back the next evening, Philpott roamed the streets (figure 2.1). Eventually, he wound up in the apartment of a slight, blond-haired, bearded young Krishna devotee named David Hoyt, who shared a house—his share was a large closet—with a lesbian commune. Philpott asked Hoyt if he had ever read the Bible; he said that he had "read sections of it when [he] was high which had confused [him] even more." Hoyt talked for hours about his beliefs as Philpott, describing himself simply as "a follower of the Lord Jesus Christ," politely listened.[26]

Hoyt, it turned out had gotten his start in the direction of Krishna consciousness in the California prison system. A native Southern Californian of Southern family stock, he was the product of a broken home who had spent years in foster homes and juvenile detention facilities and had served time in Lompoc Federal Penitentiary for smuggling marijuana from Mexico. After a bad experience with heroin shortly after being sent to prison, he adopted a fierce self-improvement regimen; tried to turn his life around; immersed himself in the writings of Eastern yogis, Zen Buddhism, and Scientology; and experimented with LSD. Paroled in September 1966, Hoyt was soon invited to San Francisco by prison acquaintance

FIGURE 2.1 Kent Philpott (r.)
Courtesy of the Archives, Hubbard Library,
Fuller Theological Seminary

Luther Greene, who had become a leading light in the emergent hippie community as the co-owner of the Straight Theater.[27]

With his background in Eastern spirituality, Hoyt found himself captivated by the Haight-Ashbury scene. "It was like the hope of man," Hoyt later wrote, "launching out desperately against materialism, hypocrisy, hatred, war and inpersonalism [*sic*] trying to find the real way and live it."[28] He soon began spending a lot of time at the storefront temple opened by A. C. Bhaktivedanta Swami Prabhupada, the founder of the International Society for Krishna Consciousness (ISKCON).[29] Enthralled by the swami's lectures on Vedic literature and the Krishna chants, he became a full-fledged devotee and was enmeshed enough in the life of the Haight to serve as the Krishna representative on the Summer of Love planning council.[30]

Hoyt's initial meeting with Philpott was the first of several discussions about their respective beliefs. After one meeting, Philpott asked Hoyt if he would be interested in having him lead a Bible study in his apartment. Hoyt agreed, but because of increased duties due to Prabhupada's absence, asked that the study be moved to the Krishna Temple itself. Thus, over the next few weeks the bespectacled Baptist seminarian met weekly with Hoyt and several of his fellow Krishna devotees in a weekly examination of the Apostle Paul's teachings on salvation by grace as set forth in the Epistle to the Ephesians.[31]

The breakthrough with Hoyt came when Philpott brought along a fellow seminarian named Timothy Wu. Wu unleashed a barrage of verses about false prophets, idol worship, and the exclusivity of Christ's claims. He later cornered Hoyt in a small room next to the temple kitchen, prayed for him to stop chanting his demonic mantras, and prophesied that within two weeks Hoyt would leave ISKCON. Hoyt was shaken by this and by rising doubts of his own ability to reform through Eastern teachings and rituals. One night in the temple basement, he had a vision of Jesus gathering people from every country and ethnic group.[32] As he remembered it years later in an interview:

> Somehow in the sky there was like the arms and face of Jesus and you could see the nail-prints and the hands; and people were being raised off the Earth, and I didn't know what to make of that, all I know was I looked at my feet and my feet were right on the ground, I wasn't going anywhere—I was still in the group of seekers.[33]

The final straw came a few days later during a morning *kirtan* service when a Krishna altar near his bed caught fire and set his room alight. He ran downstairs and snatched the only object he could reach amid the flames—a Bible. By the time the fire department came to put out the fire, he was on his knees asking Jesus to save him.[34] Helping the other Krishna devotees clean up after the fire, Hoyt painted a message in six-inch letters on the Temple wall:

> I HAVE FOUND THE TRUE AND LIVING GOD AND I THANK YOU LORD JESUS FOR SAVING MY SOUL. LORD HELP ME TO FOLLOW YOU FAITHFULLY EVERY DAY.[35]

Hoyt called Philpott later to tell him what had transpired. When he swung by to pick up the new convert, he found the place in an uproar. Sizing up the situation, he began to ease Hoyt out the door when the angry devotees seized upon Philpott as the source of their troubles and Hoyt's sudden, unexpected defection. Philpott recalled that he pulled Hoyt out of the temple while being hit, kicked, and choked all the way by angry Krishnas, saved from a major beating only by the intervention of a San Francisco fireman. Philpott took Hoyt home to live with him in seminary housing and began to disciple him in the rudiments of the Christian faith. The still scruffy-looking Hoyt spent his days wandering around the Golden Gate campus, munching on Krishna-style snacks, and mysteriously dropping into classes. In the evenings, he would accompany Philpott on evangelistic treks into San Francisco.[36] A second beachhead of what would become the Jesus movement had been established in the Haight.

The "House of Acts" in Novato

The establishment of the Living Room mission on Page Street turned out to be only part of the Wises and friends' larger vision for a radical, hippie-friendly New Testament Christianity. Shortly before the opening of the Mission, the Wises and the other three couples in their circle had finally moved full steam ahead into communal living, cramming into the house in Mill Valley that the Heefners and Doops had rented, with the Wises and Sandses and their four children camping out on mattresses in the home's two-car garage. Happily, between Steve Heefner's check from his new station, Ted Wise's small stipend from Evangelical Concerns, and small gifts the group received, money didn't appear to be a problem. The couples decided to keep a communal purse in a drawer in the kitchen. "Money went into a box on the wall, with 10% taken out and put into the bottom section to give back to God," recalled Sandy Sands years later. "There were no restrictions on the drawer," Jim Doop later wrote. "Anyone could go to the drawer and take money out or put money in." Key to this arrangement was a commitment not to question each other's drawer-based transactions: "Everyone had to make money decisions for themselves."[37]

By the time the Living Room/Mission was up and running down in the Haight, the group had finally come across a house that would suit their needs—an old two-story, four-bedroom, two-bath farmhouse ("The House")—in the middle of a new subdivision in Novato, about ten miles further north in Marin County. Rented at $200 a month, the house had a big front porch, a large fenced yard, and a fireplace in the living room to add a bit of homey charm. Each couple was allotted a bedroom, with the kids in one big room in bunk beds, and the kitchen, living room, and part of the downstairs area designated as common turf for meetings, meals, and "guests."[38] Soon after the families moved in, a visitor from First Baptist of Mill Valley came with cases of pocket New Testaments he was donating to the group's efforts in the Haight. Looking around at what was going on, he suggested what would become the name by which it was later publicized—the "House of Acts," because they were living like the first Christian community.[39]

No sooner had the four couples moved in than their financial situation became suddenly less stable. Steve O'Shea, after only three months on the job at KYA, had managed to get himself fired yet again because—in John MacDonald's words—he had "freely witnessed to his new life in Christ" between songs on another major market AM rock station. This time, Heefner made no attempt to find another radio gig and simply plunged ahead, devoting himself full-time to the group's work. Existing now largely on Wise's small salary, random gifts from church folk, and short-term odd jobs they picked up here and there for cash or services (for example, the men built a wall for a local dentist in exchange for dental work), the group decided that they would depend on God to supply their financial wherewithal. This proved all the more an act of faith as the group's core expanded—eventually Lonnie Frisbee and Connie Bremer (soon to be Frisbee) moved into the house. Rick Sacks then came along with his wife, Megan. Numbers shifted with comings and goings, but it was not unusual for the core group in the household—not counting the teens who would crash there for the night—to number a dozen adults and seven children.[40]

Life at The House quickly settled into a whirring routine. The men commuted to the city to staff the Living Room and make evangelistic forays into the streets of the Haight. Meanwhile, to feed the commune and make the huge pot of soup the men took with them every day into the Haight, the women stayed back in Novato and cooked, made near-daily rounds of Dumpster-diving, negotiated hand-outs of day-old bread and canned goods from local business owners and sympathetic grocery clerks, and cultivated a garden. At the same time, they were also charged with taking care of their children and caring for, advising, and mothering an ever-growing houseful of guests. Connie Bremer Frisbee remembered that in her case, the women at the House provided the first stable family life she had ever known. Coming out of an abusive family situation, she saw her time at the Big House as "the first time" she "ever had the feeling of being safe....I couldn't get enough of their love."[41]

It was not unusual at any one time for the commune to be hosting fifteen to twenty kids: runaways brought over from the Haight, hippie hitchhikers passing through, and a sizable influx of local teenagers and runaways seeking a sympathetic-but-hip adult ear. Sandi Heefner remembers that in the early days, many of the kids were bright and there were a surprising number of "pastor's kids." But as the months went by, the runaways they housed were "a rougher crowd" that required a little more supervision. Sandy Sands remembers that sometimes their guests were "so rough that [she] would take the kitchen cleaver and sleep across the door of the kids' room."[42]

As a result, the local police department knew the place well, as did the neighbors. However, unlike most of the relationships in those days between members of the counterculture and the straights, this one was remarkably good. After some initial suspicion, the police came to see the residents of The House as a positive resource for dealing with troubled teens, and on several occasions the "Brothers" at the House rousted unsavory characters out of town. Local parents, meanwhile, came to view the House's Bible studies and assumed antidrug thrust to be distinctly preferable to the attractions of Haight-Ashbury.[43]

As the Living Room made contact with a steady stream of hippies and the big house bulged at the seams with runaway teens, Evangelical Concerns began to promote the group among the churches in the Bay Area. Ted Wise and a revolving mix of the Living Room men were frequently slated for guest appearances at Sunday night services and pastors' meetings. As exotic to the audience as any missionary returned from New Guinea, they would give their testimonies, tell about their work with the hippies, and field questions from teens and adults alike. A January 1968 appearance at Thornton Avenue Baptist Church in Fremont, California, was described in a local newspaper:

> Ted Wise…was accompanied…by two more converts, "Steve" and "Dan." All three wore typical hippie garb—corduroy trousers, wide belts, casual shirts without ties, and black boots. Dan added a leather jacket decorated with long fringe, and Ted sported a wooden ornament on a long leather thong around his neck. The trio also wore their hair long and had over-sized moustaches.

The story continued with the tale of "Dan" (not Dan Sands), a recent Living Room convert, and how he had come to know Jesus:

> A runaway at 10, a dope addict at 13, he had reached rock bottom last fall.…A miracle, he is sure, led him to Ted. He told Ted that he was in need of a "fix" or he'd be violently ill. "But," Dan continued, "Sandy [sic] who is Steve's wife, put her hands on the needle marks on my arms, and she prayed. I slept, which was most unusual, and I wasn't sick. The next day in Golden Gate Park I accepted Jesus as my Savior."[44]

The conservative churches' reaction to the hippie Christians seems to have been mixed. Although the Mission's operators occasionally received some money or other offers of assistance, some forays—like the time they drove over 200 miles down to Fresno and were given a couple of dollars for a meal at McDonald's—ended up largely being exercises in hoping that a few straight Christians would be inspired to reach out to hippie youth. At this juncture, though, it appears that most of the pastors and congregations were not buying what they were selling. Steve Heefner recalled in a 2007 interview that at one time he had "counted 54 or 55 churches that members of the group had gone to, mostly the guys, sometime all of us—and we never got invited back to one damn church."[45] One woman's response about a request to house one of the hippie kids that they were trying to get off the street spoke volumes of the attitudes of many conservative church members. Evangelical Concerns board member Ed Plowman remembered that after he had made the request, the woman just stared at him in disbelief and blurted out: "Pastor—THAT [person] between my clean sheets?"[46]

Publicity for the "Psychedelic Christians"

Their connections with the board of Evangelical Concerns was, obviously, the key factor in helping the Wises and friends make their way onto the radar screens of Bay Area evangelicals. But by the end of 1967, they actually earned some nationwide publicity in the form of an article in the evangelical monthly *Christian Life*. A solidly respectable periodical based in the holy city of the Midwestern, Billy Graham–style postwar evangelical movement, Wheaton, Illinois, *Christian Life* filled the mailboxes of tens of thousands of subscribers each month with news of victorious evangelistic campaigns, devotional reflections, Bible study aids, tips on child and family life, and advertisements for baptismal tanks and vacation Bible school curricula. However, the cover of the January 1968 issue promised a major jog from the magazine's usual image of evangelical propriety: staring at subscribers was Ted Wise, his longish hair, handlebar mustache, and slightly amused look miles away from the middle-class respectability of the famed pulpiteers and Bible teachers who usually graced the magazine (figure 2.2).[47]

Inside, the cover story, "God's Thing in Hippieville," contained the impressions of Maurice Allan, a conservative thirty-two-year-old English Congregational minister who had been in the States for a while and studied at the Moody Bible Institute and Winona Lake (now Grace) Theological Seminary. Somehow while visiting the Bay Area that summer, he heard about the hippie Christians hanging around at First Baptist in Mill Valley and came calling on John MacDonald with an idea about doing a magazine piece on what was going on there. The Baptist minister told Allan about the exciting growth in the group and the quickly evolving nature of the just-founded Evangelical Concerns, and he put him in touch with Ted Wise. Over the next several weeks Allan traipsed along with the group on their rounds in the Haight (even, it turns out, going with them on a visit to Lou Gottlieb's famous Morningstar Ranch, where Jim Doop did a little contextual sharing of the gospel in the nude amid the unclothed hippies there), and he and his family spent a lot of time with their families up at the house in Mill Valley before departing in the fall.[48]

The magazine hit subscribers' mailboxes in mid-December. Allan presented the story of Wise's troubled marriage and extensive drug use, as well as the fact that in "a strange way, LSD had speeded up Ted's conversion to Christ." Although the article—given the intended audience—could not help but paint the Living Room group and its hippie environs as eccentric and exotic (the article included a helpful glossary of hippie terms and phrases for the enlightenment of its evangelical readership for such things as *blow the mind, groovy,* and *pot*—"usually smoked in *joints*"), its overall tone was overwhelmingly positive. Allan saw the contextual need for workers to evangelize the hippies, arguing that "psychedelic evangelists like Ted belong in this culture. It is part of them; they are part of it...these men are *in* as not even Billy Graham could be." Beyond this, however, there was something about their style and spirit he found oddly attractive:

> I like to think of them as a kind of evangelical Robin Hood and his merry men. With their different costumes, communal ghetto-style living, and anti-authoritarian ways, they outwardly resemble the mythical English

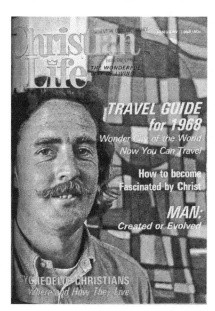

FIGURE 2.2 Ted Wise, "Psychedelic Christian," on the cover of the January 1968 issue of the evangelical monthly, *Christian Life.*

folk-hero. Also, like him, they are essentially on the right side of what is righteous and good. Sideburns, para-military jackets, thigh-high dresses, red Indian motifs—they dig these and/or other tell-tale marks of the interstitial culture of the psychedelic scene. Strongly pacifist, not unduly patriotic, yet they love Jesus Christ, and their allegiance to Him is undeniable.[49]

He figured that many readers would be concerned "because this group doesn't conform to their standards of behavior or rules of dress." Yet, he held out hope that the San Francisco street Christians were young and would mature, as well as that "some lessons about happiness, love, community and peace will get through" to the squares, hoping that "if they are patient enough, some of us might even get groovy."[50]

For their part, Wise and friends seemed to find Allan's article "fair, accurate, and very important to our ministries."[51] Ted Wise even went so far as to thank *Christian Life* for sending Allan to them and to recommend him to the brethren; in a letter to the editor published a few months after the original article appeared Wise wrote:

From Ted Wise, a servant of God through Our Lord Jesus Christ, to Robert Walker, his friends and brothers at Wheaton, also to those who in the foreknowledge of God the Father, are to read this. I commend to you my brother Maurice Allen [*sic*] for what he taught us and for writing about what the Lord Jesus has done in our lives.... In this way he convicted us of

all we were that was not of good report and virtue. He fastened our attention upon things from above, as the Lord said to do (Colossians 2:20–3:2).
In Love, Ted Wise, Novato, Calif.[52]

John MacDonald was, however, less sanguine about the article and about Allan,
feeling as he did that his countercultural charges were a fragile lot. Writing in
1970, he concluded from his "observation" that, at bottom, the average hippie was
a product of "emotional problems" and that "longtime emotional illnesses, in
varying degrees of severity" were present "among these young people."[53] Thus it
was that he thought Allan had gotten carried away with his assignment; in 1998,
he remembered that he had tried to get the young Englishman to view his sub-
jects more as he saw them—inclined toward exaggeration and loving the media
spotlight:

> I tried to get [Allan] to listen to me because I realized that our group of
> people were susceptible to having reports that were exaggerated or spec-
> tacular. But he turned me off and he went ahead and wrote what he wanted
> to write.... It was overdone, and I personally didn't appreciate it. It was
> of course very exciting for these folks to see themselves in print and in
> pictures and all.[54]

News of Wise and friends' existence seemed to touch a nerve within the evangelical community. After the article ran, *Christian Life* editor Robert Walker noted in
his "From the Editor" column in the magazine's April issue that they had received
"quite a number of letters and telephone calls" about "God's Thing in Hippieville."
As proof, the letters section featured a number of responses under the heading
"Storm over Hippieville."[55] As might be expected given the magazine's conservative, evangelical constituency, many of the letters were very critical of both the
hippie Christians and the magazine.

Thomas O. Grams, an Assembly of God minister from Lomita, California, noted
that the concept of "psychedelic Christians" caused him "great concern.... I'm
afraid I can't identify this type of Christianity with the Gospel of Christ." Similarly,
Rev. Robert Bartless of Philadelphia expressed his "disappointment": "Someone
should be given equal opportunity to point out why a change of attitude, culture
and dress should take place at the time of conversion."[56]

Thomas Smart of Hot Springs, Arkansas, was outright "shocked" by the article:
"To get down in the gutter and wallow in filth is not like my Christ," he argued,
maintaining that the clarion call to "Come out from among them and be ye separate" (2 Corinthians 6:17) was the guide in such instances. New York City's Glad
Tidings Tabernacle's pastor, R. Stanley Berg, went Smart one better. A bulk sub-
scriber to *Christian Life*, Berg was none too pleased that the magazine had devoted

"11 pages to explain what the 'make-love-not-war' flower children were accomplishing through their culture." It was "too far out" he punned, "from any New Testament standard" to be of any use to him, and he was returning his January bundle of issues back to Wheaton.[57]

But not everyone was put off by Allan's portrait of Wise and the Living Room group; others—mostly laywomen, interestingly—wrote approvingly of this new gospel venture. Mrs. C. A. Kuhn of Sugarcreek, Ohio, thanked *Christian Life* for the "insights into our own failures to reach our new generation." The secretary of the First Baptist Church of La Crescenta, California, Mrs. Ruth Baker, inquired about obtaining reprints of this "most enlightening and thought-provoking" article. Mrs. M. C. Harvin of Louisville, Kentucky, wrote in to testify how she had been moved by the article. "Several days after reading 'God's Thing in Hippieville,'" she wrote, she had been unable to sleep and had "prayed until after 2:30 A.M.," the result of God wanting her to "give a Christmas gift to Ted Wise for his work among the Hippies."[58]

The letters kept coming in the months that followed, until Walker had to announce in his June 1968 issue that he was calling a halt to the editorial debate. Most of the follow-up letters printed in the May and June issues demonstrated a sizable wellspring of positive feelings within *Christian Life*'s readership toward the efforts to spread God's Word to the counterculture. From Denver, Mrs. Silas Correa wrote to say she was "so happy to learn of the ministry of Ted Wise among his 'own people.'" She shared how her pastor had made a group of hippies feel welcome at her home church and hoped "that many Christians who sincerely love the Lord will seek to win the hippie population to Christ."[59] Others wrote in to express their dismay at some of the negative letters that had appeared in the April issue. Thelma Stahor of Hershey, Pennsylvania, wondered "how can we not love...those who are still sinners and enemies of God, if we are truly the followers of Jesus Christ? He kept company with harlots, publicans, and sinners and was condemned by the 'churchmen' of His day....Lord, grant us the grace to work together for the Kingdom of our God...."[60]

Checking Out the Hippie Evangelists

Even before the appearance of the *Christian Life* article, a small but steady stream of local pastors, evangelists, and field-workers from groups like the Navigators had begun to troupe into the Mission to check out what was going on there. Sometimes they were genuinely interested in understanding the outreach to the hippies, and in other cases, they were intent on making sure that the group was toeing the line on the various behavioral taboos—including the new preoccupation with the length of men's hair—that reigned within the evangelical subculture.[61]

One visit that caused a particular stir was a December 1967 expedition by Assemblies of God evangelist David Wilkerson, author of the book *The Cross and the Switchblade* (1963) and head of Teen Challenge, an organization targeting street gang members and drug addicts.[62] The increased use of drugs associated with the counterculture had opened a new dimension in Wilkerson's ministry, and he came to San Francisco intent on checking out the local scene for a new book and for a film he wanted to show at his speaking engagements. After a quick stop at the Living Room, he made an appointment to visit the communal house in Novato and showed up with a film crew in tow.

Initially open to "being in the movies," Wise and friends' enthusiasm quickly melted away under the hot lights and Wilkerson's interrogation. The Pentecostal preacher asked them several questions about whether a hippie could come to Jesus and still smoke pot or take LSD and then asked them if they were telling the hippies to stop all drug use, cease and desist "free sex," and cut their long hair. Steve Heefner recalled that Wise said something to the effect of "We tell them about the Lord Jesus Christ" and that when it came to cleaning up a person's life, the individual in question and Jesus could "get together on that"; the folks at the Living Room were "not in that business."[63] After Wilkerson asked the group if they practiced free love in their communal living arrangement, Wise and the others exploded and ordered them to turn the cameras off and leave. That evening Wilkerson called, apologized, and asked to make another attempt at an interview down in the Haight—and offered a $100 donation as a gesture of his sincerity. Seeing him as repentant and convinced they should forgive him, they agreed to meet him the next day down on Page Street.[64]

The next morning, they found not only Wilkerson and his film crew waiting for them back at The Mission but also a TV news crew from Channel 2 in Oakland. "Channel 2 came in filming Wilkerson," said Heefner, "who was filming us." After taking footage of the mission, they sat down with both sets of cameras rolling. Again, Wilkerson opened up with the same line of questioning. After initially playing along with the questions and joking about taking drugs during their Bible studies, Wise and friends finally just stopped the interview and threw Wilkerson and the TV people off the premises.[65]

But damage had been done. That evening, footage of the interview ran in the Bay Area, and the group heard reports that it had been picked up by a few stations across the country. Wilkerson then went on a local Christian radio station to "expose" the hippie mission and contacted the editor of *Christian Life* about the dangerous group they were promoting.[66] Wilkerson incorporated snippets of the interviews into a film he showed in conjunction with his speaking engagements across the country in late 1968 and 1969. And in his new book highlighting the perils of hippie drug use—*Purple Violet Squish*—Wilkerson referenced his encounter at the Living Room:

I had a shocking conversation with four psychedelic ministers. They told me they "dropped acid" (took LSD) before they undertook Bible study. They were especially intrigued by their study of the book of Revelation under the influence of LSD. One said, "Man, what a blast—even the beasts come to life." Under the influence of psychedelics this generation of hippies is questioning the old truths of the Bible....They seek salvation in a pill.[67]

The flap over Wilkerson's accusations caused no little stir within the advisory board of Evangelical Concerns. As MacDonald related the story, the board grilled Wise, Sands, Doop, and Heefner on the accusations and, assured by their denials, issued statements that bluntly refuted "the use of any hallucinogens or narcotics" by the Living Room's staff. But despite their pleas of innocence, MacDonald later learned that "regrettably...there was some substance to the criticism."[68]

As Ted Wise remembered the situation, the problem was that the preachers had "made the assumption that we weren't doing anything." There was still a fair amount of drug use going on, and marijuana was routinely trotted out down at the Page Street Mission. One of the basic factors was that a social joint was an aid to evangelism: "It gave me the opportunity to share the Word," Jim Doop later stated. Indeed, an unwillingness to smoke grass often proved detrimental to their witnessing efforts in those early days, as wary hippies were prone to suspect that anyone who would not partake in the counterculture's primary social lubricant was "a narc." And drug use was not just happening down at the Mission. Wise remembered one Bible study in particular at The House that MacDonald led, during which a neighborhood teen stowed away some grass down in the basement. "Slowly," he recalled, "people began to get up and meander downstairs where the pot was" until MacDonald was left practically by himself upstairs. Afterward, Wise felt bad, wanting to explain to the Baptist pastor that "it wasn't his teaching—it was pot in the basement!" But, according to Wise, they were ultimately not trying to pull a fast one on their friends in Evangelical Concerns: "He had never asked," he said of MacDonald. "We would have told him, nobody was hiding it." As Jim Doop wrote years later, "They never considered that there was anything wrong with smoking [pot]" in and of itself.[69]

Nonetheless, the group had begun to have some misgivings about their drug use by this time. One problem they encountered was financial. Early on into the start of their evangelistic mission, they had decided, on the basis of proper stewardship, that they could no longer see their way to buying grass and would only partake of freely proffered pot. "We didn't have the money to buy drugs," explained Jim Doop years later, and in light of those circumstances they "felt that it was inappropriate to use God's money in that way."[70]

By the time of the Wilkerson visit, however, the principals at the Living Room had started deciding that other drugs were off the table as well. Rick Sacks related one incident from sometime in late 1967 that was key to his own move away from psychedelics. One afternoon they had finally had a breakthrough with an early frequenter of the Page Street mission—one Stefano—who had finally accepted Jesus as his savior. Elated over this straying sheep having been brought back into the fold, one of the extended members of the group said he had just gotten his hands on "some fresh acid" and wondered if perhaps they should celebrate Stefano's entry into the Lamb's Book of Life by taking some. They thought this was a splendid idea, piled into a car, and took a drive out to Land's End on the west side of the San Francisco peninsula, where they proceeded to drop the LSD and marvel at the wonder of God's creation. Rick Sacks remembered:

> I [was] in…this little hole in the side of the cliff just so stoned I couldn't talk. And I'm watching God spinning clouds around and imagining seeing His finger reaching down and touching the clouds and giving 'em a swirl, and God's displaying His power and majesty for me.…All of a sudden Stefano gets up and he's about to jump off this cliff—and I couldn't talk. I remember praying and saying "God, I realize that I'm doing something that's preventing me from saving this guy's life and don't know what to do—help him." And Ted started talking to him and Ted talked him through it and Stefano sat down. And that was my last time taking LSD. It was then that I realized I couldn't do what God was calling me to do…because of this thing I thought I was doing to get closer to God.…I was here as an ambassador with a job to do.[71]

Just as acid had come to be viewed as bad form among the group, the influence of their sustained study of the Bible and their contact with establishment evangelicals—and probably their experience with Wilkerson—gradually convinced them that perhaps their pot smoking also had to stop. Dan Sands, on the strength of scriptural exhortations not to be "a stumbling block" to others, began to strongly voice his concern that their fondness for marijuana was indeed "stumbling [their] brothers" in the churches. And as Ted Wise recalled, there was also a growing concern about biblical injunctions urging Christians to be of a sober mind. Concerned with the fact that smoking grass was considered a "bad witness in some people's minds," they decided it was best that they change their ways. From that point forward, drugs were—for the most part—left behind.[72]

The Soul Inn

While the evangelistic work of the Living Room and the work of the commune in Novato went on and attracted backing from, and visibility within, the Bay Area's evangelical community, Kent Philpott and his hippie associate David Hoyt struggled on in the shadows without much immediate help from straight sources. At one point, Hoyt left the Bay Area for several months for an abortive attempt to enroll in California Baptist College in Riverside (the Southern Baptist administration there was put off by his longish hair and his new preference for dressing completely in white) and a subsequent call to help put together a drug rehabilitation commune called "The Way Inn," which was housed in a dilapidated tuberculosis sanitarium outside Lancaster, California. Meanwhile, Philpott was forced to alternate two-week stretches between the Haight and Southern California, where his wife and children were now living with his in-laws and where he would work as a laborer for his father-in-law's construction company. Then he would hitchhike back to the Bay Area to continue witnessing to the hippies, having convinced the pastor of the tiny Lincoln Park Baptist Church on Balboa Avenue in the city's Richmond district to let him sleep in the church sanctuary. "I had no money to eat," Philpott later reminisced. "I took advantage of the free stuff in the Haight." Wearing his old Air Force boots and a ragged jean jacket over old clothes, he would walk three miles to the Haight, arriving in the hippie district in the early afternoon, and most days not return until after midnight to his sleeping bag stored behind the Lincoln Park Baptist pulpit.[73]

When Hoyt returned to San Francisco late in the summer of 1968, the pair resumed working together; Kent Philpott kept a diary during most of this time. An excerpt from the early fall of 1968 gives a picture of both the Haight and the challenges facing the two countercultural evangelists:

Spent morning doing visitation in Haight and talking to people as we found them.

 . . . .

Talked to Luther, co-owner of the Straight Theater who David had known in his "before Christ" days. Heavy witness, and Luther wanted to talk more in the near future.

Mark, a devotee at the Krishna Temple. Brother David encountered him and was able to give him a full Gospel testimony. Mark actually was shaking as he walked away.

Fillmore: very late at night in a tough neighborhood for a lone white person. Two guys tried to rob David but since there was no silver or gold, David gave them the Gospel.[74]

 . . . .

A girl named Space, actually demon possessed, we found in a trance right out on the street . . . a young beautiful girl had her whole body painted in weird designs. She was staring at an older grey haired cat who was controlling the trance. People on the street thought the whole trip was cool. . . . She was so bound inside she could hardly talk. There was a chain of nails and pins around her neck. We approached her, praying hard, and

stepped into the line of sight between Space and the older cat. This move
shut down the trance. We began praying in the Spirit and knowing only
God could intercede. . . . At last she began to break down and she started to
cry. When she began speaking she started telling us she was God. She was
bound and trapped by horrible people who used her as they would, and all
the hips thought it was good she could do her thing.[75]

. . . .

. . . we ran into a far out guy named Charlie. He started preaching to us
what he called "God's Ultimate Truth." He was barefoot, dirty, had alcohol
on his breath, and was just coming off an acid trip. He became very violent
when we assured him that he wasn't God.[76]

. . . .

We went over to see old friend named Ileen. We found ourselves seated
around the kitchen table with about eight lesbians. Many of the girls had
been delving into various Oriental teachings. There was a very heavy confrontation and any preaching of the Gospel was tough. However, for about
one hour, they heard the Word of God as the Holy Spirit blessed. One girl
named Robin seemed very interested. They had so many cats that the smell
of their droppings nearly made you sick. Also, God made opportunity to
sing a few Gospel songs. These girls are somewhat afraid of men, but they
are very precious people and God loves them so much.[77]

. . . .

Visited Louis and Jenniene. Everything was so good and two hours later
little Jenniene accepted Jesus as savior.[78]

By this time, Philpott and Hoyt had established fellowship with Ted Wise and
the Living Room set, a relationship facilitated by the fact that the leadership
of Evangelical Concerns knew many of Philpott's Golden Gate Seminary and
Southern Baptist connections. For his part, Philpott admitted to being of a similar mind to many of his Baptist brethren in MacDonald's Mill Valley church in
that he "didn't really get along too good with Ted and those guys, they were all
acid head intellectuals. . . . I was too straight." Philpott realized, however, that—
like David Hoyt—they were "better . . . in talking the hippie language" than he was
and "were very effective" and thus he would often bring people to them, because
he thought some of his more "hardcore" hippie contacts "would be better off talking to Ted and [those] guys."[79] For their part, the Living Room group saw Philpott
and Hoyt as Christian brothers and happily worked with them, although, oddly
enough, they looked back years later and seemed to think they actually got along
better with the straight Philpott than with the former Haight resident, Hoyt. To
their minds, Hoyt had a tendency toward dogmatism and asceticism; he often
rubbed the free-thinking Wise the wrong way, and Steve Heefner recalled that they

"tangled" a few times. Still, while there was no formal linkup, a working relation-ship emerged, and Philpott and Hoyt often dropped by the Page Street mission or went out to the "Christian House" in Novato for a meal or to drop off a convert in need of a place to sleep. Likewise, sometimes Lonnie Frisbee, Danny Sands, or Rick Sacks would join Philpott and Hoyt in their street-witnessing excursions.[80]

Out of desperation for a place to house the converts and seekers they encoun-tered, Philpott, with considerable help from Golden Gate Seminary's Dr. Francis DuBose, was eventually able to persuade the pastor of Lincoln Park Baptist Church on refitting a pair of Sunday school rooms for his work. With a little paint, a new shower, some cots and blankets borrowed from the Salvation Army, and a sign painted by David Hoyt, the Soul Inn opened in late 1968. The facility had a capacity of about twenty and served as a combination shelter and halfway house, with day-to-day activities overseen by two proven converts, David Palma and Paul Finn.[81]

A House Divided

By the summer of 1968, the communal living arrangement at the House of Acts in Novato had begun to wear a bit thin. As might be expected under such cir-cumstances, the constant level of activity, the tension of making ends meet, the crowded living conditions, and the long months of living cheek by jowl with the same old people and their same old shortcomings proved a long-term corrosive force. But there were other contributing factors.

One of the irritants was a creeping legalism that gained entrance through the group's intense desires to hew close to New Testament instructions. Tobacco use was one point of contention. Although the Wises, their friends, and their extended circle had by this time pretty well ejected drugs out of their personal vice inven-tories, tobacco was one addiction that plagued some in the group. Judy Doop, particularly, had been a fairly heavy smoker and had a tough time kicking the habit. In an attempt to help her—again, in the spirit of avoiding being "stumbling blocks"—an edict was passed that no one was allowed to smoke in the house or on the grounds. This caused no small degree of personal aggravation, sneaking around, and hassles with nicotine-addicted prospects.[82]

Another source of tension came in the area of male-female hierarchies within the group. Although duties in Novato rather naturally fell into line with postwar cultural norms and assumptions that cast women in traditional roles concerned with housekeeping and children, an increasing tendency to set the men aside as "spiritual leaders" (based on biblical injunctions such as Ephesians 5:22: "wives submit unto your own husbands as unto the Lord") came into evidence within the group. At some point, the men decided they needed extra time for prayer and discussion and would gather together in one of the bedrooms behind closed doors, excluding the women. After a while, the woman began to chafe at this new direction, and one evening, after the men had returned from the Haight, they marched out of the kitchen in single file, dressed in long dresses, and wearing pot holders on their heads (I Corinthians 11:5a, "But every woman that prayeth or prophesieth with her head uncovered dishonoureth her head"). The men laughed hysterically and got the point, but the underlying problem persisted.[83]

Pastor Wierwille Comes Calling

While these personal, social, and theological issues all undermined the commune's solidarity, another major difference began to pull the couples apart: the influence of a tall, middle-aged Midwestern pastor. In the early spring of 1968, an out-of-town visitor from Ohio, Dr. Victor Paul Wierwille, dropped in to see John MacDonald at his church in Mill Valley. Wierwille told MacDonald that he had read the *Christian Life* article and that he was interested in the ministry the "Psychedelic Christians" had among the hippies. MacDonald later recalled that they enjoyed a very amiable visit and that "he presented himself as an active minister running a camp in Ohio." Wierwille told him of his background in the old Evangelical and Reformed denomination (which had merged with the Congregationalists to form the United Church of Christ in 1957) and his past coursework at the University of Chicago Divinity School and Princeton Theological Seminary. MacDonald "took it in" and heartily encouraged Wierwille to visit the Living Room to see the group in action.[84]

Wierwille had misrepresented himself, however. Although he had indeed taken courses at Chicago and Princeton, his 1948 doctorate came from a Denver-based diploma mill called Pike's Peak Bible Seminary (which would be chased out of the state of Colorado not long after Wierwille's San Francisco trip). And Wierwille's ties with the Evangelical and Reformed Church had been severed back in the mid-1950s as he touted a growing roster of beliefs and emphases (speaking in tongues, ultradispensational views on prophecy, an increasingly nontrinitarian view of Christ, a rejection of water baptism, and the conviction that the New Testament was originally written in Aramaic, not Koinonia Greek) that were out of sync with scholarship and the church's theology and traditions. Since the late 1950s, he had presided over his own independent organization, The Way, Inc., headquartered at the Wierwilles' old family farm in New Knoxville, Ohio, about seventy miles southwest of Toledo. Wierwille's "Power for Abundant Living" (PAL) lectures and the *Way* magazine attracted a steady trickle of supporters over the next decade, but, overall, his group's contacts were in the low four figures when he set out for the West Coast to investigate the street Christians.[85]

One day soon after his visit with MacDonald, Wierwille dropped in to the Mission and met Ted Wise. He thought the Midwestern pastor seemed "OK" and invited him to the House in Novato: "We had lots of interesting people [come to the House]," Wise later recalled. "We figured if they were Bible-believers that was fine—studying the Bible was fun to do." Wierwille came to Novato and told the crew about his institute back in Ohio, explained his theory how the phrase "a few" in the Scriptures always meant "eight," and expounded on the work of the Holy Spirit (which was followed up with a quick group exercise in speaking in tongues). Two nights later he came back, armed with an impressive housewarming gift for a struggling community operating on a shoestring budget—fifty pounds of hamburger meat. Wierwille spent that evening tape-recording interviews with the inhabitants. Jim Doop noticed that he seemed to be inordinately interested in his and his wife's former involvement with the Sexual Freedom League—"the only person who ever asked us specific questions about it." Later that evening, Wierwille trotted out a movie projector and showed the newly filmed introductory installment of his PAL course. The result was pretty much a disaster. The cinematic talking head Bible lecture—spiced up with several interruptions for repairing film breaks—"went over like a lead balloon." Overall, Wierwille came off badly—the "Ohio farmer straight guy with a skinny tie" reminded many of those gathered of a "used car salesman." After he left, Steve Heefner remembered that all assembled "had some good laughs at his expense."[86]

Although his foray into countercultural San Francisco had gone less than smoothly, Wierwille, for his part, left the Bay Area impressed with the Living Room group and their potential for evangelizing youth. He returned to his headquarters in New Knoxville, determined to woo some of the group into closer contact with his Midwestern ministry. Over the next several weeks, he bombarded his chosen contact—radio veteran Steve Heefner—with personal messages and invitations to attend a special summer discipleship course in Ohio, eventually sending him a special delivery letter and a tape of a Way service, asking him to reconsider his invitation. Heefner was unimpressed with the tape's corny music: "It was like getting a letter from the [WLS] Barn Dance, or the Grand Ole Opry," he remembered.[87] And although "he certainly didn't like the idea of going to humid Ohio" in the summertime "to talk to a bunch of squares," Heefner was in the midst of a round of prayer and fasting when the packet arrived and interpreted the timing as divine guidance.[88] In spite of earlier misgivings, in June 1968 he headed out to the Midwest with his wife, Sandi, planning to stay for three weeks. As it turned out, the couple—exposed to their first intensive, long-term, sustained study of the Bible—were impressed by the ministry and ended up staying in Ohio for the bulk of the summer. Particularly of interest was the information he picked up from the pastor about "discerning devil spirits," a skill he felt would serve everyone in the Living Room group well in their encounters with the stranger side of life in Haight-Ashbury.[89]

In late August, Heefner returned to the Bay Area raving to the other members of the House of Acts about the wonders of the teachings they had received in Ohio (including learning that the Apostle Paul's much speculated-upon "thorn in the flesh" in 2 Corinthians, chapter 12, was actually just "other people").[90] But the group—particularly Ted Wise, who distrusted Wierwille and thought him a hopeless square after the PAL movie debacle—was less than impressed. With the exception of Jim Doop, the proto-Jesus People in Novato expressed little interest in Wierwille's teachings and soon demanded that the Heefners quit talking about their Midwestern adventure.[91]

The split over Wierwille's influence exacerbated earlier problems. By this point, the tensions and differences had led some in the group to begin referring to The House in Novato as "The Big House"—as in penitentiary. At this juncture, connections the group had established through their work in the Haight also began to open up new opportunities, which further served to pull the group apart. Steve Heefner had quietly found a job with Evangelical Concerns board member William Mansdoerfer's employer, the Family Radio network. The Heefners seized the opportunity "to go over the wall" and, with help from John MacDonald, found a house to rent and moved out.[92]

At about the same time, Jim Doop was offered a position as the youth pastor at All Saints Lutheran Church in Novato, and in mid-September, he opened a drop-in center in the church's fellowship hall. Soon thereafter, they, too, moved out of the old House of Acts. Both couples continued to assist with the mission in the Haight for a while but were soon consumed with their other activities. The Heefners also began to hold Bible studies at their new home that emphasized many of the teachings they had imbibed back at Wierwille's headquarters in Ohio. The Doops dropped by some of these classes and, with a couple of other people from Heefner's meetings, went east in January 1969 to take one of Wierwille's classes. Like the Heefners before them, the Doops returned from New Knoxville energized by what they had learned, arranging for Wierwille to come out to California for a special four-day spring seminar.[93] Although both Heefner and Doop remained with their new employers for several more months, the two couples had clearly moved away from the influence of the Baptists in Evangelical Concerns and into the orbit of Victor Paul Wierwille's The Way, Inc.

Conclusion

The exit of half of the group's original members—along with Lonnie Frisbee's earlier departure because he felt God had called him to return home to Southern California—signaled the end for the Living Room/House of Acts group. Both the mission on Page Street in the Haight and the communal house in Novato continued on for a few months, but the group's essence had evaporated. The Haight was now long past its golden moment, and drug abuse and crime had turned it into a countercultural version of skid row. Likewise, the new hip Christians moved on. In early 1969, the Living Room closed, and the House of Acts commune broke up. The Sands family moved out, with Dan eventually enrolling at Golden Gate Theological Seminary with an eye to a degree in pastoral counseling. Ted and Elizabeth Wise moved in for a while with Pastor MacDonald and his family until they were able to find a place of their own. As had often been the case before, MacDonald's relationship with the Wises caused friction with his congregation. MacDonald recalled in 1998 that their pastor's living in this "communal" arrangement caused "something of a problem, because not everybody in the church leadership was favorable to our using the parsonage in that way." After a month, the Wises were on their way, renting a house back in Sausalito as Ted tried to start up his own sail-making business, while still taking on speaking engagements with Evangelical Concerns and involvement with a group of friends he had met in late 1968 from Peninsula Bible Church in Palo Alto.[94]

Kent Philpott and David Hoyt, meanwhile, continued to work within the countercultural milieu. They kept the Soul Inn open until mid-1969 down in the city; by that time, they had created a new entity called United Youth Ministries (UYM). They established links with the pastors and laymen in the Evangelical Concerns group, and by late September of 1969, the straight organization was formally serving as their advisory umbrella and funneling some funds their way.[95] By April 1969, Philpott and his family, along with Hoyt and his new bride, Victoria, opened up a home for runaway girls called Zion's Inn, for a short time in what had been The House in Novato and then in San Rafael. Within several months, new sites had been added—including Berachah House in San Anselmo, Maranatha House in San Jose, and Home for His Glory and Upper Streams House, both in Walnut Creek.[96] Much of the leadership for these new houses was provided by veteran contacts from the old Living Room group and the early days of the Soul Inn.[97]

Thus it was that the San Francisco Bay area had been the site of the first major outcroppings of what would later become known as the Jesus People movement. These beginnings were small, but they set the tone for a series of similar interactions in cities across the United States, which by late 1968 had begun to morph into a recognizable Jesus People movement—particularly to the south, in and around Los Angeles.

3

"...and Your Sons and Your Daughters Shall Prophesy"

THE JESUS PEOPLE MOVEMENT IN SOUTHERN CALIFORNIA, 1968–1969

AMID THE HURTLING trajectory of political and cultural upheaval of 1968 and 1969, the Jesus People movement not only grew in the San Francisco Bay area but also began to appear elsewhere. During this period, the movement spread to—and achieved much greater success in—the Los Angeles area, Orange County, and elsewhere in Southern California (SoCal). The spread of the movement beyond the Haight-Ashbury neighborhood and the Bay Area was the result of a complex intertwining of the '60s zeitgeist and local circumstances and actors. In almost every instance, the rise of a local Jesus People group in SoCal can be traced back to the work of a lone wolf evangelical minister like Chuck Smith, visionary youth workers like Hollywood's Don Williams, or, in some cases, to fringe figures like the marginalized ex-Christian and Missionary Alliance pastor David Berg, people who took it upon themselves—often in the face of yawning indifference or outright resistance from their evangelical peers—to reach out to the local youth involved in the counterculture and its shadow drug culture. Quick to tolerate hippie trappings within their revamped version of 1960s evangelicalism, they unleashed zealous hippie converts who, like the former Living Room/House of Acts member Lonnie Frisbee at Calvary Chapel, in turn bolstered and authenticated a counterculturally friendly atmosphere.

The typical Jesus People ethos was dominated by several core characteristics that mixed and matched influences from the evangelical and countercultural sides of the movement's parentage. First, the new street Christians' literalistic interpretation of the Scriptures led them into a heavy emphasis on Pentecostal and charismatic phenomena such as glossolalia, prophecy, and "words of knowledge." Second, the Jesus People inhabited a supernaturally charged world chock-full of signs and wonders and a steady outpouring of what they perceived to be divine intervention in their lives. Third, their biblicism and emphasis on the supernatural reinforced a preexisting countercultural pessimism about the direction of the world, creating a pervasive conviction that they were living in the Last Days. Thus, study of Bible prophecy and an emphasis on coming judgment came to preoccupy the Jesus People and figured strongly in their evangelistic message.

At first sight, most or all of these characteristics could be seen as applying, to some extent, to a broad swath of American evangelicals and Pentecostals during the 1960s and 1970s. But what set the Jesus People apart from their straight evangelical and Pentecostal cousins was the intensity with which these characteristics marked them and were incorporated into a distinctly nonbourgeois unchurchy atmosphere that was far removed from respectable America's way of doing church. First, the Jesus People—inspired by both hippie utopianism and their interpretation of the New Testament—placed a high value on communal living. Second, the Jesus People sought out and promoted a casual, come-as-you-are atmosphere that embodied the counterculture's emphasis on authenticity and comfort. Third, God's Forever Family seamlessly blended elements of the counterculture into their lifestyle, worship, and evangelism. Psychedelically charged artwork; pop culture bric-a-brac such as jewelry, buttons, and T-shirts; and—most important—their freewheeling adaptation of contemporary folk and rock music helped proclaim their beliefs and identity to the world.

Taken together, these various characteristics forged an identity for the developing Jesus People movement. Even in these initial stages, however, it became clear that this new hybrid combination of evangelical religion and counterculture style had an appeal that was not limited to hardcore street people, ex-drug addicts, and full-blown hippies. Younger adolescents in high school, particularly evangelical church kids, were attracted to the emerging Jesus People style as it developed in places like Hollywood Presbyterian Church's Salt Company and Calvary Chapel in Costa Mesa. This set the stage for the growth of a truly widespread youth-based evangelical movement.

Jesus People Beginnings in Southern California

Amid the small tremors that shook the wider evangelical community in reaction to the appearance of the *Christian Life* article on the psychedelic Christians of San Francisco, evangelical youth outreaches had begun to crop up to the south in the greater Los Angeles area. Utterly disconnected from what was going on to the north, these L.A. outposts of the as-yet-unknown movement—Arthur Blessitt's His Place, the work of street evangelists Tony and Susan Alamo, youth pastor Donald Williams's Salt Company nightclub, and David Berg's Teens for Christ in Huntington Beach—were initially targeted at local youth populations rather than at the counterculture per se. However, as the counterculture's influence and visibility spread, these evangelical outposts took on a more decidedly hippie aura in their quest to evangelize L.A. area youth and runaways swept up in the drug culture.

Arthur Blessitt and "His Place"—Hollywood, California

Described by early researchers of the Jesus movement as someone who always "sought good Christian adventure," the Rev. Arthur Blessitt established one of the more visible early outreaches to the developing mid-'60s drug scene on Hollywood's famous Sunset Strip.[1] A Greenville, Mississippi-born, Louisiana-raised Southern Baptist, Blessitt was a graduate of the Southern Bapist Convention's (SBC) Mississippi College and had served in student pastorates in small churches in Brookhaven, Mississippi, and Anaconda, Montana. In 1965, he came to California to study at the Southern Baptists' Golden Gate Seminary in Mill Valley. Blessitt was not impressed with what he found. Perceiving most of his professors and fellow students as "cold in spirit" and "arch-liberals," he abruptly quit school and headed off to Nevada, where he spent a year and a half as an itinerant circuit preacher in and around Elko.[2] In 1967, he came to Southern California, where he failed miserably in an attempt at traditional crusade-style revivalism at the San Bernardino fairgrounds. It was at this point that Blessitt claimed a direct call from God to minister to the down-and-out. He and his wife, Sherry, with the help of New Orleans–born Baptist pastor Leo Humphrey, found their way to the Sunset Strip in 1967, where Blessitt began to work the sidewalks, passing out tracts and sandwiches and attempting to find help for addicts and runaways.[3]

Handsome, friendly, and possessed of a quick smile and wit, Blessitt had found his element. However, he quickly realized that he would have to adapt his looks and speech to connect with the street scene. In his 1971 book, *Turned On to Jesus*, Blessitt recalled that he soon began to let his hair and sideburns grow and revamped his wardrobe:

> A collar or a business suit wouldn't get you anywhere. The first time I walked into a trip room I wore a tie and a suit. The heads panicked. They thought I was a narc agent out to bust them. After that I switched to turtle-necks and psychedelically-patterned slacks or bell bottoms and san-dals. Then came the beads.[4]

Blessitt also began to mimic the hip argot of the street. In talking to the increasing number of hippies he encountered, he urged them to consider "the Jesus trip" and to try "getting high on Jesus." Blessitt told his hip listeners of the joys of "dropping Matthew, Mark, Luke, and John" instead of LSD and urged them to "get loaded on Jesus; 24 hours a day you can be naturally stoned on Jesus!"[5]

To serve as his base of operations, Blessitt at first rented a small, $60-a-month room in a shabby old motel on Sunset Boulevard. But as his work among the Strip's denizens began to grow, he was able to put together enough financial backing from pastors and businessmen in mid-1968 to secure a $600-a-month storefront at 9109 Sunset Boulevard. Dubbed "His Place," the storefront mission was surrounded by bars, nightclubs, and strip joints. Although billed as a nightclub, His Place was a cross between an old-style skid row mission and a psychedelic coffeehouse: one room was lit by black lights, had blinking colored lights, and featured an ongoing slide show with intermittent gospel messages. Offering Kool-Aid, free peanut butter sandwiches, and day-old bagels from a Jewish bakery, His Place quickly became a magnet for the Strip's seemingly endless stream of junkies, bikers, and runaways.[6] Open twenty-four hours a day, seven days a week, Blessitt and a slowly growing corps of ex-addict counselors, along with his Eternal Rush house band (sometimes billed as "ex-drug fiends") preached and witnessed to young people—sometimes more than a thousand—that sidewalk traffic brought their way each night (figure 3.1).[7] Among Blessitt's most prominent converts was Glenn Schwartz, guitarist for the rock groups the James Gang and Pacific Gas and Electric.[8]

FIGURE 3.1 Three important early leaders of the developing Jesus People movement in California, Arthur Blessitt (l.) of "His Place," Duane Pederson, publisher of the Hollywood Free Paper (c.), and Berkeley's Jack Sparks (r.).

Courtesy of Fr. Duane Pederson.

One of the more colorful features of the scene at His Place was the evolution of what Blessitt came to call a "toilet service." In this ritual, converts who had prayed to receive Jesus were escorted into the washroom and urged to commit his or her "cache of grass, reds, speed, or acid" to the keeping of the Los Angeles sewer system. Blessitt recalled one instance where "18 small people" crammed into the little bathroom.[9] However, not all the drugs at His Place made it into the commode—one night someone spiked the Kool-Aid with LSD and sent everyone on an impromptu trip.[10]

Blessitt attempted to get area churches on board with his effort. Although some flatly told him they wanted nothing to do with "Negroes or anyone with a hippie background," the great majority simply conceded they had no "church program that would interest [those] young people." Eventually, Blessitt began to gather some local notoriety for his ministry through appearances in local SoCal churches urging congregations—mostly Southern Baptist—to consider reaching out to disaffected youth as a legitimate home missions endeavor.[11] But even as his star rose among local churches, Blessitt's presence began to grate on some of the owners of the bars and nightclubs on the Strip. Beside the fact that his operation was draining off some of their best customers, the witnessing teams sent from His Place to trawl for converts were becoming increasingly frequent on the sidewalks outside their establishments. Perhaps even more irritating, his followers had enthusiastically seized upon a Blessitt innovation, "Reds" (a play on the street slang for a type of amphetamines), a small, circular Jesus sticker with a motto such as "Smile, Jesus Loves You" and the address for His Place underneath a combination cross and peace symbol. Blessitt's disciples took to plastering Reds all over streetlights, traffic signals, stop signs, and the doors of the Strip's nonevangelistically oriented establishments.[12]

By the spring of 1969, Blessitt was taking credit for saving "more than ten thousand souls" and closing a nearby liquor store and nightclub. It was then, he alleged, that a "campaign to annihilate His Place" began to unfold that coupled police harassment on the sidewalks, raids on the club, and pressure from the Sheriff's Department—by way of neighborhood bar owners—on his landlord (or, as Blessitt described it, "a last-ditch attempt on the part of the Establishment to sweep the Strip clean of hippies and turn it back into a happy hunting ground for straight drunks"). With his lease abruptly terminated, Blessitt searched for a new home for His Place but was unable to come up with anything else on the Strip. In late June, to publicize his plight, Blessitt erected a cross on the sidewalk, chained himself to it, issued an open letter pleading his case, and began a twenty-eight-day fast to protest his situation. The stunt attracted attention from the press and local TV, and Blessitt claimed he spoke to "thousands of people" and that "hundreds were saved," with "dozens of runaways sent home, lives rescued, rededicated, and uplifted" just through his vigil.[13] In the end, he was offered a building by a

Jewish businessman named William Penzner, and on the afternoon of July 24, Blessitt ate a celebratory meal of fried chicken on the sidewalk in front of dozens of supporters. "Four weeks of witnessing, supplication, and fasting had proved too mighty a sword for all the weapons in the establishment's arsenal," Blessitt wrote triumphantly in 1971, "a determined soldier of the cross had defeated the generalissimos of greed who commanded the Strip." Within a few weeks, His Place had relocated to a building at 8428 Sunset Boulevard, and Blessitt was back in business.[14]

In addition to his new building, however, Blessitt had also found a great deal more publicity. Blessitt's opportunities for outside speaking engagements increased, particularly within the concerts and rallies that had begun to mark the flowering of the Jesus movement in Southern California.[15] Blessitt was soon distracted by other ministry pursuits—especially a cross-bearing ministry he first undertook on Christmas night 1969 that in the years ahead took him literally around the world—and His Place would wither away in the early '70s.[16] But despite his penchant for drama, hyperbole, and over-the-top self-promotion, Blessitt's outpost on the Sunset Strip really did reach a number of young runaways and kids looking for an exit from alcohol abuse and the drug culture. The visibility of his work proved to be an important early element of what would become the Jesus People scene in the Los Angeles area.

Don Williams and the Salt Company—Hollywood, California

Another of the influential early examples of what would become the Jesus movement was the spin put on congregational youth ministry by Don Williams, college pastor of the First Presbyterian Church of Hollywood (at the time, the nation's largest Presbyterian church). A native of Glendale, California, with a degree from Princeton Theological Seminary and a freshly minted PhD in New Testament from Columbia University, Williams was recruited to the position in 1967 by Henrietta Mears, a towering figure in evangelical Christian education whose protégés included Dawson Trotman, founder of the Navigators, and Campus Crusade for Christ founder Bill Bright. Mears died a few months before Williams's arrival, but whatever guidance he may have lost may have been made up for by his independence: "I was a lot more on my own than I had anticipated," Williams later reflected.[17]

Starting out with a class of "easily 200 college students" on Sunday mornings but frustrated by the fact that the church was miles from any campus, Williams set out to expand his group by starting Bible studies on the campuses of USC and UCLA. He especially targeted campus leaders and celebrities in his efforts, the so-called key kids concept advanced by Mears and by groups such as Campus Crusade and Young Life. Although this strategy seemed to work well, he was increasingly aware that youth culture was in the midst of a dramatic change. Several teens who did not fit the typical Hollywood Pres college student mold drifted into Williams's class and introduced him to the world of the counterculture. One, a pregnant teenage girl named Sarah Lemley, was particularly influential. Once converted, she "literally dragged [Williams] onto the streets of Hollywood," he recalls. "I began to meet hippie tribes....I began to go to these coffeehouses" where he became familiar with Arthur Blessitt's ministry.[18]

What really began to get his attention, however, was the role that music was playing among the alienated youth. "My deepest listening came at the point of music," Williams wrote in 1972. "Here I began to feel the full weight of the cultural revolution, and here I found a great secret: music is the key to this generation because music is the one place in the mass media where kids editorialize to kids."[19] Although Williams would describe himself as being in his "Late Ray Coniff Era" then, one of his students—Bob Marlow—introduced him to the music of Bob Dylan, and Williams was soon fascinated with the singer-poet. Dylan, recalled Williams, was "the single most important influence" on his thinking about what was going on in the youth culture at the time "in terms of understanding [the generation's]...idealism on the one hand...and then the anger on the other hand."[20] Eventually, in the fall of 1967, Williams decided to do a special Sunday evening service titled "The Gospel According to Bob Dylan," with Marlow singing songs such as "Blowin' in the Wind" and "It Ain't Me, Babe," interspersed with Williams's commentary. The college group handed out flyers on Sunset Strip to publicize the event, but nobody, Williams included, expected the response they received: the usual Sunday evening crowd of 300 mushroomed to over 1,400, many of them from L.A.'s hippie street culture.[21]

By this time, Williams had a set of thirty to forty counterculturally oriented kids in his college-age group, many of them musically and artistically inclined. These hippie-friendly youth came up with the idea of a coffeehouse to reach their own kind more effectively. Familiar with the concept from poking around the folk clubs in Greenwich Village, Williams backed their plan to the church board. "The incredible thing," Williams remembered, "was that this church—which was an upper-middle-class, high-profile church, lots of city leaders as members...opened the door for us to do it." With the aid of $10,000 to $15,000 from the church and donated labor from a wealthy contractor, the upstairs of an adjacent apartment building was remodeled and christened "The Salt Company," complete with the "best sound system money could buy at the time."[22]

Opened during the summer of 1968, the Salt Company nightclub blended a rustic hip ambience, refreshments, and music the folk- and rock-attuned youth could appreciate. The new operation was a success from the start, routinely cramming in a hundred teenagers for each of two shows every Friday and Saturday evening.[23] With the help of a $1 cover charge, the club was even a financial success. By the end of the first year, Williams recalls that they were able "to give back a big pile of money to the church.... It was fun, I felt a little vindicated."[24] Over the next few years, the Salt Company led the way for Williams to widen the scope of Hollywood Pres's youth programs, including several communal houses, a Sunday morning worship service in a more informal style, an "underground" Monday night service that attracted upward of 150 youth each week, and occasional weekend concerts in the church's 2,000-seat sanctuary.[25]

While it was certainly successful in its own right, the Salt Company's biggest influence was its role as a prototype for counterculturally friendly youth ministry. Besides directly spinning off new coffeehouses in Newport Beach (The Carpenter's Shop) and Santa Monica (The Crossroads Coffeehouse), Williams and his assistants served as mentors to others interested in doing similar work, as pastors, youth workers, and concerned laypeople visited the Salt Company or corresponded with Williams to learn "how it was done."[26] "We didn't turn out books and how-to's and run seminars," Williams later remembered, "but I literally...had to set aside at least once a month...two to three hours for pastors and youth leaders to meet me to tour through the facility and talk about leadership." At some point when publicity about the Jesus People was at its height, Williams recalls an attempt to estimate the number of coffeehouses that may have been directly inspired by the Salt Company, and he put the number—at the least—at about 400.[27] Whatever the exact numbers, Williams's Salt Company was a major influence on the proliferation of Christian coffeehouses later on in the 1970s.

Tony and Susan Alamo's "Alamo Foundation"

Tony and Susan Alamo (pronounced "Ah-LAH-mo") may have been the most unlikely shepherds of any band of hippies and runaways to emerge from the era of the counterculture and the Jesus movement. Tony Alamo, aka Bernie Lazar Hoffman, of Romanian Jewish background, was a native of Joplin, Missouri, whose family later moved to Montana. He left Montana for California as a teenager and stumbled around Los Angeles as a small-time singer (taking the name Tony Alamo, he claimed, because of the success of all the postwar Italian crooners), record promoter, and public relations agent for more than a decade. Alamo claimed that in late 1965, Christ appeared to him in his bedroom and again when he was in the midst of a business meeting promoting pop singer P. J. Proby. According to Alamo's account, Jesus demanded that he tell his colleagues the Second Coming was at hand, which, somewhat understandably, threw the meeting into an uproar.[28]

It was a bit later—as Alamo told the story—that he ran into a casual acquaintance in a downtown restaurant: a divorced, platinum blond, itinerant Pentecostal evangelist named Susan Lipowitz. The estranged wife of a small-time union enforcer for the L.A. mob named Sol Lipowitz, "Susan" was the former Edith Opal Horn, a native of Arkansas who had come to Hollywood in the late 1940s in hopes of becoming an actress or singer. She claimed to have had Jewish parents and testified of a miraculous childhood conversion, complete with a healing and visions of the End Times. According to her daughter Chris, she was also a con artist who, when they were really down on their luck, would tell her daughter: "'Put on your dress, we're gonna do a church.' She'd say, 'I have a message from the Lord and I need to speak.' I would sing and she would speak and they'd do a love offering and we'd leave with money...that's pretty much how we survived." To her mind, the meeting of Susan and Tony was a meeting of two con artists trying to size each other up.[29] But according to official Alamo accounts of their restaurant meeting, Susan answered Tony's biblical questions and took him under her wing to lead him into a more complete understanding of his Christian commitment.[30]

What happened to them during the next two years or so is cloudy, but it does seem that the couple married in 1966, that Tony soon began claiming that he had been ordained, and that by December 1968, they had formed a not-for-profit corporation (called simply the Tony and Susan Alamo Foundation).[31] At some point during this period, they became regulars on Hollywood Boulevard, passing out tracts to the runaways and druggies. Eventually, they helped out and converted a drug dealer named Ed, who helped the couple begin to attract a following among these teens. After they rented a house on Crescent Heights Boulevard, dozens of kids would gather in the home's living room several nights a week to sing and hear Susan's impassioned, old-style Pentecostal preaching, with converts taken downstairs to seek the gifts of the Holy Spirit.[32] Plagued by quarrels with neighbors, the Alamos were able—with the help of a visit to a Full Gospel Businessmen's Fellowship (FGBMF) meeting in Santa Monica at which Tony and Susan pleaded their case—to move their group to another neighborhood. In early 1970, as that situation also proved unpopular with the locals, the FGBMF helped them relocate again, this time to a ramshackle abandoned restaurant on 7.5 acres in the desert town of Saugus, about forty miles northwest of the city (near where the Manson family holed up in a remote canyon during its infamous 1969 rampage).[33]

From Saugus, the Alamos established a routine that continued for the next several years: busing teams of followers into L.A. youth haunts such as Hollywood Boulevard and the Sunset Strip, where they would work the sidewalks passing out "turn or burn" leaflets emphasizing the coming judgment and the availability of a free meal and shelter in Saugus. In the evening, that day's crop of youth would load onto one of the Alamo's various VW buses, trucks, or a red, white, and blue bus (with its destination sign reading "Heaven") and head back out of the city.[34] After the promised meal, the seekers would be ushered into the nightly service, where they were met by an orchestra described by writer Tim Cahill as "a disparate collection of about sixty tubas, trombones, saxophones, flutes, and clarinets dominated by an electric bass, an electric organ, and three sets of drums" that would lead out on "standards like 'The Old Rugged Cross' and country devotions like 'My Savior Leads the Way.'" The tenor of the meeting that followed was fire and brimstone with a heavy dose of the Apocalypse, led by one of the Alamos or one of their chosen exhorters: "Hell," Cahill observed, "seemed to be the big selling point for salvation and it beat out heaven in terms of mention about ten to one."[35]

Once converted, the Alamo acolytes entered a strict, no-nonsense regimen designed to steel them against End Times persecution. In line with fundamentalist taboos, alcohol, drugs, and social dancing were forbidden, although tobacco—one of Tony Alamo's vices—was tolerated. To keep passions from boiling over, the sexes lived at opposite ends of the Saugus property. "Decency" in clothing was vigorously enforced, physical contact was absolutely forbidden, and males and females could converse only at meal times. All marriages had to be approved by the Alamos themselves, and each prospective couple had to undergo a ninety-day separation prior to their wedding.[36]

The Alamo Foundation was basically run as a commune, although the Alamos themselves resisted that label due to the contemporary perception that such arrangements usually meant free and easy sex. Members were forbidden to work outside the foundation and were rarely allowed or encouraged to pursue higher education. The average Alamo follower's main tasks were threefold: (1) Bible study—the King James Version—as taught by a hand-picked core of overseers, (2) street witnessing and tract distribution, and increasingly, as the years went by, (3) working at the group's growing train of offices and business enterprises.[37]

The Alamos and their bus ministry maintained a prominent presence on the Sunset Strip for several years, and their Saugus compound was an important stop-off for anyone making the Southern California Jesus People research circuit in the early to mid-1970s. However, the insular Alamos had few if any dealings with other Jesus People or other evangelical groups after 1970, and their following never grew much beyond 400 to 500 full-time adult members. Isolated in their canyon stronghold, the group did not establish any major branches outside the Los Angeles area, and by the late 1970s, the Alamos moved most of their operations to rural northwestern Arkansas.[38]

Teens for Christ and the Children of God (COG)

A fourth early manifestation of the Jesus People in the Los Angeles area was David Berg's Teens for Christ—later renamed and better known as the Children of God (COG)—in Huntington Beach, Orange County. The group's founder, David Berg, was the son of two preachers, Hjalmer Emmanuel Berg—an evangelist and later professor at Westmont College, an evangelical school in Santa Barbara,

California—and Virginia Brandt Berg, a Christian and Missionary Alliance evangelist and radio preacher. After graduating from high school in Monterey, California, and a stint in business school, the younger Berg married and tried to follow in his parents' footsteps by helping with their evangelistic work and then becoming a pastor in the Christian and Missionary Alliance. But after a few struggling years at a small church in Valley Farms, Arizona, Berg left the pastorate. According to Berg, it was because the whites in his multiethnic congregation were racists opposed to his "integration attempts and radical preaching that they should share more of their wealth with the poor." His estranged daughter Deborah, however, later maintained he was forced out due to allegations of sexual impropriety.[39] After a short stint as a schoolteacher, Berg found a position in 1955 as public relations director and booking agent for Pentecostal evangelist Fred Jordan's Los Angeles–based radio and television shows. But, after nearly a decade in Jordan's employ, a personal squabble caused Berg to sever ties with him in the mid-'60s.[40]

Now in his late forties, Berg gathered his family together and headed out on the road as an itinerant evangelist, traveling from Texas eastward, including a stint of evangelism at the 1966 New York World's Fair. During this period, his preaching was something of a sidelight to a youth singing group and evangelism team that featured three of his children (Paul, Jonathan, and Faith) and a daughter-in-law. For months, the group traveled around visiting various Pentecostal, Baptist, and independent churches, billed as "Teenagers for Christ...[that] like to witness instead of Watusi, preach better than protest, and win rather than sin—a teenage witnessing revolution to prove that Christ is more than the Monkeys [sic]."[41] The group apparently made no great impression on most church or street meeting crowds, and by December 1967, Berg accepted an offer from his mother to join her in Southern California. There, Mother Berg was working part-time with a coffeehouse just off the oceanfront in Huntington Beach called "The Light Club," originally founded by David Wilkerson's Teen Challenge organization and taken over as a mission by the FGBMF.[42]

Berg's mother died in early 1968, and her son's family became the main staff at the coffeehouse. Not having experienced much success with the place, the FGBMF happily turned the mission over to Berg and his Teens for Christ rent-free.[43] Within a short time, Berg attracted several converts from the hippiesque beach bum element. Berg's daughter Linda remarked that "Teens for Christ had discovered the secret to gathering lost and wayward youth: free peanut butter sandwiches and live music."[44] These earliest disciples, along with Berg's four children and their spouses, formed a close-knit group that would eventually become the leadership of the COG.[45]

But Berg's group hardly entered Huntington Beach as some sort of countercultural evangelistic team. Kent Philpott and David Hoyt from the Jesus movement scene in San Francisco recalled visiting the Light Club sometime during 1968 and being struck by the incongruity of what they saw there. The place was, they remembered, packed with scruffy, barefoot kids listening to Berg's surprisingly austere ministry team. "I'll never forget," said Philpott in a 2002 interview. "He and his sons were all dressed in black suits...we thought that was very peculiar...wall-to-wall kids...and here's this guy dressed in a black suit." In a 2008 interview, Hoyt echoed Philpott's recollections: "They were dressed up kinda like church people," and their program was "kinda contemporary but it was just very different" than what he was used to. And unlike the broadly cooperative evangelical spirit that characterized the relationship between hippies and church-based straights in the San Francisco scene, Philpott and Hoyt found no sense of brotherhood or welcome from Berg. Hoyt recalled that Berg "seemed like he was off into his own world...[like] they didn't really interact with too many other ministries." Philpott's recollections were blunter: "We didn't like him and he didn't like us...we were not gonna be involved with these people and it was real clear...there was no 'Lord bless you.'"[46]

But Berg's group, whether influenced by Philpott and company's visit or just by Berg's continued observations of the kids on the beach, took more of a countercultural turn in the months that followed. As Berg recalled in a 1979 newsletter:

> I saw something was really happening and was really going to explode! I just knew it! I saw the Lord was really doing something! That's when I began to come down and teach in my dark glasses, beret, baggy pants, old torn jacket and tennis shoes, looking more like an old beatnik instead of a hippie![47]

With Berg leading the way, long hair and beards, blue jeans and long granny-style dresses became the typical style among the Teens for Christ. But dress and hair styles were not the only changes that became evident within the Light Club. With Berg's declaration of a "Revolution for Jesus," he began to pitch his message to an alienated hippie audience, endorsing their rejection of American society, their parents' middle-class aspirations, and the thoroughly rotten "system." Envisioning an imminent Communist takeover of America by the lights of his literalist interpretation of Bible prophecy, Berg anticipated the destruction of the United States sans the pretribulation Rapture of the church, the escape clause many evangelicals relied on. A 1970 Berg parody of the Pledge of Allegiance perfectly captured both his and many of his followers' views on the status of the American dream:

> I find disillusionment in the standard of the Divided States of America, and in the autocracy to which it has degenerated: one Confusion, without God, totally divided, with Slavery and injustice for nearly all.[48]

In his general denunciation of an America soon to be judged for its sins, Berg did not leave out the organized church—particularly the conservative evangelical church. They, too, would reap the judgment of God. Although he would continue to laud various evangelical ministers and leaders, their work, and their writings until his death in 1994, Berg retained a smoldering resentment toward "Churchianity." In a 1972 reminiscence, Berg noted that by the mid-1960s, he had become convinced that:

> church members were a bunch of old hypocrites...[they were] much more interested in getting a fancier church building, swankier preacher, and more high-falutin' fancy choir and organ music, and showing off fancy clothes at meetings...membership had become a status symbol and a business necessity for the affluent society, a social club for the rich and well-to-do, to do their dainty little duty for God to the tune of dainty little ditties to God! Church was disgusting and a bore....Most of them were whited sepulchers full of dead men's bones, and the only way they reached Heaven was by their spiritual stench![49]

By the time he hit Huntington Beach, Berg claimed he was "so bitter against the churches for their hypocritical, do-nothing religion, their multi-million dollar Gospel entertainment business, and their multi-billion dollar fancy church buildings" that he was "ready to declare war on the Church System!"[50]

These sorts of sentiments against "System-Addict religion and the Educational and Commercial System in general," combined with exhortations to abandon all for the sake of God, began to win Berg new converts from hippie ranks.[51] By early 1969, the group had increased to about fifty members who devoted their full-time efforts to evangelism and lived communally at the club. Although life was certainly a hardscrabble affair, they managed to feed themselves by provisioning food from sympathetic establishments and culling leftovers and day-old products from grocery stores and fast-food restaurants' garbage bins.[52]

In contrast to other local manifestations of what would become the Jesus People, Berg's group stood out by their thirst for publicity and confrontation. In early January 1969, the group began a guaranteed headline-grabber, usually unannounced visits to straight churches during their Sunday morning worship services. Barefoot and clothed in hippie regalia, Berg's followers marched into a church, usually crowding toward the front of the sanctuary, and boisterously shouted "Amen!" and "Praise the Lord!" during the sermon. After the service, they chatted with the regular churchgoers about radical discipleship.[53] Awkward faux pas were inevitable, such as the service at St. James Episcopal Church in Newport Beach, where one Light Club worthy shouted his praise during communion to the horror of a flabbergasted congregation. Berg, for his part, later

remarked that they were "usually treated with great kindness, favor and tolerance," although their "welcome" usually was warmer "in the larger, more liberal
churches" as opposed to the "more conservative ones," where the reaction was "a
little fearful" (figure 3.2).[54]

And indeed it was during a string of visits to conservative evangelical churches
that the Sunday morning visits ran aground. At the First Assembly of God in Santa
Ana, the pastor threatened to throw Berg and his group out when their praises and
exhortations got too loud. At Anaheim's large Garden Grove Community Church
(later better known by its 1970s-era architecture as the Crystal Cathedral), pastor
Robert Schuller called Berg a "publicity-mad false prophet" and forced the group
to leave the sanctuary on the grounds that they were dressed inappropriately. The
rudest reception came at Melodyland Christian Center in Anaheim, an influential
force within the emerging Charismatic movement. There, Pastor Ralph Wilkerson
(no relation to Teen Challenge's David Wilkerson) had been denouncing Berg from
the pulpit, and when the Huntington Beach group showed up the next Sunday, he
promptly had them thrown out of the building, allegedly ripping Berg's clothes
and spraining his ankle in the process.[55]

Not surprisingly, Teens for Christ began to receive a fair amount of press in
Orange County. Around this time, some of Berg's charges began to visit local

FIGURE 3.2 David Berg.
Courtesy of The Family International.

campuses—including Cal State–Long Beach (CSLB) and Huntington Beach's new junior college, Golden West College—to pass out literature. At Golden West, six Teens for Christ—including Jonathan Berg—were arrested. While Berg told reporters that the "same things are happening to us as happened to Jesus and his 12 hippies" and that they would not be deterred from their church visits, all of the publicity was attracting a great deal of attention from local authorities, which was beginning to make life uncomfortable.[56] As a result, the FGBMF became quite vexed with its tenants at the Light Club and notified Berg that they would soon have to vacate the premises. Amid all these happenings, several of Berg's followers believed they had received a revelation from God that California was in imminent danger of destruction from an earthquake.[57]

With no roof over their heads, the group went on the road. After brief stays in Palm Springs and Tucson (in the latter city, the group attracted a number of new followers and nearly doubled in size), they spent the next eight months moving from place to place: Quebec, Virginia, Florida, and back west to Houston. The group established a trail of short-lived coffeehouses as they travelled but had to close them all, in Berg's words, "because of persecution."[58] This period, in the estimation of sociologist Robert Ellwood, became a central motif in the group's internal mythology, comparable to the Children of Israel's wandering in the desert.[59] It was also during this time that a newsman first called them the "Children of God," a name Berg liked and began to use.[60]

In February 1970, the literally bedraggled and emaciated COG—now numbering about 200—found refuge when Berg's old employer, Fred Jordan, offered them the use of his Los Angeles skid row mission and a rundown ranch in Thurber, Texas, about seventy miles west of Fort Worth.[61] For the next eighteen months, Jordan's organization provided the COG with much-needed food and shelter, and in exchange, they stoked his ministry among Pentecostal straights, frequently appearing on his L.A.-based television show as the fruit of the evangelist's work to turn around America's wayward youth.[62] All in all, the alliance with Jordan provided for the COG's physical needs, as well as a secure base from which they would be poised to expand in 1970–1971. The Children of God were set to become an important, visible, often controversial part of the early Jesus People movement.

Calvary Chapel, Costa Mesa, California

The largest single embodiment of the developing Jesus movement in Southern California was Calvary Chapel in Costa Mesa. Its pastor, balding, middle-aged Chuck Smith, had tired of denominational politics and bureaucracy and left the International Church of the Foursquare Gospel, the denomination founded by Aimee Semple McPherson. After building a home Bible study into the 150-member

Corona Christian Center (aided by a daily fifteen-minute radio broadcast over KREL, a small AM station), Smith was persuaded to take on the struggling Costa Mesa congregation in December 1965. The church membership numbered fewer than thirty people when Smith arrived. But by the spring of 1968, the church was a middling-sized independent congregation in conservative, middle-class, heavily Republican Orange County, southeast of Los Angeles. Under his leadership, the church underwent a modest renaissance, seeing its attendance climb to nearly 200 per week and a building program put in place.[63]

As Smith went about the business of shepherding his suburban flock, his wife, Kay, began to express an increasing concern for the hippies gathering at nearby Huntington Beach. Armed with an Orange County conservative's revulsion for hippies and all they stood for, Smith would go with his wife to gawk at the long-haired youth. "I saw them as parasites upon society," recalled Smith during a 2000 interview. "My original thought was 'Why don't they cut their hair and get a job and live a decent life?'" As far as he was concerned, "They were definitely a threat to society...they were radicals, smoking marijuana, dropping LSD...disrupting things, challenging the status quo," and he wanted nothing to do with them.[64] Eventually, his wife's concern for the

FIGURE 3.3 "Papa Chuck": Calvary
Chapel's Pastor Chuck Smith.
Courtesy of Calvary Chapel.

hippies' temporal and eternal needs began to melt Smith's resistance, and he began to think about how they might make contact with these prodigal youth (figure 3.3).[65]

Through his teenage daughter and her fiancé, Smith was introduced to a number of the beach hippies, including the newly arrived Lonnie Frisbee, a Costa Mesa native who had just come for a visit home from the San Francisco Bay area and his involvement with the House of Acts/Living Room. To Smith's surprise, Frisbee turned out, in spite of his flower child appearance, to be an enthusiastic Christian. Impressed by Frisbee's "love of Jesus and his Spirit-filled personality," Smith eventually asked him to serve as something of an unofficial missionary to the Huntington Beach hippies, giving Smith a chance to learn about the current crop of kids and "what [made] them tick." Frisbee agreed and began to preach and testify at Huntington Beach and other local hippie hangouts. Soon, Frisbee convinced his reluctant wife, Connie, to leave the Big House up in Novato, and the pair relocated to Orange County to work with Calvary Chapel.[66]

The slight, Jesus look-alike's evangelizing proved effective, and soon Frisbee and a growing corps of long-haired, casually attired, barefoot or sandaled youth were beginning to troopin amid the button-downed straight congregation at Calvary Chapel.[67] Given the rootless, runaway status of many of these young people, however, it became apparent that ministering to them would entail more than the opportunity to avail themselves of Calvary Chapel's regular services and meetings. Many of the new converts needed a place to live, food to eat, and an atmosphere where Bible reading and prayer could replace drugs and sex as their main pastimes.

In response to this need, Smith started talking to another young convert who had linked up with Calvary Chapel. John Higgins was a twenty-nine-year-old Irish Catholic from New York City; managing a door-to-door magazine subscription crew, he had been converted in May 1965 after reading a Gideon Bible in a hotel room. Frustrated by Catholic priests' lack of response to his questions about the Bible and prophecy ("they really literally just laughed at me," Higgins remembered), he was brought to a Bible study hosted by Chuck Smith in late 1966 and eventually underwent the baptism of the Holy Spirit. "My eyes were opened," he recalled years later, "like they had never been before, [Roman Catholicism] is just a waste of time...go [to Calvary Chapel] and serve the Lord." Interested in the hippies, he grew out his hair and added a beard to begin evangelizing local youth. Inspired by hearing youth worker David Wilkerson speak at nearby Melodyland Christian Center in Anaheim, Higgins was interested in starting up some sort of group living center similar to Wilkerson's Teen Challenge and began taking new converts into his house.[68]

Smith then invited Higgins to bring his house idea into Calvary Chapel and operate under the church's aegis. Working together, Smith and Higgins found an apartment in late April 1968 to house some of their born-again hippies. It rapidly proved too small, and an old two-bedroom house in Costa Mesa was rented as Calvary Chapel's first communal house, the House of Miracles, which opened on May 17, 1968.[69] Lonnie and Connie Frisbee were then brought in and, along with Higgins, were appointed coleaders. Calvary Chapel paid $50 of the monthly $90 rent and provided living expenses for the house staff and perhaps an occasional portion of the money needed for utilities and food. But the assistance was not nearly enough to handle the flood of kids who piled into the modest bungalow— within the first week more than thirty new hippie Christians needed to be fed. Connie Bremer Frisbee recalled that life in the house was tough: "I would have to borrow a bicycle to go dumpster-diving...we got given canned food; I would walk around and solicit help from people." Neighbors seethed about the swarm of scruffy kids descending on their subdivision.[70] The overcrowding intensified as one runaway girl named Cherise was converted—by herself, she was responsible for bringing more than fifty people to the house in one three-week period.[71]

This early success and the arrangement with the church people at Calvary Chapel apparently proved daunting to Frisbee, and he sought advice from his former mentors in the Bay Area. In response, Kent Philpott, David Hoyt, and others from the Evangelical Concerns–backed group piled into a car and drove to Orange County to investigate the arrangement. While they knew Frisbee was gifted in dealing with people one-on-one, they were unsure about his leadership potential: "We didn't feel real strongly about Frisbee," recalled Philpott. "I had never even heard him speak to a group because he was a nobody, he would never [have been] entrusted [even] to lead a Bible study [back in San Francisco]." One evening, the San Francisco group sat down with Frisbee and Chuck Smith and his elders at the House of Miracles: "They sat in chairs and all had coats and ties on, we all sat on the floor," remembered Philpott. As they listened to the details of the situation, the Bay Area street Christians were convinced that Smith's guidance would be a real plus. Reassured, Frisbee plunged full-ahead into his role as "hippie evangelist" at Calvary Chapel.[72]

There was much to do. With the House of Miracles overflowing and people sleeping in the backyard, a search quickly began for other facilities to house the growing stream of converts and inquirers. A sympathetic evangelical judge stepped forward with an old rundown motel he owned in Riverside, fifteen miles to the east. With materials provided by some of Smith's contacts and labor from the hippies, the motel was made inhabitable in early June. With four elders (two of them under twenty) in charge, the new facility absorbed the overflow from the Costa Mesa house. The Riverside house's residents quickly set to work witnessing and preaching on the city's streets. Within a week, sixty-five young people had been saved and subsequently baptized in the motel's old fish ponds. By the end of the summer, it was claimed that more than 500 young people—including several members of the Diablos motorcycle gang—had been converted through the efforts of those at the old motel. Still, the commune was forced to close down early that fall after problems policing drug and alcohol use among some visitors and a power grab by one of the elders.[73] Nonetheless, the work among the hippies continued : the Risen Son coffeehouse was opened across from the Greyhound bus terminal in Santa Ana, and the communal houses overseen by Calvary Chapel—Philadelphia House, Mansion Messiah, I Corinthians House, and another dilapidated motel in Newport Beach, the Blue Top—multiplied in and around Orange County.[74]

As Calvary Chapel's string of Jesus Houses prospered, the church itself was increasingly dominated by its ministry among the hippies, and its Sunday services and weeknight Bible studies reflected their presence. At first, very traditional gospel music was used in services; John Higgins recalled that early on, he used to intentionally arrive late in order to miss the musical portion of the service.[75] But eventually the presence of the hippies led to the incorporation of more informal, folk-style songs and choruses that proved to be a big hit. Future megachurch pastor and evangelist Greg Laurie was a junior at Costa Mesa High School in the fall of 1969 when he was converted by Lonnie Frisbee. He recalled in his 2008 autobiography that he was not a fan of Calvary Chapel's music as music, but something about it made a huge impact on him:

> Let's just say that these songs the Jesus people sang did not have a whole lot of complexity. There were about four chords. Simple lyrics, repeated again and again. In spite of the simplicity—or maybe because of it—the songs intrigued me. The kids weren't singing for themselves; it seemed like they were singing to someone. That was strange.[76]

But the musical situation quickly picked up, even for a serious teenage rock 'n' roll fan like Laurie. Within a few months, musical groups such as Children of the Day, Country Faith, and Love Song emerged from within the church.[77]

But music was not the only way Calvary Chapel stepped away from traditional evangelical church services; befitting its new constituency, the overall atmosphere of the church had also became more informal, as the kids came to the church in patched blue jeans, T-shirts, football jerseys, peasant dresses, bare feet, sandals, and sneakers. And the new-style congregation was not content to sit primly in the pews and look at the backs of the heads in front of them. An average service at Calvary Chapel found young people sitting cross-legged in the aisles, standing and swaying as they sang, and afterward forming impromptu prayer circles and greeting friends and visitors with warm embraces.[78]

Calvary Chapel's appeal went beyond matters of style. Smith, with his engaging smile, paternal manner, and warm, radio announcer's voice, became a father figure, "Papa Chuck." His main strength lay in his role as Bible teacher, particularly in leading the youth into the "deeper truths" of Bible prophecy as contained in the complex premillennial dispensational theology he fervently espoused. The imminent Second Coming of Christ and the secret Rapture of the church before the horrors of the seven-year period of Tribulation and the Battle of Armageddon were key to Smith's biblical worldview. Indeed, Smith had embarked on a lengthy, verse-by-verse study of the Book of Revelation just before Calvary Chapel's contact with the local hippie community began.[79] Within the context of campus unrest, the sexual revolution, race riots, and the Vietnam War, an explication of John the Revelator's apocalypse attracted the attention of disillusioned, questioning young people.

However, it was the the hippie preacher, Lonnie Frisbee (figure 3.4), clad in bellbottoms and speaking in the vernacular of the street, who seemed to be key in pulling in the crowds of young people during Calvary Chapel's early expansion. A young hippie, David Rosales, remembers coming to Calvary Chapel for the first time and that it "blew [his] mind...the teacher was Lonnie Frisbee and he was a real hippie."[80] Kent Philpott, who had initially thought of the young Frisbee as a "nobody" and a "weak personality," was floored after actually seeing Frisbee speak in front of a Calvary Chapel audience:

> It was amazing to see Lonnie Frisbee in action, you just have no idea, he attracted hundreds if not thousands of kids...he looked like a picture of Jesus, he had the hair, the beard...if he had wanted to he could have passed himself off as the reincarnation of Jesus...here was an authentic hippie kid, when he got up to talk, I don't know to use the word mesmerizing, or hypnotic, or whether it was just the Holy Spirit. I don't think I've seen that kind of power...it was incredible....[81]

Oden Fong, an ex-member of the Timothy Leary–associated Laguna Beach–based Brotherhood of Eternal Love and son of Hollywood character actor Benson Fong (perhaps best remembered as Charlie Chan's "Number One Son"), was convinced that Frisbee was the story at Calvary Chapel in the early days. Asked if he was something of a "lodestone" for young people, Fong replied, "Yes, absolutely...just because of his personality anywhere he'd go he would draw people like he was a pied piper." Yet he could not quite put a finger on what it was about Frisbee that was so appealing, noting that it certainly wasn't his expertise that intrigued people: "I don't think he knew the Bible all that well," he remembers. "He was a horrible worship leader...he was awful." Looking back, Fong was at a loss: "You couldn't really explain if you sat around and tried to look through his merits...except that he had so much boldness and conviction...his message was very simple."[82]

Hollywood Presbyterian's Don Williams echoed Fong's impression. Recalling his first-ever visit to Calvary Chapel sometime in 1969, he vividly remembered that Frisbee "had trouble reading the Scriptures, he stumbled all over the words—he

FIGURE 3.4 Lonnie Frisbee.
Courtesy of Jack and Betty Cheetham.

was reading out of the King James Version...he just slaughtered the text. He then started to preach from it and he woefully misinterpreted [the passage]." But to Williams's surprise, Frisbee "went on to preach one of the best evangelistic sermons" he had ever heard. At the end of the sermon, Frisbee gave an invitation, and Williams remembered that "all over the place, people stood up."[83]

Greg Laurie relates an anecdote that gives some insight into Frisbee's style but also reinforces the mystery of his impact on audiences. He remembers once being invited over to the Frisbees' house for dinner before a Wednesday night Bible study. Lonnie told him he was thinking about preaching on Jonah that night and asked Laurie to read a passage from the Book of Jonah while they got ready to go to the meeting. "Every once in a while he would ask me to reread a passage," he stated, but the real puzzler was that "this seemed to be all the preparation he was doing." Later that night, Laurie watched as Frisbee gave his sermon on Jonah. "I listened, thrilled," he said, "but then I realized that some of his facts weren't quite right. Parts of the story weren't exactly like it was in the Bible. They were just little differences...but they made me wonder." Nonetheless, Laurie remembers that "when Lonnie finished his message and gave an invitation for people to receive Christ, dozens of kids came forward." The experience convinced him that "Lonnie Frisbee might be the human instrument, but it was *God* [emphasis his] who was at work here."[84]

One contributing factor to Frisbee's magnetism was undoubtedly his emphasis on the Pentecostal-style baptism of the Holy Spirit and the accompanying signs and wonders, such as speaking in tongues and being "slain in the Spirit." Frisbee was perhaps most truly in his element leading an "afterglow" service in a side room after services in the Calvary Chapel sanctuary. The side room meeting was apparently Chuck Smith's idea. Although raised within Aimee Semple McPherson's International Church of the Foursquare Gospel, Smith had long been dismayed by what he felt were the excesses of Pentecostal fervor. As a result, he tended to interpret glossolalia as a private spiritual exercise and downplayed other signs. One writer who mentioned that he had heard tongues in a Calvary Chapel service wrote the following description of Smith's response: "He frowned. 'Well, you shouldn't have. People know my policy on that.'" Indeed, he was perceived by more than one observer—as well as by Frisbee himself—to be "keeping the lid down" on Frisbee's penchant for boisterous charisma.[85]

Although the church experienced impressive growth under the two preachers' very different styles, not all of the old-timers were happy with Smith, his young hippie protégé, or Calvary Chapel's new direction. Some members were scandalized by the dozens of youth who would plop down on the church's lawn after Sunday morning services, reading their Bibles while enjoying a relaxing cigarette. Others were concerned after moving into their new—and already outgrown—300-seat sanctuary that the hippies' dirty feet and blue jeans would soil the plush new carpet and padded pews. Before one Sunday morning service, several church members put up a sign that read "No Bare Feet Allowed in the Church." Smith was incensed and promptly took it down. After services that morning, there was a hastily called meeting of the church board; what happened there was undoubtedly a pivotal turning point in the history of Calvary Chapel and probably for the entire Jesus movement. Smith told his elders in no uncertain terms that if the church had to turn away young people because of bare feet and dirty clothes, they would be better off ripping up the carpet and removing the pews and replacing them with steel folding chairs. With this figurative line drawn in the sand, Smith won over his board to a no-reservations approach to their ministry among the hippies.[86]

For the most part, the old-line membership of Calvary Chapel agreed—Smith remembers the departure of only a few people—and the church's already impressive growth continued.[87] But a new and important development was beginning to manifest itself at Calvary Chapel. In addition to the hard-core hippie element, the church was proving an even greater attraction for rank-and-file Orange County teenagers for whom the informal style, music, and acceptance of hippie fashion nicely dovetailed with the currents of contemporary youth culture. Lonnie Frisbee and Kenn Gulliksen had begun Bible studies at nearby Costa Mesa and Harbor High Schools, and the appeal of the new, hip version of evangelical Christianity proved popular there, too. As one woman recalled, the impact on her peer group

FIGURE 3.5 Pastor Chuck Smith baptizes a young convert at one of Calvary Chapel's mass baptisms at Corona del Mar in 1971.

Courtesy of Hugh Steven.

at Costa Mesa High in 1969 seemed to happen "overnight": "I used to go out to the field and smoke a joint with my friends, one day they were reading their Bibles instead."[88]

By mid-1970, the church was running three Sunday morning services that together attracted about 1,500. Additionally, a Sunday night service pulled several hundred every week, as did weeknight Bible studies on Tuesday, Wednesday, Thursday, and Friday nights.[89] Monthly baptisms held along a rocky beach called Pirate's Cove at Corona del Mar State Park—an event that would become a staple image of the Jesus movement in popular press coverage—were a popular feature of Calvary Chapel's program, often bringing out more than 500 young people to be baptized in the Pacific Ocean (figure 3.5).[90]

By the end of 1969, Calvary Chapel and the other prominent pioneering Jesus People groups were hardly alone in Southern California. Christian coffeehouses and outreaches to hippies and their teenaged admirers had begun popping up all over the region. Just off the campus of UCLA, former Campus Crusade staffer Hal Lindsey had established the JC Light & Power House, a combination communal house and Bible training center with an emphasis on Bible prophecy.[91] In Redondo Beach at Bethel Tabernacle, Pentecostal evangelist Lyle Steenis and former hippie Breck Stevens had gathered a following of youth from the local drug culture that numbered in the hundreds.[92] In blue-collar Covina and West Covina in eastern Los Angeles County, Ron Turner's Agape Force had begun coffeehouses, communal houses, and a "Church in the Park" in Valencia.[93] Dave Anderson straddled mainline denominational youth work, the charismatic movement, and the developing Jesus movement with his Van Nuys–based group, Lutheran Youth Alive.[94] San

Diego had The Lost Coin and Light House coffeehouses.[95] And back in Hollywood, a mild-mannered conservative Minnesota Baptist and would-be-vaudevillian, Duane Pederson, brought the new movement into the media world after being handed a copy of the underground *Hollywood Free Press* on Sunset Strip. Pederson reasoned that if the heathens could reach people through these newspapers, Christians could, too. With a typewriter and black marker, he created his own "Jesus Paper," which he dubbed the *Hollywood Free Paper* (HFP). With his Christian version of a hippie underground newspaper, Pederson attracted support from local evangelical businessmen; the paper was soon being handed out in the tens of thousands and established its own printing operation.[96]

The movement continued to grow over the next year, and by the summer of 1970, there were, at the very least, more than 100 Jesus People groups and centers functioning in Southern California. However, despite the fact that the emerging movement was informal, far-flung, and unorganized, there were several readily identifiable markers—some clearly evangelical in origin, others stemming from the countercultural side of the ledger—that most of these groups shared, setting the Jesus People apart as an actual movement with a readily recognizable form to those on the inside and outside.

The Pentecostal Ethos of the Jesus People

Not surprisingly, given the evangelical backgrounds of the movement's straight sponsors, the Jesus People thoroughly reflected the fourfold definition of evangelicalism as classically set forth by British historian D. W. Bebbington, which sees evangelicals as sharing across time and geography a set of four markers—bibliocentrism, conversionism, crucicentrism, and activism—that sets them apart from other Protestant groups.[97] The street Christians were certainly bibliocentric (and strongly fundamentalist in their interpretation of the Bible), placed a heavy emphasis on conversion and the atoning, substitutionary role of Christ's death on the cross, and were decidedly gung-ho in their activist inclinations to help, evangelize, and disciple their peers. Certainly, no contemporary observers of the American religious scene were confused about where the Jesus People fit in the spectrum of American Christianity. As scholar and former Episcopal priest Robert S. Ellwood put it in the introduction to his 1973 analysis of the movement, *One Way*, the Jesus movement was made up of "young people in considerable numbers" who were "rejecting both conventional Christianity and counter culture religions" to "take up with evangelical Christianity."[98] But within its broadly evangelical contours, there were specific aspects of the evangelical subculture that characterized the Jesus People.

The first was the role that the baptism of the Holy Spirit, speaking in tongues, and other Pentecostal distinctives played within Jesus People circles. Not all Jesus

People groups or ministries were Pentecostal in their orientation, and it would be incorrect to simply dub the Jesus People as Pentecostal. Indeed, as Detroit-based journalist Hiley Ward commented in his 1971 tour of Jesus People communes, a sizable minority of the movement struck him as "Baptist"[99]—something that the involvement of the Baptists connected with the original Evangelical Concerns group and Southern Baptists like Arthur Blessitt, Sammy Tippitt in Chicago, and Richard Hogue and the SPIRENO ("Spiritual Revolution Now") network in Houston exemplified. Other prominent Jesus People groups, while not explicitly Baptist, such as Berkeley, California's Christian World Liberation Front (CWLF, originally created by ex-Campus Crusade staffers), the Los Angeles area's Agape Force, and many of the later church-based manifestations of the movement, had a more generalized evangelical, non-Pentecostal ethos.

But the majority of Jesus People groups—particularly those emerging within hardcore countercultural constituencies—seemed to be awash in a Pentecostal ethos of glossolalia, prophecy, "words of knowledge," "singing in the Spirit," and divine healing (figure 3.6). Although part of this was the direct result of interaction with Pentecostal and charismatic ministers and evangelists, as well as books like John Sherrill's *They Speak with Other Tongues* and David Wilkerson's *The Cross and the Switchblade*,[100] much of the impetus arose simply from the Jesus People's literal understanding of the Bible. The early church in the Book of Acts had spoken

FIGURE 3.6 The Children of God meet for a morning Bible study at an encampment in northern Virginia during their wandering phase, November 1969.
Used with permission, AP/Wide World Photos.

in tongues, and the Apostle Paul spoke of various "gifts of the Spirit": the Jesus
People thought it only natural that they, too, would experience these things—a
dynamic apparent from the movement's earliest beginnings in San Francisco,
as reflected in Ted Wise and the Living Room group's chasing after the gift of
tongues—much to the discomfort of many of their Baptist and baptistic evangelical mentors.[101] Likewise, even the Baptist seminarian Kent Philpott embraced
a Pentecostal reading of the New Testament and experienced the baptism of the
Holy Spirit in a mysterious, unexpected middle-of-the-night "filling" while sleeping in the sanctuary of Lincoln Park Baptist Church in 1968.[102]

The experience of the Pentecostal baptism and the practice of glossolalia was
a given of the Jesus movement as it spread. In public meetings, in small house
groups, and in individual encounters, Jesus People claimed they were being filled
with the Holy Spirit and speaking in a heavenly language. The experience of "Jeff,"
a seventeen-year-old recent convert at Bethel Tabernacle in Redondo Beach was
typical of thousands of other Jesus freaks:

> One night my friend said he could pray me into the Baptism if I really
> wanted it, and I told him go ahead. We did it on the beach. I knelt down and
> he put his hands on my head and prayed in tongues. It didn't take five min-
> utes. The Spirit hit me like a ton of bricks. I fell right over. Then I started to
> pray in tongues. It was terrific. I never felt so great.... My friend and I were
> both crying and hugging each other. People thought we were crazy.[103]

Research for this study gives an idea of just how pervasive the acceptance and
experience of Pentecostal-style phenomena within Jesus People ranks truly was.
In a web-based survey, former Jesus People were asked if they had personally experienced, participated in, or observed people having the baptism of the Holy Spirit.
More than 75% of the 812 respondents replied in the affirmative (table 3.1).

Likewise, nearly as many claimed to have personally spoken in tongues or
observed the practice of speaking in tongues (table 3.2).

These numbers, while not definitive, certainly show how deeply Pentecostal
beliefs and practices ran among the Jesus People. Between the influence of
Spirit-filled straights and their own desire to follow and relive the Book of Acts,
the Jesus movement was markedly Pentecostal in orientation.

Table 3.1 Did you participate in or see the "Baptism
of the Holy Spirit" in your JP involvement?

Participated	76.6%
Saw	17.2%
No Answer	6.2%[104]

Table 3.2 Did you participate in or see "Speaking in
Tongues" in your JP involvement?

Participated	72.2%
Saw	23.2%
No Answer	4.6%[105]

The Miraculous World of the Jesus People

Just as the literalist approach of the Jesus People led them to expect direct, supernatural encounters with God during their worship, so, too, the movement was characterized by a larger acceptance of and preoccupation with signs, miracles, instances of divine provision, and encounters with the forces of spiritual darkness. Accounts of miraculous events, strange happenings, immediate answers to prayer, angelic encounters, and confrontations with demons provided a common source for praise and wonder in the corporate and personal testimony of those involved in the movement. Probably the most common brush with the miraculous reported by Jesus People occurred when a prayer was answered "immediately" by the seemingly miraculous supply of a need or answer. Scott Ross, from the upstate New York commune and ministry the Love Inn, believed God answered a specific prayer for the donation of a red-and-white Volkswagen minibus, and another when a load of donated cement for a kitchen foundation arrived just as they needed it. Once, Ross wrote in his 1976 book *Scott Free*, a much-needed commercial freezer arrived in mid-prayer.[106] Craig Yoe, leader of a Jesus People group in Ohio, reminisced about a rickety old furnace that had quit running and, when prayed over, jumped back to life.[107] Members of a Shiloh communal house claimed that they had run out of heating oil in the middle of the winter but miraculously "experienced no drop in temperature."[108] One of the most common stories among the Jesus People was the nick-of-time delivery of a bag of groceries or provision of a meal just as a group was sitting down at mealtime, when no food was to be had.[109]

These kinds of stories, while convincing to the favorably disposed, could easily be chalked up by skeptical outsiders and in-house doubting Thomases as coincidence or fortuitous happenstance. However, the Jesus People made claims about other miracles by whose standards these stories were merely scratching the surface of what they thought God was doing in their midst. Not only was God supplying groceries; many Jesus People believed that at times he was actually multiplying the ingredients on hand.

Marlon Finley remembered being at a Christian commune in Paducah, Kentucky, and seeing "one box of beef stroganoff...[feed] twelve people to capacity."[110] Brad Davis was living at a "discipleship house" run by the Agape Force in Southern California and claimed that more than thirty young people were fed by a single can of tuna.[111] Kent Philpott recalled an incident at the Soul Inn in San Francisco in which he claimed that a single can of beef stew cooked over a hot plate fed dozens of homeless hippies—an experience that left him reaching for the phone years later to verify with a former coworker that he had not simply dreamed the incident.[112]

Within the ranks of the Shiloh organization, "the PBJ miracle" was a famous story of God's provision in the group's early days. One afternoon, Cathy Stewart recounted in a 1977 issue of *Shiloh Magazine*, she and another sister in the House of Miracles in Fontana, California, made a number of peanut butter and jelly sandwiches for their housemates' lunch. Having planned for two sandwiches per person, they were dismayed to suddenly see "all these people from the Riverside house [charge] in the front door." They were amazed that, when all was said and done, no one had gone hungry:

> When we went into the dining room to clean up, a whole bunch of sand-wiches were left on the platters. It was like seeing something you knew log-ically couldn't exist. Everyone had two [sandwiches] and some brothers had eaten six or seven. It was just like the miracle of the loaves and fishes.[113]

James K. Foley belonged to a communal house ministry in Burlington, Vermont, that reported a similar experience. Foley claimed that "at one meal...24 pieces of chicken were put in front of 20 people; everyone had at least one piece, some as many as four, and there were nine pieces left over. No, you wouldn't believe it even if you saw it!"[114]

Food was not the only area in which the Jesus People saw the miraculous at work. As in other Pentecostal circles, cases of divine healing were also noted, although, given the younger age of the movement's participants, such stories did not get as much emphasis as they did among older Pentecostals. Mary Anne Miller, a volunteer secretary at the Fire Escape Coffeehouse in Stanton, California, claimed she was immediately healed of a painful ganglion cyst on her wrist after being prayed for on the way to a Calvary Chapel baptism at Corona del Mar.[115] A twenty-two-year-old West Virginia woman with a severe case of hearing loss was reportedly healed and "heard the sound of music for the first time in her life" at the Jesus '73 festival in Ephrata, Pennsylvania.[116] The members of the Love Inn community in upstate New York reported eye-sight restoration, reversal of infertility, and even the healing of dental cavities among its constituency.[117] A 1971 wire story about a Shiloh communal house in Charlotte, North Carolina, noted that healing was a routine part of their day-to-day life:

Ed McIsaac, 23, the group's pastor leads the nightly Bible study sessions.
He and other members of the group heal headaches, colds, and various
minor ailments by laying on of hands. Ask them if it works and they just
laugh. "Of course it works," they say. "If you believe, and if you pray, it
works."[118]

There were even Jesus People who spoke of lives being miraculously spared from
certain death and of auto accident fatalities inexplicably being brought back to
life. Peter Romanowsky of the Crown of Life coffeehouse and Agape Church
groups in Marin County, California, claimed he and his brother Romnik witnessed a boy who was hit by a car and "[thrown] out of his socks and shoes." The
boy had stopped breathing but, when prayed over by the Romanowsky brothers,
began breathing again and survived the accident. Dennis Knotts of Simi Valley,
California's Lighthouse coffeehouse claimed that he was the victim of a "fatal auto
accident,"[119] in which he was the fatality. He remembered "standing on the side of
the road watching them carry my body out of the back of the van" and claimed that
as he "stood there," he heard "a voice from behind" that he "could only describe as
the voice of Jesus" say to him, "You're not done yet."[120]

Keith Swaine stated that he was not yet in the Christian fold when he was on
Sunset Strip in the spring of 1971 and shoved a witnessing Jesus freak off the
sidewalk into oncoming traffic. "I waited to push him until he couldn't help but
be hit," and yet somehow the car stopped. "My friend and me saw the bumper up
against the guy's belt buckle and we just shrugged at each other," Swaine said,
later coming to believe that "God did a miracle and saved that guy!" The incident
led to his conversion.[121]

Kevin Newman was attending Calvary Chapel in Costa Mesa and related that one
time following a Sunday evening service they decided to play a mischievous trick on
a friend and removed his auto's distributor coil wire, which normally would have
made the car impossible to start. Moving over to the far side of the parking lot to get
a quick giggle out of their friend's distress, they were amazed to see him climb into
his car, start it up, and drive away. "Just then," Newman states, "a pickup truck ran
off the road" and struck a power pole that crashed right down "on the spot where
he had been parked." Newman reported that the incident "freaked [them] all out."[122]

At times, it seems, the perception of miraculous protection could even lead to a
near-biblical expectation of supernatural provision. The brethren at the Lighthouse
Ranch in Eureka, California, told of an incident at their logging mill when one
worker was pinned down by a number of massive logs. Uncovering him, his
coworkers said a prayer over the apparently mortally injured brother and hurried
him to a local doctor, who not only pronounced the man alive but somehow—
when all was said and done—not too much worse for the wear. A few months later,
the 115 people living at the ranch left to attend a local church function, leaving

twenty-three-year-old David Peterson to serve as watchman over the commune property. At some point in the evening, he was struck and killed by a drunken driver cutting through the commune's parking lot. When told the news, one member, who knew of the earlier "miracle," was overheard by a reporter to earnestly ask, "And the Lord didn't raise him from the dead? I expect he would have."[123]

While these stories bespoke the Jesus People's belief in divine responses to prayer, they were also convinced that God was reaching out to them through faith-affirming, other-worldly signs and angelic ministrations. One man involved with a coffeehouse in Harrisonburg, Virginia, recalled being in a room praying, when suddenly he and others noted that "the room filled with a mysterious bluish light."[124] Jackie Alden claimed that in one instance at the Cave Adullam coffeehouse in Tacoma, Washington, a group of local gay teens called the "Wiz Kids" entered the building and were startled to "see" the Holy Spirit hanging "thickly" in the air like a cloud.[125] Scott Jacobsen snapped a photo of Jesus People music artist Barry McGuire at a coffeehouse in Wichita, Kansas, and claimed that when the picture was developed, the symbol of the Holy Spirit, "a dove appear[ed] to be resting on [McGuire's] shoulder." He found this curious because, as he remembered it, Jacobsen did "not recall seeing a dove on [McGuire's] shoulder" during the concert or "when [he] snapped the photo."[126]

Visual signs were complemented by tales of aural wonders from the angelic realm. A girl who frequented Calvary Chapel and the One Way Coffeehouse in Norwalk, California, was positive that on one occasion her brother was augmented by an angelic choir as he played his guitar and sang praise songs in the backyard. "There is no doubt in my mind," she later stated, "that a huge choir of angels joined his singing."[127] Others told similar stories, and northern Californian David Ruffino claimed to have had an experience that paralleled the author of the Book of Hebrews' insistence in 13:2 that believers' kindnesses to strangers could involve "entertaining angels unawares." Ruffino stated that once he "minister[ed] to an angel," the down-and-out stranger's status becoming clear "after he disappeared in front of my eyes."[128] His tale recalled a story printed in an issue of the *Cincinnati Jesus Paper* that bears more than a little resemblance to the popular 1970s urban myth, the "vanishing hitchhiker":

> Recently it has been reported to the police of Eugene, Oregon of twelve different occasions of a man approaching individuals on the street and proclaiming the gospel of Christ. These people accepted Christ and as they came out of their waters of baptism they saw the man disappear before their eyes. Angel? Another Phillip experience? Kinda hard to take![129]

The sense that the supernatural world was immanent in the day-to-day lives of the Jesus People also meant that they believed they were grappling with the powers of darkness. Just as Jesus, the power of the Holy Spirit, and angels were present and working, so, too, were Satan and his legions of demonic helpers—a fact that Jesus People believed was manifest in the late '6os and '7os upsurge of interest in witchcraft and the occult. The struggle between the forces of light and dark-ness was not simply fought on the grand scale, either; it intimately involved the Jesus People and their quest to proclaim the gospel and "be a testimony" to those around them. Kent Philpott and David Hoyt's diary of their days on the streets of Haight-Ashbury is peppered with satanic opposition and demon-possessed street people. One woman in Washington state recalled encountering a chilling woman she could only describe as being "of the devil" in the prayer room at a local coffee-house. Rebuking the interloper in the name of Jesus, the stranger "immediately stopped talking, began to shake, sat up and left!"[130] Dale Yancy, an early Calvary Chapel follower, claimed that the "casting out of demons" was a feature of life at the Burlington, Vermont, commune he helped found in the early '70s. In one particular instance, Yancy believes that he was "given a word of knowledge" that a particular individual that had begun coming to his meetings "was a Satanist," that "had come . . . to try and destroy our work."[131] Sandi Heefner claimed a similar expe-rience back in the days of the House of Acts in Novato. Once faced with letting in a frequent visitor to the commune when local teens were at the house, she claimed God gave her a revelation in which she saw the top of the man's skull lift off his head to reveal a nest of snakes crawling around his brain. Convinced the man was on drugs and a threat to everyone there, she refused him entrance.[132] Clearly, the Jesus People were convinced that the landscapes of their day-to-day lives were a spiritual battlefield.

Just how big a role did this supernatural warfare play in Jesus People circles? Print sources and conversations with former Jesus People are replete with such stories and references, but the extent to which these encounters occurred on the ground is also hinted at by the results from the web-based survey. When asked if they had ever participated in, or seen examples of, demonic possession or exor-cism, slightly more than 60% of the respondents replied that they had contact with these sorts of occurrences (table 3.3).

Taken together, these stories of supernatural intervention, demon possession, angelic choirs, and miraculously multiplying fried chicken might indeed strike the rational outsider as well beyond the pale of credibility. However, to the Jesus People who fully expected such things and believed in them—and sometimes to

Table 3.3 Did you participate in or see "Demon Possession/ Exorcisms" in your JP involvement?

Participated	30.4%
Saw	30.6%
No answer	39%[133]

the individuals they proselytized—such incidents and stories were powerful testimonies of God's power and provision. Whatever the case, the widespread tales of signs, wonders, and the supernatural bespeak the miraculous sensibility that underlay the Jesus People movement.

The Apocalyptic Orientation of the Jesus People

Another key characteristic of the Jesus People movement was the apocalyptic fervor that pervaded the movement. *Maranatha*, the Aramaic word meaning "the Lord cometh," was on their minds, lips, and bumper stickers. This expectation not only played a major role in their devotional life and study but also profoundly affected the urgency of their evangelistic efforts and served as a filter through which they perceived the cultural, social, and political world around them. Almost without exception, the movement confidently expected the Second Coming of Jesus Christ to take place, if not momentarily, probably in the immediate future, and surely within their lifetimes. This again is reflected in the results of the survey of ex-Jesus People: Nearly 80% of those questioned about their beliefs at the time responded that they believed the return of Christ would occur within the near future (table 3.4).

As seen in the case of Chuck Smith's teachings at Calvary Chapel, the overall movement for the most part fully imbibed the dispensational premillennialism that characterized so much of the larger evangelical and fundamentalist subcultures. That particular interpretation of the Scriptures' prophetic passages had received an extra boost in the postwar period because of its emphasis on the role of the Jewish people and a reconstituted nation of Israel. With the founding of the Zionist state in 1948 and the nation's seemingly miraculous series of triumphs in the Six-Day War in 1967 and its recapture of Jerusalem, the dispensational approach to understanding the Bible appeared to have been vindicated. When coupled with the cultural chaos of the 1960s, the dispensational view's pessimistic perspective on the world's slide into the End Times seemed to be right on target, not just to the straights in the pews at First Assemblies of God, but to the Jesus People down at the Mustard Seed Coffeehouse as well.

Table 3.4 **Were you convinced that Jesus' return was imminent during your involvement with the JP movement?**

Yes	79.2%
No	9.8%
Not sure	7%
No answer	4%[134]

One reason for the Jesus People's acceptance of premillennial interpretations of the Bible was a sweeping pessimism about the future that reinforced both their old countercultural and newfound Christian perceptions. Many hippies who had condemned the Establishment for its greed and violence had become disillusioned about the direction and nature of the counterculture. Bad drug trips, dishonesty, selfish behavior, and violence among youth seemed to make a mockery of the mantra of "peace and love." The new Jesus People had an explanatory framework that made sense of the downward spiral of both straight and hip culture.[135]

Another reason for the Jesus People's enthusiastic embrace of dispensational teachings was the countercultural penchant for esoteric philosophical, occult, and religious literature. In some ways, the hippie Christians merely shifted cultural gears. Before, many of them pored over the *I Ching*, *The Tibetan Book of the Dead*, *The Urantia Book*, and the works of Carlos Castenada for clues to meaning and spiritual enlightenment; now they could indulge their mystical bent by studying the symbolism and hidden prophetic clues in the writings of the Old Testament prophets and John the Revelator.

However, a more important influence on their apocalyptic leanings was the direct impact of evangelical mentors and literature on the movement. In almost every instance where an evangelical pastor, evangelist, or youth worker helped establish or supported a Jesus People group, they brought dispensational teachings with them. There were exceptions, of course—the Presbyterian Don Williams at Hollywood Presbyterian, for instance. But in general, whether in Bible studies, sermons, informal raps, or tapes and literature, straight evangelical collaborators and enablers of the Jesus movement, like Chuck Smith at Calvary Chapel, regularly turned to the prophetic to snare audience interest. In the process, they presented them with the full gamut of dispensational teachings, such as the importance of Israel, the secret Rapture of the church, the appearance of the Antichrist, and the horrors of the Tribulation.

The ubiquity of dispensational doctrine among the Jesus People was cemented with the 1970 appearance of Hal Lindsey's breezy, best-selling analysis of Bible prophecy, *The Late Great Planet Earth*. The book achieved remarkable penetration within the ranks of the Jesus movement, in part because its author had honed his material on college students and counterculture types at the JC Light & Power House in Los Angeles. As Robert Ellwood observed in his travels among the Jesus People in the early '70s: "The book *The Late, Great Planet Earth* is one of the few volumes besides the Bible found in virtually every movement commune, home, and church parlor. Next to the Scriptures, probably no other book is more read."[136] Ellwood's take was reflected in the web-based survey of ex-Jesus People; *The Late, Great Planet Earth* was far and away the most frequent response to a query about influential books.[137]

Taken together, these influences made the belief that humankind was in the prophesied last days a leitmotif of the movement. Jesus People tracts and street papers were filled with headlines of "Get Ready!" and prophecy articles on "Daniel's Seventy Weeks."[138] Painted warnings and bumper stickers proclaimed "Maranatha!" "Guess Who's Coming Again?" and "Be Prepared: Jesus Is Coming at Any Moment... Driver Will Disappear!" on Jesus People vehicles.[139] And many of the popular songs of the new "Jesus Rock," such as the group Love Song's apocalyptic "Cossack Song," Larry Norman's "I Wish We'd All Been Ready," and Randy Matthews's "Evacuation Day," addressed the last days and the Second Coming.[140]

The Jesus People's fascination with the End Times undoubtedly fueled their enthusiasm for evangelism. But it also—for the short term at least—seems to have had a major impact on day-to-day living, as well as on the life and career expectations of many within the movement. During a retreat, Pat Cordial of the Fishmarket coffeehouse in Lawton, Oklahoma, slept through a tornado warning that sent everyone in the camp into a shelter. His immediate assumption on waking was that the Rapture had taken place and "everyone else had been raptured."[141] Such was their concern over the imminence of the Rapture that many Jesus People feared they would never experience many of life's basic joys. One man in the Midwest recalled, "I remember being afraid I may never get married before the Rapture."[142] Others surveyed the roll call of expected End Times horrors and came to the conclusion that it would be prudent to avoid marital entanglements. One Canadian woman involved with the Toronto Catacombs group recalls being so convinced by rampant last days speculation that she "once considered calling off [her] wedding and refused to have children because [she] was so terrified of what was about to happen!"[143] As historian Paul Boyer demonstrated in his seminal 1992 volume, *When Time Shall Be No More*, interest in Bible prophecy and speculation about the Second Coming are a central feature of the larger American evangelical subculture, characterized by waves of interest that vary in intensity.[144] However, it is clear that for the Jesus People, the expectation of the Second Coming played a crucial role in defining the nature, emphases, and urgency of the movement.

The Communal Tendency of the Jesus People

Although the preceding characteristics of the Jesus People movement make up an evangelical cluster of attributes, the next three could be classified as inherited from the countercultural side. One of the most obvious and widespread was the penchant for communal living, an inclination visible from the get-go among the first identifiable groups of Jesus freaks in the San Francisco Bay area. While most Jesus People did not live communally, the ubiquity of communal houses and communes within the movement was so radically at odds with normal American lifestyles that it definitely set it apart as something different.

Communal living was, seemingly, a natural development within Jesus People circles. There were three major reasons for this communal reflex. The first was the tantalizing glimpse of utopia offered in the second chapter of the Acts of the Apostles, which tells how the early church in Jerusalem "were together and had all things in common...[selling] their possessions and goods, and parted them to all men as every man had need."[145] Taking the Scriptures at their word and believing that the straight church had strayed from this truth, many Jesus People were eager to reclaim first-century authenticity in their living arrangements, as well as with spiritual gifts. Ted Wise, the early Bay Area movement leader, summed up this attitude best: "[We] agreed on one thing: that we ought to live out the Book of Acts like a script."[146]

A second factor was the dire financial condition of many of the hard-core street people who joined the early Jesus movement. It was not without reason that prayers for the miraculous provision of food and basic supplies and free or cheap handouts of food were a staple of Jesus People group life; money was almost always in short supply. The street Christians themselves were, of course, overwhelmingly young; a large number were runaways, and even more were just coming out of the drug culture. There were not many more destitute groups in postwar American society, and communal living was a practical strategy (as it was in the counterculture more generally) that allowed impoverished Jesus People groups—and the straight evangelical laypeople, churches, and organizations that struggled to support many of them financially—to keep their young cohort fed and in some semblance of decent shape (figure 3.7).

A third factor was like the second: Given the characteristics of many of the people the movement was reaching, there was a real need for order, discipline, and a watchful eye to maintain progress in converts' Christian walk and to keep them from relapsing into their old ways. Communal life provided an extended opportunity to teach babes in Christ and to see to it that they learned not only basic Christian doctrines and behavior but also, in many cases, basic life skills. Many communal Jesus houses, like the Sheepfold House in Milwaukee, Wisconsin, had an extensive list of rules, regulations, and expectations of its members:

> Consideration for the brethren: Quiet before rising hour, after 11 P.M. Keep music pleasing to God. See elders about overnight guests. Dress to come downstairs. Fellows and girls meet downstairs, not in rooms. Keep your own room neat—clean up after yourself. Be responsible for chores assigned. Let your elder know where you are at all times. Smoking guests use porch. Use pay phone for personal calls. Praise the Lord in all things![147]

All in all, the communal dimension of the Jesus People subculture played a major role in the movement's internal culture and image. According to historian Timothy

FIGURE 3.7 House of Zion girls' house in San Rafael, California, ca. 1969: far left, David Hoyt, far right, Kent Philpott.

Courtesy of Kent Philpott.

Miller's 1999 study, *The 60s Communes: Hippies and Beyond*, there may have been as many as several thousand Jesus People communes in existence at one time or another.[148] Some groups operated multiple communal houses, and largely communal groups such as the Love Inn in upstate New York and Jesus People USA (JPUSA) in Chicago numbered their members in the hundreds and operated multiple businesses and ministries as well as daycare centers, clinics, and schools.[149] The Oregon-based Shiloh commune, founded by John Higgins, eventually had more than 175 communes around North America and accumulated millions of dollars in property and equipment.[150] While communal living proved difficult or ultimately undesirable to many, nearly all Jesus People groups had at least part of its constituency—often its most committed members—involved in some sort of communal arrangement at some point in its history.

Come (Dressed) as You Are to Jesus

A second major characteristic the Jesus People inherited from the counterculture was a preference for informality in dress and behavior, which they carried over into their worship and evangelistic pursuits. Jesus People were just as likely to wear their workaday blue jeans, T-shirts, and tennis shoes or sandals (or bare feet) to a worship service as they were to a rock concert. Women—while urged by most groups to dress chastely—frequently sported much the same attire or inexpensive dust smocks or granny dresses. All of this was, of course, a far cry from the

reigning attitude among churchgoing Americans who had traditionally emphasized wearing one's Sunday best to the Lord's House.

The Jesus People's continued embrace of hippie fashions smacked heavily of
countercultural attitudes about comfort, authenticity, and living a natural lifestyle.
Within hippie circles, this often devolved into a celebration of, or excuse for, nudi-
ty.[151] Obviously, this was not an option for the Jesus People, but they nonetheless
persisted in countercultural sensibilities that saw no merit in tight, uncomfortable, formal clothing that—particularly within a context of Christian humility and
chastity—frequently served as the bearer of vain statements about one's status,
income, taste, or physique.

But it was more than just clothing that the Jesus People were relaxed about.
Posture and the arrangement of the congregation in Jesus movement gatherings
were also decidedly informal. As the good parishioners of Calvary Chapel had
discovered to their perplexity and sometimes discomfort, the young enthusiasts
were given to plopping down on the floor cross-legged and sprawling out as space
would allow. Used to the informal coziness of Bible studies and prayer groups in
communal houses and private homes, circles and face-to-face arrangements were
often preferred where the size of the gathering, acoustics, and logistics allowed.

But even as straight evangelicals and middle-class churchgoers were scandalized or discomfited by the dress and seating preferences of the Jesus People, the
relaxed wardrobe and informal atmosphere proved to be a major attraction not only
to hippies but also to their younger wannabe admirers. Dan Brookshire, who was
involved with communes in the Charlottesville, Virginia, area, remembered how
he "liked going to a church where long-haired, barefoot, music-loving folks like
myself were welcome."[152] Barb Link, a South Dakota teen, recalled how the atmosphere in the Aldrich House group contrasted favorably to her "stuffy, formal and
totally irrelevant" church: "I could wear my long granny dress and waffle-stompers
and odd jeans with patches and embroidery and not feel out of place or looked
down on. It was an incredibly liberating experience."[153] Similarly, a teenage girl
in Michigan looked back at her experiences with the Lord's House in Livonia,
acknowledging, "My best friend and I were interested in going there because we
wanted to be Jesus followers and they said we could wear blue jeans to church!"[154]

The Jesus People and Popular Culture

A third and perhaps most important characteristic the Jesus People carried over
from the counterculture was much at odds with the reigning attitudes and practices within the evangelical subculture: their comfort with (and often ironic) utilization of popular culture. Unlike their evangelical brethren who had been battling
to keep popular culture and worldly entertainments at arm's length for years, the
Jesus People used various elements of popular culture both within the movement

and in their attempts to connect with their peers. The resulting hybrid, while striking many within both the straight church and the hard-core counterculture as, by turns, curious, outrageous, and ridiculous, nonetheless positioned the Jesus People much closer to the world inhabited by American youth.

The Jesus People happily decorated their world with artwork, posters, bumper stickers, and buttons. Artwork—from thrift-store paintings of Christ to homemade murals to an ever-increasing retinue of Jesus posters—and Bible verses in Day-Glo letters frequently covered the walls. Their buildings were not the only thing they decorated. The Jesus People festooned themselves in colorful buttons announcing "Jesus Is Lord" or "Have a Nice Forever," as well as religious jewelry (generally anathema to most evangelicals up until this time), ranging from simple wooden crosses on leather straps to—as the movement matured—silver ΙΧΘΥΣ (ICHTHYS, "fish": the old Greek acronym for "Jesus Christ, Son of God, Savior") and One Way pendants and pins. Meanwhile, their ever-present Bibles became objects of beautification via hand-tooled leather bindings and leather and fabric Bible covers.[55]

FIGURE 3.8 An issue of Duane Pederson's
Hollywood Free Paper, summer 1971.

Courtesy of the *Hollywood Free Paper*.

Another aspect of pop culture was found in the splashy, often colorful under-ground newspapers the Jesus People created. Dozens of these street papers appeared between 1969 and the late 1970s, including the *Hollywood Free Paper* (figure 3.8); Buffalo's *Dust*; *Truth* from Spokane; Denver's the *End Times*; *Cornerstone*, put out by the Jesus People USA (JPUSA) in Chicago; and the Berkeley-based Christian World Liberation Front's (CWLF) *Right On!* Even the *Oracle*, Haight-Ashbury's original underground newspaper, which had given up the ghost in 1968, came back as a Jesus paper in 1971, when the Mendocino, California–based commune to which several of the paper's originators had fled was converted.[156] The quality, circulation, and life span of these papers varied because of the interplay of local personalities and circumstances, yet their general tone and content was similar. Chock-full of artwork, cartoons, ads, and the occasional photograph, the Jesus papers were multipurpose tools within the Jesus People community—at once evangelistic broadside, venue for edifying literature, news source, and advertising forum for regional and national movement resources.

Given that the Jesus People's generation had been raised on movies and tele-vision, it is not surprising that they went beyond the use of print media in their public ministrations. Many Jesus People groups utilized skits, street theater, and drama troupes as a routine part of their meetings, worship services, and evange-listic efforts. Thus it was not unusual to encounter mimes from the CWLF's Street Theatre group performing in Cal Berkeley's Sproul Plaza; to see Akron, Ohio's Avalon group stage an Eastertime Passion procession on a downtown street, as members passed out nails tipped in red paint to onlookers; or to find members of JPUSA's Holy Ghost Players staging a play in a suburban Chicago park about a helmeted, tin-foil-encrusted alien wondering what all the fuss was about this Jesus.[157] At Merv and Merla Watson's Catacombs in Toronto, several student mem-bers of the Canadian Ballet and other artsy youth (including future Pentecostal televangelist Benny Hinn) who had come under the influence of the Jesus move-ment regularly contravened standard evangelical mores with evangelistic and worship-oriented dance routines as part of the Shekinah dance troupe.[158]

However, probably the most important way in which the Jesus People appro-priated elements of the larger popular culture was their adaptation of the musical sounds and rhythms of the contemporary youth culture to worship and evange-lism. Everywhere one went in the Jesus People movement there was music, from strictly amateurish folk-guitar plunking at a local Bible study to full-blown rock 'n' roll (Jesus Rock) concerts and festivals. And by and large, it was altogether new music that arose from within the movement itself. "Rarely do you hear any of the old-time hymns," wrote one contemporary evangelical observer who was struck by the "preoccupation of the Jesus People with new music."[159]

As we have seen, many of the earliest evangelical mentors of the Jesus move-ment—Don Williams, David Berg, and Chuck Smith—recognized the vital role of folk and rock music within the youth culture and brought it center stage in their efforts to reach out to teens. Former Maranatha! Music head Chuck Fromm has gone so far as to contend that music played an even more central role within the Jesus movement than it had in earlier evangelical revivals.[160] Indeed, wherever the Jesus movement really flourished, there were probably at the least—as had been the case at the Salt Company and Calvary Chapel—a few competent guitar-strumming singer-composers or worship leaders on site, if not a house band(s) or soloists of near-professional quality. Whatever the case, music would only continue to grow in its influence within the movement as it matured into the new genre of Jesus Rock that began to ape the elements of the larger music business.

Conclusion

By the end of 1969, the phenomenon of the hippie street Christian had become an identifiable Jesus movement in Southern California. Buoyed by the efforts of individuals like Arthur Blessitt and inspired by pioneering ministries like Hollywood Presbyterian Church's Salt Company Christian nightclub and Calvary Chapel of Costa Mesa, a far-flung network of coffeehouses, communal homes, and street ministries emerged as part of the Southern California Jesus scene. While the nascent subculture was as disorganized and decentralized as the evangelical and countercultural sources from which it had sprung, it nonetheless displayed characteristics that gave it a cohesive hybrid form that set it apart from both of its cultural parents. By 1970, however, it was becoming very clear that this marriage of the counterculture and evangelical religion was not just a curiosity of California culture.

4

Unto Seattle, Milwaukee, New Jersey, and the Uttermost Parts

THE JESUS PEOPLE GO NATIONWIDE

THROUGHOUT MOST OF 1968, the Jesus People scene was mostly a California phenomenon. But by late 1968 and into 1969, it became evident that sunny Southern California did not hold a monopoly on the requisite cultural tinder to kindle the fires of a Jesus People revival. New outposts of the movement sprang up at points north in California, Oregon, and Washington State. At the same time, street Christians began to surface across the United States, from Wichita to Detroit, Kansas City to Milwaukee, and Atlanta to northeastern New Jersey. Sometimes the result of an evangelical pastor's burden to reach local youth, occasionally the result of Johnny Appleseed–like planting by migrating Jesus People from the West Coast, and as often as not, a seemingly spontaneous eruption of old-time religion within local hippie populations, the movement spread in all directions, an almost inevitable result of the counterculture's rubbing cultural shoulders with the ubiquitous presence of evangelical Christianity across America. Because of local and regional factors, varying circumstances, and unique personalities, no two groups were exactly alike. But it was increasingly clear by 1970 that they had enough in common to constitute a new national movement that was expanding even as its parent hippie culture was beginning to fade.

The Christian World Liberation Front (CWLF)

While Southern California had become the new epicenter of the emerging Jesus movement, the street Christians in and around the San Francisco Bay continued to expand their efforts, often with some sort of helping hand from, and relationship to, the nonprofit Evangelical Concerns group. Near the end of 1969, the Soul Inn was still in operation in San Francisco, eight communal houses were hosting new converts, and several evangelistic workers (including Ted Wise, Kent

Philpott, and David Hoyt) were being helped out through Evangelical Concerns' auspices. The organization was in good shape. With a balance of nearly $4,500 in the bank and donations flowing in, its directors began to dream of becoming a major nonprofit evangelistic ministry.[1] Much of the optimism stemmed from the establishment of contacts with new independent works, such as the Antioch Ranch in Mendocino, a combination Christian youth hostel and retreat center begun in June 1969 at a small farm owned by a Presbyterian high school teacher, Jerry Westfall.[2] Even more encouraging was a new Jesus People–style operation on the east side of the bay in Berkeley incorporated into the Evangelical Concerns family in mid-1969—the Christian World Liberation Front.

This outpost of the Jesus People movement amid the very heart of the 1960s New Left traced its roots to the efforts of four former staff members of Campus Crusade for Christ (CCC)—Jack Sparks, Pat Matrisciano, Fred Dyson, and Weldon Hartenburg—who desired to reach radical students with the gospel. Sparks was the group's leader. An Indiana farm boy and Army vet with degrees from Purdue and Iowa, Sparks was teaching math at East Leyden High School in Franklin Park, Illinois, in the mid-1950s, when he was converted at a Bible church in nearby Bensenville. He completed a PhD in education at Iowa in 1960 and spent several years as head of Colorado State's Bureau of Research Services. In 1965, he accepted a position teaching statistics at Penn State and became a part-time staffer with CCC. The Penn State CCC chapter quickly became the largest on the East Coast, and Sparks left his academic position there to go full-time with Campus Crusade.[3]

In the fall of 1968, Sparks and his friends announced to Crusade leadership that they felt a call to establish a hip ministry on the Berkeley campus. Crusade's leader, Bill Bright, was less than enthusiastic about the plan. Back in the spring of 1967, CCC had targeted Berkeley for a massive evangelistic effort—partially bankrolled by archconservative businessman Nelson Bunker Hunt—to counter the growth of leftist elements on the University of California system's flagship campus. Hundreds of workers descended on the area, a lot of money was expended for publicity and literature, and the event, "The Berkeley Blitz," culminated in an appearance by Billy Graham. But for all intents and purposes, the campaign was a colossal flop.[4] Nonetheless, Bright liked the enthusiasm of his four staffers and agreed to fund their effort until it was up and running, an agreement that suited Sparks, who sensed that visible connections with an establishment group like Bright's could only undercut their efforts.[5]

The quartet arrived to scout out Berkeley in February 1969 and found the entire city caught up in the Third World Liberation Front's (TWLF) campus strike. Deciding there was no time like the present to plunge into the Berkeley scene, they drew up leaflets and made placards bearing messages such as "Pig State No, Anarchy No, Jesus Yes!" and "It Takes Guts to Follow Jesus the Real Revolutionist!"

Wandering into the middle of a demonstration, they were rudely welcomed by the marchers, some of whom cursed them and spat on them. To add insult to injury, when the inevitable clash with police came, they were teargassed and brutalized with the rest of the demonstrators.[6]

Despite their less-than-successful initiation into the world of radical Berkeley, they moved their families to Northern California at the beginning of April 1969. In the weeks and months that followed, the group sat in on radical meetings and demonstrations and began to learn how to mimic the speech and methods of the New Left (figure 4.1). They also underwent a style makeover: hair was grown longer, beards were grown out, and the proletarian jeans-and-workshirt chic of the campus radicals became their de rigueur attire. Playing off the TWLF, they created a new organization they christened the Christian World Liberation Front (CWLF). Meeting the radical left on its own ground, the CWLF held their own, winning converts in heated sidewalk arguments and quiet classroom talks, often baptizing new believers in the fountain on the Berkeley campus's Sproul Plaza.[7]

As word of their new methods and appearance got back to some of the CWLF's original evangelical backers, not all of them were pleased. One friend of Sparks's back in Pennsylvania withdrew his financial support and warned him that he was "cutting himself off from the good people of America...the people who are the backbone of this country" with his new look and strategy. Convinced that he was faithfully contextualizing the gospel for the radical crowd, Sparks could not be dissuaded from his mission.[8]

With a new radical-sensitive group identity in place, the CWLF became a persistent presence on campus, attending nearly every demonstration and student action that took place in and around Berkeley. In addition to a regular sign- and banner-wielding presence, the CWLF also began to branch out into other areas of ministry. A hotline for drug counseling was put in place, CWLF members regularly passed out food to the local homeless population, and a Christian youth hostel was established on Berkeley's Telegraph Avenue. Several CWLF houses that provided a transitional, family-like environment for new converts were also begun.[9]

In late 1969—months after CCC had stopped its initial financial support—the CWLF was accepted into Evangelical Concerns and supported as one of its main ministries. In addition, a growing mailing list of sympathetic friends was bringing in well over $4,000 a month by the summer of 1971.[10] By early 1970, the CWLF was able to acquire a new retreat about 150 miles north in Garberville, the Rising Son Ranch, as a place for freshly minted Berkeley Christians to "be free from distractions...and really set their minds on the Lord."[11]

Probably the most important tool that the CWLF developed was *Right On!* the group's street paper, which began with an experimental four-page, 20,000-copy run in the fall of 1969. Addressed to the student population at Berkeley, *Right On!* was undoubtedly the most sophisticated of the underground newspapers

FIGURE 4.1 A famous poster of the Jesus People movement, Berkeley's Christian World Liberation Front's adaptation of a hippie original as printed in their paper, *Right On!* ca. August 1970.

Courtesy of the *Hollywood Free Paper.*

sponsored by the Jesus movement. Articles dealt with local problems such as the People's Park dispute, as well as such big issues as women's liberation, ecology, and racism. Special features examined the tenets of Eastern religions, and book, movie, and record reviews became regular fixtures of the paper.

As the CWLF attempted to grapple with the New Left and the counterculture, it attracted a growing number of converts and inquirers who attended regular week-night CWLF-sponsored Bible studies and weekend seminars. They also began to attract a growing group of bright, committed evangelical young people who saw it as a model for a more culturally engaged, intellectualized form of Christianity than the evangelical subculture in which they had grown up.

One such addition to the CWLF was Sharon Gallagher, a 1970 sociology gradu-ate of Westmont College in Santa Barbara. Born into a conservative Plymouth Brethren pastor's family in suburban Los Angeles County, Gallagher was a child of the evangelical movement—she had attended Billy Graham's breakthrough 1949

Los Angeles Crusade as an infant in her father's arms. Gallagher came to the
CWLF after being heavily impacted by a summer at L'Abri, the Swiss communal
retreat of emerging evangelical intellectual guru Francis Schaeffer. For Gallagher,
who "really wanted to prolong [her] L'Abri experience" before entering a master's
program in psychology at the University of Southern California, the CWLF was a
way to continue engaging the political and cultural change around her through
a Christian prism. Originally coming for a one-year stint, she ended up working
on *Right On!* and found a new career as a journalist and editor. With a group
of like-minded peers who continued to embrace evangelical Christianity as they
drifted slowly to the left culturally and politically, Gallagher would end up staying
in Berkeley for the duration of the CWLF's history.[12]

The Shiloh Communes, Oregon and Elsewhere

One of the earliest major components of the Jesus People movement outside
California was the Shiloh Youth Revival Centers movement. One of the two most
thoroughly studied elements of the Jesus movement (the Children of God being the
other), Shiloh developed out of the House of Miracles and the early Jesus Houses
operated by Calvary Chapel in Orange County, California. House of Miracles
cofounder John Higgins had dreamed of a network of self-sustaining Christian communes, a vision that differed from the more utilitarian outlook of Calvary Chapel,
which saw the houses as a short-term discipleship solution for people emerging
from the drug culture. As the Calvary Chapel network of houses expanded in late
1968 and early 1969, several communes came under Higgins's management.[13]

In the spring of 1969, Higgins claimed that the Holy Spirit had instructed him
to establish communes outside California after invitations from the Open Bible
Standard Church and the FGBMF asked him to consider coming north to Oregon
to work with students on the campus of the University of Oregon in Eugene.
Calvary Chapel's Chuck Smith—who was relieved to pass on the responsibility
for Higgins's communes[14]—encouraged the move, and with a group of fourteen
men, women, and children, Higgins set out for Eugene, Oregon. With the help
of the local Salvation Army and the Goodwill Industries store, they equipped a
house they dubbed Shiloh—the first Messianic title given in the Old Testament—
after seeing a local street with that name.[15] A second house was soon added as two
brothers (one a former follower of Charles Manson) equipped with sixty-five cents
between them entered a local hippie commune, converted most of its members,
and took it over. Quickly developing a reputation as dependable, hard workers,
the Oregon Shiloh houses made ends meet by hiring out members as fruit and
vegetable pickers to farmers sympathetic to the Shiloh youths' Christian values.[16]

At about this time, Higgins claimed God sent him "a vision of a man coming out
of a white building from the north and he was going to bring incorporation to us,

and he was going to ordain me."A month after he revealed this vision to his follow-ers, an older man named Nick Gray, a native Texan who ran a small ministry in Portland called the Oregon Youth Revival Centers, visited the Shiloh group, along with his son John, who owned a saddle shop in Eugene. The elder Gray told Higgins and his leadership that he believed God was telling him to ordain him. Scurrying to ascertain what color the man's building was painted, the commune rejoiced when it verified that it had indeed been repainted white about two weeks earlier. Reassured that this was God's leading, Higgins visited Gray, who then offered him the corpora-tion. Shiloh filed for 501(c) status and found its nonprofit status immediately helpful in organizing its ten existing houses and saving money on its fruit-picking profits.[17]

Late in 1969, Shiloh learned of an opportunity to purchase a ninety-acre tract about twenty miles outside Eugene for $55,000. Although the group was poverty-stricken, Higgins decided to go ahead with the purchase after being offered an option to pay off the mortgage without interest if it was paid within one year. In what they perceived as a miracle, they managed to raise more than $100,000 in less than six months, paying off the bank note in May 1970 and using the remaining money to begin construction of housing and offices at what was now called "The Land."[18]

By this time, Shiloh had well over a hundred full-fledged members in its vari-ous houses. Each commune generally had a two-level structure of pastors and members, with the former group containing gradations of rank, including assis-tant pastors, deacons, and sometimes deaconesses. Yet a further division of the commune was the internal differentiation between brothers and sisters that reflected their beliefs—common also among most of their evangelical and funda-mentalist contemporaries—that women were (according to the interpretation of New Testament passages such as Ephesians 5: 22–24 and 1 Peter 3: 1–7) "weaker vessels" who must submit to male leadership.[19]

Day-to-day life in the communes depended on whether one lived in the city or on Shiloh's rural holdings. City-based members divided domestic housekeeping tasks largely along gender lines and frequently worked in Shiloh-created moving, construction, or painting businesses or held jobs in the community.[20] At a recently opened Shiloh home in North Carolina in 1971, for instance, of the eleven youth (six men and five women), two worked at a discount store, one was a kitchen worker, another a maintenance man at a hotel, and two of the women were employed as maids.[21] Each member of a Shiloh house would turn over whatever outside income they made, which was then sent to headquarters and subsequently dis-tributed back to the houses as needed for food, clothing, housing, medical needs, and small allowances. At The Land or other operations in the countryside, life was organized around the seasonal demands of agricultural work and the needs of the community and was based in part on an expedition of Shiloh leaders to observe the Hutterites in action. As the group grew, The Land shifted to a training and Bible school for new members, with a tightly scheduled regimen of work, classes, study, and recreation that occupied trainees from 6:30 in the morning until lights out at 10:30 P.M.[22]

During 1970 and 1971, Shiloh attracted many new members and opened a number of new houses averaging about twenty members each in Oregon and California, as well as in Idaho, Washington, Colorado, and back east in Georgia, Tennessee, and North Carolina.[23] In Oregon, The Farm leased a 110-acre berry farm in the summer of 1970, which was soon joined by a Shiloh-owned goat dairy, a seventy-acre sheep farm, and an eighty-acre orchard. In Eugene itself, a former fraternity building near the University of Oregon campus was purchased to house financial and organizational offices. Other operations included a printing business, a cannery (which in 1973 would can over 170 tons of fruit and vegetables, largely for commune consumption), a touring drama troupe, and several groups of traveling hippie evangelists.[24] Often Shiloh sent out a small group to a particular city to establish a house and perhaps begin a coffeehouse and/or a small fellowship worship center. By 1971, Shiloh's full-time membership was more than 1,000, and the group had become truly a nationwide organization, among the largest of the communal groups that had grown out of the hippie movement.[25]

The Jesus People Army—Washington State

Another early bastion of the Jesus People movement arose in the Pacific Northwest, beginning in Seattle and branching out to cities such as Spokane, Yakima, and Everett, Washington, and Vancouver, British Columbia. The movement there had its earliest roots in John and Diana Breithaupt's outreach to young dopers in Seattle's University district. A Conservative Baptist logger from rural northwest Washington, Breithaupt had come into contact with the charismatic Episcopal priest Dennis Bennett in the early 1960s and had received the Pentecostal baptism in the Holy Spirit. Believing God wanted him to abandon his lucrative logging business for some as-yet-unspecified work, Breithaupt moved his family to Seattle in early 1967. Within a short time, Breithaupt felt led to the hippie district's University Avenue, "the Av," where he talked to the young hippies and gave them an occasional helping hand.[26]

True to his core operating principle (what Breithaupt termed "the eleventh commandment—thou shall not hassle"), he refused to preach to the street people or pass out tracts. "I never carried a Bible," Breithaupt remembered. "I just dressed in a pair of jeans and a T-shirt, and sometimes packed a guitar and wore a pair of sandals." He did not let his hair grow, however, and in the early days, Breithaupt "was accused of being a narc many times." But after a while, he recalled that "the Lord opened the door and through that contact they began to accept me as different but not looking down on them...just a friend."[27] Breithaupt's breakthrough with the University Avenue crowd came when a well-known denizen of the sidewalks,

"Little Rich," crashed one night at Breithaupt's house and subsequently spread the word that he was all right. With the financial help of an older couple from Bennett's St. Luke's Episcopal Church, the Breithaupts opened up the House of Zaccheus (named after the family's pet dachshund) in the fall of 1968, accommodating up to twenty young people at a time. Within a few months, a coffeehouse—"Zach's House"—was opened a few blocks away.[28]

Representative of the teens the Breithaupts impacted was Linda Gebaroff, an eighteen-year-old high school dropout from a Lutheran background, a denizen of the Av, and a one-time Haight-Ashbury runaway. After one particularly depressing evening, she was surprised to bump into a group she could only describe as Christian hippies at a countercultural Seattle hangout called the Last Exit on Brooklyn. Intrigued by the conversation and the presentation of the gospel from the charming, good-looking leader of the group, Bud Moegling, she decided to try to find them the next day. Eventually, she was directed to a white house on the corner of Forty-Fifth Street. There were a lot of kids there, and at first she thought she was in a hippie hangout, but then she found out that everyone—hippie or straight—was a Christian.[29]

At some point, this "regular family—an old guy, wife and four kids" (the Breithaupts) came through the door, and the man sat down at the piano and immediately began playing a hymn. That was it for Gebaroff; she broke down crying, and Breithaupt counseled her into accepting Jesus. Within a few weeks, she was a full-blown hippie Christian, living at the House of Zaccheus and attending St. Luke's Episcopal Church, which struck her as "so cool" because they could be "dressed like hippies" and yet "come to church."[30]

Another woman among the early visitors to the Breithaupts' operation was also named Linda—Linda Meissner—a young, intense Pentecostal who came to Seattle with a reputation as a spiritual warrior. An Iowa farm girl, Meissner dropped out of the Assemblies of God's Central Bible College in Springfield, Missouri, in the early 1960s after hearing the young evangelist David Wilkerson tell of his work with Brooklyn's street gangs in a school assembly. Heading east, she spent two years with Wilkerson's Teen Challenge (a period covered in his 1963 book, *The Cross and the Switchblade*).[31] Trading off her connections to Wilkerson's work, she and two friends—Treena Layman and Becky Lozano—traveled about speaking and singing as the Teen Harvester Trio in local churches before being recruited by the FGBMF for a series of evangelistic trips to Hong Kong, the Philippines, and South Korea.[32] During her travels, Meissner claims she was bombarded with a series of visions in which God told her she should go to "Seattle, Washington. . . . I will raise up a mighty army of young people, and you'll go forth and speak the words of life." Hedging on whether this was a revelation or some sort of a "brainstorm," she claimed that later in Mexico City she had another vision about Seattle:

The Spirit said that there would be a great youth revival....It showed me about the coffeehouses, although I didn't know a thing about coffeehouses at the time. It told me to get a location, about painting the tables different colors, about building a stage, and to go out in teams throughout that city inviting kids to this coffeehouse. And hundreds, literally thousands of young people who didn't know Jesus before were going to ask Him into their hearts—an army for Jesus that glorified His name.[33]

In 1968, Meissner was invited by Roy Johnson to come to Seattle's Philadelphia Church to conduct a three-day revival meeting. Finding some success with speaking engagements there and in other churches, Meissner resolved to start a Teen Challenge–like work in Seattle. Opening a short-lived counseling center called The Ark, she made little progress with Seattle's hippie teens with her combination of Pentecostal austerity and already-outdated East Coast perceptions of with-it youth culture. Recalled one girl:

There was this jukebox playing funky New York–type music...there were these two chicks [Linda and a friend] in bouffant hair styles, wearing black dresses and high heels and trying to tell us that dope was hell and Jesus could take us out of that hell. We laughed because the music was so ridiculous that it blew our mind.[34]

It was shortly after this that Meissner made contact with the Breithaupts and observed them in action, while continuing to cultivate a backing in local churches. In early 1969, she established a coffeehouse she called The Eleventh Hour at the corner of First and Madison downtown. Meissner's charismatic speaking ability and "sold-out-for-Jesus" message soon made an impact, and she began to gather a small following of zealous Pentecostal youth and converted street people, which she ambitiously called the Jesus People Army. The ranks of Meissner's army were strengthened in late 1969 and early 1970, when she picked up a new trio of effective coworkers: Jim Palosaari and Sue Cowper, a pair of counterculture-savvy converts from San Francisco, and Louis St. Cyr, a former member of the Seattle Black Panthers. "By this time," Palosaari later reminisced about Meissner, "she was starting to wear a little buckskin" and was looking more "with it." With the help of her new assistants and her street corner-, park-, and church-based rallies, Meissner's JPA ventured into the suburbs and nearby cities like Yakima in an attempt to witness to local youth (figure 4.2).[35]

As Meissner's group grew, she was given the opportunity to take over some warehouse space at Fifth and John, across from the city's famous Space Needle. Soon thereafter, she opened the Catacombs coffeehouse, which eventually would host sometimes up to 2,000 people on the weekends to listen to Meissner's talks

FIGURE 4.2 Jesus People leaders, left to right: Linda Meissner of the Jesus People Army in Seattle; Duane Pederson, publisher of the *Hollywood Free Paper*; and Jack Sparks, head of Berkeley's Christian World Liberation Front.

Courtesy of the Archives, Hubbard Library, Fuller Theological Seminary.

and a rock band called Glorious Liberty.[36] In 1970, the group began to print their own underground newspaper, *Agape* (10,000 copies of which they once dropped on a local rock festival from an airplane that circled overhead),[37] and opened two communal houses—the House of Esther for girls and the House of Caleb for boys. One of the JPA's innovations during the Easter weekend of 1970 was the Jesus March, a public demonstration that gathered several hundred youth for a march in downtown Seattle.[38] In early 1971, the JPA undertook an "evangelistic blitz" in the western portion of Washington state that led to the establishment of JPA branches, communal houses, and coffeehouses in Tacoma, Everett, and Vancouver, British Columbia.[39]

About a year prior to the '71 blitz, Meissner had established a working relationship with a new ally, Carl Parks from Spokane in the eastern part of the state. The son of a pair of Assembly of God evangelists, Parks walked away at the age of thirty-one from a position as the regional representative for a correspondence school to pursue a calling to Christian ministry. Meeting members of the JPA during a trip to Seattle, Parks investigated the Catacombs and talked with Meissner. Imbued with a new vision for work in Spokane, Parks went home and, with the help of a few friends, soon attracted a following and started the I AM coffeehouse, several communal homes, and a well-produced Jesus paper, *Truth*. Parks adopted the Jesus People Army name and used it in his work, and Meissner adopted *Truth* as her Seattle paper's name; the two groups worked together often, but the official connection was an informal one.[40] One of Parks's early coups was to convert the members of Wilson-McKinley, one of the Spokane area's leading rock groups. With this solid attraction in his pocket, Parks had no problem drawing a crowd to his coffeehouse and outdoor evangelistic meetings.[41] Parks's corps of the Jesus People Army eventually grew to include half a dozen communal houses in Spokane alone, along with the Jesus Free Store, a pay-as-you-are-able thrift store. In addition, Parks was able to establish outposts of his group in Walla Walla and Yakima, as well as Coeur d'Alene, Idaho, and Portland, Oregon.[42] Between his and Meissner's groups, the Jesus People movement was well entrenched in the Pacific Northwest by the start of 1971.

Scott Ross and the Love Inn Community, Freeville, New York

Far removed from the hippie magnet of California's beaches and mountains, the beginnings of the Jesus movement in central New York took place amid woodlands and dairy farms in response to a radio show combining rock music with spiritual banter, interviews, and phone calls from the audience. In July 1968, televangelist Pat Robertson's Norfolk, Virginia–based Christian Broadcasting Network (CBN)—at the time a UHF TV station and a single FM radio station— received a notice from a telecommunications company announcing that it was selling five signal-overlapping FM stations in upstate New York. At $500,000, the stations—which made it possible to drive the 300-mile distance between Albany and Buffalo and always be within range of a signal—were a broadcasting windfall. Robertson quickly contacted the company and convinced it to donate the stations in exchange for a tax write-off. Linking the stations together in a network, CBN sent twenty-eight-year-old disc jockey Scott Ross to Ithaca in September to serve as caretaker, transmitter operator, and nighttime announcer.[43]

Charles Edward "Scott" Ross, a young Scottish immigrant with a Pentecostal background, had come to America shortly after the end of World War II and grew up in New Jersey and Maryland. He arrived at CBN in mid-1967 after a meteoric but short-lived career as a rock 'n' roll reporter and disc jockey in New York City. Originally a producer for WINS's star disc jockey, Murray "The K" Kaufman, his career received a major boost in early 1964 when his girlfriend, Nedra Talley, a member of the popular female singing trio the Ronettes, introduced him to the Beatles. Taking a liking to the Glasgow-born Ross (who had strategically "reacquired [his] Scottish accent" for the occasion), the Beatles gave him a series of interviews that made him a major commodity. As a result, he landed a regular show in which he interviewed pop stars, as well as a syndicated newspaper column, "Scott on the Rocks." Hanging around the likes of Bob Dylan (who introduced him to marijuana); Peter, Paul, and Mary; Eric Burdon; and the Rolling Stones' Brian Jones, Ross quickly became swept up in the fast-moving world of rock music and its regimen of sex, alcohol, and drugs. He even became involved in music management, teaming with Beatles manager Brian Epstein in a stake in a band called the Lost Souls that featured future Apple Records artist Jackie Lomax. Ross was going to accompany the band to London to record their first album until an argument with Epstein on the way to the airport (a fight Ross claimed was triggered by his acid use) brought on an angry split.[44]

In late 1966, Ross was arrested for marijuana possession and lost his radio and newspaper jobs. Devastated and reduced to part-time announcing, he began to reinvestigate his family's Pentecostal heritage. Marrying Talley, he moved home to Hagerstown, Maryland, and took a low-level job at a local station. Soon thereafter, Ross and his wife underwent a conversion experience and spoke in tongues. Attending a meeting of the Full Gospel Businessmen's Fellowship (FGBMF) in Baltimore a few months later, he met Robertson, who invited the young disc jockey down to Virginia Beach for an interview and subsequently offered him a job with CBN.[45]

As Ross began his upstate New York assignment, he was mindful of the negative reaction he had received from his superiors in Virginia when he had attempted to play spiritually sensitive music by the pop-folk group Peter, Paul, and Mary. That incident—in which the station manager stormed into the studio and pulled the power cord out of the socket to stop the transmission of sinful music over the air—along with subsequent incidents had made it clear that secular folk and rock music was verboten on CBN. "The fire fell," Ross remembered in a 2002 interview; "this was sacrilege, they wanted me off the air, the phones would light up, people would threaten me, I mean physically—all for the glory of God, of course." Robertson, however, defended his young charge and encouraged his attempts to reach out to a younger audience.[46]

Now, several hundred miles from his Tidewater critics, Ross's hopes revived of putting together a program to reach a younger audience by utilizing the serious new sentiments that were appearing in rock 'n' roll. Playing songs such as Barry McGuire's "Eve of Destruction" and others by Bob Dylan, the Beatles, and other rock musicians, Ross interspersed the music with banter about God and the meaning of life and took phone calls from his audience. "I would go for hours," he recalled. "I went on the air around 4 or 5 o'clock in the evening and sometimes go to midnight....I remember a few times going all night long because all the phones lit up." Within a few months, 7,000 people showed up to hear him speak in Syracuse.[47]

But Ross also sought a way to begin an off-the-air ministry in the area around Ithaca. When a cold spell caused the pipes in his mobile home to burst, Ross put out a call over the air for alternative housing. He received a call from Peggy Hardesty, a Baptist widow who owned a small farm in nearby Freeville and claimed that she had been healed of arthritis on the first night she had listened to his show. She offered him her barn to use for his ministry. Ross visited the site, thought the place had potential, and accepted her offer. Then he told his listeners about his efforts to turn the barn into a hip meeting place for local believers. That summer, Hardesty donated the barn and an adjacent thirty acres to the new nonprofit group they labeled "Jesus People, Inc." With the help of dozens of his newfound fans, Ross cleaned up and renovated the barn, adding a stage, a stone fireplace, a kitchen, and small meeting rooms.[48]

By the fall of 1969, the Love Inn was hosting regular weeknight Bible studies and coffeehouse nights on weekends. Almost immediately, it began to attract young people as a place to crash while hitchhiking through the area and as a place for new converts to get their heads together. Eventually, a commune was established with Ross at its head. The scope of the group expanded as Ross began to syndicate his nightly *Scott Ross Show* to stations across the country. Soon, one of the members began to manage Hardesty's farm for the commune, and a secretary moved from New York City to handle the radio program's growing correspondence.[49] The commune's membership varied between fifteen and forty in its first two years or so (and eventually topped out at over 250 in the mid-'70s). It became well known in the East as a counterculturally friendly outpost of evangelical Christianity through the impact of Ross's radio program and through the hundreds who visited the Love Inn's Bible studies and music nights.[50]

The Way West and East: Mill Valley, California, and Rye, New York

Part of the Jesus movement's spread during 1969 and 1970 was the growth of the Victor Paul Wierwille–connected groups, The Way West and The Way East. Wierwille's successful recruitment of two of the four main couples—Steve and Sandi Heefner and Jim and Judy Doop—involved with the Bay Area's Living Room mission and House of Acts commune signaled a major watershed in the development of his Ohio-based Way International. The change was immediately apparent during the summer 1969 visit of the Heefners and Doops and the two dozen kids they brought with them from California. The presence of the colorful young West Coast hippies electrified the compound in New Knoxville, changing its atmosphere from that of a somewhat grim, middle-aged Midwestern church camp to a vibrant biblical ashram full of young countercultural truth seekers. One Way staffer remembered it as "an invasion of hippies" amid "some very straitlaced people. . . . The Heefners were lovely people, but they were hippies, they were long-haired and the women wore no bras and so on. It was quite a shock to the staff."[51]

But despite the cultural disconnect, Wierwille realized that he had found the constituency that would be the key to The Way International's sustained growth for the next decade. "The momentum of the ministry really picked up among a new group...young people, unaffiliated, street people," Wierwille was quoted as saying in 1974. To his mind, one characteristic made this "whole new audience" especially attractive: "Many of [them] had not been raised in a particular denomination or church" and thus had much less "difficulty believing because they didn't have all those years of wrong teaching to get rid of first."[52]

At the end of the summer, both couples returned to the Bay Area, Doop to his position as a Lutheran youth pastor and the Heefners to unemployment and Bible studies with Mill Valley hippie youth. In October, Heefner received an offer to join the launch of a major new FM station in New York City (WCBS-FM), and he and his wife left abruptly for the East Coast.[53] Jim and Judy Doop took over their Bible studies, and by late 1969, Jim had decided to leave his position at the Lutheran church and establish a Wierwille-affiliated group he named The Way West. According to a critical history of The Way written by ex-member Karl Kahler, Doop told him that he incorporated the group independent of a cautious Wierwille at the latter's insistence, just in case the hippie crowd did "anything that would embarrass him." Doop, for his part, agreed to split class registration and book sales sixty-forty and to set aside 10% of any general offerings that were collected to send back to New Knoxville—a tithe that soon went up to 15%. But from the beginning, it was clear that the only embarrassing aspect of The Way West may have been Wierwille's low expectations. The Doops' seminars and PAL classes "grew like wildfire," attracting mostly college-age youth in sessions that often attracted 200 to 300 people.[54]

Meanwhile, the Heefners adjusted to their new life in New York and had little direct involvement with either their previous ministry in the Bay Area or The Way in Ohio. But several months after their arrival in the East, they were contacted by some kids from tony suburban Westchester County they had met in New Knoxville the previous summer. Inviting the kids to their city apartment, they were stunned to find themselves hosting a mixed group of suburban teenagers and recently converted bikers—one of whom had a broken arm that was reputedly healed that night.[55] Meetings were soon moved out to one of the teens' parents' multicar garage in suburban Rye. Within weeks, the Heefners themselves moved to Rye, where their house "exploded with teenagers" looking for counseling, Bible study, and the PAL classes. Aided by Rev. Joseph Bishop, the pastor of Rye Presbyterian Church, whose son had been brought back from drugs by his contact with the Heefners, the disc jockey/youth minister and his wife quickly found space at the church for meetings, as well as entrée into dozens of local churches. By early 1971, Heefner had left his job at the radio station, officially incorporated The Way East, and played a major role in fanning the flames of Jesus People publicity when their group was featured in a *Life* magazine spread, "The Groovy Christians of Rye, NY."[56]

With the flood of publicity from the Jesus movement, The Way had by mid-1971 begun to successfully open up new centers in different parts of the country. But Wierwille was apparently chafing at the bit to tighten his control over the two most successful units associated with his movement: the bicoastal ministries begun by his San Francisco recruits. He began to negotiate for a bigger role in Doop's West Coast organization, even as he seemed to suddenly be booking "himself in a lot of engagements" in Heefner's turf in the tristate area. A final bone of contention was a record company Wierwille wanted to start to harness some of the young musical talent that had begun to filter into The Way. Heefner, with his experience as a dj and his relationships with numerous artists, insisted on having complete artistic control over the label, and "that," Heefner recalled, "just sent [Wierwille] right over the top." Wierwille then began to move behind the scenes, browbeating the other officers of Doop's and Heefner's organizations into coming to New Knoxville to draw up new incorporation papers that put him in their place as chief executive.[57]

In early March 1972, the hammer fell on The Way West at a Sunday night meeting in a school auditorium in front of a crowd of 500 people. As Doop waited to speak, one of Wierwille's executives informed him that the Ohio pastor was now in charge of The Way West and that he (Doop) had been ousted. "Howard Allen, the general manager of The Way International in New Knoxville, walked into the room where I was sitting," Doop recalled years later, "and said, 'God bless you. You are no longer the President of The Way West.'" After the Doops left the building, Wierwille, accompanied by two of his lieutenants, walked into the room and up to the stage and made the announcement that he was the new president of The Way West and that the "Doops were moving on."[58]

Coming as it did after the coup in Marin County, Wierwille's takeover of The Way East several weeks later was anticipated. Heefner, for his part, was more than willing to step aside, fed up with what he felt was a growing "cult" and the "personality structure" Wierwille was building around himself. After sitting quietly through the meeting when the Rye faithful learned of the new setup, Heefner told "the Man of God" (as he was now styling himself) that he was "bush league" and that he would be receiving a bill for moving Heefner's household back to the West Coast.[59]

After the Ways East and West came under Wierwille's control, the group lost its tentative relationship with the larger Jesus People movement and was branded a cult by the evangelical mainstream—a judgment cemented by Wierwille's 1975 book, *Jesus Christ Is Not God*.[60] During the next decade, the organization continued to exploit the youth demographic that the street Christians of the Haight had initially marked out for Wierwille. In 1975, The Way purchased the Presbyterian Emporia College in Kansas (redubbed The Way College) and, by the mid-1980s, were taking in $35 million in annual revenue from a following estimated at about 40,000.[61] Throughout this time, however, the group was plagued by a growing stream of accusations, including unorthodox theology and interpretation of the Bible, dictatorial control and economic exploitation of members, rampant sexual misconduct and abuse among its leaders (particularly Wierwille, who died in 1985), anti-Semitic teaching, homophobic paranoia, rumors of armed bodyguards and paramilitary arms training at Way compounds, and troubles with the IRS. By the early 1990s, defections and reform-minded splinter groups would drain away perhaps as much as 75% of its following.[62]

David Hoyt and the House of Judah: Atlanta and the Southeast

The major arrival of the Jesus People movement in the South began as the result of a short speaking tour of several Southern Baptist churches and colleges during the fall of 1969 by Kent Philpott's ex-Hare Krishna colleague, David Hoyt. Despite the heavily churched, evangelical ethos of the South, Hoyt was "gripped" by the need for a hippie-sympathetic "out-front ministry" in that part of the country. Atlanta "seemed like it was a migration point like the Haight for kids in the South who had any kind of interest in the drug culture, or the music of the day," recalled Hoyt in a 2008 interview. Believing God wanted him in the South, he and several others began praying about their next move when they returned to California. The call to head to the Southeast only got stronger after he attended the disastrous Altamont Speedway Free Festival in early December. Within a few weeks, Hoyt received an offer from the First Baptist Church in suburban Decatur, Georgia, to open an outreach center in Atlanta's hippie area. After a final round of prayer, he and several associates were convinced that God was calling them to the South, and Hoyt announced his resignation from Upper Streams, the Evangelical Concerns–related group he was leading in Walnut Creek.[63]

In the spring of 1970, Hoyt, his wife, Victoria, and several other members of the Upper Streams group piled into a Volkswagen van with "God is Love" painted on its sides and drove east. With help from their Baptist backers, they secured a lease on a sprawling, run-down, two-story house on Piedmont Avenue, about a block from Atlanta's drug district. The church footed the bill to rework the house's electrical wiring, fix the porch, replaster and paint the walls and ceilings, and refinish its hardwood floors.[64] Proclaiming it the House of Judah, Hoyt and company announced their mission to Atlanta by placing a hand-painted sign in the front yard: "Jesus Loves Viet Cong & G. I.'s, Parents & Cops, Rednecks & Freaks and YOU!"[65]

Their first major endeavor after getting established was a first aid ministry at the Atlanta Pop Festival over the July Fourth weekend. Backed by the church and a volunteer team of doctors and nurses, they drove sixty miles south to the festival site in Byron equipped with two tents, cots, blankets, medical supplies,

food, water, and Bibles. Over the gathering's three days, the Jesus People–
Baptist partnership helped scores of people suffering from drug overdoses,
bad cuts, and heat exhaustion. When all was said and done, they had prayed
with dozens of hippies to receive Christ and returned to Atlanta with about a
dozen new believers in tow.[66]

With the new converts added to the original group that had come from
California, there was now enough of a critical mass to begin evangelizing the
Peachtree City's hippie population. So successful were Hoyt and friends in
winning converts from within Atlanta's countercultural enclave that the House
of Judah was soon filled (figure 4.3) and shortly thereafter joined by two other
facilities, the Lighthouse and the Temple of Still Waters. All in all, Hoyt's
Atlanta Discipleship Training Center eventually counted more than eighty
full-time, live-in Jesus People.[67]

Life in the Atlanta houses revolved around a regimen of Bible study, worship,
and street evangelism, combined with housekeeping chores and gender-specific
lessons in skills such as carpentry and knitting. Despite their determined efforts
to straighten out the new converts' wayward behavior, the group's purpose was not
to turn them into prospective Chamber of Commerce members. This much Hoyt
made clear in a letter he wrote supporters from the straight churches in which he
described the demands being placed on the new converts:

> We suggest and encourage our new brothers and sisters who are somewhat
> freaky in dress, hair, and general appearance to ask the Lord in prayer for
> a balance. We do feel that the beads, bells, and various astrological signs
> along with the no-bra philosophy of the Hip Scene should be forsaken. We
> do not believe, however, that a shave and a haircut make you a Christian
> any more than long hair and sandals.... We are not rehabilitating people
> to melt back into society as good, clean-shaven and well-spruced American
> citizens, but rather to learn to follow Jesus Christ and do the will of the
> Father.[68]

In December 1970, a donor turned over to the group a fast-food restaurant and cafeteria in the heart of downtown Atlanta. Christened the Bread of Life Restaurant,
the establishment provided work and evangelism opportunities, if not much profit.
Soon, they opened up the Chamber Gates Lightclub in the Bread of Life's basement, offering music and Bible raps on Friday and Saturday evenings.[69] Perhaps
most important for the visibility of the Jesus movement, Hoyt's lieutenants began
fanning out to other Southern cities to work within local hippie enclaves. By early
1971, the group had helped establish communal houses in Nashville, Knoxville,
Chattanooga, Birmingham, Gainesville, and Jacksonville.[70]

FIGURE 4.3 The House of Judah in Atlanta, ca. summer 1970; David Hoyt, upper right.
Courtesy of Kent Philpott.

Maranatha Coffeehouse and Church, New Milford, New Jersey

Adjacent to New York City, the suburban districts of northeastern New Jersey, with their heavily Catholic and Jewish populations, have, since the late nineteenth century, hardly been a promising environment for evangelical Protestantism. But here, too—a few miles west of the Hudson River—the Jesus movement emerged, seemingly out of nowhere, during 1969 and 1970. In this instance, the youth revival occurred under the unlikely pairing of a by-turns bold and uptight perfectionist Nazarene pastor from the Midwest and a guitar-playing, Beatles-worshipping Italian American Jersey kid.

Paul Moore was a native Midwesterner and the son of a Church of the Nazarene pastor. A gospel musician who was tiring of the road, in January 1969 Moore found himself at a struggling Nazarene church in the New Jersey suburb of New Milford in central Bergen County, just south of the New York state line. With a recently purchased building and parsonage to pay for, the congregation of roughly a dozen souls was desperate for a pastor and invited the likable Moore to fill the church's empty pulpit in exchange for free housing. Suddenly finding himself a pastor, one of Moore's first halting steps as a man of the cloth was an attempt to evangelize the local youth. In the fall of 1969, he opened a coffeehouse in the church basement where he offered a "mixed program" of pizza, soft drinks, and music—usually live rock bands from New Milford High School interspersed with records by southern gospel groups. While the free refreshments and local secular bands attracted pretty good crowds, Moore's sermonettes and southern gospel music were greeted with benign amusement and tolerance at best. Within a few months, the novelty had worn off, and the coffeehouse folded—after Moore's stereo and other items had been stolen.[71]

However, Charlie Rizzo, a guitarist in one of the bands and a thoroughly hip-pified speed freak, continued to come around and talk with Moore. Rizzo liked Moore, describing him as "looking like the legendary Clark Kent" and in spite of his being "a typical, corny Midwestern pastor."[72] In the summer of 1970, Rizzo ran into a small group of ex-druggie Jesus freaks who finally connected and made sense of what Moore had been telling him. Undergoing a conversion experience, the excited Rizzo came to Moore with the news and surprised Moore by returning his stereo. One of the first steps Rizzo took to remove any stumbling blocks to his newfound faith in Christ was to smash his $450 Gibson guitar to pieces. Over the next few weeks, Moore counseled a bit of patience and eventually convinced Rizzo that perhaps he could use his musical skills—even as a rock 'n' roller—for the furtherance of God's Kingdom.[73]

By early October 1970, Moore had rethought his original coffeehouse effort and reopened the newly christened Maranatha Coffeehouse with a "clear Gospel emphasis." Rizzo, who years later remembered that at the time "he had no idea about the Jesus movement on the West Coast," was talked into forming and leading a Maranatha house band, and this time it all clicked. Within a couple of months, the coffeehouse was jammed and stayed that way. Shortly thereafter, a special Jesus concert at a lodge hall in nearby Hackensack attracted a crowd of more than 500 teens. But more important, Moore and Rizzo had begun to harvest souls. A second concert at Washington High School saw sixty-five teens converted. Soon New Milford Nazarene had been tagged by locals as "the hippie church," as a now longer-haired Moore preached to two Sunday morning services packed with a mixture of grade-A hippie converts, more mainstream teenagers, and twenty-somethings who found the music, relaxed dress code, and all-out com-mitment to their liking.[74]

By early '71, the success of the youth revival at New Milford had attracted the attention of the Nazarene Church. Jack White, the thirty-plus-year superintendent of the New York District, visited and found a church consisting nearly entirely of hippies and young people, replete with rock music and drum sets. White's initial reaction was one of horror, but after a few visits, he knew he could not argue with the results. In an interview in 1979, he recalled the scene in New Milford:

> Thirty and forty people coming to Christ every service...lines of people to be baptized every week! God [was] at work. I saw those young people accept Christ and their decisions were real! I [did not] understand it...but I [was not going to] stop it![75]

Maranatha the coffeehouse and Maranatha the Jesus rock band were the leading edge of a blossoming Jesus People presence in the New York metropolitan area in 1971 and 1972. Coffeehouses popped up in northern Jersey in towns like Morristown, Plainfield, Montclair, and West New York, as well as in southern Connecticut towns like Ansonia, Danbury, and Norwalk. A few Jesus People outposts even opened up in Manhattan, Queens, and on Long Island.[76] Jesus music festivals sprang up around the area, with the biggest splash made by the Maranatha-sponsored Jesus Joy Festivals held at Madison Square Garden on April 16 and Labor Day, 1972, which attracted crowds of around 3,000 youth from the tristate area to hear the likes of Rizzo and Maranatha, Andrae Crouch and the Disciples, Danny Taylor, and Love Song.[77]

Such was Maranatha's unlikely success in its New Jersey setting that eventually the Church of the Nazarene's leadership embraced the new Jesus People movement in their midst. Locally, they put up money to start three "New Milford-influenced" Nazarene church plants in nearby Hackensack and Washington, New Jersey, and Monticello, New York. On a national level, films and slide programs were created to promote—and defend—the New Milford revival. The church hierarchy even sent Moore, Rizzo, and the Maranatha band on the road to EXPLO '72; regional Nazarene youth conventions in Sacramento, Des Moines, Oklahoma City, and Atlanta; and the denomination's 1972 General Assembly in Miami Beach. The example of what was going on in New Milford not only influenced a number of Nazarene churches to tolerate the Jesus People as a model for youth ministry but also encouraged a number of congregations—such as the First Nazarene Church of Detroit and its Salt Company—to open their own Jesus movement-friendly youth outreaches.[78]

Fort Wayne, Indiana: The Adam's Apple

The beginnings of another Jesus People center began to emerge in early 1970 in northeastern Indiana in the city of Fort Wayne. There John Lloyd, a freshly converted, guitar-playing, ex-drug-using, recently discharged soldier in his mid-twenties, had just returned to work as a model artist at the local International Harvester plant. Lloyd began to attend a large Pentecostal church called Calvary Temple and soon started a Bible study in his apartment. The meetings proved

popular with some of the church youth and began attracting students from the Fort
Wayne Art Institute. As the Bible study grew, Lloyd approached Calvary Temple's
pastor, Paul Paino, with a vision to begin a coffeehouse that coming summer in
an attempt to reach the kids in the local drug culture. Paino agreed to the plan and
promised to provide some financial backing.[79]

Believing God was guiding his steps, Lloyd quit his job at International Harvester
and took Paino's offer of $100 a week to pilot the new youth outreach. He quickly
found an old warehouse fronting the Wabash & Erie Canal in a downtown area
called the Landing. Turning some of his born-again artists loose to decorate the
place, he secured a soda machine and kitchen equipment to help feed the hungry
teens. Christened the Adam's Apple, the place was open days and evenings, allowing teens to drift in and out for conversation and meet their friends. For Friday
night concerts, he hired secular rock bands from the area that promised not to
smoke, curse, or bring any drugs into the venue. Their sets—featuring songs like
"Mississippi Queen" and "Spirit in the Sky"—provided the backdrop for Lloyd's
Bible raps and invitations to those interested in Jesus to come chat with him and
his staff in an adjacent inquirer's room. The formula apparently worked; the coffeehouse soon became Fort Wayne's happening teenage hangout for the summer
of 1970, and dozens of kids were converted.[80]

But not everyone was thrilled with the new teenage gospel venue. The Adam's
Apple was attracting lots of scruffy-looking kids to the downtown area, and some
of the city's civic leaders objected. A particular opponent was Joan White, the wife
of local businessman Edward White, whose Bowmar Company would introduce
the world's first handheld calculator ("the Bowmar Brain") the very next year. Joan
White was a "special advisor" to a group called the Landing Association, which
had been formed in 1968 with an eye to restoring the former glory of Fort Wayne's
Columbia Street. Unfortunately, the sudden appearance of the Adam's Apple was
an unexpected monkey wrench in the association's grand strategy. Speaking to a
reporter about the group's overall progress, White noted that there was one place
in the district—the Adam's Apple—that the board was definitely "not happy with."
"There are hippies hanging around, 200, 300, 400 of them. It just gets out of
hand. It is not a playground out here." Touting the Landing as a "showcase for
anything the city—the people of Fort Wayne—want," it was clear she assumed the
citizens wanted no part of a place like the Adam's Apple. The story made it plain
that while the association had no power to expel an "undesirable establishment,"
they would "strongly suggest" to the landlord that he "reconsider" his tenant.[81]

By the fall of 1970, the Landing Association's pressure had apparently made
life uncomfortable enough for the warehouse's landlord that the Adam's Apple
was forced to leave the downtown area. The group retreated to the basement of
Calvary Temple for several months and took over a house the church owned for
twice-weekly Bible studies. In Lloyd's estimation, this time actually solidified the

group, recalling in a 2010 interview that the change of venue allowed them to see "who was *into* rock and who was *on* The Rock" (his emphasis).[82]

By early 1971, the Adam's Apple had reopened in its coffeehouse incarnation, at first in a leaky old revival tent on the church grounds and later inside a church-owned building that housed Calvary Temple's printing press and an auto body shop. By that summer, the Adam's Apple had pretty much crowded out the other tenants in their building and was again attracting hundreds of kids to its weekly Bible studies and concerts. In addition, they started their own Jesus paper (*Hard Core*) and commandeered one of Calvary Temple's school buses—colorfully bedecking it with the Adam's Apple logo, cartoons, and the message "Jesus Loves You, Yes He Do." Enhancing the appeal of the ministry was a growing stable of in-house musical talent including Lloyd, a quirky six-foot-plus female singer named Oreon Trickey ("Oreon"), the Adam's Apple's secretary and worship leader, Nancy Henigbaum (known as "Honeytree," a literal translation of her German surname), and a hard-rock band calling itself Petra that was fronted by a guitar-playing convert from Ohio, Bob Hartman. By the mid-1970s, Calvary Temple had erected a new physical plant, and the Adam's Apple took over the majority of the church's old building and—with a little squeezing—could accommodate a crowd of 2,000 kids. With its sizable local constituency, musical talent, and newspaper (which at one point had printing runs estimated at 200,000 per issue), the largely self-supporting Adam's Apple became an important resource for other Jesus People coffeehouses and ministries in the eastern regions of the Midwest.[83]

Milwaukee Jesus People, Milwaukee, Wisconsin

The origin of the Jesus People movement in the Milwaukee area was perhaps the textbook example of how the movement was transplanted from one area to another by zealous counterculture converts. The group that came to be known as the Milwaukee Jesus People had its origins in Linda Meissner's Jesus People Army in Seattle. Jim and Sue Cowper Palosaari, who began and led the Milwaukee group, were Jesus People missionaries commissioned by their Washington state brethren to evangelize the Midwest.

Jim Palosaari, a second-generation Finnish American, was born in 1939 in the Upper Peninsula of Michigan. From the age of ten, he was raised on a small farm outside of Oconomowoc, Wisconsin, twenty-five miles west of Milwaukee. After graduating from high school in 1957, he drifted around the United States as a salesman and bartender and worked as a part-time actor in Chicago, Detroit, and New York. By 1967, he had left behind two wives and children and was living in Haight-Ashbury. Always much more into alcohol than any of the new drugs that were all the rage, he eventually picked up some work in a bar near San Francisco State, where he met a young woman named Susan Cowper.[84]

Cowper had come to the Bay Area in 1962, following a married sound engineer with whom she was having an affair—Augustus Owsley Stanley III, the grandson of a Kentucky senator, and the Bay Area's future psychedelic chemist-in-residence, and soundman for the Grateful Dead. Raised in a solidly respectable upper-middle-class family in South Pasadena, California, Cowper experimented with psychedelic mushrooms in her first year at a local college, met Stanley, and then ran away to San Francisco. Bouncing between life with Owsley—where day-to-day life brought "people...through the door...that were out of a Fellini movie"—and the middle-class propriety of an aunt and uncle's home in the suburbs, Cowper eventually worked her way free of the burgeoning psychedelic scene, dabbled in the antiwar movement, and returned to college.[85]

Soon after meeting in the summer of 1969, Palosaari and Cowper decided to get away from the Bay Area. Selling her old Volkswagen, they bought a van and set out camping their way up the Pacific coast. By the time they arrived in Washington, they were broke and looking for a free place to camp. They wandered into a tent revival in the village of Cathcart (a few miles outside Seattle) that was being led by Russell Griggs, an associate of Linda Meissner's. He convinced the two to stick around, and after attending a few meetings, the two were converted and underwent the baptism of the Holy Spirit.[86]

Their lives suddenly turned upside down, and having no particular plans, Palosaari and Cowper went to Seattle and were introduced to Meissner. Palosaari recalled her as coming off as "kind of a straight-looking person" who "didn't know what to do with us" but "didn't want to let us go."[87] Linked up with the JPA, they were among the first residents of her new communal houses. Within a few months, the pair had become an integral part of Meissner's leadership team, working with evangelistic street-witnessing teams and organizing and governing the JPA's growing corps of Jesus houses. Along with Meissner, Palosaari helped plan the early 1971 evangelistic blitz that resulted in new JPA operations in several western Washington cities.[88]

By that time, however, Palosaari had notions that God had called him to be a Jesus People missionary to his native Midwest. Meissner, the native Iowan, flirted with the idea of picking up a large chunk of the JPA and heading to Chicago to serve as a countercultural corollary for the big Billy Graham Crusade that was planned for the following June. Ultimately, she decided to stay put but gave her blessing to Palosaari's efforts.[89]

In February 1971, he and Sue—now married—departed for the Midwest, initially heading to Chicago. But after a quick visit to Palosaari's hometown of Oconomowoc, the couple stopped to visit Milwaukee and within a few days had received what they felt was divine assurance that they should drop anchor in the Beer City. They met a man who had two large adjacent houses he was willing to let them use and just as quickly picked up five new converts to put into the newly named Power House—Milwaukee's first Jesus People group house. Within a few months, the group had dozens of members, including some local rock musicians. Throwing together a Jesus rock band, The Sheep, the Palosaaris used them as a focal point for a series of recruiting and evangelistic swings into northern Wisconsin that summer that further enlarged the group.[90]

By the fall of 1971, aided by their band and two attention-attracting appearances by Linda Meissner at well-publicized rallies, the Milwaukee Jesus People (MJP) had grown to more than 150 full-time members. To house the group, Palosaari was able to secure a lease on an abandoned 315-room hospital near the city's center. That facility not only became the MJP's megabarracks but also housed its Jesus Christ Power House Coffeehouse, its new *Street Level* Jesus paper, and a Jesus People's version of a Bible college, the Milwaukee Discipleship Training Center (figure 4.4).[91]

This latter program was a direct reflection of Palosaari's conviction that an overemphasis on a salvation experience at the expense of committed study and discipleship was undermining the entire movement. The Training Center was designed as a forty-week program that alternated seven weeks of classwork

FIGURE 4.4 A member of the Milwaukee Jesus People passes out copies of their paper *Street Level* in front of the Jesus Christ Power House coffeehouse, July 1971.

Used with permission, AP/Wide World Photos.

with intensive three-week evangelistic excursions to nearby Midwestern cities. In these three-week missionary pilgrimages, the trainees—or better yet, disciples—followed a program modeled after Christ's instructions to the twelve in the tenth chapter of Matthew. Broken into small groups, the students were given just enough money to make it to, say, Eau Claire or Cleveland. Once there, they were expected to stay "in the field" witnessing, evangelizing, and relying on the Lord—and his people—to provide them with food, housing, and the means to get back to Milwaukee. All in all, more than seventy fervent young trainees turned out in the fall of 1971 and completed the course in the school's first and only year in operation.[92]

By late 1971, Palosaari was able to create two large witness teams, replete with their own rock bands—The Sheep and Charity—and sent them out on the road for extended evangelistic campaigns. The groups hit Springfield, Missouri, and the Quad Cities area in Iowa and Illinois in late 1971 and early 1972, as well as Duluth, Minnesota. The Duluth revival was particularly successful, with meetings that ran for over six weeks, produced hundreds of converts, and received a good deal of publicity in the evangelical media.[93] Through these efforts and other evangelistic activities, the MJP proved to be a key player in directly inspiring the creation of Jesus People groups, ministries, and coffeehouses throughout the Midwest in 1971 and 1972.

Jesus Is Lord, West Chicago, Illinois

The Chicago area would become one of the largest strongholds of the Jesus People movement during the early and mid-1970s. The most important early, home-grown manifestation of the movement in the Windy City emerged in its western suburbs around the end of 1969. Jesus Is Lord revolved around the maverick ministry of Ron Rendleman, a handsome, well-built former advertising copywriter and salesman turned successful model and commercial actor for accounts such as La-Z-Boy, John Deere, Quaker Instant Oatmeal, and Nescafé. Raised a Catholic in Chicago, Rendleman had undergone a born-again experience in 1966 during a Sunday morning mass, after having been given some evangelical literature by a sales client. After a period of time in which he was mentored by evangelical pastor Lud Golz from nearby Wheaton, he came under the influence of some local charismatics and underwent the baptism in the Holy Spirit and spoke in tongues.[94]

Emboldened, Rendleman became a fixture in the business districts of towns throughout the western suburbs on evenings and weekends, handing out tracts and evangelizing passersby. The biggest response by far to Rendleman's efforts came from the teenagers—particularly the disaffected hippie types—he encountered on his evangelistic forays. Eventually, he began holding Bible studies and meetings in his West Chicago suburban home. Starting out with a handful of interested teenagers, within a few weeks, he and his wife were hosting more than thirty kids, and within six months, more than a hundred teenagers crammed into their sprawling ranch home every Sunday evening.[95]

As often happened within the Jesus movement, the West Chicago gathering attracted a divergent mix of countercultural types and hard-core ex-druggies with a counterbalancing crowd of high schoolers and church kids dissatisfied with youth group games and promotions. In a memoir published in 2003, Rendleman recalled that his meetings were anything but a soft sell. "We taught the fundamentals over and over: commitment to Christ, water baptism, baptism in the Holy Spirit, and discipleship."[96] Rendleman later estimated that he and the other "older brothers" in Jesus Is Lord baptized more than 1,000 young people during a three-year period. Baptisms took place either in the pond on Rendleman's property (smashing through the ice with a sledgehammer during the winter on some occasions), in the nearby Fox River, or in an old red-painted horse trough he lugged to various outdoor events in his pickup truck.[97]

As an extension to the Jesus Is Lord group's street witnessing and discipleship ministries, in early 1971 Rendleman decided to begin promoting Jesus rock concerts featuring Midwestern-based Jesus bands such as the Sheep, Hope, Crimson Bridge, and, most frequently, "e" from Indianapolis. The concerts attracted crowds (frequently more than a thousand) of Jesus People, church kids, curious high schoolers, and a few inquisitive parents. All in all, Jesus Is Lord sponsored nearly forty such events in venues such as the grounds of a suburban Catholic seminary, Chicago's downtown Civic Center Plaza, the quad at the University of Illinois at Urbana, and towns in Wisconsin, Iowa, and Indiana within manageable driving distance of the western suburbs.[98]

In one typical concert held on May 29, 1971, in the auditorium at East Aurora High School in Aurora, Illinois, a "capacity crowd" came out to hear the bands Hope and "e" rock out for Jesus and Rendleman preach. Reporter Sherry Lang wrote of the "excitement of the Jesus fever" that "circulated through the crowd and held most spellbound." Unbelievers, she noted, could easily be picked out from the crowd: "Their heads weren't bobbing, their feet weren't bobbing, nor were their fingers pointing to Christ." Many, however, were eventually affected by the "Jesus fever"; after Rendleman urged the crowd to ask Jesus to come into their lives, an estimated 100 to 150 came forward.[99]

Overall, Rendleman's Jesus Is Lord group was generally well received and became an important and visible manifestation of the Jesus movement in the Chicago area and northern Illinois. They cooperated both with other Jesus People groups as they emerged and with various adult evangelistic parachurch ministries. In early 1972, Rendleman and twenty-five of his young followers, along with members of the Palosaaris' Milwaukee Jesus People, would be tabbed by the

FGBMF for one of the few major attempts to spread the Jesus movement beyond America's borders, as they spearheaded a two-week Jesus People evangelistic foray to Sweden.[100]

Conclusion

These groups and organizations were among the largest and best known manifestations of the movement outside California. However, they were hardly the full extent of the burgeoning national footprint of what was beginning to be identified as a "Jesus movement." Jesus freak activity was popping up all over the country. New groups were emerging on the West Coast that had no direct links with older Jesus People groups. For example, in Portland, Oregon, the Maranatha Assembly of God Church had begun to implement evangelistic work and Bible studies among local hippies and created a string of communal houses on the city's northeast side.[101] Meanwhile, down in northern California near Eureka, an Oregonian contractor named Ken Smith had purchased an abandoned Coast Guard station and lighthouse compound and established the Lighthouse Christian commune in early 1970. Sure that his next mission was spreading the gospel into Hawaii, Smith turned over the ministry to a local pastor—Chicago-born Pentecostal Jim Durkin—and within several months the struggling group (now known as Gospel Outreach) had grown to more than 100 members and set up businesses ranging from an advertising newspaper to a doughnut shop to support itself.[102]

Increasingly, however, the most notable expansion of the movement was showing up in the Midwest. In the Kansas City area were a dozen Agape House communal homes led by David Rose, a KC boy who had been converted in Los Angeles at Arthur Blessitt's His Place and then spent time with the CWLF in Berkeley. Heading back home in early 1970, he made a special point of approaching pastors as someone willing to work with the "hard cases" among their young people. Operating out of the Second Presbyterian Church, Agape House sponsored rallies that drew upward of a thousand youth to hear Rose speak and listen to Jesus rockers such as the Hallelujah Joy Band and singer-songwriter Paul Clark.[103]

Another Midwestern group was B.A.S.I.C. (Brothers and Sisters in Christ), which got its start in Wichita, Kansas, when Californian Tom Rozof's car broke down on a cross-country evangelistic trek. Rozof found an ally for his work with local high schoolers in Pastor Bob Myers of Faith Presbyterian Church and in 1970 began holding rallies attracting hundreds of kids. A special series of five meetings in early 1971 featuring L.A.'s Don Williams attracted more than 10,000. Making a special attempt to connect with the parents of his followers, Rozof boasted, "We may be the only Jesus People group in the country with a P.T.A."[104]

In Detroit, a Pentecostal minister named George Bogle established a hippie-friendly outreach called the House of Prayer in 1970. Combining Jesus rock bands, black gospel groups, coffeehouse cool, and storefront mission grit, the House of Prayer attracted a racially diverse following. Bogle's outreach spawned a number of communal houses for single men and women and for married couples. By 1971, he had opened another huge House of Prayer in an old department store in suburban Pontiac, started a House of Prayer grill in Allen Park southwest of Detroit, and commissioned vans of wayfaring youth evangelists, including a band that began a Jesus People group in Topeka, Kansas.[105]

Ohio had several Jesus People–oriented ministries in operation by 1970. The Church of the Risen Christ was begun in the Cleveland area by former Teen Challenge worker Larry Hill in the late '60s. A rigid, legalistic group that Hill ran with an ever-heavier hand, they eventually relocated to a small farm about twenty miles northeast of Cincinnati. With the addition of former James Gang and Pacific Gas & Electric guitarist Glenn Schwartz, their in-house rock ensemble, the All-Saved Freak Band, and evangelistic teams became a ubiquitous presence in Ohio and adjacent states well into the late '70s.[106] Beginning about 1969, Grace Haven Farm, a retreat center near Mansfield, Ohio, began to function as a combination retreat center and quasi-commune for numerous dropouts from the counterculture seeking to "get their heads right." Founded by Gordon Walker, a former Campus Crusade for Christ worker and friend of Jack Sparks, Grace Haven worked with a number of Jesus People and evangelical campus groups in the Midwest during the early '70s.[107] And in the summer of 1970, Randy Matthews, a singer-songwriter and student at the Church of Christ's Cincinnati Bible College, combined with students from Mt. Healthy High School to begin a series of Bible raps at Highview Christian Church. The meetings proved successful enough to promote the establishment of The Jesus House, a coffeehouse responsible for well over 100 baptisms of local countercultural types and high school kids in its first year of operation.[108]

While the Midwest was becoming promising terrain for the movement, Jesus People activity was also beginning to pop up on the East Coast. In Philadelphia, a chemist named Joe Finkelstein and his wife, Debbie, were converted to evangelical Christianity in the late '60s. The Finkelsteins soon began establishing relationships with alienated kids in a predominantly Jewish neighborhood in the city's northeast section. Labeled "Fink's Zoo," their home became a magnet for dozens of hippieish Jewish youth by 1970.[109] In Kenmore, New York, just outside Buffalo, the House of Life commune published the *Together* street paper and operated the Power & Light Company coffeehouse.[110] In Washington, D.C., the Agape coffeehouse was established

in June 1970 through the backing of an adult Bible study group that included
a former assistant director of the Secret Service; within a few months, it was
attracting an average of 300 kids a night on the weekends, about half street
kids and half church youth group members.[111] In the tidewater region of
Virginia the Rock Church's Proclaim commune house, established in 1969,
had a viable presence as an outreach among the drug culture and hippie youth
of cities such as Norfolk, Hampton Roads, and Virginia Beach.[112]

In Houston, Graham Pulkingham, a charismatic Episcopal priest at the
Church of the Redeemer, established a countercultural-style coffeehouse ("The
Way In") during the summer of 1969 that attracted a bevy of musical talent
and crowds of 300 to 400 on weekend nights. Integrating the coffeehouse's
ministry to disaffected countercultural youth with his church's vision for charismatic renewal and social justice in poor Houston neighborhoods, the Church
of the Redeemer implemented a sweeping attempt at communal living. By
1972, nearly fifty communal households were home to some 350 of the church's
constituency.[113]

Houston was also an example of the increasing impact of the Jesus People on
middle-class church youth in the form of the SPIRENO ("Spiritual Revolution
Now") meetings of Southern Baptist pastor John Bisagno's First Baptist Church.
Started in early fall 1970 as part of an all-out evangelistic blitz, SPIRENO featured
the long-haired, hip-speaking, twenty-three-year-old youth evangelist Richard
Hogue at nearly fifty school-based rallies and a series of nightly meetings. Utilizing
"with it" publicity, Jesus cheers, and music from a band named Dove, Hogue readily identified with the notion of a spreading Jesus movement among the nation's
youth. Criticized by some conservatives, Hogue and Bisagno were able to beat
back protests with SPIRENO's results: over 4,000 professions of faith and more
than 600 baptisms in the space of three months. As Hogue later recalled, "I don't
know any Baptist who don't want to see folks get saved...you start winning folks
to the Lord and baptizing them...they'll pretty well put up with [your methods]."[114]

As 1970 drew to a close, then, the widespread interaction between the counterculture, youth culture, and evangelical Christianity was becoming an increasingly
common reality within American culture. Most unexpectedly, the independent,
largely unconnected groups were pulling together the disparate worlds of the hippies and the evangelical church, forming the basis of a national Jesus People movement. The result of spontaneous hippie conversions to evangelical Christianity,
direct fertilization by California Jesus People, or attempts by local straight evangelicals to minister to the counterculture, God's Forever Family multiplied itself
across the land. Until that point, the movement had been largely unnoticed—but
that was all about to change.

5

It Only Takes a Spark

THE JESUS MOVEMENT IN THE NATIONAL SPOTLIGHT

BY THE END OF 1970, the Jesus People movement was a fact of life not just in Southern California; representatives of this unlikely marriage between the hippie counterculture and old-time evangelical Christianity could now be found in towns and cities scattered all across the United States. One might think that it would have—at the very least because of its peculiarity—increasingly called attention to its existence, both to people within the evangelical subculture and to the larger overall culture. However, that was hardly the case. The story of the Jesus People did not burst into the national consciousness until early 1971—for most of the population—coming, seemingly, from out of nowhere.

Despite the lone—and controversial—article about San Francisco's Living Room group in the January 1968 issue of *Christian Life*,[1] the budding Jesus movement received scant coverage in the national press during the rest of 1968, 1969, and well into 1970. With the exception of a few stories in California on speaking engagements by the Living Room group or figures like Arthur Blessitt, the press paid the emerging movement no never-mind.[2] In fact, those articles that did appear, like a short blurb about Blessitt that appeared in the *Santa Ana Register* in August 1968, focused on the novelty of evangelistic outreaches to the counterculture ("Rev. Blessitt...is said to speak the language of today's youth"), rather than any cognizance of a distinguishable Jesus movement that was emerging among the hippies themselves. Surprisingly, even the religious press took little notice at all of the youthful street Christians in 1968.[3] The year 1969 was little different; neither the Jesus People themselves nor efforts to evangelize hippies attracted much attention in either the secular or the evangelical press. But by mid-1970, books had begun to appear from evangelical publishing houses by people who were involved with what shortly came to be known as the Jesus People movement. Arthur Blessitt led the way with *Life's Greatest Trip*, a book about his ministry on the Sunset Strip, published by the Southern Baptist–networked Word Books. A few months later, Pastor John MacDonald published his account of working with Ted Wise and friends in *House of Acts*, released by Creation House, a small evangelical publishing house in Carol Stream, Illinois. Although both volumes traded on the novelty of ministering to hippies and life in the drug culture, neither volume touted the arrival of a growing evangelical movement within the counterculture.[4]

Of the two books, MacDonald's was by far the more analytical and insightful; Blessitt's volume tended toward blustering self-promotion. Both books fit into the well-established "ministry hero" genre long popular with evangelical readers. They joined Christian bookstore best-sellers that described the depredations of delinquent youth and the problem of drug addiction, such as David Wilkerson's 1963 book, *The Cross and the Switchblade*; Wilkerson protégé Nicky Cruz's 1968 *Run, Baby, Run*; and the 1969 account of Bob Harrington's ministry in New Orleans's French Quarter, *The Chaplain of Bourbon Street*.[5]

As these books hit the shelves of Christian bookstores, awareness of a new conjunction of the hippie subculture and old-time religion began to emerge. The evangelical press was first to perceive this new development. In articles in *Christianity Today*, *Campus Life*, and *World Vision* magazine, groups such as Linda Meissner's Jesus People Army and the Christian World Liberation Front were being depicted as part of a growing network of street Christians—or, in evangelical theologian Carl F. H. Henry's description, "evangelical hippies"—that was making its presence known in the hip underground and within the evangelical church.[6] As Rita Klein described it in a June 1970 story on the "Spiritual Revolution":

> Some call it an "underground movement." Others describe it as the closest thing to New Testament Christianity this country has ever seen. But those involved—thousands of bearded, long-haired, rather unkempt former hippies—term it a "spiritual revolution."[7]

In the midst of this evangelical coverage, the phenomenon finally began to surface in more mainstream media. *Rolling Stone*, the three-year-old voice of the avant-garde countercultural rock fan, first noticed the perplexing visibility of "Jesus Freaks" in a short blurb in the April 16, 1970, issue of the magazine. In a rambling review of the Beatles' recently released *Let It Be*, reporter Langdon Winner was amazed to note that "honest-to-God long hairs" were being quoted in a local newspaper story as having left drugs and "returning to the Christian Church."[8] A little later, CBS's Sunday morning religious program, *Lamp unto My Feet*, came to the Bay Area and interviewed some of the local Jesus freaks for a program that was broadcast in late June.[9] But by far the most important coverage of the movement that year was an upbeat two-page piece in the August 3 issue of *Time*, whose religion editor, Richard Ostling, had been tipped to the existence of the movement by Ed Plowman, the new current-events editor for *Christianity Today* and a founding board member of Evangelical Concerns. Replete with photos of Arthur Blessitt carrying his cross in Manhattan and a demonstration by members of the Children of God in Los Angeles, the article described them as:

> The latest incarnation of that oldest of Christian phenomena: footloose, passionate bearers of the Word, preaching the kingdom of heaven among the dispossessed of the earth. Their credentials are ancient, for they claim to be emulating Christ and his disciples....They evoke images of St. Francis of Assisi and his ragged band of followers, or of the early Salvation Army, breaking away from the staid life of congregations to find their fellow man in the streets.[10]

The article centered on David Hoyt's group in Atlanta as its main personal interest focus but also gave a broad overview of the movement, paying attention to its San Francisco origins, the CWLF in Berkeley, Arthur Blessitt, and the Alamos' compound in Saugus, California. Although *Time* and a few other 1970 articles signaled a growing awareness of the movement, the eventual outpouring of interest and publicity that would appear in 1971 required more of a cultural push than a few magazine articles.

The Spiritual Side of Rock 'n' Roll: 1968–1970

One of the most important elements in setting the stage for the 1971 Jesus People media blitz was the movement's timely intersection with larger currents in the worlds of youth culture and popular entertainment—specifically, music. As the emergence of the Jesus People reflected religious undertones within the counterculture, so, too, the world of popular music began to evidence a new spirituality during the late 1960s, part of the serious undertaking that rock music had become for both musicians and their listeners. This new religiosity was a departure from previous content and subject matter. Although the church and black and white gospel music had served not only as a training ground and inspiration for numerous early rockers (Elvis Presley, Little Richard, Buddy Holly, and Jerry Lee Lewis, to name a few) and exerted tremendous influence on their musical and performance styles, spiritual—and explicitly Christian—subject matter and themes were extremely rare in popular music during the first decade of the rock 'n' roll era. In fact, only in the spring of 1968 were Simon and Garfunkel responsible for breaking an unwritten Top 40 rule with the first blatant naming of "Jesus" in their smash song "Mrs. Robinson" from *The Graduate* soundtrack.[11]

The year 1969 marked a turning point in this regard, however, as a flurry of spiritual tunes, many with forthright Christian subject matter and content, began to get airplay and climb up the charts: In June, "O Happy Day," a traditional gospel hymn sung by the Northern California State Youth Choir (later redubbed the Edwin Hawkins Singers) hit #2 on the Billboard Top 40; "Jesus Is a Soul Man," by an unknown Alabaman named Lawrence Reynolds, peaked at #28 in late September; and the rereleased 1967 Youngbloods' song "Get Together," featuring lyrics about "The One who left us here" who "comes for us at last," reached the #5 slot nationally in the autumn.[12] These songs were quickly followed by Norman Greenbaum's massive hit, "Spirit in the Sky." Greenbaum told *Hit Parader* magazine that "Jesus Christ is popular" and that he had decided "to write a thing called a religious song."[13] His "religious song" rocketed to the #3 spot in the nation by February 1970.[14]

Now that it was apparent that religious themes could make it, there was an industry-wide OK for the release of more songs with spiritual themes. The success of spiritual rock continued apace during 1970, with songs like the Hollies' "He Ain't Heavy, He's My Brother," Ray Stevens's "Everything Is Beautiful," and Simon and Garfunkel's massive hit "Bridge over Troubled Water," which spent six weeks in the #1 spot.[15] Also hitting the charts that year were the Byrds' "Jesus Is Just Alright" from the soundtrack of the smash film *Easy Rider*, the Pacific Gas & Electric Company's apocalyptic "Are You Ready?" "Fire and Rain" by new singer-songwriter James Taylor, and George Harrison's #1 "O Happy Day"–inspired repetitive ode to a Hindu deity, "My Sweet Lord."[16]

While none of these hits had any direct link to the Jesus Movement at the time, their success demonstrated that a large segment of early '70s American youth and rock music fans were sympathetic to spiritual matters. But it was the release of another record in November 1970—Andrew Lloyd Webber and Tim Rice's rock opera, *Jesus Christ Superstar*—that provided the cultural momentum to help make the Jesus movement a natural for the national stage.

Jesus Christ: Superstar

Rock operas were another new emblem of the seriousness of rock 'n' roll as an art form, and the success of the British rock group the Who's double-disc effort *Tommy*, released in the spring of 1969 on Decca Records, had that label's executives casting about for another hit in that format. In December 1969, a preview copy of "Superstar," the pilot song from a yet-to-be-written recording project by the unknown British duo of Andrew Lloyd Webber and Tim Rice, was released as a 45 rpm single in the American market. The majority of stations refused to touch it because of its lyrics, but a few major FM stations in New York, Miami, and Cleveland did, signaling hope for the project.[17]

The double album of the complete rock opera was released in the United States in November 1970 and greeted with a mixture of rave reviews from critics and outrage from conservative Christians. The reviewer in *Rolling Stone* admitted that when he got the album in the mail, he laughed at what he considered its preposterous premise—a rock opera about Jesus. But in the end, he concluded: "*Superstar* is basically a superior musical anchored by a very tight and together conception....A beautifully organized package" that he believed had "enough clout to bail out" rock music from what he considered a "sagging musical period."[18] The critic in the music industry's *Billboard* prophesied: "This brilliant musical...is destined to become one of the most talked about and provocative albums on the pop scene,"[19] and *Newsweek* arts critic Hubert Saal saw it as a triumph that spoke not only to religious questions but also to the current political and social climate in the United States:

> *Jesus Christ Superstar*...is nothing short of brilliant—and reverent....Without any heavy-handedness the opera makes it natural to see Jesus as a superstar, the new Messiah, who's at "the top of the poll," with Mary Magdalene as his chief groupie, Judas as conniving manager, the Apostles his turned-on band, the priests the blind guardians of rigid law and order, Pilate a kind of smooth university president, Herod governor of the state....[20]

Syndicated religion columnist Louis Cassels even saw *Superstar* as the perfect tool for catechizing disaffected teens bored with church: "If your teenagers balk at Sunday School or reading the New Testament, buy them this album. It is more likely to draw them to Christ than a thousand conventional services."[21]

Many religionists, however, saw the endeavor as anything but reverent. For their part, many Jewish groups felt it smacked of anti-Semitism, with *Superstar*'s villainous portrayal of the Sanhedrin and bloodthirsty Jerusalem mob like something out of a medieval passion play. The criticism from conservative Christian quarters was even more intense. Frank Garlock, of the music department at the fundamentalist Bob Jones University, criticized the rock opera for emphasizing the humanity of Christ and "deliberately trying to portray a man who was *only* human and not God."[22] A reviewer in an evangelical periodical lamented that youth were being targeted with a false view of Christ and his mission on earth:

> The wordless finale, entitled "John Nineteen Forty-One," leaves Christ in the grave. No faith and no victory emerge from this weary music, but the relentless quest remains, haunting and hollow. Here is a work that sets the standard for full-length rock—and an idiom for reaching this generation. Perhaps some Christian composer will take the cue and produce a rock opera about Christ that ends not with hollow questions but with triumphant answers.[23]

Overall, the tremendous reaction proved the old public relations axiom that there is no such thing as bad publicity: The record became a genuine religio-cultural phenomenon. By early February, the expensive double album (retailing for $12 at a time when most single LPs went for $4 or $5) reached the #1 spot on *Billboard's* Hot 100 U.S. album charts, a position it twice recaptured. Overall, during the course of 1971 *Superstar* racked up over $15 million in North American sales.[24] It was so popular that many radio stations did the unthinkable—scheduling special presentations of the entire piece without commercial interruption.[25]

By the spring of 1971, several unauthorized touring troupes were presenting a staged version of the rock opera's music until forced to cease and desist after Webber and Rice and MCA/Decca threatened legal action. In July 1971, an authorized production hit the road and drew large crowds and rave reviews across the country: 12,000 came out to the Charlotte Coliseum; 15,000 saw the production at the Boston Garden; and more than 20,000 turned up at the Ravinia concert grounds north of Chicago.[26]

In late October 1971, *Jesus Christ Superstar*—picketed by both Christian and Jewish demonstrators—opened on Broadway with a gaudy, psychedelically surreal set under the direction of Tom O'Horgan, who had recently overseen the Broadway production of *Hair*. *Superstar* the Broadway musical was never the sensation that the record album had been. After a good but not spectacular run, the play closed in mid-1973.[27] During the same time, another hip musical play about the life of Christ—*Godspell*, based on the Gospel of Matthew—had opened and soon achieved tremendous success off-Broadway at the Promenade Theatre in Manhattan. Written by two Carnegie-Mellon grad students (one Episcopalian, the other Jewish), *Godspell* featured a Jesus in a clown's greasepaint makeup, followed by a band of hippie flower children; the musical was lighthearted and upbeat in contrast to *Superstar*'s dark, brooding tone, and soon a road ensemble had taken it on the road, too.[28] The success of *Jesus Christ Superstar* and *Godspell*, along with the religious pop music of the period, created a cultural template that suddenly helped make sense of hippies who believed in Jesus and played rock music. The gate had been opened for the 1971 Jesus People media onslaught.

The Jesus People Publicity Blitz of 1971

On New Year's Day, 1971, America's premier evangelist, Billy Graham, came face-to-face with the Jesus People as he served as the grand marshal of the annual Tournament of Roses Parade in Pasadena, California, broadcast live by both CBS and NBC. Among the Jesus People in the crowd that day were a group from a Fullerton coffeehouse and a band of Los Angeles street Christians recruited by Duane Pederson to hand out 200,000 copies of the *Hollywood Free Paper*. Both groups were augmented by a large Nazarene youth choir. As Graham and his wife,

Ruth, rode down the boulevard in their convertible, they noticed that a number of young people were holding up placards and standing "with raised index finger lifted upward" shouting "One Way!" Graham returned the gesture and began shouting back, "One Way—the Jesus Way!" The scene duplicated itself all along the parade route as Graham continued to hold his finger aloft and thousands amid the throng responded in kind. At the end of the parade, Graham commented that he and Ruth felt as if they had "been in a revival meeting."[29] The event certainly caught Graham's attention. Not only would he soon set to work on a new book built around the theme but also he and his staff made plans to incorporate it in their upcoming summer crusades. In the meantime, Graham talked positively about the wonderful youth revival he saw "sweeping across the country."[30]

Graham's New Year's Day epiphany had far-reaching implications, particularly for evangelical cognizance and acceptance of the Jesus People. But it was the coverage in the mainstream secular media in the first half of 1971 that ensured the movement its place in the national consciousness. Crucial was a two-hour documentary on NBC's *First Tuesday*, broadcast in late January. Focusing on the Children of God's (COG) encampment near the north-central Texas town of Thurber, the broadcast pulled no punches in depicting the group's Spartan lifestyle, rigid morals, and fanatical dedication to worship, Bible study, and evangelism. Nonetheless, the COG's single-minded devotion to God proved attractive to a number of viewers. For days afterward, NBC was swamped with requests for information about the group, and the first of what became hundreds of eager young recruits began showing up at the COG's Texas compound.[31]

Close on the heels of the NBC special, *Look* magazine carried a major spread in its February 9 issue titled "The Jesus Movement Is upon Us." The article was structured around large photographs of Calvary Chapel's ocean baptisms and intense, grainy pictures of young people in the throes of charismatic worship. Reporter Brian Vachon summed up what must have been the feelings of many:

> This is a movement that started subtly—almost secretly, as if religion's widespread unfashionableness made faith a bit felonious. But signs began to appear, little obscure signs that seemed almost to be teasers from some clandestine underground. A bumper sticker on an occasional car: "Have a Nice Forever."...Popular music began getting slightly religious and then obviously so. Two teen-agers would pass each other on the street and exchange a private signal. The new sign: the forefinger pointed heavenward. An instant, unprefabricated way of relating was being developed. "I'm a Christian. Are You a Christian? Oh, wow. Praise the Lord."[32]

The movement received another fresh gust of publicity on February 13, when a crowd of 7,000 to 8,000 young people turned up in Sacramento for a Jesus

FIGURE 5.1 8,000 Jesus People march toward the California State Capitol building in Sacramento on Spiritual Revolution Day, February 13, 1971.

Courtesy of the Archives, Hubbard Library, Fuller Theological Seminary.

March on Spiritual Revolution Day, which had been approved in a California
State Senate resolution the previous summer. Carrying signs with messages like
"Jesus Lives," "Spiritual Revolution Now," and "Uncle Sam, Jesus Wants You," the
orderly, Jesus-cheering, "Amazing Grace"–singing marchers gathered on the steps
of the state capitol to hear speakers such as Duane Pederson, Arthur Blessitt, and
Burbank State Assemblyman Newton Russell call California to trust Jesus. Stories
and pictures of the event were played up in the print and broadcast media in
California, and the story went nationwide on the wire services (figure 5.1).[33]

In the next several weeks, the Jesus movement was featured in several other
leading papers and magazines, including a front-page story in the *Wall Street
Journal* on March 2, an article in *Newsweek* later that month, and a feature on Steve
and Sandi Heefner's Way East Jesus People group in suburban New York in the
May 14 issue of *Life*.[34] While almost all the stories highlighted the Jesus People's
curious—and highly photogenic—mixture of the counterculture and revivalism,
the coverage was characterized by a surprisingly upbeat, perhaps even charmed,
sensibility. In many ways, the advent of the Jesus People must have seemed like
an oasis in a desert of several years' worth of distressing news about the younger
generation. The Jesus movement had, as one article put it: "an uncommon morning freshness a buoyant atmosphere of hope and love along with the usual rebel
zeal. [A] love [that] seems more sincere than a slogan, deeper than the fast-fading

sentiments of the flower-children."[35] For adults buffeted by several years' worth of bad news about the sexual revolution, the rise of the drug culture, the generation gap, the domestic chaos and violence surrounding the civil rights movement, and the seemingly intractable nightmare that was the Vietnam War both "over there" and on the home front, the Jesus People were a refreshing bit of good youth news.

By June, the Jesus People were a big enough story to merit the cover of the nation's premier newsmagazine, *Time*. In an eight-page feature story, "The New Rebel Cry: Jesus Is Coming!" the *Time* writers portrayed the Jesus Revolution as a major new force in both youth culture and American religion. Although noting the movement's faddish trappings such as bumper stickers and buttons, the article concluded that the Jesus People showed evidence of considerable staying power: "The movement is something quite a bit larger than a theological hula hoop, something more lasting than a religious Woodstock. It cuts across nearly all the social dividing lines ... [and] its appeal is ecumenical."[36]

In the summer, CBS News did an extensive story on the Jesus movement, covering a Jesus music festival in Indiana that featured an interview with singer Larry Norman. Syndicated talk show host Phil Donahue did a show featuring folks from the Jesus People Center in Phoenix, and in July, NBC's *Today* had a special show featuring short clips from the earlier *First Tuesday* special on the COG; an examination of Jesus People buttons and posters by hosts Hugh Downs and Barbara Walters; a panel discussion featuring a Catholic priest, Harvard Divinity School's Harvey Cox, and Arthur Blessitt; and interviews and musical numbers from the authors and cast of *Godspell*.[37]

Readers of the nation's local newspapers were learning about the Jesus People as well: AP wire stories with headlines such as "Jesus People Theories Appear to Be Billy Graham Explained by Timothy Leary" appeared across the United States.[38] Newspaper columns by syndicated writers such as David Poling and George Cornell, as well as broadcaster Paul Harvey, provided upbeat assessments of the new movement to people in Nevada, Louisiana, and Montana.[39] Even those checking out syndicated psychic Jeane Dixon's July predictions learned that she had seen that the "'Jesus People' ... [were] a coming force for good in our country."[40]

While wire stories provided information, local newspaper editors outside the movement hotbeds on the West Coast were eager to print stories about Jesus freak activity in their own areas. A reporter for the *Idaho State Journal* did a two-page spread on Pocatello's Shiloh communal outpost. A reporter in Edwardsville, Illinois, near St. Louis described a group of about thirty Jesus People centered around Ray Darr—an ex-member of the SDS chapter at Southern Illinois University–Edwardsville—that had begun meeting at an Assemblies of God church in town. A tiny newspaper in rural Iowa eagerly printed an "eyewitness account" of a "Jesus Festival" held fifty miles east of Sioux City, where "50 youth were baptized in a

mass rally" on a Sunday afternoon. The imminent opening and story behind the
Power House Jesus Center coffeehouse in Jefferson City, Missouri, appeared in
the pages of that city's *Post-Tribune*. An article in the *Post* of Frederick, Maryland,
weighing the rise of the Jesus Movement duly noted that the "effects...[could]
be found right...in Frederick" at the Jesus coffeehouse on Fourth Street and in a
"Jesus Hotline" telephone counseling service.[41]

The ample coverage of the Jesus movement in the nation's local newspapers,
national magazines, and electronic media both reflected its growth and amplified
it as a major cultural event. Such was the story's salience in the culture that members of the press were out beating the bushes hoping to find the Jesus movement
in their area. Ray Renner, Vietnam veteran and a new student at Anderson College
(affiliated with the Holiness-leaning Church of God–Anderson) in Anderson,
Indiana, about twenty-five miles northeast of Indianapolis, had been converted
during a campus revival in early 1970. A member of a rock/folk gospel group called
the Fishermen, he helped start a Christian coffeehouse called Solomon's Porch in
January 1971. Local reporters were delighted to learn that Anderson was part of a
national trend and descended on Solomon's Porch to learn everything they could
about the Jesus freaks in their midst. But although they fit the profile, Renner
and his brethren had no idea what they were talking about. "They were asking us,
'Are you guys the Jesus Movement of Anderson?'" Renner recalled in an interview
many years later. "And we didn't know anything about a Jesus Movement. Well,
Jesus is moving and we're trying to move with him, so I guess we are."[42]

Evangelical Coverage of the Jesus People

The flood of Jesus People coverage in the mainstream media dramatically displayed the impact of the Jesus Revolution in the country. But if the movement sent
tremors throughout the national secular media in 1971, the evangelical press ran
with the story for all it was worth, trumpeting the good news that the long-awaited
national revival was in progress in the most surprising of places: among America's
unruly youth. The story that had barely registered among evangelical journalists
in 1970 received top billing in 1971.[43] During the year, nearly every major evangelical periodical, denominational magazine, and organizational publication featured news of the movement and/or highlighted an institutional, organizational,
or denominational connection to the amazing revival that was taking place among
the nation's young people.

Leading the way in evangelical coverage was *Christianity Today*, with over three
dozen features, stories, or items on or with connection to the movement.[44] The
pipeline for much of the magazine's information was news editor Ed Plowman.
Indeed, Plowman served as something of a press liaison between the movement
and the straight press.[45] His support was reflected by the magazine's executive

editor, former Fuller Seminary professor and pugnacious guardian-of-the-truth Harold Lindsell, who, while cautious about the movement's lack of theological sophistication, nonetheless endorsed the Jesus People in strong terms and urged his fellow evangelicals to do likewise:

> ...to the extent that the new believers are out to integrate belief and experience in a biblical dimension they have our unwavering support. We sense that this may be the Holy Spirit's way of bringing revival to our society. If the Church turns its back, it does so to its own detriment.[46]

Other major evangelical periodicals also hyped the Jesus movement. *Campus Life*, Youth for Christ's crisp, visually appealing magazine targeting the high school crowd, devoted its entire June–July issue to the Jesus People.[47] The popular evangelical monthly *Eternity* ran five feature articles on the Jesus movement during 1971, along with several stories on the "young sounds" that were changing evangelical music.[48] *Christian Life*, finally recovering from its shell-shocked reticence about the street Christians, printed three major articles on the Jesus People in its April issue.[49] Even the Moody Bible Institute's conservative *Moody Monthly* featured photographs and enthusiastic reports about the adventures of Arthur Blessitt, the movement's growth in various cities, and the selection of a beauty contest winner who had participated in a "Jesus demonstration."[50]

The eagerness with which the Jesus explosion was covered in these general-audience evangelical periodicals was duplicated in denominational publications. The Assemblies of God's national magazine, *The Pentecostal Evangel*, happily reported a Calvary Chapel ocean baptism of more than a thousand youth, along with other hopeful news on the movement's growth.[51] A number of state Baptist newspapers and magazines such as the *Alabama Baptist*, the *California Southern Baptist*, and the *Indiana Baptist* regularly covered the rise of the Jesus People, along with signs of revival among their own youth.[52] Writing for the Christian and Missionary Alliance's *Alliance Witness*, J. Furman Miller went so far as to proclaim the Jesus movement a fulfillment of the declaration in Joel 2:28 that in the last days God would pour out his Spirit upon "your sons and daughters."[53]

Even periodicals from denominations and traditions whose theology and liturgical style were quite removed from the styles of the Jesus People and their evangelical backers carried optimistic, approving news of the movement and the renewed appeal of Christianity among the young. Father Mikulski from St. Anne's in Alpena, Michigan, told the readers of the *Catholic Weekly* that the Jesus People were "groovy." Meanwhile, a writer for the *Lutheran Standard* glowingly related how denominational youth had begun to cheer for Jesus at their meetings.[54]

Billy Graham Boosts the Jesus People

As the coverage of the Jesus Movement hit high gear in 1971 and early 1972, a number of prominent religious figures spoke out in largely favorable tones about the new wave of hippie Christians. In the summer of 1971, healing evangelist Kathryn Kuhlman featured Chuck Smith, Lonnie Frisbee, and the kids from Calvary Chapel on a series of programs; at a Youth Miracle rally at the Hollywood Palladium, she declared: "I want everyone to know that I'm a part of the Jesus Movement."[55] The guru of Positive Thinking, Norman Vincent Peale, admitted that while he was not "the type to sit around on the floor with a guitar," he was delighted that "young people [were] going for Jesus Christ in unprecedented numbers.... Jesus is back, and how!"[56] Visiting an Episcopal congregation in one of New York City's wealthier suburbs, the Anglo-Catholic Archbishop of Canterbury, Michael Ramsey, told a well-heeled congregation that the Jesus People's "ardent devotion" and their "conviction that Jesus can make a real difference to their lives" might well be something from which Anglicans could learn. In another instance, he was quoted as saying that it would not surprise him "if St. Paul himself, were he alive today, chose to be a leader in the American Jesus movement."[57]

On the Catholic side, the powerful John Cardinal Krol of Philadelphia thought the "Jesus movement among young people . . . was generally a good thing," although he feared it pointed up how many American young people grew up without any religious training.[58] The famous TV priest Bishop Fulton J. Sheen appeared to be impressed by what he had seen of the movement, openly admiring "the changed morals and lives of the young known as Jesus People," who allowed "Jesus the Victor become Victim to change their lives."[59]

But one famous American clergyman carried more weight than any of these otherwise prominent ecclesiastical figures and was particularly important to the nation's conservative Protestants—Billy Graham. Continuing what had begun on New Year's Day in Pasadena, the Jesus People movement would receive a highly visible place on the national religious stage as "America's evangelist" made the youth revival the major theme in his 1971 summertime crusades.

Consistently voted among the nation's most admired men and a close friend and spiritual adviser to President Richard Nixon, Graham may well have been at the zenith of his national influence in the early 1970s.[60] However, his decision to embrace the Jesus People was not without risk. Lending support to a movement that seemed to legitimatize long hair, beards, rock music, and informality in dress and worship went against long-held fundamentalist and evangelical taboos against worldly fashion and entertainment and was definitely on the other side of the cultural barricades manned by the Nixon-Graham Silent Majority. At the very least, he could expect (and he received) a fresh salvo from those fundamentalists who had criticized him in the past.[61] Yet, for an evangelist who utilized the headlines for maximum audience impact, the movement was too inviting to ignore—evangelical Christianity was now culturally relevant to the American masses in a way that it had not been since the 1920s. Billy Graham would not be one to miss such an opportunity.

Graham's domestic crusades in the summer of 1971 were slated for Lexington, Kentucky; Chicago; and Oakland. References to the new interest in Jesus became more prominent with each meeting. In Lexington, the major headline getter of the crusade was a Jesus March that attracted 1,200 banner-carrying, sign-waving high school students. Graham—and no doubt many of his backers—noted with satisfaction that this was "about three times the number who staged a protest demonstration" a year earlier after the Kent State shootings.[62]

The Greater Chicago Crusade began in early June. The influence of the Jesus movement was readily apparent throughout the crusade. Graham flashed the "One Way" sign for photographers in Mayor Richard J. Daley's office; the meetings featured music and guest speakers aimed at youth, as well as sermon topics such as "Youth's Hang-ups" (about the long-haired rebel Prince Absalom), "Jesus Christ: Superstar," and "The Gospel in Modern Youth Jargon."[63]

At the meetings, the Jesus People were in full evidence. Ron Rendleman's DuPage County–based Jesus Is Lord group and members of the Milwaukee Jesus People were camped outside the McCormick Place Convention Center underneath a homemade wooden cross and handing out copies of *Street Level* and "Jesus Loves You" stickers to the crowd. But not everybody in Graham's audience was happy to see them. Ron Rendleman remembered that people filing by were reluctant to make eye contact and refused the Jesus stickers they were passing out. Sutton Kinter III, a member of the Milwaukee Jesus People, had similar memories: "It was difficult to hand out a copy of the paper, let alone engage in any conversation with the people."[64]

The fifth crusade meeting on the evening of June 8 attracted a crowd of 27,000, and that night the audience received a special demonstration of Jesus Power. Ingrid Spellnes, a junior at Glenbard West High School in suburban Glen Ellyn, attended the crusade that night at the invitation of her classmate John Ayers, the son of a Commonwealth Edison executive and the younger brother of infamous SDS Weatherman Bill Ayers. Hoping to get a few laughs, Spellnes and Ayers's group arrived late and found themselves sitting at the back of the auditorium "among probably about 200 hippies," who were later described by a Chicago newspaper as 200 to 300 Chicago-area Yippies, hippies, leftists, and self-described Satanists. Spellnes remembered thinking this "was a pretty cool group of people" and that she "enjoyed" the "happy, smiling, joking" group, even though she could hardly hear Graham over their banter, catcalls, and random shouts.[65]

Graham, for his part, prayed for the miscreants from the platform and reminded the vast bulk of the audience that they had come to listen to the sermon in a hall for which the Billy Graham Evangelistic Association had paid the freight. Were things to get even more out of hand, Graham warned darkly, "I'm sure you will know what to do when the time comes—and there are enough of you here to do it." At the first notes of Graham's invitational hymn, "Just as I Am," the protesters, led by a high-stepping young man wearing a cape and wielding a baton, surged into the aisles with shouts of "I wanna be saved" and "Power to the People!" The mob moved forward, and one youth broke out a fiddle and began to play as ushers moved to block the aisle. It was then that a cluster of about thirty hand-holding, praying Jesus People from Rendleman's group suddenly appeared and surrounded the leaders of the protest. Spellnes remembered that the Jesus People joined hands and were singing, "We are one in the Spirit, We are one in the Lord." Some of the Jesus People prayed fervently, while others entreated the radicals to "Join the Jesus Revolution!" or prayerfully chanted, "Jesus, Jesus, Jesus, Jesus." It was Rendleman's lieutenant Ken Downey, Spellnes recalled, who warmly placed his hand on the shoulder of the hippies' apparent spokesman and told him, "Jesus loves you, you can trust Him, Jesus loves you, man."[66]

At that point, the Chicago Police edged into the crowd with batons at the ready, when suddenly from somewhere in the midst of the demonstrators a smoking, sputtering cherry bomb sent everyone scattering. With the explosion, a scuffle began, and the police swooped down into the melee. Believing someone had been shot, Spellnes later related that she was impressed by the Jesus People's peace amid the chaos: "These people...[were] willing to die for what they believe[d] in. That's what [I wanted]." Meanwhile, two of the agitators were handcuffed and dragged away— one of the offenders receiving a broken nose for his trouble. As this was happening, hundreds of young people left their seats to bolster the ranks of the ushers and Jesus People. Under the watchful eye of the Chicago Police, the Graham backers slowly edged the protesters back down the aisle and out the exits.[67]

After the service, an exultant Rendleman passed word through the press to the evangelist from his "One Way" security force: "Tell Billy Graham: 'The Jesus People love him.'" But the affection was not a one-way affair; Graham had endorsed the Jesus People in the meetings and had asked those assembled to pray for the young Christians and their evangelistic efforts. His endorsement proved to be an immediate charm with the churchgoing establishment types in the audience. "The difference in the response of the people attending the crusade after that endorsement was like night and day," recalled Milwaukee Jesus People member Sutton Kinter III. Suddenly, they were much more willing to fellowship with their young Jesus freak brethren:

> People smiled, blessed us and even took the [copies of *Street Level*]. Several times people gave a contribution without taking the paper...there was lots of blessings and promises of prayer. Most people asked if we were some of the Jesus People that Rev. Graham had mentioned. When we said "yes," you could see the visible relief in their faces. Most times they were very eager to talk further.[68]

Moving west for the Northern California crusade, Graham was ebullient about his Chicago experience. Over lunch with Governor Ronald Reagan in Sacramento, he related the story of the protesters and the Jesus People, suggesting that Reagan might want to try this newly developed technique with student demonstrations in California.[69] However, with the exception of a few Viet Cong flag-waving antiwar demonstrators and someone bearing a "Gay Lib Now" sign, there was no need for a special outpouring of the Jesus Power that had been called for in Chicago. Nonetheless, the Jesus Movement and its symbols were in abundant supply at the meetings. A bright neon yellow-and-purple "One Way" symbol—the upraised arm and index finger superimposed upon the cross—served as the podium backdrop. The crowd did "spell yells" for J-E-S-U-S. Berkeley's CWLF chartered a nightly bus bedecked with a banner proclaiming the "People's Committee to Investigate Billy Graham." Duane Pederson, editor of the *Hollywood Free Paper*, was an honored platform guest.[70] Graham even informed his stadium and television audiences that sheets of red "One Way!" stickers were available "by the hundreds if you want them" to anyone who would write to him. He noted that his youngest son, Ned, had "pasted the hotel with them" and urged the applauding audience to "cover America with little tracts and little signs and symbols to let people know that God is at work in this country."[71]

One of the services from the Oakland crusade was televised nationwide later that year. In his sermon "The Jesus Revolution," Graham set forth his vision—partly glommed from the *Time* cover story about the movement—of a genuine revival with potential for bringing America together:

> …the "straights" and the "far outs" are finding common ground in a personal relationship with Christ. … Every American should thank God for this new breath of fresh air that is sweeping the country among the youth. It has not yet affected the majority of American young people but the minority is growing by leaps and bounds. Spiritual renewal is coming among the young. Perhaps the prophecy will come true, "A little child shall lead them."[72]

The results of the Oakland crusade gave Graham and his staff reason to believe that God was indeed at work. The ten-day campaign resulted in 21,000 confessions of faith (12,000 of which were by high school or college-age youth), the highest number of converts per capita of any of Graham's American crusades to that point.[73] It seemed that the Jesus People movement had served Graham well as a focus for his 1971 crusades.

The Evangelical Jesus People Book Parade

While the Jesus movement may have provided the entrée that made the Oakland crusade such a success for Graham, he shared his vision of the contemporary youth question and the potential role of the Jesus People in a spiritual revival in his *The Jesus Generation*. Published that fall by Zondervan Publishing,[74] the book sold more than half a million copies, just one of a sudden deluge of books on the movement from evangelical publishing houses eager to capitalize on the new phenomenon (figure 5.2).

The dozen books that appeared during 1971 were much different from the Arthur Blessitt and John MacDonald books published the previous year. The Jesus People themselves and the prospect of a national, generational revival were now the story. Some of the new volumes came from within the ranks of the movement. Arthur Blessitt was back with a second volume, *Turned On to Jesus* (Hawthorn). *Jesus People* (Compass Press) by Duane Pederson, publisher of the *Hollywood Free Paper*, not only told Pederson's story but also surveyed the broader currents of the West Coast Jesus People scene.[75]

Easily the most unusual book, *Letters to Street Christians* (Zondervan) came out of the CWLF in Berkeley, put together by Jack Sparks and staffer Paul Raudenbush.[76] Listing the authors as simply "Two Brothers from Berkeley," the book was a paraphrase of the New Testament epistles in the argot of the counterculture. Thus 1 Corinthians 13: 4–7, long cherished by American Protestants in the King James Version as:

> Charity suffereth long, and is kind; charity envieth not; charity vaunteth not itself, is not puffed up. Doth not behave unseemly, seeketh not her own, is not easily provoked, thinketh no evil; rejoiceth not in iniquity, but

FIGURE 5.2 The Jesus People make the funnies: "Berry's World," June 30, 1971. Used with permission, United Feature Syndicate, Inc.

rejoiceth in the truth; beareth all things, believeth all things, hopeth all things, endureth all things.

became in *Letters*:

If God's love is controlling you, you will be patient and kind. You won't get jealous, won't brag about yourself, you won't be thinking about impressing people, won't have to grab at places of importance or go after things for yourself. You won't get upset by what people say and do to you or get hassled up at people who burn you. If you're being controlled by God's love, you'll be hurt to see people rip off others and you'll be really happy when things which are true and right happen. God's love can take anything that's thrown at it; it never stops trusting and never gives up hope; it just never quits. In fact, man, when everything else is smashed, God's love still stands.[77]

Surprisingly—and perhaps fueled by the phenomenal sales of Kenneth Taylor's 1970 *Living Bible* paraphrase or by a bevy of evangelical parents and youth pastors seeking to interest their teens in reading the Bible—the Two Brothers' paperback paraphrase turned out to be something of a best seller in evangelical publishing circles, ringing up more than 100,000 sales that year.[78]

The depth, range, and insight provided by the new wave of books about the Jesus People varied quite a bit. Easily the most detailed and informative of the books was Ed Plowman's *The Underground Church* (later retitled *The Jesus Movement in America*) from the evangelical publisher David C. Cook.[79] With information on the origins of the Jesus People, the coffeehouse and commune scene, the campus dimension, the underground Jesus Press, and Jesus Rock, Plowman's book provided an accurate—if unapologetically favorable—overview of the contours of the movement. The book was well received by the evangelical public, selling about 180,000 copies in just four months.[80]

By contrast, *The Jesus Freaks* (Word) by Jess Moody, a Southern Baptist pastor from West Palm Beach, Florida, was unclear on the entire concept. Although the book contained a few brief interviews with youth who might genuinely fit the Jesus Person mold, its overwhelming focus was the hippie view of the world. Confusing the matter all the more—and stretching the paperback's length from a flimsy 85 pages to a workable 127—was the inclusion of a gratuitous index of "liberated churches" that listed an odd assortment of struggling mainline Protestant congregations in the inner city, Catholic Worker communes, and left-wing "urban action centers."[81]

Billy Graham's book, although the top seller among the new books, likewise contained little information on the movement itself. Evangelistic in tone, the book focused on the shortcomings of drugs, sex, and politics as solutions to the problems that faced modern youth. However, while *The Jesus Generation* did not provide much insight into the movement, it did provide an invaluable service for teen-age evangelical Jesus People wannabes by giving the Graham imprimatur to parents who may have had serious doubts. Conceding that the critics who suggested that the movement was sometimes superficial and too emotional had a point, he nonetheless argued: "Most of the characteristics of the Jesus revolution [were] good" and that most of the Jesus People seemed to be "genuine in their commitment." Moreover, Graham was delighted by what he saw as the movement's positive points: It centered on Jesus and demanded an experience with him; it was Bible-based ("For them...it's the ultimate 'how-to' Book, like the very ambitious manual of an automobile mechanic"); it put a renewed emphasis on the Holy Spirit and Christian discipleship; it displayed "an incredible zeal" for evangelism and had introduced a renewed emphasis on the Second Coming.[82]

Other volumes from evangelical publishing houses, such as William Cannon's *The Jesus Revolution* (Broadman Press), Dick Eastman's *Up with Jesus* (Baker Book House), Pat King's *The Jesus People Are Coming* (Logos International), and Roger Palms's *The Jesus Kids* (Judson Press), while focusing on the participants in the movement, echoed Graham's enthusiastic view of the movement and its potential as the basis for a great national revival.[83] Typical of these books was *Jesus People Come Alive* (Tyndale House) by Walker L. Knight, head of the Southern Baptists' press office in Atlanta, who compiled reports from SBC observers across the country. Examining not only hard-core Jesus movement centers such as Calvary Chapel and the soon-to-be-discredited Children of God, the book also included a close look at the 1970 revival at Wesleyan Asbury College in Wilmore, Kentucky, as well as pastor John Bisagno and youth evangelist Richard Hogue's SPIRENO (Spiritual Revolution Now) Southern Baptist youth revivals in Houston.[84] Underlying the whole was the hope shared by many adult backers of the movement that the Jesus freaks were just the tip of the revival iceberg:

> The explosion of revival spirit is not just among the young. The revived interest in the Holy Spirit and the out-front, Jesus-centered evangelism currently penetrating every denomination is clearly a parallel expression of the Jesus Movement which is rolling outside the institutional church.... But what is fueling the blazing revival spirit in the public eye is the "Jesus Generation" these glowing, hip kids with their testimonies of sudden cures from drugs and fleshtrips and aimlessness, their irresistible smiles and simple "Praise Gods" and the way they seek to share the joy of their experience.[85]

Amid all of the celebratory prose, only one book published during the 1971 publicity blitz struck a negative note. *The Jesus Trip*, published by the mainline Methodist Abingdon Press, generally criticized the movement even as it sympathetically portrayed several of the leading Jesus People and others with whom the author, Lowell Streiker, had come in contact.[86] Streiker was a Jewish-born convert of 1950s Youth for Christ in Chicago and a former editor at conservative Moody Press who had gone on to obtain a PhD in religion at Princeton.[87] Perhaps not surprisingly, the things that troubled him about the Jesus Movement were also perceived characteristics of the fundamentalism he had left behind for the more liberal Lutheran Church in America: the authoritarian control of groups like the Alamo Foundation and the Children of God; the overbearing presence of leaders like the CWLF's Jack Sparks; the Jesus People's anti-intellectualism and emotionalism; the movement's apolitical, individualist emphasis; and its escapist concentration on the End Times. In his summation of the movement's possible future impact, Streiker mused:

> Perhaps the hundreds of small Jesus movement groups will discover that the really hard work of being a Christian comes after conversion for both the convert and the convert-maker. Perhaps the Jesus freaks will learn that if every man, woman, and child were to accept Christ, the task of solving America's social, political, moral and ecological problems would only have begun.... "Youth is a wonderful thing," a wise man once mused. "What a pity that it's wasted on the young." In a few years will we ruefully add, "Christianity is a wonderful thing. What a pity it was wasted on the Jesus freaks"?[88]

Debating the Jesus People: A Backlash?

Looking back over the religious events of 1971 for the journal *Theology Today*, University of Chicago church historian Martin Marty acknowledged that the Jesus People had been the story of the year. But he wondered if the movement and its evangelical backers had made something of a Faustian bargain in the process of eagerly utilizing media publicity. "Why do the adherents find it so important to let one know they are important because the press has said so?" Marty asked, wondering whether "the fate of the movement" was now "inextricably tied to its fate in the media." Sizing up the situation, he had a word of advice for the Jesus People:

> Somebody would serve [the Jesus People] well by offering to be a public relations expert in reverse, one who will hide them from the press and the camera. In almost any other period such a religious force or sectarian cluster would do what it could to find a crevasse or niche out of view somewhere. From such a place people could carry on creative subversion, do some sorting; get things together, and then sally forth...they have sold just enough of their soul to make their finitude and mortality begin to be visible. Welcome them, then, to the human race.[89]

As 1971 turned the corner into 1972, it was becoming clear that Marty had a point. It was increasingly apparent that there had been some media overkill and that not everyone was smitten with the Jesus freaks. Criticism came from both inside and outside the church.

Among the most vocal critics were the nation's fundamentalist Christians. From the pulpit and in their publications, leading fundamentalists blasted the Jesus People for their long hair, beards, clothing, and regard for rock music, all of which smacked of the godless radicalism and worldly youth culture from which, they believed, all true Christians were beholden to separate themselves. In an article titled "I'm a Jesus People" in the Bible Baptist organ the *Baptist Banner* (later reprinted in the fundamentalist paper *The Sword of the Lord*), Rev. Elwood Hensley of Calvary Baptist in Crestline, Ohio, conceded that some of the "freaks" were true followers of Christ. Yet, he also believed "that Jesus saves idiots, and some are so feeble-minded that they remain so, not being responsible for their mental condition." To Hensley's mind, this was no excuse for the allegedly sound of mind: Change, he believed, was the defining reality by which one normally evaluated Christian commitment, and on this score, the Jesus Freaks were not passing muster:

> The so-called "hippie" and "yippie" washes his dirty feet, puts on shoes, throws his filthy garments into the washing machine, jumps into a bathtub filled with soapy water, scrubs and washes and rinses until scum and stench goes down the drain. He will cut his hair to the point of respectability and look clean and groomed. That's what being a "Jesus People" does for you.[90]

The Sword of the Lord's regular "Teen Talks" columnist, Dr. Bud Lyles, took after the Jesus People on several occasions. In Lyles's opinion, male participants' refusal to cut their hair was not only a direct rebuff of Paul's statements in 1 Corinthians 11:4 (which reads in part, "if a man have long hair, it is a shame unto him") but also an implicit endorsement of antisocial behavior. Pointing to a statement by radical Jerry Rubin that long hair was a badge of rebellion against the establishment and a thumbing of the nose at American values, Lyles wondered how someone could claim to be a Christian and yet "identify themselves with the rebellious crowd." It was clear that there was one solution to this problem:

> What truly saved "Jesus People" need is a good basic course in the Bible. By reading and studying the Bible they would learn that God established the differences in the sexes and He meant for them to be maintained. They would learn that God favors respect for authority. He favors the local church. He favors decency and morality.[91]

Dr. Bob Jones III, president of the ultraconservative "world's most unusual university" that bore his grandfather's name, published a booklet titled *Look Again at the Jesus People* that, in the space of sixteen pages, made a broad case against the "undeniably wicked" Jesus movement. While admitting that it was hard to peg the movement because it was so decentralized and pointing out that some Jesus People had "indeed, been regenerated," he relied on a string of anecdotes to argue that the movement rejected the established church, largely did not believe that Jesus was God, venerated the Gospels to the exclusion of the rest of the Bible, and refused to separate themselves from the immoral lifestyles of "the world." Appalled at photos of beach baptisms with "girls dressed in bikinis no bigger than postage stamps," Jones raged that "in their blasphemy and irreverence the Jesus Freaks 'out-devil' the Devil." It was clear, then, that any "preachers, evangelists, [or] religious leaders" who were looking to the Jesus People as "a symbol of revival in our land could not be more mistaken."[92]

Even at the local level, fundamentalists took out after the Jesus People. In Holland, Michigan, a man named Andy Gras got so fed up that he took out display ads in the *Evening Sentinel* newspaper to share his concerns about the movement. Gras complained that "all these new Jesus Freaks and Jesus People" were making him "sick," and he railed against "the perverted, damnable, and cursed ideas" of the "modern-day (Bible-believing?!), religious mad, 'Jesus' generation of adults and youths," judging them to be "but a nauseating stench in the nostrils of the Lord God Almighty." Particularly offensive were the popular culture-friendly ways of the "'Jesus' People" and their "bumper sticker slogans, and rotten picture posters, theological comics and cartoon gospels, 'gospel' rock and 'Jesus' Freaks." Truly, he wrote, the Jesus People were a walking embodiment of Isaiah 66:3—"yea, they have chosen their own ways and their soul delighteth in their abominations."[93]

One did not have to be a fundamentalist to eye the Jesus People with suspicion, however. The Jesus People's identification with the fashions of the counterculture was enough to make many older Americans lump them in with the riffraff tearing the nation down. An exchange of letters to the editor in the Frederick, Maryland, *News-Post* in the spring of 1971 reflected these suspicions. The debate began with a short letter lauding the new Jesus freaks. Its publication drew an angry response from Darleen Hoff, who protested the "letter comparing Jesus to bearded freaks." To her mind, these Jesus freaks were no role models: She knew "a few people" that she regarded as "Christ-like...SOME of them even wear long hair, but they also wear skirts to go with it!" Donna Yinger agreed: "If God and the long-haired freaks were so much alike, then how come the freak is not in the Bible?" A teenager named Sharon Phelps rushed into the gap to defend long hair and beards and helpfully pointed out, "Isn't there a picture of Jesus in the Bible? Doesn't he have long hair?" Norman U. Taylor would have none of Phelps's arguments justifying the long-hairs who "do not have the courage to face life squarely without the use of drugs and [the] leadership of communistic agitators." As far as he was concerned, he did not "see how any person attending church as you say you do would associate the name of Jesus and these freaks in the same letter."[94]

Conclusion

As the months went by, it was obvious that in some quarters the Jesus freaks had outlived their welcome. But although not everyone was convinced that the Jesus People were the answer to the nation's ills, it was undeniable that during 1971 they had registered on the nation's cultural radar screen. In a little more than a year, the Jesus movement had gone from the fringes of the counterculture and obscure sectors of America's evangelical church to a largely warm and accommodating national spotlight. No longer simply a California religious curiosity, the Jesus People could now be found in sizable groupings in cities and rural areas alike in many parts of the United States, and people had noticed. This growth had come during a cultural moment when the expression of explicitly Christian sentiments had begun to proliferate in the world of rock music and the advent of the rock opera *Jesus Christ Superstar* had mixed the seemingly exclusive worlds of first-century Palestine, hippies, and rock 'n' roll into a cultural template against which the Jesus People could begin to make some sense to the wider culture.

The Jesus People story made sense to a lot of people in 1971. For the secular media who covered them, they were an invigorating shot of youthful good news. To many average citizens, they were an encouraging sign that despite all the recent years' intergenerational strife, America's youth were not totally rejecting their elders' values and traditions. For evangelicals they were this and much more—God's Forever Family, a sign of possible national revival, and even a sign that the end of the age was at hand.

6

The Jesus Kids

THE JESUS PEOPLE MOVEMENT BECOMES EVANGELICAL
YOUTH CULTURE, 1971–1974

IN THE WAKE of nationwide publicity in both the secular and religious press, the Jesus People showed up in nearly every corner of the United States in the early 1970s. In the process, it was transformed from being a religious expression of the counterculture to a widespread evangelical youth culture of choice. While the movement continued to make converts among the remnants of the counterculture and drug culture—providing the necessary streetwise bona fides and color for the movement—increasingly, the Jesus People's demographic became younger and more middle class. All across the nation, teens, often with the support of evangelical pastors, youth workers, laity, and parents, adopted the Jesus People persona. With its slogans, symbols, enthusiastic worship style, and—not insignificantly—its accompanying acceptance of hip hairstyles, fashion, and music, evangelical teens created a Jesus People–based youth subculture that vied successfully with the larger youth culture. No longer just a strange religious offshoot of the counterculture, the Jesus movement evolved into an attractive mass identity suitable for a large segment of the children of Nixon's Silent Majority.

This sense of a group identity was abetted by several factors, including the growing availability of a wide range of popular merchandise—decals, bumper stickers, T-shirts, posters, and jewelry—that demonstrated one's Christian commitment and willingness to self-identify as a Jesus Person. More important, however, for the viability of this new evangelical subculture was the proliferation of Jesus People coffeehouses that sprang up all over the country. Whether operated by a local church, an evangelistically minded group of laypeople, or a fervent group of evangelical youth, the coffeehouse provided a face-to-face meeting place where local teens could identify with the larger Jesus People movement.

As a result of the grassroots penetration of the nation's churches, a positive image of the Jesus Revolution as an appropriate spin on contemporary American youth culture was conveyed even deeper into the evangelical subculture. And as the movement took firm hold among evangelical youth, more and more of their parents' and grandparents' generation were optimistic that a longed-for national revival was underway: The "Jesus Generation" was a comforting reassurance that the nation's moral and cultural future was in good hands.

Jesus People in the Heartland

With the publicity wave of 1971, the Jesus People movement began to appear all across the United States.[1] But it particularly caught fire in the Rust Belt region of the Midwest, extending from Minnesota east to Wisconsin, Illinois, Michigan, Indiana, and Ohio and into Pennsylvania and northward into Ontario.[2] Indeed, *Christianity Today* news editor Ed Plowman, intimately involved in the movement's beginnings in the San Francisco Bay area, ventured to say in a 1975 article that the Jesus movement was probably stronger in the Midwest than it had ever been in California. A 2005 observation by former Myrrh Records' head Billy Ray Hearn on the sale of the then-new Jesus music supports Plowman's mid-'70s observation. In Hearn's recollection, "the best areas" for sales of Jesus music albums were not just located on the West Coast "but [in] Pennsylvania, and the Chicago area." Taken together, this presents a radical reimagining of the Jesus People movement in terms of long-standing academic and lingering popular perceptions. The vital Jesus People movement that existed elsewhere in the United States and in parts of Canada has been obscured over the years because of the heavy California-centric nature of the publicity and research surrounding the movement, most of which appeared in 1971 and early 1972 and then petered out just as the movement was beginning to explode in the nation's heartland (figure 6.1). But if California was the home of the Jesus movement in 1970, by 1972 and 1973, the Jesus People's center of gravity had shifted eastward to the Midwest.[3]

Some of the movement's growth in the Midwest and elsewhere in the country can certainly be traced back directly to cross-fertilization from California, often in the form of kids returning from extended visits to the West Coast or California kids uprooted by family relocation. For instance, the Feast of Tabernacles communal house in Waterloo, Iowa, traced its roots back to founder Bill Webber's 1969 encounter in a city park with a girl from California who told him that God had sent her to Waterloo. Intent on finding out about God he went west, converted, joined a Christian commune, and came back to Waterloo in December 1970.[4]

Similarly, the House of the Living Water coffeehouse group in El Paso, Texas, was the result of Steve Walker's sojourn in Southern California and time spent at Calvary Chapel. Returning home to El Paso, he found a group of about fifteen churchgoing teenagers sympathetic to what he told them of the Jesus movement.

FIGURE **6.1** Jesus People march in downtown Cincinnati in the fall of 1971. Courtesy of Gary Sweeten.

The group expanded; enlisted help from Methodist, Christian, and two Baptist congregations, eventually formed a band ("The Gospel Truth"), and opened a coffeehouse.[5]

The Power House Jesus Center in Jefferson City, Missouri, meanwhile, had gotten its start via the influence of a teenager from California. A former drug user and hippie-wannabe, he had stopped using drugs under Jesus People auspices. Upon relocating to Missouri, he talked up the Jesus movement and its SoCal coffeehouses to his friends, which eventually led to the formation of a group pushing to start their own coffeehouse.[6]

However, the bulk of the movement's growth in this region from 1971 through 1974 had no direct connection to California and was seemingly a spontaneous local and regional occurrence. As had happened in the earlier period on the West Coast and elsewhere, hippie types were running into evangelical pastors and youth workers and being converted, moving out of the drug-dominated counterculture, and in turn winning their friends and associates to Jesus. The story told by social scientist Sally Dobson Bookman of one teen named "Peter" was typical.

Raised in a single-parent family in Rockford, IL, Peter had been in and out of state-run youth homes; he was constantly in trouble and eventually began using and selling drugs. "I've done every kind of dope there is, just about," he told Bookman in a 1973 interview. "I used to sell reds like hotcakes, $2.00 a hit, boy. Man, I used to rook people so bad." Eventually, some of his old drug friends became Jesus People and began to try to convert him. "The guys were trying to talk to me for a long time about Jesus and saying 'You gotta get off this dope.' . . . [I told them] just get away from me." But eventually, their work began to pay off. Peter broke down and prayed: "I just said, 'God, I want you to do this for me, man. . . . God I'm messed up. Jesus, I've never been anything but a bum all my life. . . . I'm willing to give up anything for you.'" Feeling as if a tremendous burden had been lifted, he remembered, "I went home—I ran home, I was so happy. Hallelujah! I ran upstairs and I had dirty posters all over my room. I tore 'em all down and put Jesus posters up in their places 'cos those guys had given me some."

He then went to school and began to tell everybody about Jesus: "I said, 'That Jesus man, he done messed me up. I quit dealing dope, I quit everything.'" Peter related how some of his former druggie friends eventually came calling:

> I [knew] a whole lot of junkies in town, a whole lot of dudes that deal dope and mesc and microdot acid, all that kind of stuff, and they come calling on me and said "I've got about two pounds I want you to deal." And I put a Bible in his hand, and I said "Hallelujah." He says "What's the matter with you, don't tell me you're a Jesus Freak?" I said, "I'll tell you the truth, I'm a freak for Jesus. I'm never going to leave Jesus." I was never so happy in my whole life.[7]

While Peter was a typical teenager enmeshed in the early-'70s drug culture, Craig Yoe was a local leader among the hippies in Akron, Ohio. A talented artist inclined toward left-of-center politics, Yoe, along with his young wife, Janet, operated a drug paraphernalia store ("head shop") and a hippie music club in downtown Akron. In the late fall of 1970, the Yoes were persuaded to attend an old-fashioned revival meeting in a place known simply as "The Barn" out in the countryside between Akron and Youngstown. There Craig found a crowd of about a hundred hippies sitting around, as Yoe remembered, "enraptured" by the singing and preaching of a small contingent of straight Pentecostals. Yoe said that it "seemed . . . almost surreal" but that at the end he felt "an overwhelming feeling of love, spiritual rebirth, and ecstasy" and he started "hugging . . . people, hippies, and black people, and [women] with beehive hair-dos" and spoke in tongues.[8]

Back in Akron and trying to process their experience, Yoe and his wife maintained their businesses for a while but inevitably began moving them in the direction of the Jesus Revolution. "On fire for the Lord," the Yoes began to talk to their friends about Jesus and even went so far as to name their dog "Repent" so they could stand in the city's parks and shout the canine's name and their message at the top of their lungs. Yoe eventually came into contact with a local Assemblies of God pastor, whom he invited to begin holding Wednesday night Bible studies in the nightclub. On the weekends, they continued with their regular hippie bands but added a local Christian musician as well and began to spend time talking with the clientele about Jesus. Within a short while, a number of his friends and customers had come "to know the Lord." Eventually, Yoe decided to move the Bible studies and Christian content to Friday nights, too, and then Saturdays, as well.[9]

Soon, they had transformed their headshop into a Diggers-like "Jesus Free Store" for Akron's hippies and poor people. Within a few months after converting a core group of forty to fifty of their former hippie friends, customers, and teenagers, they rented an old theater (the Avalon, after which the group took its name) and turned it into their headquarters. Besides assuming control of two former hippie communal houses adjacent to the theater (one for men, one for women) and turning them into Jesus-based houses for those seeking to escape the drug lifestyle, the group had its own house band ("The Peculiar People"), began hosting concerts by better known Jesus musicians such as Phil Keaggy, Larry Norman, and the 2nd Chapter of Acts, and started their own comics-heavy Jesus paper (*Jesus Loves You*). Over the next few years, the Yoes' Akron group helped establish branch groups and provided support and resources for sister fellowships throughout northeastern Ohio, including the Phoenix in Massillon, the Antioch in Coventry, the Gospel House in Bedford, the Upper Room in Columbiana, and the Jesus People Center in Canton.[10]

Similar patterns occurred throughout the Midwest during the early and mid-1970s. In Adrian, Michigan—fifty miles southwest of Detroit—Denny Keitzman, a thirty-year-old former druggie, became the driving force behind the Living Water coffeehouse. Employed as a salesman by J. C. Penney, Keitzman double-dipped as a drug dealer and operated a headshop on the side. Arrested for selling drugs in the spring of 1973, he was fired from his department store job. By this time, he had reached the end of his rope: "Reality [was] crashing all around me…[it] caused me to say 'This isn't right, I can't keep going this way.'" Converted after a soul-searching day with his Bible "and a few joints" in the countryside, he closed his headshop and got involved with a local Free Methodist church. After a short jail sentence, Keitzman linked up with several other recent ex-druggie converts and "formed an exploratory committee" to consider opening a coffeehouse. After visiting a few regional coffeehouses such as the Adam's Apple in Fort Wayne, Indiana, they "cherry-picked" a number of ideas for their vision. Eventually, the Salvation Army gave them a huge unused building—rent-free with utilities paid—where the Living Waters coffeehouse set up shop in early 1974. For the next four years, Keitzman's group sponsored weekly music nights and concerts with Jesus music artists like Randy Matthews, Honeytree, and the band Selah, as well as a crisis pregnancy center, a counseling hotline, and a local jail ministry.[11]

As these sorts of scenarios were being repeated in places across the Midwest, one of the major institutional developments that helped spread the Jesus movement in the nation's heartland was the partition of Jim and Sue Palosaari's Milwaukee Jesus People in the spring of 1972. By that time, the Milwaukee group had grown to about 200 full-time members and had just come off successful campaigns in Davenport, Iowa; Benton Harbor, Michigan; and, particularly, Duluth, Minnesota.[12] Early in 1972, the FGBMF approached Palosaari about putting together a Jesus People–based evangelistic campaign to reach European youth. Palosaari accepted their invitation and selected about twenty group veterans to make an extended trip to Scandinavia.[13]

This decision obviously implied big changes for the year-old group, which led to a recall of the various ministry teams from elsewhere in the Midwest and meetings to discuss future directions. Opting to extend their evangelistic outreach as much as possible, it was decided to formally divide into four separate parts. Under the leadership of Frank Bass (an evangelical layman brought back with the returning Duluth evangelistic team), a small group of about thirty was set aside to keep the home fires burning in Milwaukee. The second branch was Palosaari's Europe-bound cohort of about twenty members plus the group's band, The Sheep. A third group of about thirty plus a new band, Charity, was put under the leadership of John Herrin Sr., an ex-alcoholic pastor from the South with previous ties to the Advent Christian Church and the Assemblies of God. Along with his wife, Dawn, Herrin was attracted to the Milwaukee Jesus People after their teenage children became involved with the group. The largest segment of the Milwaukee group—almost a hundred, and most relatively new converts—were put under the supervision of Bill Lowery, an Assemblies of God Bible school dropout from central Illinois who headed up a traveling tent revival ministry called "Christ Is the Answer." After a combination graduation service and farewell on April 23, 1972, the Palosaari group headed off to Scandinavia, and the other groups went their separate ways.[14] Palosaari's group would go on to a series of adventures in Europe and play an important role in bringing the Jesus People movement to the United Kingdom over the next two-plus years.

Now without the Palosaaris and having lost a sizable percentage of their constituency, the Milwaukee group, plagued by uninspiring leadership, a quirky following (described by one former Milwaukee Jesus People member as made up "of the youngest and the weirdest group of people"), and a growing pile of bills, began to thin even further as some members joined newer Milwaukee Jesus People outfits, were absorbed into the city's evangelical churches, or simply drifted away. In early November 1972, the Milwaukee Jesus People formally called it quits.[15] The groups headed by Herrin and Lowery, however, began to grow and played an important part in the ongoing history and evolution of the Jesus movement.

Jesus People USA (JPUSA)

John Herrin Sr. dubbed his new group the "Jesus People USA Traveling Team" and spent the balance of April and May 1972 in the Lake Michigan corridor running south from the Milwaukee area, down through Chicago and its suburbs, and east around the lake to the Benton Harbor region in Michigan. During this period, they developed their own street paper (*Cornerstone*) and spent the bulk of their time in street evangelism and impromptu Jesus rallies with their increasingly hard rock Jesus band, which had changed its name from Charity to Resurrection (aptly described in their slogan, "Music to Raise the Dead"). Herrin and his followers believed the Lord had called them to go to the South, so in June they piled their people and belongings into a few cars and a ramshackle red-and-white school bus with "JESUS" emblazoned on the side and wended their way south through Kentucky and West Virginia, down through the Southeast, and eventually into Florida.[16]

In Florida, the JPUSA group landed first in Jacksonville. After spending most of August there, they decided to move fifty miles southeast to Gainesville, home of the University of Florida. They managed to find temporary housing in a large, well-worn house that had until then been occupied by the local chapter of the Vietnam Veterans against the War, before settling in another house just abandoned by the Hare Krishnas. The JPUSA quickly opened a coffeehouse next door in a former synagogue and also began sponsoring a weekly meeting in the basement of one of the university's dorms.[17]

After a few months, however, it appeared that Gainesville and north-central Florida seemed pretty immune to JPUSA's efforts, as the "Northern hippies" did not seem to be winning over either the area's hard-partying students or its conservative Southern churchgoers. By the end of 1972, the JPUSA vehicles were caravaning back north so its members could spend Christmas at home with their families. They fully intended to return to Florida, where they had left many of their meager belongings and been promised use of an empty church building. But before returning, they reconvened in January 1973 back in the Benton Harbor, Michigan, area and then moved on to a series of rallies and revivals in Michigan's cold, snow-buried Upper Peninsula. In the frosty environs of northern Michigan in towns like Ontonagon, Houghton, Ironwood, and Marquette, they hit their stride. "When we were up there, so many people got saved," reminisced one JPUSA member in a late-1980s interview, "We would stay for a week in a town, playing every night at a high school, witnessing in the street.... We realized, 'Boy, this is the place to be! The Bible Belt didn't need any evangelism, but up here the people are really open.'" John Herrin Jr. recalled in a 2009 interview for one scholar how in Ontonagon on a freezing winter night "probably about eight hundred people" crammed the local high school gym, "and this [in] a town of a

thousand!" Reaffirmed by their success in Michigan, JPUSA's leadership decided
that God's calling had moved north.[18]

After several months on the road, JPUSA began to look at Chicago as an ideal
central location for a Midwestern outreach. The group made the city their perma-
nent home beginning in May 1973 (the popular legend had it that they had been in
transit to a rally when their ancient Jesus bus broke down while passing through)
by the good graces of a local member of the FGBMF who pulled some strings
to allow them to set up temporary headquarters at Faith Tabernacle, a large but
sparsely attended Pentecostal church on Chicago's North Side. Some thought that
their coming to that spot was no accident: Faith Tabernacle stood on the corner of
Grace and Broadway. Settling down, JPUSA would make the church its temporary
home for more than two years, with single men sleeping in the church's auxiliary
meeting room while the single women occupied one end of the church's spartan
concrete-block basement, with married couples in temporary rooms on the opposite side.[19]

As JPUSA settled down into its new home, it was hardly the first or only Jesus
People presence in Chicago or the surrounding area. But its committed membership, artsy bent, and hard-core countercultural edge quickly made it the movement's premier bastion and the go-to Jesus People resource in the Windy City and
its sprawling suburbs. The commune's Resurrection Band headlined numerous
rallies and concerts in the area and began to expand its fan base in evangelistic
concert tours around the Midwest and, increasingly, to distant regions of the country. A drama troupe, the Holy Ghost Players, frequently accompanied Resurrection
on tour when not frequenting Chicago-area coffeehouses, parks, and streets. And
JPUSA's colorful, well-designed paper, Cornerstone, became the Jesus People paper
of record in the Midwest.

But JPUSA's first years in Chicago were not without trouble. In 1973, a crisis erupted when the young commune's forty-something head elder, John Herrin
Sr., developed an obsession with the young wife of another member. The woman
reported his advances to Herrin's wife, Dawn, who, in turn, went to JPUSA's
young deacons and deaconesses. A six-month-long attempt to resolve the situation eventually led to a decision to send Herrin to a Charismatic Christian coun-
selor who specialized in "fallen pastors." The attempt failed, however, and Herrin
was asked to leave the commune in March 1974, eventually leaving his wife (who
sued him for divorce), son, and daughters (his daughter Wendi had by this time
married Resurrection guitarist Glenn Kaiser and become the band's lead vocalist)
behind at JPUSA and leaving the ministry altogether.[20]

Even through this trying period, however, JPUSA continued to grow. Nearing
the 200 mark in full-time membership, the group desperately needed to escape
the inadequate facilities at Faith Tabernacle. By the spring of 1975, they were able
to pull together enough resources to put a down payment on a six-flat apartment

building on Paulina Street in the city's Ravenswood neighborhood. By that time, they had begun a painting and decorating business (J.P. Painters) to support the ministry, which soon branched out into moving (J.P. Moving), carpentry (J.P. Contracting), and graphics (J.P. Graphics). To house their *Cornerstone* offices and provide a worship space for the group on Sundays, they rented two storefronts on North Halsted Street.[21]

Thus set, the members of Jesus People USA were positioned to remain a familiar sight on the streets of Chicago throughout the mid and late '70s. Airline passengers going through the various terminals at O'Hare International Airport would come to know them as the Jesus freak counterbalance to the ubiquitous presence of the Hare Krishnas.[22] More important, they increasingly became a resource for the area's evangelical churches and their various youth outreach programs.

Christ Is the Answer

The biggest group derived from the division of the Milwaukee Jesus People, Christ Is the Answer (CITA), was surely the largest troupe of perpetually traveling Jesus People in the movement's history. Other Jesus People ministries or bands might spend extended time on the road in an effort to save souls, but the road was pretty much where CITA lived. The group cut a colorful swath through a large part of the United States during the 1970s, and its combination of long-haired Jesus freaks and old-time tent revivalism was always a sure-fire attention getter that won a number of converts in the process.

Bill Lowery had little real contact with the Jesus movement until his involvement with an FGBMF-sponsored trip to Scandinavia in late 1971, where he met Jim Palosaari. In the spring of the next year, Lowery received a call from Palosaari asking for his help over in Davenport, Iowa. Lowery had not been in town long, however, before his tent was irreparably damaged in a windstorm and he was forced to call a halt to most of his activities.[23]

Palosaari's decision to "take the Jesus Revolution to Europe" pulled Lowery into the mix as he was in the Beer City teaching some classes at the Milwaukee Discipleship Training Center while waiting for his new tent. As the details were hashed out, CITA was designated as the landing spot for anyone who did not want to stay in Milwaukee or accompany John Herrin's group to the South. Lowery apparently left the meeting with the idea that he might see a few of Palosaari's people turning up in Davenport. But within a few days, ex-Milwaukee Jesus People began streaming into his camp. "Next thing I know," Lowery reminisced in a 2010 interview, "I had 30 to 40." Within another few days, that number had doubled, and Lowery, who had been used to traveling around with his family and a few workers, suddenly had a small village to care for.[24]

Over the next several months, Lowery's primary challenge proved to be trying to house, feed, bathe, and transport his new Jesus People disciples while CITA held evangelistic campaigns in cities such as Topeka, Tulsa, and San Antonio. To house single men and women, he bought two moth-eaten forty-foot by sixty-foot tents; camping tents provided shelter for married couples and single women with children. To provide for basic living needs, a damaged semitrailer was reequipped as a commercial kitchen, and another old trailer was remade into a shower facility with one section partitioned off for the brothers and another for the sisters. Additional vehicles, of course, had to be secured to haul all the equipment and people, and within a few months, CITA traveled in a caravan of more than fifty vehicles, including seven tractor trailers (most having been purchased from the estate of the recently deceased Pentecostal evangelist A. A. Allen). Eventually, CITA even began a school for the Lowerys' children and others who traveled with the group.[25]

Feeding the group—which eventually peaked at about 250 people—was a continual struggle: "Give us this day our daily bread, that became a very serious prayer," Lowery remembered. "A lot of the fare back in those days were what we called 'Jesus People steaks'...peanut butter and jelly sandwiches." Donated bread, hot dogs, chicken (or, in one instance, the contents of a local turnip field), and other assorted groceries from local churchgoers was CITA's lifeline. With their lack of resources, there were inevitably a lot of rough times, like the day they rolled into Anaheim, California, for a series of meetings and dined on a load of out-of-date Twinkies that had been originally slated to feed the local farmers' pigs.[26]

But signing on to travel with CITA meant not only rough living conditions and gastronomic sacrifices but also acceptance of a lifestyle marked by discipline and hard work. Lowery ran "the camp" like a military base: Each day started at 6 A.M. with the entire group turning out for "formation." There they would pray, read the Bible, and sing, as well as receive their assignments for the coming day. After breakfast and another meeting, most of the group would disperse throughout the community to witness, pass out the group's Jesus paper (Free Manna), and invite people to that night's meeting. After several hours, they would return, eat supper, and take part in the evening service. Between 11 and midnight, "lights out" was ordered, and four posted guards both kept an eye on CITA's equipment and made sure "nobody was slip-sliding around and going into each other's trailers...it kept everybody's feet to the fire." For his part, Lowery realized the regimen was tough but looked at it as a nod to stone-cold necessity: "Hey, you got a bunch of ex-drug addicts, everything imaginable, alcoholics...you had to have discipline in the camp."[27]

The traveling caravan inevitably made quite a splash when it arrived in town, especially among local youth. Mark Hollingsworth, son of a conservative Presbyterian pastor, was seventeen years old in the summer of 1972 when the

CITA Jesus People rolled into Decatur, Illinois. He was taken with the entire experience—the hippie Christians witnessing on the streets, the tent, the Jesus bands like Joyful Noise and "e," and especially the now-bearded and long-haired Lowery's energetic sermons, sense of humor, and call for total commitment. "They turned [Decatur] upside down," he remembered in a 2002 interview, and later that year it seemed like "one out of three kids [at Eisenhower High School] were carrying Bibles every day." As a direct result of CITA's visit, Hollingsworth estimated that the youth group at his father's Woodland Chapel Presbyterian Church grew "from about 8 to 10 kids to 40 to 50."[28]

Lowery's group soldiered on throughout the '70s and eventually sponsored a series of Jesus People missions through a loose affiliation of Christ Is the Answer–sponsored mission teams to Italy, India, the Philippines, and several other countries.[29] But as time went on, groups like CITA and JPUSA that were made up primarily of recruits from the counterculture and the drug culture were less and less the norm for the larger Jesus movement. From 1971 on, the pure hippie dimension of the phenomenon was increasingly eclipsed by a grassroots, high school–age cohort of youth—frequently church kids—who were claiming the Jesus People name and image. As the movement spread into the highways and byways of North America in the early 1970s, this element more and more began to define God's Forever Family.

The Jesus Kids

Greensburg, Kentucky, was a small town of about 2,400 in 1970. Situated in the center of the state roughly a hundred miles from both Louisville and Nashville, one could hardly have predicted the rural seat of Green County (roughly 10,000 inhabitants) to become a hot spot for anything remotely countercultural. Yet by May 1971, the new teenage, church kid–friendly guise of the Jesus movement had worked its way into the isolated rural community. A revival among the town's youth was underway that—while very different from the purist countercultural form of the Jesus movement that had first emerged in the late '60s—was certainly like nothing the good folks in Green County had seen before.

Everything began during a weekend of youth meetings at Greensburg's 141-year-old United Methodist church. The invited speaker was Jerry Matney, a soft-spoken, bellbottom-wearing, twenty-four-year-old Greensburg native attending seminary at Vanderbilt Divinity School. Quickly, however, the meetings turned from routine youth meetings to red-hot revival. Matney's rambling ruminations about life's purpose and Jesus greatly affected his teenage audience. Tearful converts crowded the altar, word spread, and soon the 250-seat sanctuary was packed. The weekend stretched into two weeks, becoming the talk of the town. When it was over, more than 350 conversions had been reported.[30]

Although the town was used to a regular schedule of planned, church-sponsored revivals, the shape of this revival was different from anything the locals had seen before. It was characterized by the exuberant hallmarks of the Jesus movement: Matney's talks were interspersed with his guitar-accompanied "God-heavy folk songs"—indeed, he seemed to "[sing] more than he preached." Bob Durham, a junior at Greensburg High that spring and president of the Methodist church's youth fellowship, remembered in a 2007 interview that Matney's musical selections (such as a version of the new hit song "Put Your Hand in the Hand") were a big hit compared with the church's usual musical fare. "We didn't relate to those hymns as much as to what he was singing!" Particularly conspicuous within the audience were "the area's long-haired sandal set" and "the boozers and dopers" among the high school crowd. The atmosphere, in contrast to the traditional Sunday-go-to-meeting ethos of the area, was informal, with swaying, hand-holding, singing and boisterous "Jesus cheers" ("Give me a 'J.'"). Students at the local high school held evangelistic rallies, convened lunch-hour Bible studies, scrawled pro-Jesus slogans on blackboards, and sported "Join the Jesus Revolution" buttons.[31]

Although some of the local traditionalists criticized the boisterous cheers and informality, for most adults, the turnaround of local long-haired delinquents like seventeen-year-old Billie Judd (who told a reporter, "You just don't know how it is to have Jesus until you've experienced it") was both welcome and a challenge to their own assumptions. Greensburg's mayor, George Huddleston, speculated that the older generation's "formalities, rituals, and programs [were] poor substitutes for the real thing and our young people have seen through this."[32] The May 1971 goings-on in Greensburg were a telling indicator that the style and ambience surrounding the Jesus movement was working itself into the fabric of the American cultural scene. "Jesus People" was more than a movement or a network; it was an identity and a style—and the identity and style were everywhere. Much as it had in Orange County, California, earlier, the movement had worked its way into the high schools and junior high schools of suburban and small-town America, now drawing on a mixture of counterculturally oriented teens and church kids feeling the pull of both youth culture and their families' Christian faith.[33]

For many teens, the Jesus Person, Jesus People, and Jesus Freak badge became a powerful part of their personal identity. Lee Ann Powers, a young teen growing up in the Phoenix area, stated: "I...identified myself as a 'Jesus Freak.' One of my better days was when my atheist father yelled at me, 'You're just a Jesus Freak.' If only he knew how proud that made me!"[34] Ingrid Spellness from Glen Ellyn, Illinois, remembered that after being converted by Ken Downey, an assistant with Ron Rendleman's Jesus Is Lord group, she immediately began identifying with the Jesus People: "From that point I changed from pom-poms and short skirts to long dresses, big crosses and a big Bible at my high school."[35] Often Jesus People were a sizable group within a local community's youth culture. Bill Radcliffe recalled returning to the St. Louis area in May 1972 after living for a period in Europe. Then about fourteen years old, he was struck by how his teenage peers were divided into two distinct, sizable camps—Jesus Freaks and everyone else.[36]

The publicity surrounding the movement was a strong drawing card for many young people. Steve Church, a high school senior from a Catholic background in the St. Petersburg, Florida, area, "was really getting into reefer and psychedelic music" when, in 1971, he became intrigued by media coverage of the Jesus People. This led him to drop in on a free concert by a Jesus rock band in St. Petersburg's Williams Park, where he was converted.[37]

Even though most teens did not go as far as actively investigating the Jesus People, there was a pervasive curiosity and openness to the movement within the larger youth culture of the '70s. This interest is amply illustrated in the experiences of Jeff Lough, a graduate of fundamentalist Cedarville College in northern Ohio, who thoroughly identified with the Jesus People after his 1971 graduation. Lough remembers going on evangelistic "party cruising" forays with his brother during summers in the early and mid-1970s. Their usual modus operandi was to crash the party and when invited to drink alcohol tell their hosts, "We're not here to get drunk. We're here to tell you about Jesus." Amazingly enough, he recalled, the partygoers would "almost always ask us if we were Jesus Freaks and when we said 'yes' all of them would gather around to hear us tell them about Jesus."[38]

It was that sense of cultural opportunity that attracted some young evangelical Christians. Tom Medley, a convert to Pentecostalism from Roanoke, Virginia, in the state's largely rural, mountainous southwest, was involved with several Jesus People ministries during the '70s. Medley gravitated toward the movement because of his interest in evangelism. He looked back and commented: "The Jesus Movement was in the news. We wanted a piece of the action."[39]

But for most evangelical youth, the Jesus movement was attractive because it was with it in a way that existing evangelical youth clubs, activities, and programs were not. In a period when the clean-cut look had become the epitome of uncool, churchgoing kids had been thrown an adolescent life line in the Jesus movement's countercultural ethos and utilization of contemporary music. Chris Brunson, a Rockford, Illinois, teen, summed up the feelings of thousands in a letter to the *Rockford Star* in February 1972. Commenting on a rally he had attended at a local church featuring Chicago-based Southern Baptist youth evangelist Sammy Tippitt and the Milwaukee Jesus People band The Sheep, Brunson wrote:

> We saw Sammy Tippitt.... He was real good, I thought. He and his friends had long hair, yet they were dedicated to Christ. Sammy had a great singing group with him [that] sang some groovy songs they had composed. He really got to me. Sammy proved once and for all that you can be a hippie and still be a Christian.[40]

In a similar vein, Jim Sterling, a Methodist teen from rural central Kansas, remembered his Jesus People ties as being a comfortable "blend of my Christian beliefs/values" with "our changing culture."[41] Although coming from an Australian, the recollections of Phil Spence, the disenchanted son of an evangelical minister from Brisbane, undoubtedly echoed the feelings of many American evangelical kids: Here, he said, was "a Christianity I could relate to."[42]

The Jesus movement's baptizing of rock music seems to have been a particularly salient feature for many churched youth, providing an outlet for their passion for rock 'n' roll they could reconcile with their Christian faith. Growing up amid the fertile California Jesus scene as the member of a Baptist youth group, Twila Beaubien looked back to a concert in Oakland: "It was awesome! I had never heard any Christian music like that before…later I saw Love Song in concert in San Jose. It was the sound I fell in love with."[43] Similarly, Gary Seals, a youth at an Assemblies of God church in Richardson, Texas, remembers a divided existence before his participation in the Jesus movement: "I was into rock 'n' roll pretty heavy, even though I attended a conservative church." When he came into contact with "Jesus music," he was able to reconcile his two loves, becoming part of a Jesus rock band named Mephibosheth.[44] In much the same way, Tim Harris, a young member of a Baptist church in Oakboro, North Carolina, recalls that he was initially "drawn mostly by the music and later by the message" of the Jesus movement.[45]

Yet while cultural relevance and group identity carried a certain measure of appeal, it must not be forgotten that the movement ultimately rose and fell on its ability to deliver some type of spiritual meaning and fulfillment to its participants, many of whom were struggling with various adolescent problems and emotional crises (figure 6.2). It seems apparent that a lot of young people—from both evangelical and other backgrounds—were introduced to the Jesus People's Jesus and came away feeling that they had found a new sort of hope, meaning, and connection with God. One young teen from the Gerry's Place Jesus People group in Anderson, Indiana, testified to a local reporter about how his life had turned around:

> My life before I found Jesus was a real bummer. I was doing a lot of dope, booze and had low morals. My idea of a good weekend was a hit of acid, a good-looking chick, and all the booze I could hold. But since then I have died and been reborn….[I'm] free![46]

In a similar vein, a twenty-two-year-old man at a coffeehouse in Rockford, Illinois, told an interviewer about how meeting some local Jesus People—and then their Jesus—delivered him from a penchant for theft and its attendant guilt:

> I was Joe-Ripoff, y'know. I'd go into a store and if I saw anything I liked I'd steal it. I was terribly guilty….One night I stole $17 out of a swimming pool locker and I was going to spend it all and have a lot of fun. I stopped in at the headshop…and bought a Jesus button….I was wearing it around and this

FIGURE 6.2 Two high school church youth in full Jesus freak mode at a rally in downtown Chicago ca. 1971.

Courtesy of Ron Rendleman.

guy said "You're a Christian, aren't you?" And I said "Oh, I don't know"...and he said "Well, anyway, how'd you like to come to a Bible study tonight?" And I said "I don't think so." But, I took a couple of tracts he had and I read them and God just shouted at me through 'em, and I knew then that I was going to hell. I knew my only hope was in Jesus Christ. I just saw this light guiding me, so I came down here and I was sitting over there by that table and...August 13th, 8:31 PM (everyone laughs), and I prayed, and I felt Jesus come down and forgive me all my sins. And this terrible burden—this heaviness that was laying upon me was taken away. Everything was filled and I've never been lonely since....And well, I just can't praise the Lord enough....[47]

In a 1974 issue of the St. Louis–based *Zoa Free Paper*, a teenager named Kerry Moore wrote about her spiritual journey. Although no doubt modeled on the conversion stories she read in other Jesus People and evangelical sources, it nonetheless conveys a real sense of what she felt before and after her own encounter with Jesus:

I had been an atheist since I was ten....I would put on a plastic mask and pretend that I was having fun, but deep down inside, when the party was over and the crowd had gone home, I would lie on my bed and bury my face

in my pillow and cry...sometimes I would have a few drinks and smoke
a few joints to forget, but in the morning the emptiness was still there. I
tried to fill this vacuum inside me, but nothing seemed to work....I stuffed
the holes inside me with intellectual highs and self-pity and freaky spiritual
trips like the Hare Krishna religion or ESP....I've been a Christian almost
three years....Now my life has meaning and purpose and I have a reason
to live....I still have questions, but I know that Jesus is the answer....[48]

Rick Peterson, a high school senior in Spokane, Washington, expressed the sense
of spiritual connectedness that ultimately imparted a larger meaning for many
youth in the movement. In the pages of the underground Jesus paper *Truth*,
Peterson wrote that soon after he had been converted, he had been unable to find
a summer job. "My parents were really bugging me to get a job. I'd been looking
for a month with no luck." One night he decided, "I can't find a job any other way.
Here goes...Jesus...." Peterson reflected: "Man, it felt mellow and peaceful just
to rap with Jesus like that. Before, praying had been just a lot of words. But now I
realized I was talking to a real dude. Sleeping was real easy that night." Peterson
found a job as a dishwasher soon after his prayer.[49]

Aided by the massive publicity the movement had garnered in 1971, the Jesus
People persona had clearly found its way down through the various eddies and
substrata of American youth culture. Teens on the margins of the drug culture,
troubled high schoolers looking for stability and meaning, clean-cut kids in church
youth groups, and gung-ho evangelical youth intent on winning their generation
to Christ—all were finding a place within the Jesus People movement in the early
and mid-1970s. Mixed together, they made a powerful—and very visible—national
youth movement.

Equipping the New Jesus People Saints

An important dimension of the growth, maintenance, and group identification
of the Jesus movement was the thriving material culture that grew up around it.
From the outset, the movement had been nothing if not visual. Indeed, much of its
early impact stemmed from an inherent cultural-visual dissonance: Encountering
long-haired, jeans-clad, sandal-wearing, countercultural-looking youth being
baptized or engaging in Pentecostal-style worship was, for Americans in the late
1960s and early 1970s, literally a sight to behold. The Jesus People added to this
initial visibility a penchant for visually reinforcing their Christian commitment
through the use of artwork and a wide variety of buttons, decals, stickers, posters,
T-shirts, and a new evangelical liking for crosses and religious jewelry.[50] With the
help of an enterprising network of evangelical organizations, publicists, and entre-
preneurs eager to capitalize spiritually, emotionally, and financially from the Jesus

movement, they would create an iconic universe that contributed to the movement's overall growth and vitality.

An appreciation for the need to make their faith visible was in evidence from the days of the earliest Jesus People. In this, they combined the worlds of high art, social commentary, and Madison Avenue in a way that reflected both the counterculture's romantic emphasis on artistic expression and its whimsical pop-art sensibilities.[51] Yet, the hippie approach to art was not simply an ethereal "art for art's sake"; there was a decidedly public component to the materials they created. Peace-sign medallions, posters, bumper stickers, and buttons were all part of conveying the hip message—whether it was dope, sex, or stopping the war—to the rest of society. The Jesus People simply carried on in the same formats with their proclamations about Jesus.

The first major attempts to create evangelistic paraphernalia for a Jesus People audience seem to have appeared in Los Angeles. Early on, Arthur Blessitt began to use small, round, red stickers imprinted with messages like "Smile, God Loves You" and "Have a Nice Forever" at His Place on the Sunset Strip. He and his workers' tendency to plaster the Strip with these stickers was enthusiastically adopted by young believers who came into contact with his ministry.[52]

The degree to which this sort of activity became part of Jesus People life is reflected in the lyrics of "Oh My," a song by Cincinnati-based Jesus People singer Randy Matthews, in which he recounts witnessing for Christ in depressing, sin-soaked territory. Telling God that he had "talked to junkies, Lord" and "ate lunch with whores," Matthews tells how he shone a light in the darkness as he "stuck [God's] stickers, on barroom doors" (figure 6.3).[53] However, to enable tens of thousands of young Jesus People to go out "shining their lights" before the world, someone would have to begin supplying the materials that would allow them to do so.

One of the first to answer this entrepreneurial call was Duane Pederson, publisher of the *Hollywood Free Paper*, who picked up on the popularity of "reds" and other items and began to produce bumper stickers, posters, and buttons and offer them for sale as part of an attempt to subsidize the expense of printing his paper. Pederson developed this into a mail-order business, the Emporium. Although its financial success was marginal at best (for a while, Pederson apparently relied on a manager who donated his time while living on unemployment checks),[54] the widespread distribution of the *HFP* as the "national" Jesus People paper undoubtedly did much to sow the vision of Jesus stuff among consumer and entrepreneur alike.[55]

From these early beginnings, the proliferation of Jesus-related merchandise is impossible to trace.[56] Indeed, not all of it originated directly from the Jesus movement proper: The rise of the evangelical bumper sticker began when Elden W. Ferm, a churchgoing traveling salesman, began marketing a half dozen stickers (including

FIGURE 6.3 Young Jesus People parcel out Jesus stickers at a Midwest rally in the early '70s.

Courtesy of Ron Rendleman.

his classic "Our God Is Not Dead—Sorry about Yours") from his home in Elkhart, Indiana, in late 1969.[57] However, it does seem that the breakout of this sort of material coincided with, and came on the heels of, the high tide of media publicity the Jesus movement received in 1971. *Time* magazine's June 1971 cover article on the "Jesus Revolution" carried a brief mention of the visibility of Jesus People bumper stickers and T-shirts, together with the appearance of a Jesus People wristwatch made by the Los Angeles–based Jesus Watch Company, whose slogan was, naturally, "Be with Jesus every minute of the day."[58]

Soon thereafter the first ad for Jesus People–style merchandise appeared in a mainstream evangelical organ, Youth for Christ's *Campus Life* magazine. The October issue carried an ad from a small Jesus People–run enterprise, the Everlasting Studio in Chicago. Replete with a line drawing of a hippie in a sweatshirt bedecked with peace symbols and conceived as an ad for a peanut butter–like "Jesus Word Spreader," the ad was visually unlike anything else in the magazine. Reds, window decals, and an embroidered cotton "One Way" emblem were offered for sale with the assurance that they were "effective as tracts/effective as posters."[59]

By the end of 1971, a number of companies ranging from small businesses run by Christian laymen (such as Christian Lettering of Beloit, Wisconsin; Harold's Signs and Displays of Boise, Idaho; and the aforementioned Ferm Publishing) to established evangelical corporations like Grason (a for-profit corporation formed by Billy Graham aide Grady Wilson in the early 1950s to

FIGURE 6.4 Young Jesus People queue up at a van selling Jesus merchandise at the Spiritual Revolution Day march in Sacramento in February 1971.

Courtesy of the Archives, Hubbard Library, Fuller Theological Seminary.

feed profits from books and other merchandise back into the Billy Graham Evangelistic Association) were attempting to capitalize on the new market.[60] Perhaps the single most successful company dealing in "witness ware/wear" was Cross Productions of Hollywood. They offered for sale a complete line of items, including buttons, decals, posters, patches, T-shirts, bumper stickers, and even license plate holders—all emblazoned with phrases such as "Smile, Jesus Loves You," "Have a Nice Eternity," "Guess Who's Coming Again?" and "Things Go Better with Jesus."[61]

By 1972, Jesus merchandise was seemingly available everywhere (figure 6.4). The new cohort of evangelical kids turned Jesus People could now get their favorite buttons and bumper stickers through the mail or at their local Christian bookstore. Evangelical magazines, especially the youth-oriented *Campus Life*, regularly carried ads for a variety of items, including "fold n' mail" stationery, "folk hymnals," and denim-covered Bibles. All this new Jesus merchandise caused a major shift within not only the type of non-print-related merchandise sold in Christian bookstores but also its market. Whereas heretofore "Christian goods" had been marketed primarily with an eye on the Sunday school and rural housewives, in the 1970s the market shifted to the varied needs and tastes of evangelicals under age thirty.[62] Indeed, the sudden influx of youthful Baby Boom buyers was a major factor in the overall explosive growth of the Christian bookstore industry, for they were also buying books (not only books on the Jesus People but also phenomenal best sellers such as Hal Lindsey's *Late, Great Planet Earth*), Bibles (young people snapped up the new paraphrased *Living Bible* and the popular youth version, *The Way*), and an

increasing number of records and tapes.[63] A clerk at the Lighthouse Christian
Bookstore in Long Beach, California, gave this snapshot of local Jesus People's
buying habits in August 1971:

> The Jesus People are enthusiastic buyers of Bibles. They wear out the [Bibles]
> in a few months and come in for replacements. They also buy scholarly works
> on the Bible which are expensive. Many are studying the Greek Testament.
> There is also a thriving sale of bumper stickers, buttons, and jewelry.[64]

A 1973 story on local Christian bookstores in the Tucson area reported similar
findings but noted the popularity of new Christian comic books and tracts targeted especially "for Jesus freaks" and the popularity of wood and leather crosses
among the young.[65]

For the bevy of new Jesus People, Jesus merchandise became a vital means
of building group identity. A spring 1972 story about Jesus People in Winona,
Minnesota, noted the importance that outward symbols played with local high
school and Winona State College students involved in the movement. "Their
Bibles are earmarked and worn since they carry them at all times," the article
stated, noting that "most of the joyful children of the Lord wear chains around
their necks featuring crosses, or medallions showing the head of Jesus."[66]

Armed with their Bibles, books, crosses, buttons, stickers, and shirts, the Jesus
People not only advertised their faith but also emphasized the bonds they had with their
peers. The comments of one woman remembering her California adolescence and the
way she and her "friends...bought 'One Way' necklaces, *The Living Bible*, etc., for one
another" reinforce the notion that Jesus merchandise played a big part in creating a
sense of Christian identity for many teens during this period.[67] Even apparent nonbe-
lievers could sometimes be smitten by Jesus People merchandise. In December 1972,
a teenage girl in Pasadena, California, wrote to the local newspaper's "Action Line" column to ask where she could obtain an "Ichthys" (ΙΧθΥΣ in Greek) sticker—except she
had no idea what it was: "Where could I buy a decal, resembling a fish, with the letters I,
X, O (with a 'belt'), Y and sideways M? And can you tell me what it means?"[68]

To many older evangelicals, the popularity of this "witness ware" was another
positive sign of a turnaround in the culture. The expansion of the market for
"Christian youth items" was a visible symbol that the Jesus Revolution was not
just apparent everywhere the eye looked but represented a triumph over the radicalism of the New Left. Writing in the summer of 1973 in the staid evangelical
monthly *Christian Life*, one author approvingly noted:

> The connection today between Abbie Hoffman and the "Things go better
> with Jesus" bumper sticker is long since buried underneath failure and
> success: the New Left has gone away mad while their gear—youth items,

remember—has made good in Middle America. In fact, the once radical message button, T-shirt, or sticker now has been domesticated into a bona fide sales item.[69]

However, for the kids who wore the Jesus buttons and laid down money for bumper stickers, warming their elders' hearts at the sight of a "One Way" symbol was an afterthought at best. Their Jesus People bric-a-brac was primarily a message to their peers, expressing solidarity with their fellow Jesus Freaks while proclaiming their Christian allegiance to those outside the fold. As such, the new Jesus merchandise played an important role in fostering a group identity following the expansion of the movement in the wake of the 1971 publicity wave.

The Coffeehouse: The New "Human Face" of the Jesus Movement

Probably the biggest factor in the Jesus movement's move into the mainstream of American youth culture during the early and mid-1970s was the widespread adoption of the coffeehouse as a focal point for meetings, Bible studies, concerts, and evangelistic activity. Whereas in the movement's earlier counterculture-centered phase the primary organizing mechanism was generally the communal house, after 1971 the coffeehouse became its main organizational base. No longer centered on a cohort heavy on runaways and free spirits deeply immersed in the countercultural lifestyle, the movement was now tapping into more rooted kids, most of whom lived at home with their parents.

As a result, all across the United States, the Christian coffeehouse became a cultural fixture of the 1970s. So ubiquitous did it become, it is probably safe to say that every town of any size, or of any local or regional importance, had one or more coffeehouses at some time during the '70s. Coffeehouses—and Jesus People–related ministries in general—were often unstable, transitory, and subject to turnover. Getting ongoing, steady financial support was a constant struggle.[70] As a result, the size, appearance, organization, and stability of coffeehouses varied widely—from a room in the basement of a local church to elaborate, self-sustaining Jesus People concert halls. But their function was always the same, serving as places to meet informally with fellow believers, places to take inquiring friends and acquaintances, places to find acceptable Christian entertainment, and staging points for activity and assistance to Jesus People in nearby communities. For most kids who identified with the Jesus People, there was a coffeehouse (often coffeehouses) that played an important role in their involvement with the movement.

Rebecca Kelly remembered that "a Christian adult" had begun the coffeehouse in her hometown of Albany, Oregon, at which she was converted after accepting a friend's invitation. Replete with "black lights, those discarded cable-wheels as tables," it was a place where teens could "[sit] on the floors, people [played] guitars...drinking tea and talking." From that point, Kelly became fully "involved with the kids who hung out at the coffee house....I took my Bible to school every day and was a full-blown out-of-the-closet Jesus Freak. Everyone at school knew it."[71]

A researcher described the intimate atmosphere and supportive environment at a coffeehouse in Rockford, Illinois, this way:

> Physical closeness (hugging, clasping of hands, laying on of hands, and general physical contact) is practiced among participants. The coffee-house is described in positive terms by most Jesus People as being warm, friendly, understanding, joyful, loving, constructive, refreshing, spiritual, beautiful and so forth. In other words, it has those characteristics that so many youths search for in their home environment and, unfortunately, do not always find.[72]

Bill Kaffen, a founding member of the Open Doorway Coffee House in Richmond, Virginia, looked back to those coffeehouse days as the highlight of his time in the movement: "The most outstanding experience was with the fellowship and community experienced by those of us guys who were staff members at the coffeehouse...wonderful times of prayer and sharing on a daily basis."[73] Through her involvement at The Way coffeehouse in Waukesha, Wisconsin, in the mid-'70s, Elizabeth Knuth recalled she knew of prominent groups and saw publicity about what was going on in "faraway California"; however, "the folks I knew from the coffeehouse and my classmates who were 'Jesus freaks' pretty much were the movement to me. They were the human face of it."[74]

So central did the coffeehouse become to the movement that opening one became an almost reflex response to the fervor teens were feeling for the Lord. Thus it was not surprising that after getting a spiritual boost from the new Billy Graham film, A Time to Run, in the summer of 1973, six young Jesus freaks in Blythesville, Arkansas, brought The Warehouse into being.[75] Similarly, when the Jesus movement hit Carroll County, Missouri, in late 1971 and early 1972, the degree of its impact was manifested by the establishment of the His Place coffee-house in nearby Chillicothe.[76]

That the coffeehouse became such a fixture of the evangelical youth scene was yet another irony of the Jesus movement, given that its form and atmosphere originated in the postwar bohemian hangouts of the Beat movement.[77] However, the coffeehouse idea had been quickly adapted as a means for counseling and social work by a few mainline Protestant and Catholic ministries in urban drug and tenderloin districts during the '50s and '60s period of transition from the Beat to the hippie counterculture.[78] As an extension of their long-standing commitment to gospel missions, such an approach naturally appealed to conservative Protestants as well.[79] It was this approach that appears to have been the genesis of one of the earliest of the proto–Jesus People ministries, Arthur Blessitt's His Place on Los Angeles's notorious Sunset Strip.

Blessitt's seedy setting catering to junkies, prostitutes, and drifters, however, was not the model for most of the '70s Jesus People coffeehouses. A more seemly example was the success enjoyed by Blessitt's Los Angeles contemporary, Don Williams, the youth pastor at Hollywood Presbyterian Church, and his Salt Company coffeehouse. Williams's more relaxed, middle-class, youth-friendly ambience with refreshments, Bible studies, sing-alongs, and concerts was much more appealing to the majority of American teens.[80] Although several coffeehouse-type ministry centers were established as part of the original countercultural segment of the Jesus movement, it was the success of the Salt Company that triggered hundreds of imitators across the country during the late '60s.[81]

As the coffeehouse moved center stage within the movement, the evangelical establishment jumped on the bandwagon. Reflecting the mania, Bethany House Publishers released *A Coffee House Manual*, a how-to book by the brother and mother of Teen Challenge evangelist David Wilkerson.[82] Churches and concerned laypeople of every conservative theological and denominational stripe in every region tried their hand at creating a slice of Jesus movement bohemia. The First Baptist Church of Woodville in the piney flats of East Texas sponsored a coffeehouse, as did the Assemblies of God congregation in Hays, Kansas. The Salvation Army operated God's Garage in suburban Phoenix; Grace Apostolic Church in Elyria, Ohio, underwrote The Carpenter's Shop; and the First Nazarene Church of Detroit backed the downtown Salt Company.[83] The members of a Christian Reformed church in tiny Stout, Iowa, were so enthusiastic about the possibilities of coffeehouse ministry in late 1971 that they dreamed of raising $55,000 to purchase a former Pepe Taco restaurant to open The Way Station—in bustling Cedar Falls, twenty miles away.[84] Ironically, even the Belmont Church of Christ in Nashville, Tennessee—part of the literalist Churches of Christ that banned the use of musical instruments in its services—started a coffeehouse (Koinonia) that became a thriving center for Nashville's acoustic and fully amplified Jesus rockers.[85]

The names given to coffeehouses were colorful, usually a play on some biblical or theological allusion—The Belly of the Whale, The Holy Ghost Repair Service, The Mustard Seed, Koinonia House, The Upper Room, The Ark, The

Glory Barn, House of the Risen Son, and the Way Inn were typical.[86] Writing in
1985, pioneering Jesus music disc jockey Paul Baker caught the ethos of the typical coffeehouse:

> Sometimes the coffeehouses were small and quaint. But usually they were
> no more than rented-out storefronts. The interior decorations were colorful
> Jesus posters or even wall murals; the floors were a patchwork of old carpet
> sample squares in a rainbow of colors. There was usually a coffeemaker
> and a Coke machine off to one side, and there was a good chance the spon-
> sors of the coffeehouse would set up a small "Jesus People" bookstore, with
> contemporary Christian books and records, gospel tracts, bumper stickers,
> T-shirts, and miscellaneous items for sale or for handing out.[87]

This description rang true for the vast majority of the coffeehouses that popped
up during the '70s. Most were created with a small infusion of cash and operated thereafter on a shoestring budget, using financial gifts by the Jesus People
themselves and occasional gifts from local churchgoers or family members
to keep the doors open. For example, the Fire Escape coffeehouse in Gardiner,
Maine, began on the strength of a $200 gift from a local clergyman to a group of
Jesus People from nearby Waterville.[88] The Koinonia Koffee House (and attached
Bible Bookstore) in Three Oaks, Michigan, in the southwest corner of the state
moved into an old Sunoco service station and was renovated, decorated, stocked,
and staffed for an entire year for $3,500.[89] Similarly, the House of the Risen Son
in Round Lake, Illinois, was made possible by a $4,000 bank loan secured by a
young group member's certificate of deposit from an insurance settlement.[90]

Several major coffeehouses became important regional and, in some cases,
even national centers of influence.[91] The Adam's Apple in Ft. Wayne, Indiana,
was an example of this type of coffeehouse. Backed by Calvary Temple Pentecostal
church and given a building that seated several hundred people, the Adam's Apple
became home to a cluster of talented groups and singers (including the heavy
band Petra and folk stylist Nancy "Honeytree" Hennigbaum) who became important Jesus music acts of their own. With an adequate financial base, the Adam's
Apple was able to provide a regular program of top-drawer Jesus musicians and
served as a major regional node on the developing Jesus music circuit.[92] Other
coffeehouses playing similar regional roles included The Avalon in Akron, Ohio;
Koinonia in Nashville, Tennessee; the Joyful Noise in Chicago Ridge, Illinois; the
Greater Life Coffeehouse in Dallas, Texas; the Salt Company in Detroit, Michigan;
and the Holy Ghost Repair Service in Denver, Colorado.

Sometimes the coffeehouse concept could be even more specialized. For a
while, there was a Jesus People–run Ichthys Pizza in central Indiana.[93] David
Hoyt's Atlanta Jesus People group ran a fast-food restaurant they called the Bread

of Life Restaurant and later added a nightclub in its basement.[94] Perhaps the ultimate evolution of the Jesus People coffeehouse-cum-restaurant opened in the mid-1970s. The Fatted Calf was a branch of the House of Faith in the Dallas, Texas, area and featured grade-A steaks cooked over a mesquite wood fire, a salad bar, homemade bread, and a choice of three desserts. As patrons ate, one of the ministry's couples would sing and play guitar. No prices were on the menu, and a jar was placed on each table; those who could pay were asked to support the ministry, and those who needed money were encouraged to take what they needed. The Fatted Calf became well-known in the Dallas area and was twice featured on Pat Robertson's *700 Club* television show. A popular destination for church groups, people frequently stood in line for two hours for a table, and sometimes the restaurant served as many as 1,500 people a week.[95]

These relatively well-heeled regional operations were, however, but a small part of the coffeehouse phenomenon. The coffeehouse announced to towns and cities across the United States that the Jesus People had moved beyond the headlines and into the local community. Combining the roles of meeting center, fellowship hall, and evangelistic outpost, the Christian coffeehouse was the ubiquitous institutional thread that served to unite the nationwide movement in the early and mid-1970s.

"Godstock": The High Water Mark of the Jesus Movement

The national strength of the Jesus movement, its new teenage demographic, the involvement of local evangelical church youth, and the backing of important evangelical leaders were put on dramatic display during Campus Crusade for Christ's (CCC) EXPLO '72. Held in Dallas from June 12 through 17, 1972, 85,000 youth attended this five-day series of training seminars and rallies, and an estimated crowd of 180,000 gathered for the all-day Saturday closing concert. Throughout the event, the symbols, language, and—perhaps most influentially—the music of the Jesus People were front and center. After a lull of several months, smiling youth giving the "One Way" raised index finger sign were once again plastered all over the pages of *Life*, *Newsweek*, and the *New York Times*.[96]

The vision for EXPLO (short for *explosion*) had first originated in the mind of Campus Crusade's founder and leader Bill Bright well over a year before there was a national inkling of the Jesus movement. Its shape and scope—a rally for college students and laymen somewhat like InterVarsity Christian Fellowship's triennial Urbana missions meetings but stressing personal evangelism—crystallized as Bright attended the August 1969 U.S. Congress on Evangelism held in Minneapolis.[97] Bright envisioned a gathering of 100,000—the majority being college students—who would be equipped with basic evangelistic training and then return to their homes and then, in turn, train five other people in what was termed Operation Penetration. Through these new cell groups, Bright hoped to train an army of half a million local lay evangelists who would spread the gospel throughout America by the nation's bicentennial in 1976 and go on to promote the evangelization of the entire world by 1980.[98]

Much of the motivation for this International Student Congress on Evangelism lay in Bright's and fellow Campus Crusade leaders' concern about the nation's volatile political and cultural scene. Reports from various campuses had convinced Bright that radicals were targeting September 1972 in advance of the November presidential election as the date when the revolution would begin, and EXPLO would be Campus Crusade's attempt ("only three months before radicals claim the revolution will start") to help derail this calamity.[99]

Official planning for the event began in the spring of 1970, even though many within Campus Crusade's leadership were skeptical of the grandiose scheme. In a classic case of passive-aggressive internal organizational politics, Bright's lieutenants deliberately selected a young, relatively inexperienced twenty-eight-year-old staffer named Paul Eshleman to head up the project. An MBA from Michigan State, Eshleman had been with CCC for only three years and had up to that time been an assistant to the regional director for the Big Ten.[100] After initial debate over whether to hold the meeting in Chicago or Dallas, it was decided that the Texas venue would be safer and that its smaller size and Bible Belt location would allow the meeting to dominate the area.[101] Eshleman set up headquarters in Dallas in August 1970, saddled by Bright's in-house opponents with an undistinguished initial staff of fourteen that was later described by a Bright aide as "horrible." But Eshleman would prove himself more than capable in the months ahead, aided by Bright's vision for the event and an ample budget of $2.4 million, more than a million of which was reserved for the purchase of airtime for a syndicated national television broadcast.[102]

The official kick-off for the event—now renamed EXPLO '72—occurred on December 3, 1970, in a press conference featuring Bright and his protégé Eshleman. They emphasized basic facts about the size and nature of the event and Campus Crusade's plans to evangelize the nation. Careful attention was paid to denying claims CCC was in any way tied to right-wing political elements or attempting to serve as a counterbalance to campus radical organizations.[103] Despite the fact that the planning document "1972 Congress—With Training" makes it clear that in 1970 Campus Crusade wanted a link-in with President Nixon, Bright publicly pooh-poohed the notion that the president might be "just dropping in," as he had to great criticism at Billy Graham's Knoxville Crusade earlier that year.[104]

As 1971 dawned, Campus Crusade's publicity machine swung into full gear. Six million brochures were distributed across the country. Ads were taken out in every major evangelical periodical. Field representatives were recruited, and a promotional film featuring Billy Graham was made for their use. Eventually, more than 200 agents were in place distributing copies of the film and making EXPLO presentations to church groups and civic organizations. With more than 1,000 16mm prints in circulation, the film was estimated to be—up to that time—the most widely distributed and shown evangelical film in history.[105]

It was apparent that Eshleman and Bright had decided to recast the gathering with the Jesus People in mind and had begun to utilize the publicity surrounding the movement to promote the event. The suggested presentation for field reps referred to the coming assembly in Jesus People terms as a gathering of "God's Forever Family."[106] The concluding mass rally evolved into a Jesus music festival featuring a number of Jesus movement bands and singers.[107] Eshleman and his staff were surprised that an estimated 40,000 high school students—more than three times the originally projected number for that age group—signed up for the meeting.[108]

Meanwhile, the political question of Richard Nixon's involvement was still troubling Bright's staff. Despite the opposition of presidential aide Charles Colson to any attempt to "tie into the 'Jesus freaks,'" they learned that Nixon himself very much wanted to be a part of the CCC event. According to his biographer William Martin, Billy Graham, EXPLO's honorary chairman, was also in favor of having the president speak at the gathering. Bright, it seems, was fine with this, but his assistants were firm in their opposition to Nixon's presence, arguing that it would undercut the very evangelistic goals they hoped to be promoting. Eventually, Bright relented and went back to Graham with the news. Nixon aide Bob Haldemann was quoted as saying that Graham and Bright had "a stormy session re: whether to invite the President," but in the end Bright's decision to take his staff's advice won out, and Nixon's only message to the EXPLO audience would be via telegram.[109]

As the 85,000 "delegates" to EXPLO rolled into Dallas on Monday, June 12, they were greeted by placards on the city's buses; the electronic billboard on the downtown Blue Shield building carried the phrase "Something Historic Is Going to Happen Here." When attendees arrived at Fair Park, home of the Texas State Fair and the Cotton Bowl (the site of the nightly rallies), 2,000 CCC staff and EXPLO volunteers were on hand to staff 300 registration and information tables. Computer printouts covered a dozen billboard-sized bulletin boards listing the housing assignments in downtown hotels, church basements, local homes, and 14,000 vacant apartments. Nearly 1,000 city and chartered buses were on hand to transport attendees to and from meetings—when the hopelessly snarled traffic would allow.[110]

With the long lines, inevitable glitches and the omnipresent Texas heat, the event got off to a bumpy start. Even before the meetings started, a fourteen-year-old boy from East St. Louis, Illinois, drowned in a motel swimming pool. A small but vocal group of about two dozen evangelical peace activists calling themselves the People's Christian Coalition came down from the Chicago area, led by Trinity Evangelical Divinity School student Jim Wallis, to protest against the war. Meanwhile, a small group from the Children of God, who had fallen out of favor with the evangelical mainstream during the course of 1971 for their insular nature and raiding of other Jesus People groups in the Pacific Northwest and Southeast, showed up to recruit new members and were promptly shown the gate by EXPLO officials. Five hundred youth from a "Jesus Only" Pentecostal sect were also on hand to distribute literature mimicking EXPLO's brochures but pushing the need for the baptism in the Holy Spirit and speaking in tongues.[111]

But when things actually got under way, these problems were quickly forgotten. The youthful crowd proved resilient and unswervingly cheerful, dutifully attending their daily seminar assignments and providing an atmosphere nothing short of electric for the nightly Cotton Bowl rallies. The singing, slogan-shouting, Jesus-cheering, One-Way signifying crowds dominated the proceedings (figure 6.5). On the first night, the crowd on the west side of the stadium began to shout, "Praise the Lord!" In response, the east side volleyed back, "Amen!" At another time, the crowd on the north side of the field began to chant "One Way! One Way!" Soon, the entire stadium rocked to the staccato cheer, their index fingers pointed to the sky in the Jesus movement's One Way symbol. Chairman and nightly speaker Billy Graham had the honor of reining in the crowd and did so successfully as he told them that he saw EXPLO as an opportunity to "dramatize the Jesus revolution [and]...say to the whole world that Christian youth are on the march, moving forward with Christ!"[112]

Over the next three days, the 85,000 participants spent their days attending seminars on various evangelistic and spiritual themes and were twice dispersed during the afternoon into the greater Dallas area to try out the evangelistic techniques they had learned. Many packed into the downtown area where they swarmed Dallas's well-churched shoppers and businessmen with expositions of CCC's famed "Four Spiritual Laws" tract and the news that Jesus loved them. While the EXPLO contingent may not have made many converts in their downtown sallies, they managed to make a generally good impression. As one Dallas policeman volunteered, "They're great kids, I haven't been called a pig once."[113]

In their down time, many of the young people wandered the aisles at EXPLO's job fair, checking out the exhibits set up by evangelical schools and organizations. Many groups made significant contacts with prospective workers and volunteers. One of the most popular booths was operated by Intercristo, a recently hatched computerized evangelical employment and career agency based in Seattle. For a $3 fee, the prospective missionary, schoolteacher, nurse, or warehouse worker could fill out a form detailing skills, education, and interests, which was then matched to corresponding jobs and service opportunities. As many of the prospective employers were on hand in the hall, initial contact could often be made

FIGURE 6.5 EXPLO '72 leaders flash the "One Way" sign at the conclusion of the Jesus music festival on Saturday, June 17, 1972; left to right: unidentified Campus Crusade official, musician Turley Richards, evangelist Billy Graham, Campus Crusade president Bill Bright. An estimated 180,000 people attended the day-long concert.

Used with permission, Campus Crusade for Christ International.

right there. An estimated 10,000 of those attending EXPLO took advantage of Intercristo's service.[114]

On Saturday the 17th—the morning of the infamous Watergate break-in—the scene shifted to an open field between two expressways at the Texas State Fairgrounds near downtown Dallas for EXPLO's closing Jesus music festival. A platform fifty yards wide had been erected with a brightly painted, thirty-five-foot-high, three-tiered, psychedelic backdrop emblazoned with Jesus People symbols and buttons designed by New York set designer Bill Bohnert. A rock festival–quality sound system cranked 3,000 watts of power to the two dozen speaker units on either side of the stage.[115] The crowd, estimated at 180,000, assembled for a marathon round of music and testimonies that began at about 7:30 in the morning to the strains of Chico Holiday singing, "Put Your Hand in the Hand." Prominent among a musical mix that included country and both Southern white and black gospel artists were representatives of the new Jesus music—Larry Norman, Love Song, Randy Matthews, Danny Lee & the Children of Truth, Barry McGuire, and the Children of the Day. Testimonies were given by a number of professional athletes, as well as by former Miss America Vonda Kay Van Dyke.[116]

The meeting built to a crescendo in the early afternoon as Johnny Cash and his supporting ensemble (the Tennessee Three, the Statler Brothers, and Mother Maybelle Carter and the Carter Sisters)—the best known of any of the performers that day—gave a rousing half-hour performance of gospel songs.[117] Following Cash was Billy Graham. Graham exhorted the sweltering multitude to carry out the Great Commission and reach the world with the gospel: "There is more potential power to change the world gathered here on this mall than I have ever seen.... You are young. You are fearless. The future is yours."[118] Leading them in reciting John 3:16, he told the audience that Christ alone offered the solution for the problems that were besetting the world:

> Put your hand in the hand of the man from Galilee. When you do you'll have a supernatural power to put your hand in the hand of a person of another race. You have a new love in your heart that will drive you to do something about poverty, the ecology question, the racial tension, the family problems and, most of all to do something about your own life.[119]

Graham concluded by asking his hearers if they could "cheer and hold up the One-Way finger when I speak of Jesus" and, if they could not, invited them to commit to Christ. Hundreds of individuals stood in the sun as Graham led them in the "sinner's prayer." Then Graham, Bright, and the musicians gathered on stage holding hands and led the throng in singing, a capella, the chorus "We Are One in the Spirit." With that, the audience gathered their belongings, picked up the trash, and left.[120]

EXPLO: The Aftermath

As he came away from EXPLO '72, Billy Graham apparently thought he might be able to harness the Jesus People's enthusiasm to help both the nation and his seemingly pious Quaker friend, Richard Nixon. Envisioning hordes of young Christians filling the streets to counter the expected onslaught of the New Left at the upcoming political conventions, he dropped a serious hint of what he would like to see in the upcoming weeks. Speaking to a group of reporters in early July, Graham expressed his hopes that "thousands of Christian students, Street Christians and Jesus People" would find their way to Miami to "join other young demonstrators" at the upcoming Democratic convention in August.[121]

Graham's hopes could not have been more misplaced, however. God's Forever Family could be turned out in great numbers to evangelize their neighbors, soak up some heavy spiritual teaching, or listen to some great music (and, realistically speaking, probably in reverse order). But aside from a highly contextualized group like the CWLF in radical Berkeley, the Jesus People were just not terribly interested in political activism. True, Jesus People groups could turn out for the day-trip enthusiasm of a Jesus March that mimicked the demonstrations of the civil rights and antiwar movements;[122] they would, on occasion (as they had at the University of Iowa earlier in 1972), take over a campus mall usually frequented by student protestors;[123] and every now and again, as they had at a St. Louis–area mall during the Christmas season of 1971, they might directly confront a radical group.[124] For the overwhelming majority of Jesus People, however, turning out for some sort of political cause was simply unappealing because it skirted the "real" issue: how would this effort glorify the Lord or lead people to Jesus?

Thus it was that when the Democratic Convention convened in Miami in mid-July, the number of Jesus People that had taken up Graham on his suggestion was but a faint shadow of the 85,000 eager youth who had descended upon Dallas. In fact, the numbers would have been disappointing for a local Jesus People rally and concert. All in all, an estimated 500 Jesus People, most of them from South Florida, along with movement luminaries like Arthur Blessitt and Sammy Tippit and contingents of the more politically attuned CWLF and Jews for Jesus from the faraway Bay Area, made their way to Miami Beach's Flamingo Park to demonstrate, testify, pass out literature, and otherwise make their presence known.[125] A few weeks later, about the same number returned to the city to carry crosses, pass out tracts, feed radicals, print "bust" cards, and bathe the eyes of teargassed and pepper-sprayed demonstrators during President Nixon's more violent coronation at the Republican Convention.[126]

While Graham's hopes for some sort of grand Baby Boomer Christian repudiation of the radicals failed to materialize in the wake of EXPLO, the Texas gathering had nonetheless made a profound impact. In their reporting of EXPLO, the media echoed stories from the previous eighteen months that generally boosted the Jesus People and held out the movement as hope for American youth.[127] The EXPLO afterglow extended to Dallas locals, as they remembered the well-mannered, cheerful, Jesus-cheering kids. Robert Mead, director of sales at the Dallas Hilton, wrote Paul Eshleman that it was "rare for a hotel to host such a well-behaved and mannerly group of young people....Every staff member...is still talking about the smiles, hello's and thank you's they received and our lobby still echoes with the sound of their happy singing."[128] One local woman who had two girls staying at her home during EXPLO wrote CCC to tell them "our hometown was blessed to be chosen as the site for EXPLO; these young people left behind them renewed faith in the younger generation."[129] Another woman from suburban Mesquite related that the door-to-door visit she had received from two of the EXPLO youth during one of their evangelistic practicums was "one of the most heartwarming experiences" of her life. "Ruth Kaneshiro and Phil Young from Hawaii spent an hour with me...so refreshing that it completely refuted the prevailing feeling of wayward youth."[130]

Even more enthusiastic about EXPLO, however, were the sentiments of evangelical leaders who had been present at the event. "Though their music was not my kind of music," wrote John F. Taylor, executive director of Wheaton College's Alumni Association, "I fell in love with these beautiful kids. I can see a brighter tomorrow because of them."[131] Clyde W. Taylor, general director of the National Association of Evangelicals, was sure EXPLO would "go down in history." He, too, was unprepared for "the marvelous spirit of all these kids."[132] Robert A. Cook, president of The King's College in upstate New York and a past president of Youth for Christ, wrote Bill Bright that "EXPLO '72 has to stand out as the great event of our generation, so far as mobilizing youth for evangelism is concerned…one can never forget the sheer impact of nearly a hundred thousand hearts praising the Lord in the Cotton Bowl."[133] Harm A. Weber, president of Judson College in Elgin, Illinois, expressed a similar wonder to Bright and recounted the appraisal of taciturn, Ulster-born Bible teacher J. Edwin Orr, who compared the stands full of youth shouting "Praise the Lord" and "Amen" back and forth to the time when Joshua gathered the children of Israel for the reading of the Law in the Valley of Shechem.[134]

Beyond the enthusiastic response to the kids and to the event itself, several evangelical leaders were thrilled with the publicity surrounding EXPLO and its positive implications for evangelicalism. Wendell Collins, an official with Muskegon, Michigan's Gospel Films, believed "Evangelical Christianity was not only made the most visible it has ever been, but was greatly advanced because of EXPLO '72."[135] Paul Little, a prominent seminary professor and author, was heartened by "the coverage in the national press," which he felt would "increase further the openness we now have to talk about Christ in almost every place and situation."[136] Meanwhile, LeRoy Eims of the Navigators contended that the widespread participation of evangelical groups augured great things for the future. In reality, EXPLO had provided the first major umbrella networking opportunity for the broad range of evangelical parachurch organizations that had grown up in the three decades since the evangelical movement had begun in reaction against the fractious, insular fundamentalism of the 1920s and 1930s. As Eims observed:

> I am sure that there will be a greater trust and collaboration among those 210 groups that were represented at EXPLO. Many of us got well acquainted with each other and learned what others were doing and I know that will have a significant affect [sic] on the world wide vision of Christianity in the years to come.[137]

But the most significant impact that EXPLO made may well have been the impression it made on the youth who had experienced the five days that was the Godstock Nation and its rallies, seminars, and concerts. They had experienced a Jesus People high that they could carry back home with them to their parents, friends, schools, and home congregations. Lucy Kalijian of Pasadena, California, could describe it as nothing less than a "foretaste of heaven on Earth."[138] Dean Olsen of Medford, Wisconsin, told Paul Eshleman, "Boy that was a week worth living for!" Gushed

Olsen, "My plans are now to attend Dallas Theological Seminary...June 12–17, 1972, a week that will not be forgotten by thousands of people, by me, or by the history books."[139]

The immediate impact of EXPLO was extended in the weeks and months that followed. For example, one group from a Methodist church in Granville, Ohio, came home so fired up by their experience that they decided to run their own Mini-EXPLO at Harmon-Burke High School's football field to kick off the new school year. The local Jesus band Dust—at "one-fourth their usual fee"— stepped forward to provide the music, supporting speakers from the House of the Risen Son in Dayton and the Jesus People Center in Newark.[140] A delegation of forty interdenominational youth from Crossett, Arkansas, returned home and recounted their "Great Adventure in Christ" in the First Methodist Church's newsletter, the *Methodist Messenger*. Jody Hart said the main thing she took away from EXPLO was "the display of love. Every time I passed someone I could just feel God's love flowing into me.... Everyone was accepted for what he was." She resolved that "we must let God's love transform us from lukewarm Christians into red hot ones!" Tron Clark was also struck by the feelings of unity and love at EXPLO: "People [were] loving each other because we are one in the Spirit and are all brothers and sisters in Christ Jesus." Sounding like a Jesus People equivalent to a participant from another celebrated youth festival that had taken place in upstate New York a few years earlier—Woodstock—Clark reveled that the usual cliques, hierarchies, and superficialities of teen culture seemed to have been pushed aside: "No one cared how you looked, how you dressed or wore your hair.... To see 100,000 Christians gathered to praise the Lord was an experience of a lifetime."[141]

In early August, EXPLO fever was broadcast nationwide, as Campus Crusade bought airtime on nearly 200 television stations and aired three hour-long specials—two showing excerpts from the nighttime Cotton Bowl rallies and one from the Saturday Jesus music festival. Now in crisp color videotape, the nation could see the Jesus movement in action; hear the new, upbeat gospel music; and see the nation's most prominent evangelicals extol the cause of Christ. To anyone who wrote in, Campus Crusade offered a special album packed with musical highlights from EXPLO, including the new Jesus music performers, as well as a copy of Bright's book *Come Help Change the World*.[142]

While CCC continued to make hay off of EXPLO and the Jesus People into the fall of 1972, the media moment for the Jesus movement was over. In terms of public recognition and the movement's morale, EXPLO had been as big as it was going to get. Major national media coverage of the Jesus People would be pretty much nonexistent from that point forward. Publicity or no, however, the Jesus People would continue to try to win their generation for the Lord in the days, weeks, and months that followed.

Conclusion

After EXPLO in late June 1972, an uncredited reporter for New York's *Newsday* presented an analysis of the current status of the Jesus People that got at the overall transformation that had occurred in the larger Jesus movement during 1971 and 1972:

> Most recently the movement has built along solid middle-class lines. Waiting in the wings was a sizeable corps of Sunday school regulars, raised by devout Protestants to obey authority and honor America, whose funda-mentalist faith previously earned them more embarrassment than respect from their peers. When some of the hippest elements started embracing that faith, these more conventional Jesus people emerged proudly from their relative obscurity to join the cause, becoming as a class the most numerous segment of the new spiritual enthusiasts.[143]

Indeed, the shape of the Jesus People movement changed considerably after the great media fanfare in 1971. What had begun as a genuinely counterculture-based spin on traditional evangelical Christianity among the nation's hippies had evolved into a widespread movement featuring younger, teenage kids, particularly the children of America's conservative evangelical churches. The countercultural element continued to be an important—and very visible—part of the movement. Now, however, they were the colorful, eccentric older brothers and sisters and role models for a broad-based mass of largely middle-class, mostly church-raised sib-lings. But this change had definitely expanded the size, scope, and infrastructure of the movement. The large numbers of evangelical youth meant that the move-ment was now thick on the ground not only in the big cities but also in the nation's small towns and suburbs.

Division in the Camp

THE JESUS PEOPLE VERSUS THE CHILDREN OF GOD

ON THE AFTERNOON of Friday, December 3, 1971, the readers of the *Seattle Times* were greeted with a jarring front-page story concerning the local Jesus People movement. The article by religion editor Ray Ruppert and the accompanying photo highlighted an ongoing struggle between supporters of Linda Meissner's hometown Jesus People Army (JPA) and an out-of-town contingent of the Children of God (COG) who had swept into Seattle in September. The photo showed Meissner's husband, John Salvesen, attempting to gain entrance to the Danish Brotherhood's historic Washington Hall in Seattle's downtown Central district. Wrestling with him in an attempt to block his entry to the hall (which had been leased to the JPA in Salvesen's name earlier that year) was Shoshannim, one of the COG overseers who had been inhabiting the building for several weeks. Police broke up the scuffle and allowed the aggrieved JPA delegation into the building. Once inside, new confrontations broke out, as other COG members attempted to bar Salvesen and a group of JPA loyalists from snagging records and personal belongings.[1]

The early December skirmish was but the most publicly contentious episode of a sequence of events that kept the Jesus People movement in the spotlight in Seattle-area media outlets during the fall of 1971. The stories in this latest wave of publicity in the Puget Sound area, however, deviated from the stream of feel-good, informational, or "man bites dog" angles that had characterized local and national media coverage of the Jesus movement since the beginning of the year. The new spate of stories highlighted conflict and complexity within the movement, shattering any illusions that it was a tightly organized, monolithic entity. By the time the dispute had run its course in late 1972, the Jesus People had publicly disowned the COG—one of the movement's largest and most publicized elements—in a drawn-out battle that extended across the Atlantic Ocean to Britain.

Although the mainstream evangelical Jesus People came off looking better to the public than the discredited COG, the entire movement could not help
being tarred by the dispute and the public perception of the COG's authoritarian
excesses. The episode revealed the unnerving truth that the youth, inexperience,
and zeal of many of the new converts made them prime recruits for authoritarian leaders whose style approximated the old-time religion but whose theologies,
methods, and governance stood outside the pale of evangelical orthodoxy. As a
result, evangelical advisors and movement leaders stepped up efforts to clearly
mark off deviant groups such as the COG and emphasized their basic theology
and anticult apologetics to protect the Jesus People from heterodox proselytizing
efforts. The educational and publicity efforts to discredit the COG effectively neu-
tralized their sheep-stealing expeditions among the Jesus People. But the resultant evangelical apologetics and anticult crusades helped revive a long-standing
American suspicion of outside-the-lines religious groups.

The Children of God: The Cutting Edge of the Jesus Movement?

With the exception of Chuck Smith's burgeoning outreach to Orange County's
youth at Calvary Chapel, no element of the early Jesus People movement received
as much publicity as David "Moses" Berg's Children of God. Their relatively large
numbers (by various counts somewhere between 2,000 and 3,000 full-time members in late 1971), organization, commitment, and penchant for public spectacles
like sackcloth-and-ashes demonstrations made them a logical go-to group for anyone investigating the Jesus movement during late 1970 and the first half of 1971.
This held true not only for secular reporters with *Time* magazine or NBC News's
First Tuesday but also for mainstream evangelical authors who visited and interviewed the COG as part of their research. Like the interviewers who fanned out
across the West Coast to collect material for Ruben Ortega's *The Jesus People Speak
Out!* most viewed the COG as just another part of the larger Jesus People movement. Quotes from COG members such as Cornelius in Dallas and Maoch in
Hayward, California, were sprinkled throughout the book alongside Jesus People
peers from Calvary Chapel, the CWLF, and various other Jesus People houses and
groups.[2]

Other evangelical observers who came into contact with the COG lumped
them in with the movement but did notice that they stood out from the rest of
the Jesus People crowd. In *Jesus People Come Alive*, Southern Baptist journalist
Walker L. Knight devoted most of his chapter on communes to the COG. The
COG struck him as "fundamental" and "secretive" to a degree that "suggest[ed] a
hostility toward society, established churches, and even modern-day family life."
But Knight reconciled himself to these things because the COG told him that they

were expecting "a Communist takeover or a revolution sparked by disenchanted young people." Knowing that they were "preparing for life under anarchy or a dictatorship where Christians are persecuted," their self-described attempt to "live as though the nation were already under Communist rule" made sense to Knight. He assured his churchgoing readers—buffeted by years of protests and disrespect to authority figures—that the COG's vision of Nixonian America as a perfect setting for a dry run at life under Stalinist oppression did not carry with it a contempt for law and order. "The police," he assured them, were in the COG's eyes "ordained of God," and without them, "there would be many more crimes."[3]

In their early 1972 book, *The Jesus People*, sociologists Ronald Enroth, Edward Erickson, and C. Breckinridge Peters similarly considered the COG to be a part of the larger Jesus People phenomenon. As they researched their book in the fall of 1971, they also found the COG much more exclusive and antiestablishment than most of the Jesus People they ran into, holding communal living to be "an inviolable commandment of God" and seeing themselves as the "only Christians in existence who were 'one hundred percent sold out for Christ.'"[4] When they asked a COG girl they encountered on Hollywood Boulevard what she thought about "the brothers and sisters at Calvary Chapel in Costa Mesa," her "face turned to a scowl and she hissed, 'Bullshit!'"[5]

In hindsight, the growth of the COG in late 1970 and 1971 was all the more impressive, given their level of commitment, isolation, and rigorous lifestyle. Within a movement that emphasized an ideal of being "sold out" for Jesus, the Children of God were the most committed of the committed, emphasizing the need to repent and break free of "cold, dead formalism" and "churchianity" to concentrate wholeheartedly on saving souls before Christ's imminent return to earth. Therein lay their appeal to many potential converts.

But another dimension that may well have added to the COG's appeal was the fact that the COG had no visible, charismatic leader out in front of the movement serving as a lodestone for new recruits. In fact, almost all of the group's major decisions and strategy were being handled remotely—often from half a world away. The COG's founder and leader, David "Moses" Berg, was globetrotting and keeping a very low profile. From the time his 200 or so followers had begun using Pentecostal evangelist Fred Jordan's properties in early 1970, David Berg had consciously disengaged himself from regular, direct contact with the COG's rank and file. Instead, he let his core leadership—mostly his children—run the day-to-day business of the group.[6] Berg seemed so far in the background that he was almost invisible. For example, an early 1971 AP wire story about the Jesus movement identified the group as "a wandering religious tribe" but listed it as being led by Berg's twenty-nine-year-old son-in-law, Arnold "Joshua" Dietrich. Author Lowell Streiker, who visited the Children of God in Los Angeles in mid-1971 while researching his book *The Jesus Trip*, also had a distorted view of the group's leadership. Streiker came away believing that the COG was actually "an outgrowth" of Fred Jordan's American Soul Clinic and never so much as mentioned David Berg, believing that guidance for the group was being provided by Jordan's Southern Baptist assistant, Freeman Rogers.[7]

This was not just a matter, however, of the flock being closed-mouthed about their shepherd. Sociologists Enroth, Ericson, and Peters had a chance to do their homework a little more thoroughly in finishing their research and writing in the fall of 1971. They knew that Berg was the founder and leader of the group; however, the trio of evangelical scholars realized that they had a leg up on most of the COG rank and file in that regard. They observed that if one were to "ask a recent recruit if he knows David Berg" that one would "draw a total blank." Moreover, they believed that most COG members did not even "know who [prominent leaders] Joshua (Arnold Dietrich) and Jethro (John Treadwell)" were, being aware of "the elder of their own commune, but no others."[8] This level of secrecy may have been exactly what one might expect from a group convinced that the end of the age and intense persecution were right around the corner. But more controversial developments were taking place behind the scenes with "Moses" that may have prompted him to bide his time in revealing both himself and the growing series of fresh revelations he had received from the Lord.

Besides his own existence and role, the major secret that Berg was keeping from most of his followers was a startling vision he claimed God gave him that he initially shared with his inner circle of fifty or so, back in the summer of 1969 during the COG's wanderings in the East. Not only was the ragtag band of hippie Christians he had assembled God's "new church," chosen to replace the lukewarm, establishment "old church," but also the Lord had shown him a wondrous symbolic type of this mystery that was to be lived out in their midst. As a living exemplar of this new relationship, the End Time Prophet's wife of twenty-five years, Jane ("Eve"), was to be replaced by a new wife—"Maria" (Karen Zerby), a twenty-three-year-old secretary, the daughter of a Wesleyan Methodist pastor from Tucson, who had joined the group a few months earlier. Berg felt this "strong teaching" could be absorbed by his followers only after much preparation.[9]

Perhaps amazingly, the COG leadership appears to have remained collectively mum on the subject during the ensuing two years; news of this key doctrinal development seems never to have leaked out beyond the COG's innermost core. But for the most inside of COG insiders—Berg's own children—the degree and nature of this revelation may not have been as great a surprise as might have been expected and perhaps steeled them for signs that more revelations might be on their way. Berg's eldest daughter, Linda (Deborah), in her 1984 autobiographical exposé of the COG, claimed that her father had attempted to have sexual relations with her several times over the years and that her younger sister Faith had been involved with her father in an incestuous relationship for years, something "Faithy" never seemed to deny.[10] Although there may have been a dark, hidden secret kept from those outside the immediate family, Berg allegedly exhibited other peculiar sexual behaviors even before the announcement concerning "Eve" and "Maria." Sarah Glassford, the first wife of David's son Paul ("Aaron"), told New York state investigators in 1974 that she had been forced to have intercourse with her husband-to-be in front of the elder Berg in 1967 and that over a three-year period her father-in-law attempted to seduce her numerous times.[11]

Sarah fled the COG's Fred Jordan–leased Texas Soul Clinic with a baby daughter in tow in mid-1970. Aaron's next wife, "Shulamite" (Judy Arlene Helmstetler, a runaway from Los Angeles he married almost immediately after his first wife's escape), claimed to have been introduced to her father-in-law's theologically liberated libido several months after her marriage. According to an interview she gave to author Don Lattin in 2006, she glimpsed Berg's evolving teachings during a visit to a Dallas hotel around the early summer of 1971. Invited to the hotel with her husband for a meeting of core family leaders, she alleged that as the business agenda wound down, Berg began to imbibe from a bottle of wine and peeled off his clothes. "To the pure, all things are pure," she said Berg proclaimed from Titus 1:15, as he strode around the suite buck-naked. She stated that this was a cue to everyone present that it was time to exercise one of the prophet's recent revelations: "sharing." Shulamite recounted that soon "everybody was having sex." Although the activities were rather modestly sequestered ("It wasn't like an exhibition," she stated), she ended up "sharing" with someone other than her husband. Later, in the middle of the night, she claimed that David Berg himself paid her a wine-soaked visit to kiss her and inform her he was in the mood to make her—by his count—his "fifth wife." She put off his advances, she stated, but her allegations add further to the speculation that Berg's ideas about what constituted Christian community were evolving in ways that no one outside the COG hierarchy could imagine at the time.[12]

The Children [of God] Begin to Run Afoul of the [Jesus] People

As the late winter and spring of 1971 passed into the summer months, it became clearer that the insular nature of the Children of God was putting them at odds with the larger Jesus People movement and the movement's straight evangelical backers. The first major indicator of potential trouble in this regard was the COG's penchant for proselytizing not only everyday pagans but also members of extant evangelical ministries. Sheep stealing has long been an offense within evangelical quarters as taboo as horse thievery in the Wild West. The dirty little secret of many evangelical success stories over the years has been that the stunning popularity and growth of some churches and ministries often was anything but a harvest of unsaved souls: To some degree or other, it often depended on gaining bodies from other congregations. The free-market, cafeteria dynamic of American religion— going back into the mid-1700s—has long meant that attractive theology, better preaching, charismatic leadership, stronger youth programs, more appealing music, or up-to-date facilities have all combined to encourage an active circulation of church attendees. Still, within this evangelical marketplace, the active attempt to purposefully pluck souls away from a bona fide evangelical sister ministry or church in order to enlarge one's own flock was always considered a major eccle- siastical faux pas.[13]

By 1971, the COG had begun taking recruiting shortcuts beyond simply evangelizing the hippies on the street and had started actively visiting other evangelical pastures to have a go at their young sheep. One of the first recorded forays occurred in the early spring, when a group of six COG arrived on the campus of Oral Roberts University as a seminar featuring student represen- tatives from a number of evangelical Bible schools and colleges was under- way. Fresh off their appearance on NBC's *First Tuesday*, the group was warmly received and even appeared as guests on the college's *Voice of ORU* radio pro- gram. But the main attraction for the young COG members appears to have been the opportunity to preach to, and dialogue with, the students of ORU. To the "sold out" Children, the "systemites" at the famous healing evangelist's school seemed largely uncommitted and biblically illiterate. Reporting back to their comrades at the Texas Soul Clinic, Adria was amazed "at how little [the ORU students] knew," while David Berg's daughter Faith sadly declared that "there were a lot of sheep starving" and that the Tulsa school was little more than "an empty shell." But according to the "intercolonial" COG paper, *The New Nation News*, the COG's exemplification of radical discipleship had borne fruit: "Five ORU students [had] arrived at the Texas Soul Clinic and many more [were] expected."[14]

Oral Roberts University was but one of a number of campuses that received a visit from the COG during 1971. But even when visiting a secular college or university, they frequently targeted not run-of-the-mill unregenerate col- lege students, but the evangelical students and fellowships on campus. In fact, just such a visit on May 6 to the campus of Southwestern College in Chula Vista, California, produced what became the first public red flag con- cerning the COG within evangelical networks. A letter purporting to be from Southwestern's local chapter of Inter-Varsity Christian Fellowship (IVCF) responded to a contentious late spring COG visit with a mass-mailed open let- ter of warning to other IVCF chapters and Southern California Jesus People. The COG, the statement accused, treated recruits like "captives," which they "held...somewhere in Los Angeles" in order to teach them "un-Christian doctrines" and kept them "guarded at all times." Deprived of food and sleep, the letter claimed, prospects were "bussed to Arizona, taught in a hypnotical [*sic*] state, kept away from the sunlight, and filled with wickedness." The letter went so far as to proclaim the COG as the "wicked forces of Satan" and warned readers to:

> ...please be on your guard! Have the guts to say "With the Blood of Jesus Christ, and in His name, Be gone ye follower of Satan!" They will stare at the ground in shame.... Please get word around, or either you or your friends' lives may be in serious spiritual danger.[15]

The Southwestern College IVCF letter received as high a visibility as was possible at that time amid the loose, disorganized networks of the Jesus movement by virtue of being reprinted and distributed in an early June issue of Duane Pederson's *Hollywood Free Paper* (*HFP*). By that time, the *HFP* was being drop-printed in cities across the country with a printing of well over half a million copies per issue; the publication of the Southwestern IVCF letter in the *HFP* therefore constituted a major lightning bolt within the heretofore fraternal innocence of the Jesus People movement.[16] Fred Jordan denied all charges in a rebuttal letter to the editor signed "The Children of God" in the next issue of the *HFP*: "members are always free to depart...sleep regular hours and partake of wholesome and abundant supplies of food...the church certainly does not teach 'un-Christian doctrine.'" Duane Pederson had a sit-down meeting with L.A. COG leaders, and the editorial staff of the *HFP* jumped back, declaring that it was keeping neutral in the matter and that neither letter represented their position.[17] Indeed, there may even have been evidence to suggest that the original letter from Southwestern College had been written by an evangelical coed who was not even a member of the Southwestern IVCF chapter.[18] However, the letter was out in Jesus People circles and had begun the ball of anti-COG publicity rolling.

The very next issue of the *HFP* in early July only intensified the controversy. Despite the paper's earlier statement of neutrality, Pederson decided to feature an alarmist letter from early Bay Area Jesus People veteran Kent Philpott warning Jesus People everywhere that the COG were not to be trusted:

> In 4½ years of street ministry and operating Christian houses, I have never encountered so dangerous a group as that Texas-based group formally called the "Children of God."...The fruit they have left...has been confusion, snatching away of people (at times people under age), creating factioning [*sic*], demanding of followers the turning of all property and money...an unhealthy subjection of followers....Their familiar approach is to go into Christian houses or other concentrations of Jesus People and try to attract new believers.[19]

Philpott reported on recent instances in the Bay Area where the COG had been attempting to gain members, relating the story of "one guy [who] walked all night to get away" from them and who "was watched so closely that someone of the group even went to the bathroom with him."[20] Philpott carried a lot of weight in West Coast Jesus People circles, and his letter was undoubtedly taken seriously there. As a result, Evangelical Concerns went so far as to appoint CWLF member Bill Squires and Palo Alto pastor Ray Steadman to set up a group to investigate the COG.[21] Speculation continued to grow like wildfire in the following weeks, as news began to filter out about another story of alleged COG skullduggery—this time in the Southeast.

The Children of God March on Atlanta

Philpott's letter to the *HFP* came on the heels of a personal visit to Atlanta, where the COG had come close to obliterating nearly a year and a half's work by Philpott's longtime friend and associate David Hoyt. Hoyt, who had founded a string of communal houses in Atlanta and several other cities, had been featured, along with the COG, in NBC's *First Tuesday* program about the Jesus movement back in February. Most of the program focused on the COG, and when Hoyt saw the broadcast, he was impressed with what he saw of their organization and dedication. Struggling to provide direction and funding for his sprawling network of Jesus houses, Hoyt claimed that he thought the Children offered a way forward out of the constant pressure to provide for his followers:

> I knew that they were big...and I was curious as to how they handled their organization as they expanded and were able to keep up with their bills and the...practical side of running a large ministry when I was faltering in Atlanta because...I had no training...we didn't know how to sustain it all.[22]

In the spring, Hoyt headed off for a visit to the COG's Texas Soul Clinic compound in Thurber. Arriving under an assumed name, he spent several days checking out the COG, their teachings, and their system. While he was taken aback at the armed guards he claimed he found at the gates (a deterrent, he was told, to the local rednecks) and underwhelmed by the somewhat unkempt COG and their quarters, Hoyt was nonetheless impressed with their Scripture memorization, their dedication to witnessing, and the obvious commitment he sensed in their ranks. Eventually, he revealed who he was to some of the COG elders, who eagerly offered to come to Atlanta, suggesting that perhaps the two groups could even hold a joint worship celebration together and that they would bring along their crack new band with recent convert Fleetwood Mac guitarist Jeremy Spencer at the helm. Hoyt said he would talk over the idea with his leaders when he got back to Atlanta and get back to them.[23]

Hoyt returned to Atlanta in May and told his leadership about his visit with the COG and how he thought they might be able to help out their string of Jesus houses. They agreed to invite a small delegation of the COG to Atlanta in early June for a worship celebration and advice about tightening up their ministry's finances and administration. Shortly thereafter, Hoyt began receiving calls from the West Coast from Philpott and others warning him about the Children of God. To Hoyt's mind, the charges all seemed very dubious, based on sketchy information. Attempting to balance it with what he had seen, he could see no reasons to revoke the invitation, and plans went ahead.[24]

When the afternoon arrived for the COG visit, the Atlanta Jesus People were surprised to find not just a band and a few guests pulling up, but a display of spiritual shock and awe: Several of the COG's top leaders had flown in from Los Angeles along with Spencer and the worship band, a small caravan of campers and packed buses arrived from a large COG colony in Cincinnati, and a number of leaders from the Texas colony appeared as well. In short order, the COG guests outnumbered their Atlanta hosts. As the night progressed, tension grew, exacerbated by visits from the police responding to neighbors' complaints about the noise and the number of vehicles—as well as calls from a few worried members of Hoyt's group who had left the meeting.[25] He remembered that some of these disgruntled disciples later confronted him about the aggressive COG: "This group is nothing like us!" they told him. "There's something wrong—they're like zombies and Bible-memory robots!"[26]

Hoyt was reassured by COG leader Hosea (Jonathan Berg) that all was well; the surprise busloads from Cincinnati were explained as having detoured a bit for fellowship's sake while on the way to a witnessing campaign at a Louisiana rock festival.[27] Hoyt accepted the explanation, and the rest of the evening proceeded calmly as the Atlanta group's band had a chance to lead worship and everyone finally broke off to eat. As the event wound down, several of the COG leaders took Hoyt aside and waxed enthusiastic about the COG's premier Bible teacher and End Times expert, Joel (Wordsworth), who was not too far away and was someone they felt Hoyt should meet. He agreed to meet Joel and was driven out to meet him at a remote campground nearly forty miles away. The COG leaders urged him to spend a day or two while they got back to Atlanta to supervise their followers and make sure that there were no more problems with the neighbors or police.[28]

For the next two days, Hoyt and Joel discussed the Scriptures together. Hoyt was impressed with Joel's learning and observed that he expressed some concerns over certain COG policies and decisions. Their time together was brought to an end, however, with the return of Hosea, who bounced in with the news that Hoyt's people back in Atlanta were all geared up to go along with their new friends to witness at the rock festival in Louisiana. A conversation with one of Hoyt's leaders, Philip Clore, over shortwave radio confirmed the news. That evening, assured that his young daughter and very pregnant wife were fine and at home in Atlanta with the other mothers and children in the ministry, Hoyt also left for Louisiana with Joel and a few of the COG's other top leaders.[29]

By the time he arrived in McCrea in south-central Louisiana for the Louisiana Pop Festival, a brief conversation with Clore revealed that a number of the people from Atlanta—Hoyt's wife included—had wanted to visit the COG headquarters in Texas and had, or would soon be, leaving Georgia. Over the next few days amid 50,000 young people and the attendant noise, heat, and mud of the rock festival, Hoyt claimed it began to dawn on him that something was wrong. Rather than returning to Georgia, the Atlanta group was now being invited to come over to the Texas Soul Clinic, along with a bevy of fresh converts from the festival.[30] At this point, under the watchful eyes of COG leaders, without money or ready access to a telephone, with no independent transportation, and with his family in, or headed to, Texas, Hoyt later claimed in an interview he finally began to realize that he had been had: "'Oh my God' I thought...[the COG] 'have taken over this ministry!'"[31]

When he arrived at the Thurber compound, Hoyt claimed he found that his wife, Victoria, and the other Atlanta women had been deluged with attention from the COG women. His wife spent nearly all of her waking hours in a grueling 8 A.M. to 11 P.M. training regimen with "Rachel" (Barbara Kaliher), one of the group's top female leaders. The Hoyts' daughters (the second daughter had been born shortly after the Atlanta group's arrival in Texas) and the other children from Atlanta were being kept in the compound's kibbutz-like communal child care facilities, which Hoyt claimed were largely off-limits to fathers except for the occasional visit when they were given time off from their studies and chores.[32]

Meanwhile, back in Atlanta, the COG effectively took over the management of Hoyt's Atlanta houses, and COG representatives were making contact with other houses his group had started. To try to derail what was happening, Father Ed Sweeney, a Charismatic Catholic priest who had been helping Hoyt, called Kent Philpott, the only authority figure he knew within the youthful movement that he thought might be able to help turn back the tide. Philpott listened to Sweeney and hopped aboard the next available flight to Atlanta. By the time he arrived in Georgia, however, it was clear that the battle was over—Hoyt and followers were already in Texas.[33]

Nonetheless, Philpott stopped at the House of Judah and the Temple of Still Waters and encountered the COG caretakers there. Skeptical of the COG as he was, Philpott says that he, too, was nearly recruited. Arriving at the House of Judah early one morning, he was met by a young COG member who had been with the group about six months. As Philpott remembered it, the appeal of the

COG's avowed all-out commitment was very appealing. "I can't explain it to you," Philpott recalled in a 2002 interview, "it was like the Siren's Song." Had it not been for the presence of Sweeney, Philpott believed he would probably have joined the COG that afternoon.³⁴

Now having encountered the group's allure up close, Philpott was worried that the residents in all of Hoyt's affiliated Southeastern houses might be tempted to defect to the COG as well. He got on the phone and began warning the houses in Nashville, Jacksonville, Knoxville, and elsewhere that the COG had taken over Atlanta and that they were probably on their way.³⁵ In the meantime, two of Hoyt's Nashville leaders, Bud Poston and John Shurgar, had visited Atlanta and fled back to central Tennessee to further raise the alarm. By the time Hosea had recruited Hoyt to fly with him to Nashville to meet with the leaders of the 23rd Psalm House and the group of local businessmen who were its financial backers, the momentum in the Southeast had changed.³⁶ Ken Pitts, a resident of the 23rd Psalm House, later remembered that without the "heads-up," they "probably would've all gone off with the COG." As he remembered it, the Children's calls for sold-out, 100% discipleship constituted "a very tasty-sounding spiel" that, even with the warnings from Philpott and others, almost overcame their reservations.³⁷ But by the time Hosea and Hoyt exited Music City, they managed to take with them only four individuals—long-time Hoyt associates from Atlanta and California who had been assigned to Nashville earlier that spring.³⁸

A New Front Opened: The Pacific Northwest

As the contretemps in the Southeast faded away, reports about Hoyt's enlistment by the COG created an uproar in Jesus People circles and the broader evangelical world. Linda Meissner and Russell Griggs, heads of the Seattle and Vancouver branches of the Jesus People Army (JPA), however, were still looking to the COG as a potential solution to their problems. By the summer of 1971, Meissner and Griggs—like Hoyt—had misgivings about their ability to get their group to the next level of spiritual maturity and dedication. Meissner had met some of the Berg children in New York City during their "Teenagers for Christ" days several years earlier when she was still with David Wilkerson's Teen Challenge. She considered the COG as a possible solution for developing the full-time, youthful disciples she had seen in her original Mexico City vision. Discipline, the enforcement of rules, and the motivation to get people out on the streets witnessing day after day were an ongoing problem.³⁹ Griggs found things much the same: conversions were easy, but making full-time disciples was hard; his casualty rate was nearly 50%, and he was beginning to feel that "a lot of the Jesus People work [was] very shaky."⁴⁰

Hoyt's decision to join the COG, coming on the heels of NBC's *First Tuesday* special, thus made a potential alliance very appealing to the JPA leaders. For

Griggs, Hoyt's decision to join the COG made him think that maybe the Atlanta leader knew a good thing when he saw it, as he had heard that Hoyt's organization was a "very well-run work reaching radical kids."[41] In an interview years later for Jesus People chronicler David Di Sabatino, Meissner recalled that joining the COG "seemed like a completely natural thing to consider, like the merging of two churches to form another larger one."[42]

Sometime during the summer of 1971, Meissner and Griggs separately headed down to check out the COG work in the Los Angeles area. Meissner admitted to being "favorably impressed with all levels of their operation" and even took part in one of their famed sackcloth-and-ashes demonstrations (figure 7.1). "They were a big, strong, well-organized group," Meissner wrote years later. "They had excellent music, organized Bible classes, and went witnessing every day. Everything I saw was impressive."[43] She told reporter Michael McFadden at the time that she was "opening [her] heart to the Lord to see if this is what the Lord [wanted her] to do." She was "fellowshipping with them, witnessing with them, and praying with them." She was impressed: it was "very, very heavy."[44] Griggs was likewise smitten with what he saw: he was "very impressed with the efficiency, with the scriptural attitude toward everything."[45]

The Pacific Northwest leaders' favorable observations about the COG came, however, at almost precisely the same time as a rash of setbacks and negative publicity began to dog the Children. The sudden bad press lay in a growing wave of criticism from nervous parents of recent recruits who worried about the group's antiestablishment rhetoric and the implications of its "forsake all" mandate. The growing COG compounds were increasingly the site of emotional exchanges with resistant young converts, backed by communal elders, resisting family pleas to return home.

FIGURE 7.1 A COG sackcloth demonstration ca. 1969.
Courtesy of the Family International.

In August, a few of these parents formed an organization under the unwieldy title "Parents' Committee to Free Our Sons and Daughters from the Children of God" (popularly referred to as FREECOG). One of the leaders of the group was William Rambur, a retired lieutenant commander in the Navy and high school history teacher from Chula Vista, California. His daughter Kay, a twenty-two-year-old nursing student, had joined the COG after running into an evangelistic team one afternoon on the Berkeley campus. Having already lost a son in Vietnam in 1968, Rambur was not inclined to lose a daughter to the COG and tracked her down to Fred Jordan's Soul Clinic in Texas.[46] During his visit there, he came close to talking her into leaving. However, when it came time to get in the car, he reported that she began to scream, "The Devil's in that car with you. I'm not getting into a car with the Devil!" and ran into the waiting arms of her COG brethren.[47]

This episode occurred in July, and within a few weeks, Rambur had networked with about sixty other unhappy parents, mostly from the San Diego area, to form FREECOG in an attempt to spread publicity about the COG and pressure local, state, and federal officials into investigating the group.[48] A sensationalistic press release from the group penned by a Mrs. Ida Mallik painted a lurid picture of the COG's methods and its impact on unsuspecting targets on college campuses and beaches, their prime recruiting grounds. After some hymn singing to guitar accompaniment, the COG would engage in some "very unique eye usage." This eye usage resulted in "some type of hypnotic state" that caused potential converts to desert "all—home, family, car, friends" to be "carried off in a bus or van to a place where they [underwent] extensive brainwashing sessions." There, they were "taught to hate their parents, schools, churches and the government." Kept "behind locked doors in a slave-like atmosphere," the new converts were "guarded at all times...and told that if they leave the building they will die." Those parents fortunate enough to recover their children from the COG, Mallik wrote, sadly reported that their sons and daughters had "a zombie-like appearance" and spoke "as if reciting from memory some text [they had] learned."[49]

Sharlene Falkowitz echoed Mallik's picture of COG mind control. She told one author that she and her husband had lobbied for an audience with a young family friend and finally got to meet with her at the Los Angeles colony one night after midnight. Falkowitz complained that "[the COG] wouldn't let us see her alone," and while they met with her, her handlers "kept staring into [the girl's] eyes. I told her that a close friend of hers had just died and she didn't even bat an eye."[50]

But FREECOG had escalated the conflict. Key to this was one of the founding members of the group, Ted Patrick, a middle-aged African American employed as a part-time State of California community relations officer in San Diego. Patrick had first encountered the COG attempting to proselytize his high school age son and a nephew at a Fourth of July fireworks display at San Diego's Mission Beach. After investigating and then spending several days posing as a convert, he concluded that the COG were up to no good and were guilty of "psychological kidnapping" via a process akin to hypnosis. But Patrick surmised that if a young person could be "programmed," it would be possible through a reciprocally intensive process for one of these misled youth to be "deprogrammed."[51] At the behest of concerned parents, Patrick was soon literally kidnapping COG members off the streets and out of communal homes and spending hours and days breaking down their defenses through an onslaught of Bible verses and argument. Quickly enough, the COG labeled him "Black Lightning" for his stealth raids.[52]

The growing pressure from FREECOG and other irate parents soon gave David Berg's old mentor Fred Jordan second thoughts about his partnership with the Children of God. Realizing he had little or no real influence on their decisions, Jordan began to see the COG as a major source of potential embarrassment. In late September 1971, he evicted them from his California and Texas properties, causing the COG to scramble for local alternatives or set out on the road in various "family" groups.[53]

It was then that the COG came calling in Seattle. The JPA had just moved from their old coffeehouse, the Catacombs near the Space Needle. Meissner invited the COG's band and a speaker to take over a weeknight service at their new cavernous coffeehouse downtown in Washington Hall.[54] However, when the COG arrived, they began to confront the Seattle Jesus freaks about their level of commitment to the Lord's work and urged them to "forsake everything... and join the COG."[55]

From that point forward, the Pacific Northwest COG expedition moved almost en masse into Washington Hall and began squeezing out the JPA. Meissner later claimed that "one COG member confronted each of us, one on one. They placed David Berg's daughter, Deborah, on me.... Deborah declared that only those who 'forsake all' were true disciples. She asked me the questions continually.... I was not prepared for this sort of confrontation."[56] As this was going on, she called her Seattle followers to a two-day round of fasting, prayer, and Bible reading. Several times she reportedly "cut" the Bible, that is, opening it at random and picking out a portion of Scripture to read. Each time she was convinced that "it was the Lord speaking" and that he was prompting her to join the COG.[57]

To bolster their efforts, the COG brought "inside" Jesus People recruits to intensify the pressure to persuade her to join—including Russell Griggs, who had already handed over the Vancouver JPA with its chicken farm, bakery, and 150 followers to the Children.[58] Also included as part of the COG team for the Pacific Northwest adventure was David Hoyt. It seems that Hoyt had gotten over his initial suspicions of the COG as he had settled into the group; Kent Philpott remembered that Hoyt wrote him several recruiting letters.[59] Hoyt insisted, however, that by the time he arrived in the Northwest, he was wavering badly and that the COG leadership was doing its best to hold onto him.[60] This may well have been the case, as even Moses himself was pitching in from overseas. In a section titled

"Exhortation to a Former Religious Systemite" in a September 1971 "Mo Letter," Berg acknowledged Hoyt's mental anguish and lavished praise on him for some broadsides he had penned, prophesying that God was getting ready to use him in a mighty way:

> David, I loved your letter and literature.... You seem to be doing a great job.... In fact, as I was reading one of your tracts, I had quite a thrilling experience! I got something right fresh off the griddle directly from the Lord, for you personally, David H.... "Even as My mighty men of old lay down their lives, and took up their cross and followed Me...so have I chosen this one that he may perform My Will, that with his pen he may pick up the Sword and fight the battles of the Lord, like David of Old!"— HALLELUJAH! ISN'T THAT TERRIFIC, SON? YOU'VE REALLY GOT A TREMENDOUS MINISTRY AHEAD OF YOU![61]

Hoyt claimed, however, that it wasn't Berg's prophecies that inspired him to go to the Pacific Northwest but rather the opportunity to gain control over his family. When he learned about the trip to Seattle, he agreed to go along only if the group allowed his wife and children to accompany him. Hoyt said that they honored his request but sensed his conflicted mind-set and kept him on a tight leash, trotting him out only as necessary. For most of the time, they kept him sequestered in Vancouver baking bread with Griggs for the latter's bakery operation.[62]

Meanwhile, Linda Meissner—isolated from her husband and her five stepchildren—was, either by the appeal of strategic advantages, reason, persuasion, ambition, or some combination of them all, increasingly impressed with the COG. She called her leaders and asked them to bring their people to Washington Hall to hear a presentation by the visitors. One of her lieutenants from Tacoma, Richard Vicknair, recalled in a 2002 interview that he had no feelings one way or the other about the COG and made preparations to bring his sixty kids up to Seattle the next day. That night, however, he remembered having "had a nightmare...a cold sweat nightmare." When he awakened in the morning, he claimed he "absolutely knew that [he] should not bring [his] kids." Instead, he drove up with a few of his leaders and walked into a coffeehouse packed with COG, Seattle JPA members, and reps from around the region. When Vicknair walked in with only a few people in tow, Meissner was not pleased; they spoke briefly before two COG jumped in between them to monitor their conversation, demonstrating—to Vicknair's mind—a "real bad spirit."[63]

Also there that night was Jim Palosaari, Meissner's former lieutenant and head of the Milwaukee Jesus People group. Palosaari had been contacted soon after the COG had shown up and flew into town along with Jay Dalton, a higher-up in the FGBMF, in an attempt to wield whatever influence they could with Meissner.

"We'd seen [the COG's] literature and knew they were off," Palosaari recalled years later in an interview. As a result, Palosaari recalled, they steeled themselves for spiritual warfare: "We went into the lion's den all prayed up!"[64]

The meeting itself met the expectations of battle and reportedly lasted twelve hours. "It was exciting," Palosaari remembered, noting that to Jesus People eyes, the COG "were impressive—good or bad, they were impressive." Adding to their impact was the fact that, according to Palosaari, part of the COG crew dressed up in their sackcloth-and-ashes costumes, banging their staves in unison on the floor: "If you made a movie people wouldn't believe it." Meissner spoke briefly, followed by the COG leaders, who hammered on the need to commit 100% to discipleship by rejecting the system. Questions and objections came from the audience, with any negative sentiment being greeted by the COG chorus with an Old Testament–style prophetic chant of "Woe! Woe! Woe!" Vicknair stood up at one point and declared that his Tacoma branch of the JPA wanted nothing to do with the new arrangement.[65] At that juncture, Meissner, her ex-husband John Salvesen later recounted, began to take the COG's side, feeling that Vicknair and others were not being open to all the evidence. Not a little part of her defensive reaction, Salvesen claimed, was that the COG leaders had prophesied to her beforehand that her husband and her former leaders would oppose the new arrangement. Frustrated, she reportedly told the crowd, "Anyone who is going to stay with me and join the Children of God stay in the building. The rest of you get out!"[66]

From that point forward, it was chaos, as the COG and JPA squared off in pairs and small groups, proof-texting each other, cajoling, and arguing over the merits of the proposed merger. Vicknair recalled it as "an absolute frantic and crazy evening," with a number of JPA kids eventually doing anything they could to get away from the COG emissaries: "They bailed out of Washington Hall, they were actually climbing down the fire escapes." All in all, most of the Seattle JPA apparently agreed with Vicknair that the COG merger was "a bad idea." Meissner recalled, "Almost all my leadership from Seattle and Tacoma walked out at the end," and while a few of her Seattle "foot soldiers . . . decided to join the COG . . . the majority did not." Of the approximately 115 estimated hardcore Seattle members, only ten to fifteen decided to go along with Meissner and join the COG.[67]

Over the next several weeks, Washington Hall became the COG's official base in the Pacific Northwest. A total of about fifty COG made the building their home, setting up a bank of phones and using the JPA's contact lists for a telephone marketing campaign to raise funds. Members hit the streets to witness and preach, passing out a revamped version of the JPA's old paper *The Truth*, now redubbed *The New, Improved Truth*.[68] In this they were proceeding according to David Berg's advice. Writing to his leaders in the Northwest in a Mo Letter dated September 27, Berg told them that the new acquisitions offered the COG some real opportunities: "That Seattle place sounds like a great place for meetings and eatings.... From what I heard of Everett, they're doing great, and so is Burlington, God bless 'em! Sounds like Seattle would make a good head-quarters for your general offices and Vancouver will be terrific if you don't muff the whole deal by offending Russ' good business sense.... You need that front. If a printshop, why not a bakery and a radio programme and an already going famous newspaper! For God's sake let's not lose all they've gained."[69]

Berg was under no illusions, however, that their new acquisitions in the Northwest were safely in their back pocket. In another Mo Letter dated October 1, he made it clear he was not overjoyed with his leaders' performance: "You've got a problem on your hands there in Seattle with that other guy's [John Salvesen] name still on the lease. He doesn't have to release it, and he can even sue you or charge you with trespassing." In that spirit, he urged them to learn from their mistakes and "get something on paper, wherever you go, including the camp in Burlington, and the building in Vancouver" and to remember that they could not "do to the people in Tacoma what you just did to those in Seattle." Furthermore, he noted they still needed to handle Meissner with kid gloves as she was the only major Seattle leader they had recruited, and she was "not too certain." For that reason—and for public relations' sake—he urged them to "let her keep her speak-ing engagements to try to explain us to the people and give her something to do," reminded them that "she had a good going newspaper there, which was quite well known throughout the West," and recommended they "let her continue to edit it and publish it, under your supervision."[70]

While the COG attempted to solidify their new acquisitions, the remnants of the JPA and their clerical and lay supporters rallied to continue the fight. The local Charismatic pastors' fellowship was consulted, and meetings at Bethany United Presbyterian Church brought together Jesus People leaders such as Vicknair, Parks, Palosaari, and Meissner's now on-the-outside-looking-in husband, John Salvesen, with fifty Seattle-area pastors. The group found sympathy for their cause in the local media, particularly with religion reporter Ray Ruppert of the *Seattle Times* and KIRO (CBS, Channel 7) television reporter Colleen Hansen. By mid-October, an unfriendly media spotlight had begun to shine on the COG in the Puget Sound region.[71]

The heat from local newspaper and television coverage of the COG-JPA strug-gle alerted FREECOG that Seattle was the new focal point of controversy. Near the end of October, William Rambur and others steamed into town and began adding their voices to the mix. To help clear the air, the Children called a press conference in Washington Hall on Sunday afternoon, October 31. Besides the Seattle COG elders and Meissner, Griggs, and Hoyt, the group had flown in Kay Rambur to disprove her father's charges that she was being held against her will. In front of a mixed crowd of COG, Seattle Jesus People, and print and broadcast media, the two sides debated, argued, and negotiated. When all was said and done, there were no breakthroughs one way or the other: William Rambur headed back home to Southern California, Kay Rambur went back with the COG, John Salvesen went back home to his five children, and Linda Meissner stayed at Washington Hall with the Seattle COG.[72]

Although the press conference produced no startling new developments, it provided no reasons to dissuade the Seattle Jesus People, the media, or the general public from taking an increasingly sour view of the COG. Barely a week later, reporter Ed Stover of the *Seattle Post-Intelligencer* got his hands on some Mo Letters, and in an article in the November 9 edition of the paper, revealed the COG leader's pragmatic strategy for dealing with its new Northwestern acquisitions. Among the stratagems detailed was Berg's counsel to COG members to take advantage of whatever welfare or unemployment benefits might come their way to help fund the operation. As for the local Jesus People scene, the article published Berg's advice to let Meissner fulfill her speaking engagements to keep her busy and to let her and the other JPA leaders keep their titles and organizational names to make them "feel good," even as the COG moved to consolidate control.[73]

But the worst damage from Stover's piece came from glimpses into some of Berg's evolving esoteric teachings, visions, and announcement that "the great Archangel Michael himself" was now the COG's special guardian angel. What probably piqued most readers' interest, however, were the censored excerpts Stover provided from a February 1971 Mo Letter titled "A Shepherd-Time Story," which described "the happy folds" of David where the COG shepherds and shepherdesses protected the little lambs who "laugh and sing and dance and play and—...[four-letter word for sexual intercourse] and bear lots of little lambs! And the shepherds like it!" where "nobody ever had so much fun as we have—loving and living and dancing and playing and singing and [same word]—and bearing little lambs, and gathering in more sheep!"[74]

The COG leaders in Seattle were surprised when they learned Stover had the letters and reacted angrily to his request to see more. David Hoyt seemed every bit the loyal COG soldier in this instance, and when asked for his comments, replied that Stover had "got enough with the letters [he] had acquired" and that the Children were "not interested in causing any more commotion than [they] already [had]....People tore apart the Bible and I guess they'll pick apart the letters."[75] But such protestations undoubtedly did not play well to the *Post-Intelligencer*'s readers. For a generation whose religious sensibilities had been formed by catechism classes, Sunday school, and Youth for Christ rallies, the folds of David must have struck Seattle area parents as being no kind of church to which they wanted to send their kids (figure 7.2).

Following many months of generally favorable publicity, the COG had experienced a pretty bumpy couple of months. But as the negative media drumbeat picked up in Seattle and across the nation, the COG's leader prepared a counterplan that

FIGURE 7.2 COG Bible teacher Joel leads a study at former Jesus People Army camp in Burlington, Washington in fall 1971.

Used with permission, AP/Wide World Photos.

would help his followers escape the "upcoming persecution." The matter of troubled parents was really proving to be a problem for the COG, so it fought back in three ways. First, hoping to force FREECOG to back down, they filed a $1.1 million libel suit against their accusers.[76] Second, in an attempt to create some positive publicity, they formed their own small group of pro-COG parents called "THANKCOG," led by Houston businessman M. I. DuPuy, whose son, Rick, was one of the COG's upper-tier leadership.[77] Berg struck an even more positive third note, however, in mid-November as he told his leaders to instruct everyone to contact their families and tell them they would be coming home over either the Thanksgiving or Christmas holidays. In a Mo Letter dated November 21, Berg argued this was a chance to "prove we do not hypnotise, drug, kidnap, nor coerce" converts. He urged all local colonies to call their "local news media, TV, radio, and newspapers and tell them...they are welcome to come out and watch the young people while they phone their parents...or to even film them as they board various means of transportation to return home."[78] In a follow-up letter two days later, he revealed that besides providing some positive PR, this would also accomplish another valuable task: the elimination of all "the fearful, half-hearted, slothful and undetermined" within COG ranks.[79]

The news was indeed treated as a positive development, and over the next few days, wire service photos showed smiling COG members on the phone as others queued up to call their families as instructed. Over the holidays, COG members headed home, some flying back with tickets paid for by grateful parents, others heading to the interstate and hitchhiking.[80] Behind the scenes, the COG seemed to have prepared their young followers for the return home. As Maacha, a nineteen-year-old girl at the COG communal house in Hayward, California, commented to a reporter, she was looking at it as "a journey of faith...a test of our faith in God." To her mind, it was another opportunity "to take the message to my parents and to my brothers and sisters."[81]

Even Linda Meissner emerged from the old Jesus People Army–COG headquarters in Washington Hall to reunite with her husband and five stepchildren for the Thanksgiving holiday. Making her husband promise not to talk about the COG, they had an idyllic family holiday, dining at Salvesen's parents' house on one of Puget Sound's islands. Salvesen recalled that they left the kids with his parents, returned to the mainland, and spent the rest of the weekend at their house in Seattle. As far as he could tell, things were going well, commenting that "she was just as wifely as can be." After the weekend, he dropped her back at Washington Hall. Soon thereafter, Deborah Berg packed Meissner off on a plane bound for a new COG base in London. A divorce followed (at Salvesen's insistence), and a decade would pass before he saw her again.[82]

When all was said and done, the home visit gamble seemed to have paid off for the COG leadership. The overwhelming majority passed their test and dutifully returned—often with some extra cash, personal belongings, documents, and passports in hand. This last item would prove particularly useful. By early 1972, Berg had been warned by his son-in-law Jethro and daughter Deborah that NBC news was gearing up for a major exposé on the COG. Veteran NBC producer Bob Rogers felt "burnt" by his earlier positive coverage of the group on *First Tuesday* in the wake of all the bad publicity the COG had been receiving and rumors he heard of sexual immorality among its leadership. Now Rogers was preparing to strike back with a two-hour retraction for NBC's new *Chronolog* program that would reveal Berg's role as leader and prophet and feature interviews with former members, FREECOG spokesmen, and secular and ecclesiastical critics.[83]

Feeling the heat, Berg quickly began to roll out a new vision for his organization that would help them melt away into the underground. Inspired by study of the gypsies, he was intent on decentralizing, shrinking, and dispersing COG colonies across the map and, particularly, moving them overseas. The group's geographic profile changed within a few short months, aided by a string of new Mo Letters that foretold God's coming judgment on the church and America. By the fall of 1972, more than half the roughly 2,300 members COG officially claimed had relocated to small colonies scattered outside the United States, Mexico, the Caribbean, continental Europe, and the British Isles.[84]

As for Berg, he would follow soon enough. Recalling the period in a 1991 Mo Letter, he wrote: "Mama [Karen Zerby—Maria] and I needed to leave the country before that 'Chronolog' show came on, so we did! We packed and did our forsake all, kissed most of our stuff goodbye and left it all in the [camper], except for our personal clothes."[85] Where would they flee? He and Maria had spent a fair amount of time during 1970 and early 1971 in London and found much to recommend it as a haven from God's coming judgment on the United States. On April 17, 1972, Berg and Maria arrived at Heathrow. Styling themselves as a retired American businessman living with his daughter, they moved into a prim brick bungalow and began to direct COG's worldwide operations from suburban south London.[86]

The COG and the Battle for Britain

At that point, Britain was looking like an especially fruitful venue for the COG. By September 1971, the COG, with Faith and Hosea at the helm, had already established a headquarters and a publication division in Bromley, South London, with workers hitting the streets of the metropolis with their literature and picking up new disciples. Kenneth Frampton, a successful evangelical real estate developer pleased by the group's positive influence on his wayward sons Keith and David ("Samson" and "Micaiah"), encouraged the group to invite more of their people to Britain and gave them four properties in South London to use.[87]

Among those who eventually landed in London were David Hoyt and his family. Amid the chaos of what had been happening in the Pacific Northwest—including a hepatitis breakout at the COG-commandeered JPA camp in Burlington, Washington, where they had been staying—Hoyt had successfully cajoled COG leadership into giving him a vehicle so he could move his family to healthier surroundings. Hoyt headed to Northern California, hoping to spend time with old Jesus People associates who could help him sort out his future direction. But amid the hysteria surrounding the Children of God, old friends were now suspicious of him and his motives, fearing he was the advance guard of a COG takeover. The Hoyts were grudgingly taken in by friends at his old Upper Streams house in Walnut Creek, and quickly a group of COG leaders tracked him there and spooked his old Jesus People associates. Although Hoyt was able to shoo them away, they followed up with a barrage of apologetic phone calls, laying out new opportunities for a fresh start and a bold evangelistic ministry in London. The reassurances coming from the Children once again proved too inviting to resist. Within a few weeks, the Hoyts were on their way to England.[88]

As the growing COG migration from the United States shifted the geographic center of the group, another major change had begun in terms of Berg's relationship to rank-and-file COG members. Whereas for nearly two years he had been a shadowy figure, in a Mo Letter dated February 21, 1972, Berg made his special status clear to the entire membership for the first time, telling them that "to ignore the Word of the Lord through His Prophet [was] to ignore the Voice of God Himself."[89] All COG members were now expected to supplement their daily Bible reading and meditation and "have an appointment with [Mo] every day" through his letters. The alternative, of course, was to risk the Lord's displeasure:

> God made me your shepherd!—And you had better follow, or you're going to miss God and His Will!...As throughout all time, God has always required His people to follow and obey His chosen Mouthpiece, His Prophet, His man of God....Those who rejected God's leadership through His anointed ones fell by the wayside, or were destroyed! But those who believed, followed and obeyed, were blessed of the Lord, prospered, were protected and provided for, and reached their goal—God's goal![90]

Berg went on to assure his followers that they were part of God's plan, the "Jesus Revolution," and that he was its leader. "I did not start the Jesus Revolution: but Jesus did—through me!" he claimed, arguing that "Before [the COG]...there were no Jesus People." He went on to condemn evangelical youth evangelists of prior eras who he argued were trying to jump on the Jesus People bandwagon. David Wilkerson, "the Saviour of the juvenile gangs of New York City and the Beatniks of yesterday," was condemned for denouncing hippies in general, and the COG in particular, in his 1969 book *Purple Violet Squish*. And although Billy Graham—the old Youth for Christ apostle to the bobby-soxers—was credited with being "more charitable toward the long hairs," he likewise came up short as a mover and shaker in the Jesus movement because "he had nothing better to offer them after Christ but the dead stinking, body of a decaying Church System!"[91]

These new revelations were elaborated on in the next few Mo Letters, and by all indications, these stunning pronouncements appear to have been largely accepted. There is no evidence of any major rebellions or mass defections in the wake of the introduction of the new teachings.[92] However, for one relatively new disciple, Berg's pronouncements apparently reinforced misgivings that had already been plaguing him.

From the moment he set foot in England, David Hoyt claimed, he sensed that things just were not right with the COG. Reminiscing years later, Hoyt wrote:

> I'd hoped things would be different here in England, but...I knew something was drastically wrong....In worship, the yelling of short radical slogans continued along with an over-emphasis of certain pet doctrines. Added to these old things that bothered me, more time was now given to reading letters from David Berg, the movement's emerging prophet....In these letters he presented himself as God's special end-time prophet....I could hear and see the error and self-glorification woven throughout. This was [the] hardest evidence I'd had to date and the most alarming....[93]

Hoyt decided to clear things up, and in early June 1972, he wrote a letter directly to Berg to air his concerns. Berg, condemning Hoyt later that year in a Mo Letter, viewed his concerns as less theological than personal, contending that Hoyt's real desire was a larger leadership role with an eye to supplanting Hosea Berg as editor of the COG's now London-based *New Improved Truth*. Whatever the exact nature of the dispute, Berg's response came several days later when two COG leaders called Hoyt on the carpet and demanded he write a letter of apology. Hoyt refused and fought with his wife about leaving. A few days later, he returned to their room to find her gone, the door's lock removed, and two guards standing outside his door. He alleged that he was awakened at midnight by COG leaders who gave him a "last chance" to recant. Upon his refusal, they left, only to return to whisk him away to a tribunal before a larger group of leaders, where he was accused of insubordination. A long, blistering letter from Berg himself that accused Hoyt of being demon-possessed was read. Unwilling to go along with Berg's assessment, he was sent back to his quarters.[94]

A few hours later, after rounding up his passport and a few other items, Hoyt crept silently out of the building in the early morning light. When his departure was discovered, the COG lost little time in sounding the alarm, including an "Emergency Notice" Mo Letter issued on June 12, 1972. In the letter, Berg warned all COG colonies of the "departure and defection of one of our former brethren...affectionately known to us all as David H. Judah, a former Jesus People leader." Berg explained that although he had recognized his talent and zeal, the "Lord warned" him that Hoyt was "weak both physically and mentally due to his years of past experience with drugs, demons, demonic religions, and incarceration" and, if under too much pressure, was headed for "a nervous breakdown." Berg put all colonies in North America and Europe on alert for Hoyt's possible sudden appearance "looking for help, asylum, or division" and warned them not to allow anyone to "be deceived by him, associate with him, or receive him, or allow him to associate with any of our sheep, as he has at least temporarily turned traitor to the cause! Just pray for him!"[95]

But Hoyt actually stuck close to the London colony, trying to get the local police interested in helping him extract his wife and children while he lodged with a sympathetic evangelical restaurateur. Although these efforts were frustrated (in a 1979 Mo Letter, Berg would contend that the COG's efforts to hide Victoria Hoyt and her children had been inspired not by Hoyt's disputes with COG leaders, but by the need to protect her and her children from an abusive husband's violent temper), his new friend introduced him to someone he thought would find his story of vital interest: Kenneth Frampton. The English real estate magnate had been displeased with the contents of the new Mo Letters that had come his way. Now, once again concerned about his two sons, Frampton was eager to meet with Hoyt and hear his story. After a few meetings, Hoyt's take on the COG, along with a steadily growing pile of negative information and unsatisfactory responses from COG's British headquarters, convinced Frampton that they were a dangerous cult. He cut off all financial support, issued orders for them to vacate his property, and personally wrote a pamphlet titled *Beware the Children of God*.[96]

In response to Frampton's warnings, in early September 1972 the British Evangelical Alliance sponsored a press conference in London to call attention to the COG. Gordon Landreth of the Alliance offered his organization's help to any parents wanting to contact or rescue their offspring from the group.[97] Also at the meeting was Russ Griggs, the former Vancouver Jesus People Army leader who had, along with his wife, only recently fled the COG in Texas. In subsequent conversations with Frampton about his experiences, Griggs advised him that the best way "to battle the inauthentic [the COG] was with the real thing"—the Jesus People. And Griggs told Frampton he knew of a "real" group of Jesus People who were within relatively close proximity of England.[98]

The Jesus Family Comes to Britain

Since the meeting in early 1972 at which the Milwaukee Jesus People group divided into four separate units, Jim Palosaari's band—The Jesus Family, they were now calling it—of twenty-plus had been roaming around Europe and holding meetings and impromptu concerts. For the first couple of months, the group had been sponsored in Scandinavia by the FGBMF. The group was especially well received in Finland because of Palosaari's Finnish heritage, becoming a short-lived rage, receiving coverage in the papers, and appearing on state-owned TV and radio.[99] Its band, the Sheep, even cut an album—*Jeesus Rock*—which included Finnish versions of songs such as the Edwin Hawkins Singers' 1969 hit "Oh Happy Day" and "A Mighty Fortress Is Our God" ("Jumale Ompi Linnamme").[100]

But when their scheduled support from the FGBMF ended, they made a decision to stay in Europe to see if they could duplicate their Scandinavian success and trigger a European Jesus movement. For seven months, the group wandered around Europe, eking out a hand-to-mouth existence, their best bit of fortune coming in the form of the free use of an ex-brothel near the U.S. Air Force base at Lautzenhausen, near Frankfurt in West Germany. For the sake of their mission, however, they elected to turn their backs on their toiletless facilities and the free outdated K-rations they received from evangelical friends at the base, and they continued their travels. Eventually, they ended up in Holland, with the Sheep getting an occasional gig playing in local bars. By this point, the group had added a few souls to their number, making it all the harder to provide the wherewithal to adequately feed and clothe themselves.[101]

By the end of October 1972, the group was penniless and underfed and decided to sell the Sheep's drum kit to a band they had met back in Lautzenhausen. They planned to use the money to buy food for the group and airline tickets for Palosaari and his family, who would then fly back to the United States and figure out how to get the rest of them home. After dispatching a trio to go back to Germany, the rest continued to pray that God would deliver them. Discouraged and hopelessly homesick, Palosaari recalled in a 2002 interview that the group was huddled together in their quarters, having used their last money to buy *pommes frites*, and watching an old episode of *Gunsmoke* dubbed in Dutch, when their drum sales team returned from Lautzenhausen. According to Palosaari, the group had been unsuccessful in selling the drum kit but told him they had picked up a telegram for the former Milwaukee leader that had been sitting for a few days at the base. Puzzled as to who possibly could have sent him a telegram, Palosaari opened the envelope and found a message from Kenneth Frampton that contained seven words: "Come to England. Posthaste. Money no object."[102]

Delivered in the nick of time, the Jesus Family gathered in London and, after a few days of room service in a posh London hotel footed by Frampton's Deo Gloria Trust, set up two communal houses in Beulah Hill and Bromley and a coffeehouse—the Living Room—in the Upper Norwood section of South London. Within a short time, they had nearly doubled their number to about sixty (now including David Hoyt) and were printing their own newspaper, *Everyman*.[103] A particularly momentous event was a gift of £40,000 from Frampton's trust to back a musical put together by Palosaari's Jesus Family. Initially a series of narrated concerts about the Jesus People movement called *The Story of How the Jesus People Came Alive*, it was performed informally in and around London in the spring of 1973. Slowly, the presentation transmogrified into a full-blown multimedia show along the lines of *Godspell*, telling the story of hippies in 1967 San Francisco who struggle through the various drugs and fads of the Summer of Love, only to have one of their number accept Jesus as Lord and Savior and eventually win over his peers. The play was called *Lonesome Stone*, and Frampton rented out one of Britain's premier rock music venues, the Rainbow Theater in London for the summer of 1973.[104]

Lonesome Stone was heavily publicized: Ads appeared in the newspapers, a specially decorated bus plugged the show, and the members of the Jesus Family blanketed the city with flyers. Palosaari recalls that audiences reacted pretty well but that the London theater critics, jaded now on biblical musicals in the wake of *Jesus Christ Superstar*, *Godspell*, and *Joseph and the Amazing Technicolor Dreamcoat*, wanted none of it.[105] Certainly, the critics didn't help their cause. *Time Out*, London's hip guide to nightlife, opined that the play reminded them of "a joint effort by the CIA and Moral Re-Armament."[106] *Record and Radio Mirror*'s faith-friendly rock critic, Tony Jasper, was underwhelmed by the story line, music, and performances: "Right shocker this...*Lonesome Stone*. There's no story, hardly any worthwhile songs and some very amateur acting."[107] For Michael Jacob in the

Church of England Newspaper, the musical failed because it was not an up-to-date comment on the androgynous, British glam-rock "youth culture of today" that had emerged in the previous two years and, like the tract handed to patrons on the way out, "largely old-fashioned" and not the sort of thing to make for "a meaningful experience for 1973."[108] Even London's youth culture-attuned Christian paper *Buzz* (an effort of the youth-based Musical Gospel Outreach group) invited anyone who actually liked the show to write in, name a West End show they had seen in the prior year, and include a certificate of sanity.[109] Following a three-month run, the JPF shut the show down, reworked it, and took it on the road. Tweaked and now well-rehearsed, *Lonesome Stone* moved away from the cosmopolitan confines of London and apparently went down considerably better with audiences in the outlying districts of England, Wales, and Scotland in the fall and early winter of 1973. A critic for *The Star* in Sheffield noted that the show "rocked into Sheffield singing a song of love and peace.... It was one of those shows that made you want to join in."[110] Another reviewer who saw the show in Manchester in November remarked that the play managed to charm him in spite of its gospel-heavy theme: "Ignoring the religious overtones and 'the message'—and I did—'*Lonesome Stone*' was very enjoyable. A collection of good songs gutsily presented by an incredibly enthusiastic cast won me over."[111]

Despite the splash made by Palosaari's Jesus Family, their presence and major efforts like *Lonesome Stone* hardly constituted the death knell of the British COG operation. Much more serious was a new wave of negative British-based criticism. Beginning with the Evangelical Alliance's September 1972 press conference, the COG became the targets of a great deal of negative publicity in the British media. The first major blow came with a two-part story, "The Shocking Truth about the Children of God," printed in the Sunday edition of the London paper *People.* An undercover reporter had feigned joining the COG and lived in one of their homes for a couple of weeks. His report emphasized the authoritarian structure of the group, its secrecy, the rampant criticism of church and parents, and excerpts from Mo Letters that showed Berg's claims to be the End Time prophet and final authority.[112] News stories on the COG soon followed in the *London Times* and the *Daily Telegraph,* while *Home Words,* an Anglican magazine, featured excerpts from the *People* articles and Frampton's anti-COG pamphlet.[113] The coup de grace came with a BBC News documentary that was largely footage from the dreaded spring 1972 NBC *Chronolog* retraction of its original *First Tuesday* coverage of the COG. Along with interviews of Frampton, Hoyt, and others, the British version had additional interviews with COG leaders (Berg was "unavailable"), but within the larger context of the program, they came off looking bad.[114]

Although bad PR was serious enough a problem for the COG, the growth of interest in the group by the British authorities was even worse. John Hunt, Conservative MP for Bromley, urged the Home Secretary to begin deportation proceedings on all COG leaders. The Home Office ruled that while the "way of life" of the COG "may be unorthodox," local authorities had found no evidence that they had "been guilty of any breach of the criminal law" and thus Hunt's charges were not actionable. However, the Home Office noted that it would keep the matter under review.[115]

The intensifying scrutiny of the British media and the real possibility of greater government surveillance were signals to Berg that the British Isles would not long serve as an alternative home base for the COG. Although the COG would retain a presence in Britain from early 1973 onward, there was a gradual shift of operations to the Continent and elsewhere. As in America, the COG would be cut out of the picture of what constituted the much smaller British Jesus People movement, which aligned with the nation's evangelical Anglican and nonconformist churches. Groups like Palosaari's Jesus Family and the indigenous Jesus Liberation Front north of London became the major flag bearers of the movement.[116]

Although the British Jesus People movement—unlike its American counterpart—never struck deep into the British equivalent of what was left of the counterculture or into the ranks of secularized youth, it did serve as a rallying point for that nation's evangelical church youth in a very similar fashion as it had stateside. New Christian rock music, J-E-S-U-S cheers, and Jesus stickers became part of many British evangelical adolescents' coming of age in the early to mid-1970s. Not surprisingly, the British Jesus People movement was greatly influenced by the American movement—both its indigenous figures and its evangelical backers. Visits by Jesus rocker Larry Norman, who linked up with British figures such as Garth Hewitt and pop legend Cliff Richard, played out in giant rallies and concerts sponsored by both British evangelical youth organizations (the London Festival for Jesus, September 1972) and American parachurch organizations (Billy Graham Evangelistic Association and Campus Crusade for Christ Spree '73, August 1973). In August 1974, Jim Palosaari's Jesus Family revived *Lonesome Stone* as the centerpiece for a series of concerts and lectures for a festival held at a pig farm near Charsfield, Suffolk, that attracted a crowd of about 2,000. In the years that followed, this festival became the Greenbelt Festival, Britain's largest annual Christian music and cultural gathering, which often attracted between 20,000 and 30,000 people.[117]

Conclusion

By the summer of 1973, the battle for the definition of the Jesus People movement had been won by the mainstream groups identified with the larger evangelical churches and parachurch organizations. The wave of negative publicity had effectively discredited and outflanked the Children of God, having largely succeeded in painting them as a group with unorthodox and disturbingly authoritarian tendencies. However, the impact of the COG episode on the Jesus movement, the evangelical church, and the wider culture was not to be limited to that one-time face-off with David "Moses" Berg and his radical young followers. The lessons and fears that emerged during the COG scare would be magnified and broadly applied both within and outside the movement. Moreover, for the Jesus People movement itself and for the wider perception of new religious movements among American youth, the bloom was officially off the rose—the specter of cultic mind control, brainwashing, and fanatical followers had been combined with youth in the public imagination in a way it had never been before.

For the Jesus People, the COG episode revealed just how inexperienced many of its leaders were and how thin the theological and biblical knowledge of many of its rank-and-file devotees. Within the movement and the larger evangelical church, there was a growing realization that converts needed a better grip on the Scriptures and basic theological orthodoxy before being unleashed to evangelize the world. John Bisagno, pastor of Houston's huge First Baptist Church, which had reaped a significant harvest among area youth in Houston and in meetings in other Southern and Southwestern cities because of the Jesus People movement, gave voice to these concerns when he wrote in late 1971:

> Unless the church can latch onto the Jesus movement and keep it doctrin-
> ally straight, we are going to miss the greatest opportunity that we've ever
> had.... We had better accept these kids and get hold of them and indoctri-
> nate them. If we do not, we'll not only miss a great chance for real revival
> but we will also by our negligence contribute to the spawning of a lot of
> new heresies and cults out of this as these kids make up their own rules.[18]

Organizational evangelicalism provided a great deal of help for this effort. A flood of new discipleship aids—study Bibles, devotionals, Scripture memorization packets, and other items—specifically targeted young people and especially the ranks of the Jesus movement. Although the production of such materials was hardly unexpected, its acceleration in 1972 and afterward was evidence of a changing mind-set within evangelical circles. No longer was the wider evangelical culture content just to celebrate and publicize the fact of the Jesus People. They realized that to keep control of the movement and make sure its legions of teens did not wander off after their own peculiar notions or those implanted by a David Berg sort of figure, teens would need more thoroughgoing training.

One attempt to provide this training came in the form of the Shepherding movement. Originally created in 1969 as the brainchild of a group of charismatic ministers and evangelists—Bob Mumford, Derek Prince, Ern Baxter, Don Basham, and Charles Simpson—the movement (Holy Spirit Teaching Ministries and a magazine, *New Wine*) was originally developed with an eye to helping shore up the doctrinal and biblical understanding of the tens of thousands of independent charismatic Christians coming out of the ranks of mainline Protestant and Catholic churches. But the leaders of the Fort Lauderdale–based movement quickly came to see the ranks of the burgeoning Jesus movement as in need of their guiding hand. In the wake of the COG scare, many influential Jesus People figures such as Lonnie Frisbee and Scott Ross began to see the Shepherding movement, with its emphasis on a prolonged period of discipleship coupled with strict lines of authority, as a necessary safeguard for their ministries. Between 1972 and 1975, a number of Jesus People groups and fellowships across the country came under the direct authority or indirect influence of the Shepherding movement.[119]

But as they determined to hew more closely to orthodoxy and prop up their theology, the Jesus People also began to step up their own attempts to learn about and fight their competition in the youth culture's religious marketplace. From mid-1971 forward, important Jesus People papers such as Denver's *End Times*, the CWLF's *Right On!* and Chicago's *Cornerstone* were more likely to feature extensive, well-researched exposés, polemical articles, and apologetic defenses of the evangelical version of the Christian faith against groups and religions ranging from Roman Catholicism to Transcendental Meditation (TM) and from the Witness Lee Local Church to Guru Maharaj Ji's Divine Light Mission.[120] One of the most important of these efforts grew out of the work of the CWLF with the founding of the Spiritual Counterfeits Project (SCP) in 1973. Tackling a wide variety of groups, religions, and philosophies in its *SCP Newsletter* and, in 1977, its *SCP Journal*, the organization quickly became a resource for the wider evangelical community on groups with roots in evangelical religion such as the Way International, the Alamo Foundation, and Sun Myung Moon's Unification Church, as well as more exotic religious groups ranging from Buddhism to UFO cults to Scientology.[121]

The SCP became part of a larger evangelical obsession with anticult teachings and Christian apologetics that emerged during the 1970s and 1980s. Along with prominent mainstream evangelical apologists such as Walter Martin and Josh McDowell, the SCP would join in a veritable evangelical crusade to define orthodoxy and battle theological error at the grassroots level.[122] Coupled with a burgeoning body of literature aimed at exposing occult and demonic activity in America, the anticult writings signaled an unprecedented fixation within evangelical ranks on doing spiritual warfare against "the other" and protecting the faithful from their depredations.[123]

The anticult paranoia within the evangelical subculture—given a new burst of life by the Jesus People's dustup with the COG—was not limited to the born again, however. As the 1970s progressed, there was a noticeable increase in a culture-wide suspicion of new religious groups, particularly those that attracted a youthful following. Not only the COG but also groups like the Unification Church, TM, and the followers of Osho (the Bhagwan Sri Rajneesh) were subjected to extensive

media scrutiny, academic study, and—in several instances—increasing harassment from local, state, and federal authorities.[124] Deprogramming became a growing phenomenon, used even against members of groups widely considered okay
in Jesus People circles, as an increasing number of distraught parents recruited
Ted Patrick and others to rescue their loved ones; it subsided only when many
groups and "rescues" fought back in the courts and appealed to basic personal
liberty and religious freedom.[125] Eventually, the tragic mass suicide of more than
900 people at Jim Jones's People's Temple in Guyana in late 1978 would produce
a fresh burst of anticult fervor that lasted into the early 1980s.[126]

Meanwhile, the Children of God, the group that had been the focus of the
original controversy, nearly faded from view in the United States. They continued to appear periodically in the public spotlight, with a trail of increasingly lurid
news stories about internal developments—sexual sharing among the faithful,
the implementation of Flirty Fishing evangelism (young women used as bait for
evangelizing potential male converts), accusations of incest and child molestation,
and news of arrests and attempted prosecutions—appearing in the American and
foreign media from the late 1970s on, past the 1994 death of David "Moses" Berg
and into the twenty-first century.[127] Meanwhile, American academics exploring
new religious movements (NRMs)—a new subfield within religious studies and
the social sciences—made the COG (known as "The Family of Love" or just "The
Family" by the late 1970s) one of the most studied religious movements since the
World War II cargo cults of Micronesia.[128] In the process, these scholars would be
swept up into the battles between those who attacked and those who defended the
COG. Ironically, having been pushed out of the mainstream Jesus People movement years before, the COG/Family would outlive its much larger victorious counterpart by decades.

8

Sweet, Sweet Song of Salvation

MUSIC AND THE JESUS PEOPLE MOVEMENT

FROM THE BEGINNING, music was an integral part of the Jesus People movement's message and appeal. In fact, it is hard to imagine a Jesus movement without there having been Jesus music. Whether a home Bible study, a worship gathering at a commune or local fellowship, the Friday night program at a coffeehouse, or an outdoor festival attracting thousands, Jesus music was a prominent—and frequently the central—feature. As *Time* magazine's July 1971 cover story on the movement stated, "Music, the lingua franca of the young," was the "special medium of the Jesus movement."[1] Hiley Ward, the religion editor of the *Detroit Free Press*, spent several months in 1970 and 1971 visiting hundreds of Jesus People communes and coffeehouses scattered throughout North America. Ward noted the "preoccupation of the Jesus People with new music.... Rarely do you hear any of the old-time hymns." Ward observed, "[The Jesus People] write their own."[2] His observations were echoed by John A. Cerrato Jr., a Baptist pastor in Woodlyn, Pennsylvania, just outside of Philadelphia. Speaking to a local reporter in 1972 about the Jesus People of his acquaintance, he noted that coming up with new music was one of their central pastimes: "They write their own songs like mad."[3]

Given the centrality of music for the Jesus People, the movement's emergence came at an opportune time in terms of the musical trajectory of American evangelicalism, just as more upbeat, youth-friendly musical forms had begun to make some inroads into the subculture during the '60s. However, it would be the Jesus People themselves who would prove the most revolutionary musical force within much of the evangelical subculture, drawing upon rock, pop, and folk music to create their own body of Jesus music, which they used as an evangelistic tool, to enhance their worship, and as a form of sanctified musical entertainment. This baptized version of popular music provided a common ground within the movement, serving as a vehicle for its expansion to churched youth outside the movement and as a potential bridge between the Jesus People and their unredeemed peers in the world. As the movement spread across the country and gained a more solid footing, it promoted not only the emergence of more musicians playing for a growing audience but also an expanding infrastructure of local venues, homegrown promoters, and a rough-hewn recording and distribution industry that in its early days placed more emphasis on evangelism and discipleship than on marketing and sales.

Soon, however, the marketing potential of the new Jesus generation began to move Jesus music away from its informal, countercultural roots toward the trappings and business practices of the mainstream music and entertainment industries. Although it was still but a shadow of big-time rock 'n' roll, by the mid-1970s, recording contracts, improved production values, better distribution and packaging, large Jesus music festivals, and a tiny but increasing amount of radio airplay all contributed to a growing professionalization and corporate control over a formerly casual, homegrown element of Jesus freak life. But even as Jesus music changed, it provided the foundations for significant musical change within the evangelical subculture through its development of praise music and its creation of Contemporary Christian Music (CCM), the latter of which would prove a linchpin for emerging evangelical youth cultures into the early 21st-century.

The Emergence of a New, Contemporary Evangelical Music

The rise of Jesus rock in the late 1960s was not something that many observers could have envisioned—evangelicals had been in the forefront of rock 'n' roll's homegrown American critics during the 1950s. Typical of the resistance in evangelical quarters was an article by Marlin "Butch" Hardman, a YFC leader from Indiana in the *Youth for Christ* magazine in October 1958. Hardman put the matter bluntly: Rock music "had a decided physical effect...which is hardly in line with the Word of God." It was clear that "no Christian fellow or girl who really love[d] Rock 'n' Roll [could] be an effective witness for Christ. You [could not] mix oil and water, nor [could] you mix a living testimony for Christ and the driving beat...of Rock 'n' Roll." Obviously, much of the concern here was about teens—overheated by the raw, animalistic passions of rock—engaging in sexual behavior. As Hardman hinted, "What you do *after* [emphasis his] you listen to Rock 'n' Roll is the direct result of the music itself."[4] No more authoritative voice than Billy Graham himself summed up the case against rock 'n' roll for evangelical teens, writing in 1960: "If I were 17 today I'd stay as far away from it as I could."[5]

Nonetheless, music that was more appealing to young people made inroads into many conservative Protestant churches during the 1960s. Evangelical musicians, composers, and youth leaders were actively seeking sounds that would appeal to the younger generation. One of the major innovators in this regard was Ralph Carmichael, Hollywood-based composer and arranger who had worked with many mainstream band leaders (Stan Kenton, for instance) and singers (Frank Sinatra, Nat King Cole, and Andy Williams).[6] A Midwesterner raised in the Assemblies of God, he remained a devout evangelical layman and brought his ideas about commercial music to religious music as well. Carmichael stirred up controversy within conservative Protestant circles during the late 1950s and early 1960s with lush orchestral arrangements and the inclusion of guitars in his recorded versions of traditional hymns.[7] However, his compositions and arrangements actually fit in well with the developing tastes of older evangelicals who, through radio and television, were increasingly being exposed to the popular musical styles and settings used in the entertainment industry. As a result, Carmichael became a well-regarded source of new inspirational sacred music; particularly groundbreaking was the pop- and jazz-influenced music he composed for the successful 1965 Billy Graham drama, *The Restless Ones.*[8]

While Carmichael brought the influence of mainstream pop music sensibilities to evangelical circles, musical troupe leaders such as Cam Floria and Thurlow Spurr were being influenced not only by pop music but also by the late '50s and early '60s popularity of folk music. Mirroring folk groups like the New Christy Minstrels and Up with People, groups of well-scrubbed, fresh-faced evangelical youth like Florio's Continental Singers and Spurr's Spurlows toured evangelical churches playing a style of music that was in equal parts sacred, folk, and Hollywood/Broadway.[9] For many congregations, exposure to such groups was a first step to going beyond the bounds of traditional hymnody and gospel songs within a church setting.

In the late 1960s, these various trends combined in a spate of new youth-oriented folk musicals that took evangelical churches by storm. A Texas-based Southern Baptist youth choir director, Billy Ray Hearn, with composers Carmichael and Kurt Kaiser—authors of a popular new folky-sounding song, "Pass It On"—collaborated on the musical *Good News*, which debuted at national Southern Baptist youth gatherings in North Carolina and New Mexico in 1967. It was later performed by a 1,300-member youth ensemble for the SBC's 1968 national convention in Houston and shortly thereafter shown on the SBC's national Sunday morning program on network television. Released as a $2.98 musical portfolio, *Good News* went on to sell more than 250,000 booklets to church youth groups and choirs across the country, in the process starting a new fad of youth-flavored gospel musicals that would become a commonplace of church life in the 1970s.[10]

Energized by the success of *Good News*, Carmichael and Kaiser set to work on another folk musical. The result, *Tell It Like It Is*, was released in early 1970 as a record album and music portfolio and quickly became even more successful than its predecessor, eventually selling more than 500,000 copies of the musical portfolio.[11] *Tell It Like It Is* was but the most prominent of many musicals produced during the next few years, including Carmichael and Kaiser's *Natural High*, Otis Skilling's *Life and Love*, and Jimmy and Carol Owens's *If My People* and *The Witness.*[12]

By the mid-1960s, a small but growing cadre of folk-influenced evangelical musical performers and groups began to emerge. Groups modeled on Peter, Paul, and Mary and the New Christy Minstrels, as well as churchly versions of folk-singers like Joan Baez and Tom Paxton, performed folk hymns, spirituals, and original compositions for church youth groups and local denominational meet-ings. Evangelical youth organizations soon got in on the act, sponsoring their own, more polished touring singers, like Campus Crusade's New Folk group, which appeared at regional rallies and conventions.[13] By the late 1960s, a trickle of record albums—cheaply produced and often self-released—emanated from such groups as the Spurlows and the Continental Singers and solo acts like Wheaton College graduate John Fischer of Palo Alto, California, and Ohioan Gene Cotton (signed by Benson Records after the label's president heard him sing at a United Methodist youth convention in Tennessee). However, the limited circulation of these records—available via direct sales at youth rallies, church appearances, and a portion of the less hidebound Christian bookstores—meant that the vast major-ity of evangelical church youth had little or no recorded access to the new music.

Rock 'n' Roll in the Service of the Gospel?

Toward the end of the 1960s, as evangelicalism slowly warmed to the idea of a mainstream pop sound as a potentially tolerable supplement to its youth outreach, a few daring mavericks made halting attempts to harness the raucous sounds of secular rock 'n' roll for the service of the old-time gospel. Such attempts were rare and well off the beaten path of mainstream evangelical parachurch work and local congregational life. However, their very existence demonstrated an emerg-ing willingness to consider musical forms as a neutral venue for communicating religious truth.

One of the most startling examples of mainstream rock music as a vehicle for evangelism was hatched in Florida toward the end of the 1960s by Lowell Lytle, a native of Jackson, Michigan. A musician, former YFC worker, and sometime gospel magician and ventriloquist from a fundametalist Baptist background, Lytle had a great deal of experience in thinking outside the usual evangelistic boxes. Along with his brother Terry, he had been involved for several years with a pair of Christian drive-in movie theaters in Manitou Beach, Michigan, and Clearwater, Florida. In 1968, frustrated and feeling that "somehow there had to be a better way to communicate the Gospel," Lytle decided he was "going to fight fire with fire," grew his hair long, put on bellbottoms, and aimed to "go into high schools and communicate the Gospel." Putting together a small combo specializing in popular soul hits, he offered free assemblies to local high schools in exchange for permis-sion to put on nighttime concerts, where his group, Free Fare, would play and he would trot out his ventriloquist dummy, perform skits, and share the gospel.[14]

In late 1969 and early 1970, Lytle decided to expand his effort and stepped back into a managerial role, forming an organization called Young American Showcase. Recruiting enough earnest young Christian musicians to staff four versions of Free Fare, Lytle brought them to Florida for a six-week show business boot camp. Lytle insisted that the Free Fare bands not advertise their Christianity. "I would not play 'Jesus Music,'" he remembered. "I would never let the fellows wear Scripture verses on their guitar cases or crosses around their necks," lest it send mixed messages about their mandate to "play Top 40 music."[15]

The formula worked well. Singer Gene Cotton had first come across Lytle and his original unit at a high school assembly in Bradenton, Florida. He was immediately impressed by what he saw. "They were doing all this rock 'n' roll stuff and...[wore] psychedelic clothes...the kids were just going crazy." Cotton had a band at the time (including future Petra drummer Bill Glover), and Lytle asked the group to join his new expanded Free Fare lineup.[16]

In late 1971 and early 1972, Cotton's version of Free Fare played dozens of high schools in the upper Midwest, performing more-than-credible cover versions of songs like the Doors' "Riders on the Storm," Rare Earth's "Hey Big Brother," and the Hollies' "He Ain't Heavy (He's My Brother)." Their routine followed the course Lytle had mapped out: The band would first perform in a free, all-school assembly, where they would play a few songs, perform a skit or two, and urge the kids to stay off drugs. Later that night or the next, they would charge $1 or $2 at the door for an evening concert. Near the end of the concert, a band member would give a short talk and a personal testimony of his faith in Christ, and literature would be made available to the audience.[17]

The strategy proved remarkably successful—not least for its ability in a post-*Engle v. Vitale* America to gain access to public schools with an evangelical Christian message. For more than twenty years, various versions of Free Fare and other YAS-sponsored bands under names like Freedom Jam and The Edge played at literally thousands of American middle and high schools, frequently returning time and time again. The program also proved a success financially—or was at least self-supporting. "I only charged," Lytle later recalled, "[because] I felt...if it's free it can't be worth very much"—a lesson he had learned at the Christian drive-in movie theaters. "The school...the student council," Gene Cotton remembered, "would sell the tickets and make a percentage off the show....It was not uncommon for us to gross $3,000 to $4,000 a night." While the formula helped the local student council to fund its projects, the fee provided the financial wherewithal to clothe, equip, transport, feed, and house each band as it toured for months on end.[18]

The real payoff for Lytle, his supporters, and the musicians, however, came with the response to the evening concert message. In one year alone, Lytle claimed YAS bands garnered more than 40,000 decisions for Christ at their concerts. Yet for all of their practical success, the various Free Fare bands went too far for most evangelicals, and Lytle reported that many former supporters and mentors denounced his new enterprise.[19] As a result, YAS had little visibility within the evangelical community. Its direct effect on evangelical youth culture and the developing world of Jesus music and CCM—aside from serving as a venue for future band members to improve their craft—would be limited.

Better connected to the world of evangelical parachurch and youth ministry was a young InterVarsity Christian Fellowship worker in Chicago, John Ankerberg. The Ankerberg family had a long pedigree in evangelical youth work; John's grandfather Joe had been part of Chicago evangelist Paul Rader's Worldwide Christian Couriers, and his father, Floyd, was a staff evangelist and administrator for Youth for Christ. John Ankerberg followed in their steps, starting successful Bible clubs at Prospect High School in suburban Mount Prospect and then at Wright Junior College in Chicago. As a junior, he transferred to the University of Illinois's Chicago Circle campus and became the president of its InterVarsity chapter.[20]

In 1968, he was approached by the Exkursions, a recently saved three-piece psychedelic blues band featuring a young Pentecostal—guitarist Mike Johnson—who had previously worked in local bars with Chicago blues legend Mike Bloomfield. The Exkursions wanted to volunteer their services for InterVarsity's efforts, and after a successful first meeting at Roosevelt University in downtown Chicago, where the band's music drained attention away from a competing Black Power rally, Ankerberg knew he was on to something. "I wasn't into rock music, I didn't even go to movies," Ankerberg later recalled, "but there was just something that clicked, I mean it was first of all the need—I had people coming out of the nightclubs and drugs and I thought, 'Why can't we use their abilities for Christ?'" It was not long before Ankerberg had utterly gotten over any potential stumbling block in the use of rock music:

> I was interested in reaching students and all I knew was we could jam any place, at any hour of the day, and I had a chance to talk to straight pagans...we first started doing "Louie, Louie"...when I would hear that it was just like singing "Just as I Am"—that was gametime...this was the start: God was going to do business....[21]

The method proved so successful that Ankerberg and the band traveled—with full support from IVCF—to nearly eighty different Midwestern campuses. After a while, they did away with flyers and passing out handbills and simply set up and "just start[ed] the music, it was like drawing bees to honey; kids flocked in from everywhere—[and] once we got 'em there we could keep them there."[22]

While Ankerberg went on to other evangelistic endeavors in 1969, the Exkursions linked up with young English IVCF evangelist John Guest for a summer-long coffeehouse effort in Virginia Beach. The campaign was successful;

the evangelist and band toured several dozen more campuses in the eastern United States during 1969 and 1970.[23] The formula remained about the same— playing a mix of mostly secular songs and a few self-penned tunes with a spiritual thrust. Johnson recalled: "We would come into town for a week doing 'teaser' concerts [followed by] one last big bash at the end of the project" that would pre- cede Guest's speaking engagement. Johnson remembers that campus audiences were receptive in part because of the novelty of what they heard: "No one had seen anything like this...we broke down the stereotype views of Christianity."[24] Guest and the Exkursions stayed together for about two years, including stints in Fort Lauderdale during its chaotic spring break season and at a youth coffeehouse associated with Billy Graham's 1969 New York Crusade.[25]

The New Jesus Music and the Southern California Jesus People Scene

The emergence of Jesus music or Jesus rock is impossible to trace to any one singer, band, or place. However, the emergence of a widespread Jesus People youth subculture in Southern California depended heavily on Christian music with a rock-friendly beat and instrumentation. The Los Angeles–area band Agape (pronounced uh-GAH-pay) was certainly one of the first Jesus rock bands, and its story was prototypical of many groups that would spring up in later years all across the country.

The band grew up around Fred Caban, a Puerto Rican teen fresh out of Azusa High School in suburban Los Angeles County who was a member of a local acid rock band looking to hit the big time. Toward the end of 1968, Caban and his bandmates were looking for places to play in Huntington Beach and accepted an offer for a free spaghetti dinner at David Berg's Lightclub Coffeehouse. Caban was unsuccessful in getting a gig, but he came away impressed with the enthusiasm he had seen there. "That was the first time," Caban later remembered, he had "ever seen Christians that were bonkers for Jesus and that made quite an impression." He walked away with a copy of the Gospel of John and a new interest in spiritual things.[26]

That night, while camping out on the beach, he prayed "to Whomever," asking if what these people had told him was true. Caban claimed that "it felt like Jesus came up to me on the beach—physically—and put his hands on me and told me that it was true and to follow him." His fellow guitarist, Jeff Newman, had a similar experience, so the next day they went back to the coffeehouse and were marched down to the ocean and baptized. Still wet from their baptism, they went back to Azusa and began telling their friends about Jesus and soon helped form the nucleus of a small group of hip Christians.[27]

At first, music played no part in Caban's new relationship with Jesus. "I had put down the guitar," he recalled, "and told God that I was not going to play anymore until He told me to pick it up and play." This lasted for about three months until mid-1969, when he believed the Lord called him to play rock 'n' roll. With Mike Jungman, a recently converted drummer, and a female bass player named Lonnie Campbell, he formed a new band they called Agape (taken from the New Testament Greek word ἀγάπη for selfless, sacrificial love). The group played for youth groups at a few churches, but their heavy sound did not go over well with the powers-that-be—several churches shut them down. Arcadia Community Church was one such venue, but there they met a youth pastor, Ron Turner, who was interested in reaching the hippie kids in the area. Joining forces, Turner became their de facto manager and began strategizing free gigs in the surrounding area.[28]

The band's modus operandi was simple and straightforward: go to some park, college campus, or side street near where the kids hung out; set up their equipment (often on a flatbed truck); start to play instrumental versions of songs like Albert King's "Born under a Bad Sign"; wait until an audience gathered; play their songs about Jesus; share their testimonies; and then Turner would give a concluding salvation rap. "We'd jam…and then boom, we'd start preaching…and they'd stick around and listen!" Caban recalled.[29] Their music was bluesy rock, and its message was simple and to the point:

> I come on behalf of the King of Kings
> Come and listen to the message that I bring;
> The message is peace and love, yeah.
> Not like the world gives,
> But which could only come from above.
> The King is Christ,
> And His death is your life.[30]

When not playing impromptu concerts at the beach or at public parks, Agape increasingly found their way to the Jesus People centers that were popping up in and around Los Angeles. Probably the most important venue they found was Hollywood Presbyterian Church's Salt Company nightclub, which had first opened up in late 1968. Although its initial musical thrust was in the more folk-oriented hootenanny style via its in-house Salt Company group and singer-guitarist Mike Barlow, the club quickly began to take a more counterculture-friendly turn as solo artists such as Dennis Agajanian, converted hippie runaway Verne Bullock (known simply as "Verne"), and bands like Agape became more involved with the weekly performances.[31] Later, the Salt Company expanded its program by sponsoring occasional concerts in Hollywood Presbyterian's main sanctuary. "The sanctuary seated 2,000," Don Williams later recalled, "[they] jammed the place out.…Kids would be lined up waiting to get in two hours before we opened up the doors."[32]

Later that year, the Salt Company program was joined by a regular series of Jesus concerts at the Hollywood Paladium hosted by Duane Pederson, publisher of the newly created *Hollywood Free Paper*. The Paladium concerts highlighted not only musical talent from the Salt Company but also a growing body of Jesus music artists from throughout Southern California—singers like Larry Norman and Randy Stonehill, as well as groups like Agape, the Dove Sounds, Harvest Flight, Morning Star, and Ron Salsbury and the J.C. Power Outlet. These concerts proved popular with both the countercultural Jesus People and church youth and were later successfully held elsewhere in the state.[33] While the Paladium concerts and the Salt Company continued as a fixture in the Southern California Jesus People scene, they were shortly surpassed by musical developments several miles to the south in suburban Orange County.

The Role of Calvary Chapel in the Emerging Jesus People Music Scene

The growing outreach to hippies at Chuck Smith's Calvary Chapel in Costa Mesa had a profound effect on shaping what came to be identified as Jesus music. Strangely, Smith made no initial attempt to cater to the musical tastes or utilize the musical aptitude of his hippie audience. John Higgins, one of the original overseers of Calvary Chapel's House of Miracles communal-living discipleship program, recalled that at first the music at Calvary Chapel was straight "out of the hymn books and it wasn't something that made you just leave and go into another world." In fact, Higgins found the music "rather boring" and admitted that he "came late sometimes just to avoid the music."[34]

But within the newly founded communal Jesus houses, something very different was taking place. "We sang every day," Higgins recalled. "People were making up new songs all the time. Some would even write lyrics to things like Coca-Cola commercials."[35] According to Higgins, the first guitars soon began to show up at Calvary Chapel, and eventually some of the communal house efforts were incorporated into the services, adding a growing contemporary flavor to the music.[36] As Smith's outreach among the hippies grew, so did the upbeat music in Calvary Chapel's worship—along with a growing stable of countercultural converts eager to use their musical talents for the Lord.

Among those attracted to Calvary Chapel were the five drug-imbibing members of a metaphysically tinged, down-on-its-luck rock band, Love Song. Its leader, Chuck Girard, was a native of Santa Rosa and a veteran studio musician and singer who had played a major part in two made-in-the-studio "surf and hot rods" bands that had scored hits in the early 1960s: the Castells and the Hondells (the latter's 45 single "Little Honda," penned by Beach Boy Brian Wilson, hit #9 in the national charts in late 1964).[37] Intrigued by the psychedelic revolution and the counterculture, Girard ended up in Las Vegas, where he met a Bible-thumping, drug-taking vocalist named Denny Correll and a self-styled hippie guru known only as "George." "We got this big intersection of Jesus, and drugs, and Bible, and Eastern philosophy...all at the same time," recalled Girard in a 2010 interview. He and several bandmates followed the guru to Hawaii and then eventually to Salt Lake City. While in Utah, Girard tried to put together a band that dabbled in weighty philosophical lyrics. After a bad LSD trip, Girard forswore psychedelics and George, moving with his band to Laguna Beach, where they rented a house, smoked grass and hashish, and got work in the L.A. recording studios.[38] But as a group, the band found no answers and little success. Bass player Jay Truax recalled: "We went into bars and everything. We had some songs about Jesus and about other things." However, the good-time patrons of these establishments were usually not impressed by the band: "We'd get kicked out...no one could even relate to us at that point."[39]

The band was living together in late 1969 when band member Fred Field ran into a Campus Crusade for Christ worker down at Huntington Beach and was converted. Hearing about the hippie preacher Lonnie Frisbee and the "great things" that were happening over at Calvary Chapel, Field pestered his bandmates into attending one of the evening services. The speaker that night was Chuck Smith (Girard was shocked to see a "straight guy"); the band was greatly impressed with his relaxed, informal talk and, in Chuck Girard's words, "the cozy and warm atmosphere." And they were also impressed with the music that was being sung. "I remember being very deeply affected by the music," remembered Girard, "and wondering why, because technically it wasn't that great...." Within two weeks, everyone in the band had undergone separate conversion experiences, and by early 1970, all were in regular attendance at Calvary Chapel.[40]

About a month after they had been baptized, Lonnie Frisbee encouraged the band to see Chuck Smith one Wednesday afternoon to tell him they had written some new songs they would like to play for him. Agreeing to hear them, Smith accompanied the band to the parking lot, where they brought out their guitars and played several songs. Smith reportedly began to weep, telling the band, in the memory of lead guitarist Tommy Coomes, he had "been praying for something like this for a year."[41] That night the soft rock, country-tinged sound of Love Song became part of Calvary Chapel, and soon they became a regular feature of Lonnie Frisbee's Bible studies.[42]

But Love Song was hardly the only band at Calvary Chapel. Converted rock 'n' roll musicians joined with musically inclined church youth to create a host of acts that filled up worship services, Bible studies, and evangelistic events. Love Song shared the bill with groups like Children of the Day, Good News, Gentle Faith, Selah, Blessed Hope, Mustard Seed Faith, The Way, and Country Faith and solo singers like Karen Lafferty, Debby Kerner, Ernie Rettino and Kenn Gulliksen.[43]

Inspired by the surfeit of musical talent at their fingertips, Smith and Frisbee decided in early 1970 that special concerts were the next logical step in their outreach to young people.[44] On a Friday evening in the spring, Calvary Chapel rented the auditorium at Milliken High School in Long Beach for the first of what would become a multiyear run of near-weekly concerts. The initial shows were a stunning success. One concert at Long Beach's Woodrow Wilson High School filled its 1,700-seat auditorium and packed another 1,000 into the school gymnasium as five bands on the program shuttled back and forth all evening. While the concerts went on inside, a local newspaper reported that an estimated 2,000 more teenagers unable to fit inside milled around outside the school. But sheer attendance was a distant second goal to the concerts' main purpose—at the end of one Love Song performance, an estimated 600 young people came forward at the invitation to accept Christ.[45] Soon, the concerts were switched to Saturday nights and moved to the giant circus tent Calvary Chapel had purchased to contain the crowds that outgrew their two-year-old, 300-seat sanctuary.[46]

Musically, the "Calvary Chapel sound" was all over the map: folk, light pop, soft rock, country. But one thing it was not was hard rock. As Chuck Smith told journalist Ed Plowman in an interview, he personally favored the term "contemporary gospel" to "rock" and was leery of music that "moves the body more than the soul."[47]

Much of what was being played and sung at Calvary Chapel was a new type of music that would later come to be called praise music, aimed at creating a corporate worship experience. This new style was an amalgamation of simple Scripture songs and choruses that were influenced by both contemporary folk music and old gospel choruses dating back to late-nineteenth-century revivalism. Another inspiration was the "singing in the Spirit" phenomenon associated with the Pentecostal and charismatic movement. John Sherrill described singing in the Spirit in his 1964 book, *They Speak with Other Tongues*:

> As the music continued, several people at the tables began to sing "in the Spirit." Soon, the whole room was singing a complicated harmony-without-score, created spontaneously. It was eerie but extraordinarily beautiful. The song leader was no longer trying to direct the music, but let the melodies create themselves: without prompting, one quarter of the room would suddenly start to sing very loudly while the other subsided. Harmonies and counter-harmonies wove in and out of each other.[48]

Love Song member Tom Coomes remembered that the simple intuitiveness of the music he heard at Calvary Chapel had impressed him on his first visit. "I knew each line even before it was sung," he recalled. "I wasn't used to simple music like this, but it blew me away! It was a music which drew people into the Lord's presence!"[49] Songs like Coomes's "Holy, Holy, Holy," Karen Lafferty's "Seek Ye

First," and Marsha Stevens's "For Those Tears I Died" became staples at Calvary Chapel and moved out with the church's armada of touring musical talent and the many non–Calvary Chapel youth who attended the Saturday night concerts.

Stunned at the impact music had on Calvary Chapel's ministry, Chuck Smith wondered if somehow the effect could be bottled in the recording process. Very early in 1971, he took $2,500 from his own pocket and arranged to record an album featuring the best of the Calvary Chapel talent—Love Song, Debby (Kerner), Children of the Day, Country Faith, and three other groups. The result, *The Everlastin' Living Jesus Music Concert*, was an adequately engineered studio album that sold thousands of copies at Saturday night Calvary Chapel concerts, by the artists themselves at their respective gigs, and by mail. This led Smith to create Maranatha! Music later that year. Over the next decade, Maranatha! recorded nearly forty albums by their artists and simultaneously oversaw evangelistic ministry tours of Calvary Chapel bands that ranged up and down the West Coast and eventually all across the country. As a result of the distribution of its records and its bands' relentless touring, Calvary Chapel became the major purveyor of praise music, influencing Jesus People—and the wider evangelical church—around the nation.[50]

Regional Developments in the Early Jesus Music Scene

The early 1970s marked a general flowering of Jesus music. Every local node on the national Jesus People landscape seemed to have its own band(s) and musical artist(s) that served as unofficial representatives and drawing cards to both the believing and nonbelieving. In the Pacific Northwest, where the movement had a strong presence through the work of Linda Meissner's and Carl Parks's Jesus People Army in Seattle and Spokane, the rock band Wilson McKinley became the regional champions of Jesus music.

A secular rock band formed in 1967, the Spokane-based Wilson McKinley had an early affinity for the country rock that attained great popularity by 1969. In mid-1970, three members of the band came into contact with Jesus People from Parks's group, were "baptized in the Spirit," and committed themselves to join the JPA. For the next three years, Wilson McKinley was a staple of Jesus People events in Washington, Idaho, and Oregon. Reportedly turning down a recording contract from a major secular label, they cut low-budget albums such as *Spirit of Elijah* and *Heaven's Gonna Be a Blast*, which were marketed mainly to the Jesus People in the Northwest via concerts and in Parks's Jesus paper, *Truth*.[51]

Other areas had their local Jesus music stars. In the Northeast, Danny Taylor forged a regional following out of upstate New York's Love Inn community, and Mike Johnson—formerly of the Exkursions—was a frequent headliner in and

FIGURE 8.1 A publicity shot for a leading Midwestern Jesus band: "e" of Indianapolis ca. 1972.

Courtesy of Ron Rendleman.

around Boston in the early 1970s.[52] In Cincinnati, the major figure was Randy Matthews, a student at the Church of Christ's Cincinnati Bible College and son of Monty Matthews, one of the founding members of Elvis Presley's backup group, the Jordanaires.[53] In the Atlanta area, the prominent Jesus music balladeer was a young singer-guitarist named Pat Terry from Smyrna, Georgia.[54] And in Texas, the bands Hope of Glory and Liberation Suite were the major purveyors of Jesus music.[55]

In the Midwest, several bands played important roles. Hope was a talented, hard-core hippie band from western Wisconsin that played throughout the Midwest in the early '70s and even had an album out on the A&M label after being converted.[56] From Indianapolis came a band that simply called itself "e" ("e" being short for "everything"). This band—including vocalist Greg X. Volz (who later achieved a degree of fame with the band Petra and as a solo CCM artist)—converted as a unit in 1970 and played concerts all over the Midwest until 1974 (figure 8.1).[57] Further to the north, Milwaukee's Sheep, part of Jim Palosaari's Jesus People group, was the dominant musical voice in that area until their departure for an evangelistic tour in Europe in 1972.[58] When part of Palosaari's group became Chicago's Jesus People USA (JPUSA), its new Resurrection Band led by blues guitarist Glenn Kaiser became the dominant musical expression of the Jesus movement in the Windy City.[59]

An unlikely hotbed of the new Jesus music proved to be the city of Fort Wayne in the middle of rural northeastern Indiana. There, centered in the Adam's Apple, a number of Jesus music acts emerged in the early 1970s. One of these groups was Petra (a play on the Greek word for "rock"), led by guitarist Bob Hartman. A former student at Kent State and veteran of several local bar bands, Hartman was converted and headed to Fort Wayne to enter a discipleship-based school at the Adam's Apple. Shortly thereafter, he fashioned a group with a particularly heavy rock sound, reminiscent of secular groups like the James Gang and the Allman Brothers.[60] In contrast to Petra's hard rock sound were the soft ballads of one of the few women in the early Jesus music scene, Nancy Hennigbaum—"Honeytree" (a literal translation of her German surname). The Episcopalian daughter of an Iowa college orchestra conductor, she converted while visiting an older sister who had become involved with the Fort Wayne Jesus People. Equipped with only an acoustic guitar and her voice, Honeytree moved from handling the secretarial load to singing on weekend programs.[61] By late 1971, the Adam's Apple had become a major Midwestern anchor for a network of local fellowships, churches, coffee-houses, and Jesus People nightclubs that made for a vaudeville-like circuit for Jesus People musical artists. The regional flowering of Jesus Music was laying the foundation for a national Jesus music scene.

The Giants of Early Jesus Music: Love Song and Larry Norman

As the Jesus music scene began to take hold, its two most influential artists proved to be Calvary Chapel's band Love Song and the Los Angeles–based singer Larry Norman. As a group of polished, veteran rock 'n' roll musicians before their con-version, Love Song and its leader, Chuck Girard, had a clear leg up on most of the other musical talent at Calvary Chapel. For that reason, they stood out from the beginning, quickly became the central attraction of Calvary Chapel's musical stable, and were in demand for concerts up and down the West Coast. "We didn't know we could say no," Girard recalled in a 1998 interview. "If the phone rang with an invitation to play somewhere we felt it must be God. We would sometimes play 2 to 3 times a day in those days. We would just get in our vans and take off. We never knew what we were getting paid or how big the crowd would be; it was just an opportunity to preach the gospel."[62]

Soon, the group began to attract the attention of major record labels such as Columbia and Warner Brothers.[63] The group opted, however, to record their own album in late 1971 under the Good News label and signed a distributing deal with United Artists. That first album, a compilation of tunes the band had been working on since they first came to Calvary Chapel, was titled simply *Love Song*.[64] "Little Country Church" was a song about Calvary Chapel itself; however, it reso-nated with anyone who had come into contact with the Jesus People movement:

Little Country Church on the edge of town
Doo-do-do-do-do-do-do...
Preacher isn't talkin' 'bout religion no more,
He just wants to praise the Lord...
And it's very plain to see,
It's not the way it used to be...
Long hair, short hair, some coats and ties,
People finally comin' around,
Lookin' past the hair and straight into the eyes,
People finally comin' around.[65]

Another popular song from the album, "Front Seat, Back Seat," addressed the problem of the young believers' refusal to put God in control of one's life. Probably the most popular ballad on the album was the simple tune "A Love Song," which asked hearers to listen to their hearts as they reflected on the message of forgiveness and salvation. The album did very well and not just in California: One independent national subdistributor reported that at one point he shipped 20,000 copies of the album in just two weeks.[66] To the group's astonishment, "A Love Song" was released as a single and received extensive airplay in the Philippines, becoming the number one song in Manila in the fall of 1972, prompting a quick trip to play five sold-out concerts and revival meetings in the capital city's baseball stadium.[67]

Although Love Song never had close to that kind of secular chart action in the United States (aside, perhaps, from a brief stint atop the album charts in Wichita, Kansas), one estimate puts the sales of its debut album at more than 250,000 copies (figure 8.2).[68] Whatever the numbers, the impact of their first album was profound. Competently produced, professional sounding, and unapologetic in its message, *Love Song* was good listening fare for young Jesus People, while also providing a model for would-be Jesus musicians and bands across the United States. Moreover, its sound was not so aggressively rock 'n' roll as to alienate many pastors, youth group leaders, and parents who were open to the idea of the Jesus Revolution. Indeed, it may not be an exaggeration to argue *Love Song* played a pivotal role within the Jesus People movement and evangelical youth culture.[69] In a Web-based survey compiled in 2004 from responses submitted by former Jesus People, *Love Song* was overwhelmingly cited as the single "most influential" Jesus music album by nearly a four-to-one margin over its closest competitors (see Appendix).

While Love Song epitomized the quiet, melodic side of the developing genre, the oeuvre of Larry Norman was the embodiment of its raucous rock 'n' roll edge. A quixotic, elfin figure with shoulder-length blond hair, Norman was too religious for the secular rock world and too moody and unpredictable for many would-be

FIGURE 8.2 The Calvary Chapel–based band Love Song ca. 1972; top, left to right: Bob Wall, Chuck Girard, Tommy Coomes; bottom, left to right: Jay Truax, John Mehler.
Courtesy of Calvary Chapel.

evangelical fans. Nonetheless, he stood out as a unique talent amid his Jesus music peers.

Born in Corpus Christi, Texas, of Oklahoman parents in 1947 and raised in a conservative Southern Baptist home in the San Francisco area, Larry Norman dropped out of college to join the San Jose–based band People! in 1966. Although he considered himself a believer, a visit to a Pentecostal church sometime in 1967 brought forth what he described as "a fullness in the Holy Spirit."[70] Meanwhile, People! experienced moderate success in the Bay Area at the same time that bands like the Grateful Dead and Jefferson Airplane were the center of the Haight-Ashbury psychedelic scene. The group signed a record contract with Capitol Records late in 1967, and their second single release, "I Love You (But the Words Won't Come)" with Norman sharing the lead vocals, rose to #14 on the national charts in April 1968.[71] Their first album, featuring a cover of country singer Wayne Raney's "We Need a Whole Lot More of Jesus, and a Lot Less Rock n' Roll," was released in spring 1968. However, the moody Norman, squabbling with management and bandmates, quit People! the day the album was released.[72]

During the next eighteen months, Norman stayed mostly in Los Angeles, working on new music and becoming increasingly visible through his popular performances at Hollywood Presbyterian's Salt Company and the *Hollywood Free Paper*'s Paladium concerts.[73] In 1969, after turning down the lead in the L.A. cast of *Hair*, he signed another contract with Capitol, the result being *Upon This Rock*, an imaginative album with an unmistakably rock 'n' roll sound, Beatlesque harmonies, clever lyrics, and good production values.[74] Within the context of the period, it certainly had a commercial sound. The problem was it was unapologetically Christian in a market where religious music was still something of a commercial taboo. Typical was "Sweet, Sweet Song of Salvation":

> *Sing that sweet, sweet song of salvation,*
> *And let your laughter fill the air;*
> *Sing that sweet, sweet song of salvation,*
> *And tell the people, everywhere;*
> *Sing that sweet, sweet song of salvation,*
> *In every land, and every nation;*
> *Sing that sweet, sweet song of salvation,*
> *And let the world know that Jesus cares.*
> *Lisssstennnn, Satan....*[75]

"Moses in the Wilderness" was a light-hearted novelty song about the Exodus story; "Forget Your Hexagram" condemned the growing fascination with astrology and the occult. One song on the album, "I Wish We'd All Been Ready," would become Norman's signature song and quickly spread through Jesus People circles and into church youth group networks. A heartfelt ballad about the Second Coming, "I Wish We'd All Been Ready" was a glimpse into the dispensationalist vision of the horrors and heartbreak for those left behind after the Rapture:

> *A man and wife asleep in bed,*
> *She hears a noise and turns her head,*
> *He's gone; I wish we'd all been ready.*
> *Children died; the days grew cold,*
> *A piece of bread could buy a bag of gold;*
> *I wish we'd all been ready.*
> *There's no time to change your mind,*
> *The Son has come, and you've been left behind.*[76]

Capitol released *Upon This Rock* in December 1969 and, not quite knowing what to do with it, sold the album rights in 1970 to Heartwarming/Impact Records, a subsidiary label of Nashville-based Benson Records that specialized in Southern gospel music.[77] Impact had visions of reaching a younger audience and had just released an album by Gene Cotton,[78] but the persona of Larry Norman was something for which they were unprepared. The company had no coherent plan for marketing an album of unabashed gospel rock 'n' roll, and simply listing the album in their catalog or sending out sample copies to their normal clientele (as they might do with a Southern gospel group like the Stamps Quartet) might have been counterproductive. For many conservative bookstore owners, one look at the album cover with its picture of a shirtless Norman in a Superman-like flying pose, his long blond hair streaming behind him, and the case was closed. When all was said and done, *Upon This Rock* sold few copies, and Norman was left without a record label.[79]

Back in Los Angeles, Norman continued to be in major demand in the local Jesus People scene, appearing at coffeehouses and rallies and occasionally taking up the pen for a column ("As I See It") in the *Hollywood Free Paper* (figure 8.3).[80] Buoyed by a loan of $3,000 from born-again entertainer and recently Spirit-baptized Charismatic Pat Boone, Norman and his protégé, Randy Stonehill, had after-midnight access to a recording studio and worked on *Street Level* (released in two versions, 1970 and 1971) and *Bootleg* (a two-record set of music and interviews, 1972), along with Stonehill's first album, *Born Twice* (1971).[81] The albums were sold mostly at concerts and by mail, and none of them sold more than 25,000 to 30,000 copies.[82] Although Norman's record sales were less than spectacular, his prior work with People!, the quality of *Upon This Rock*, his mention in the July 1971 *Time* cover story on the Jesus movement, and his subsequent interview on a national news program

FIGURE 8.3 The "Father of Christian Rock," Larry Norman, performing at the Hollywood Paladium ca. 1970.
Courtesy of Archives, Hubbard Library, Fuller Theological Seminary.

segment on the Jesus People were more than enough to keep the record industry interested.[83]

In early 1972, Norman was signed by MGM's Verve label and went to England to record an album. There, with input from the Beatles' legendary producer George Martin, he recorded an album that many CCM critics and insiders considered the best Christian rock album ever recorded: *Only Visiting This Planet*. The opening song, "Why Don't You Look into Jesus?" Norman later said, had been inspired by seeing an inebriated Janis Joplin's backstage behavior during his days with People! The song set the tone with a pronounced rock setting and a graphic, in-your-face advocacy of Jesus as an answer to the sordid underbelly of life in the counterculture:

> *Gonorrhea on Valentine's Day (V.D.),*
> *And you're still lookin' for the perfect lay;*
> *You think rock n' roll will set you free,*
> *But honey, you'll be dead before you're 33;*
> *Shootin' junk 'til you're half-insane,*
> *A broken needle in your purple vein,*
> *Why don't you look into Jesus, He got the answer.*[84]

The album went on to use a wide variety of musical settings to address issues from a distinctly counterculturally tinged, evangelical perspective. The driving rock of "Six O'Clock News" was a swipe at the Vietnam War and the surrealistic media coverage of the "living room war." "The Great American Novel" was a Dylan-like ballad that criticized everything from American racism, to hypocrisy in the churches, to the enormous amounts of money expended on the space program.

Perhaps *Only Visiting This Planet*'s defining moment, however, was Norman's high-energy, 1950s-style rock 'n' roll anthem, "Why Should the Devil Have All the Good Music?":

> *I want the people to know, that He saved my soul,*
> *But I still like to listen to the radio.*
> *They say rock n' roll is bad,*
> *We'll give ya one more chance,*
> *I say I feel so good, I gotta get up and dance*
> *....*
> *I ain't knockin' the hymns,*
> *Just give me a song that has a beat;*
> *I ain't knockin' the hymns,*
> *Just give me a song that moves my feet...*

> *I don't want none of them funeral marches—*
> *I ain't dead, yet!*
>
> . . . .
>
> *I feel good every day, I don't wanna lose it;*
> *All that I'm really tryin' to say is:*
> *Why should the Devil have all the good music?*
> *I've been saved, I feel O.K.!*
> *Jesus is the Rock, and He rolled my blues away!*[85]

While enthusiastically received by those fans who did happen to bump into the album, Verve, like Capitol and Impact before it, did a poor job of promoting and marketing the album. As a result, *Only Visiting This Planet* did little in the way of sales in its first year of release.[86] Nonetheless, it set a mark for quality and, along with the appearance of Love Song's debut album, proved to be an encouraging sign of Jesus music's potential.

Growth of a Jesus Music Industry

By the early 1973 release of *Only Visiting This Planet*, it was clear that Jesus music had begun to establish itself as a separate genre apart from both secular rock 'n' roll and the sanctified world of sacred music. In addition to the growing numbers of Jesus People singers and bands, there was an influx of converted performers with established connections to the music industry. At the same time, a modest but expanding recording and distribution network was coming into existence that delivered the music to its growing fan base despite the skepticism of secular music executives and the disapprobation of some evangelical leaders.

One important dimension of the expanding genre of Jesus music was the growing visibility of established rock musicians who were identifying themselves and their music with the Jesus movement. Some of these musicians had prior ties to evangelical religion and sought to bring their pop music aspirations into line with their religious sympathies. More often, however, it was a conversion experience that compelled them to use their musical talent for Jesus. The infusion of these talented professionals expanded musical resources and industry connections, added to Jesus music's credibility among both secular and Christian young people, and raised the bar musically. Among these figures were Jeremy Spencer of the rock group Fleetwood Mac (although his involvement with the controversial Children of God soon removed him from the public eye); Southern gospel rocker Mylon LeFevre, the long-haired, mutton-chopped black sheep of the Singing LeFevres gospel group; and guitarist Glenn Schwartz, formerly of the James Gang and the Pacific Gas & Electric Company, whose song "Are You Ready (To Sit by His Throne)?" became a hit in the summer of 1971.[87]

Three imports from the world of secular music proved of particular importance: Noel Paul Stookey, Barry McGuire, and Phil Keaggy. Stookey, the Paul of the famous folk trio Peter, Paul, and Mary, had been turned onto the Bible by Bob Dylan ("It's a heavy book," Stookey claimed Dylan told him) and underwent a conversion experience after talking backstage with an evangelical believer at a 1968 concert.[88] His new religious inclinations soon showed up in his music, including the 1971 solo hit "The Wedding Song (There Is Love)." As the 1970s progressed, Stookey turned out a series of albums that combined winsome insights into childhood and family life with religious sentiments and convictions.[89]

Stookey's friend Barry McGuire also joined the ranks of the Jesus movement. An original member of the New Christy Minstrels, McGuire helped write and sang lead on their early '6os hit "Green, Green."[90] After leaving the group, he posted a number-one hit in the fall of 1965 with the ultimate anthem of Cold War angst, "Eve of Destruction"[91] and then for a while was the male lead in the Broadway production of *Hair*. After bottoming out on drugs back in Los Angeles, he picked up a copy of the American Bible Society's modern translation of the New Testament, *Good News for Modern Man*, at a friend's house, which eventually led to his early 1971 conversion. For a while, he turned his back on music, but living in the midst of the Los Angeles Jesus music scene soon led to playing his new Christian songs at worship services and coffeehouses. His 1973 album, *Seeds*, and the 1974 *Lighten Up* became classics of the early Jesus music genre.[92]

Ohio native Phil Keaggy was not near as well-known as either Stookey or McGuire in the early '70s but was destined to play a much larger role in the ongoing annals of Jesus rock and its offspring, CCM. Keaggy was the lead guitarist for Glass Harp, a "power trio" that attained a regional following in the Midwest and served as a frequent opening act for major acts. Keaggy became a born-again Christian in 1970, and although his two bandmates, Dan Pecchio and John Sferra, did not share his religious enthusiasm, they let him freely indulge his predilections in the group's music. The band cut three albums for the Decca label between 1970 and 1972 featuring such Keaggy-penned tunes as "David and Goliath," "It Makes Me Glad," "The Answer," and a rocked-up version of the old spiritual "Do Lord."[93] After Glass Harp disbanded in late 1972, Keaggy moved to Freeport, New York, and became something of an artist in residence at Scott Ross's Love Inn. While at Love Inn, he recorded his first Jesus music album, *What a Day* (1973).[94] Keaggy soon forged links with other Jesus rockers, including Love Song—touring with them in 1974—as well as the 2nd Chapter of Acts and A Band Called David, with whom he toured extensively in the mid-'70s, recording what enthusiasts consider a classic three-disc live album, *How the West Was One* (1977).[95]

Selling Jesus Music

With the addition of these established musicians to popular acts like Love Song and Larry Norman, it became increasingly clear that Jesus music was something more than just an internal worship resource or Saturday night coffeehouse fodder: It was tapping into a major industry that fed on mass media exposure and capital-driven distribution.[96] Both the music's creators and its consumers expected that Jesus music would be readily available and accessible—just like the rock 'n' roll of the larger secular youth culture—in the form of records and tapes, along with radio airplay. In light of the evangelistic imperatives of the Jesus People, the development of these support structures seemed all the more necessary.

But mere desire or desirability did not translate into the economic wherewithal to bring this about. The worldly entertainment and recording industries and secular radio stations offered little in the way of encouragement. But there was another possibility: For the sake of evangelizing the nation's youth—and the chance to make a dollar or two—there were straight evangelicals who would be willing to provide the economic backing necessary to ensure the creation and flow of Jesus music to its growing constituency.

As of the late 1960s, the evangelical recording industry was a pale reflection of the larger secular one. Within a market that produced more than $1.3 billion in sales in 1967, the largest evangelical record company—Word Records—mounted sales well under $10 million—a lightweight in comparison to the huge numbers of even a single major secular company like Columbia Records.[97] One of the central reasons for this situation was that the evangelical record companies severely limited themselves in their mode of operation—sacred and gospel records were sold through religious bookstores, by mail order through advertisements in religious magazines, and by the artists themselves as they toured and performed. Rarely could one find an album from an evangelical record company in a record store or in the record bins at a five-and-dime, drug store, or department store.[98]

But this situation began to improve by the end of the 1960s. Triggered by the availability of extra dollars among a prospering evangelical population, there was a related growth of the evangelical publishing and bookselling industries. For evangelical record companies, this meant the addition of crucial new outlets for their product, just as a maturing music-listening, record-buying, Baby Boom population arrived within evangelical circles and the Jesus People movement was spreading.[99]

One of the first companies to cater to this evangelical youth audience was Los Angeles–based Creative Sound, Inc., formed in 1966 by Bob Cotterell. A member of Bel-Air Presbyterian Church in his late twenties and a former salesman for Sacred Records, Cotterell provided manufacturing and packaging assistance, as well as distribution resources. As a result, Creative Sound's early catalogs featured albums from evangelical labels like Word and Benson, as well as self-produced albums from traditional evangelical singers and younger acts in the folk-singing Up with People vein.[100]

As the Jesus People movement arose, Cotterell was enthusiastic about both the new music and its impact on young people and sought out as much of the Jesus music as he could for his catalog. With few other viable options, the company quickly became a relatively inexpensive choice of first resort for Jesus music artists; Larry Norman used Creative Sound's manufacturing and distributing network to market his homegrown One Way Records. Cotterell also pressed and circulated albums by such California Jesus People grandees as Arthur Blessitt and Duane Pederson, signed a deal to subdistribute *Love Song,* and offered Chuck Smith's Calvary Chapel Maranatha! Music acts in his catalog. It was Creative Sounds that manufactured and distributed 175,000 copies of the EXPLO '72 concert soundtrack for Campus Crusade for Christ. Jesus music artists from outside Southern California also found their way to Creative Sound and its connections to more than 700 U.S. Christian bookstores that were bold enough to carry their records.[101] In 1972, Cotterell began a mail-order record club that marketed its offerings through advertisements in magazines like *Campus Life* and eventually accounted for about 20% of the firm's sales.[102]

While Creative Sound was a first step toward getting Jesus music into the hands of its existing audience, it offered little hope of establishing a major market presence or, more important, providing the initial investment necessary to produce and record albums that were up to industry standards. Here, the cash-poor Jesus music artists were at a major disadvantage. As early as 1964—at the dawn of Beatlemania in America—the average production cost for a new record album from a mainstream record label was in the neighborhood of $15,000.[103] With the subsequent advances in multitrack recording technology and the growing move toward art within mid-sixties rock, the cost of production exploded. By the early '70s, it was not unusual for leading rock artists to spend hundreds of thousands of dollars in turning out a record, with the average album coming in at around $40,000.[104] The early budgets behind Jesus music, on the other hand—such as the $2,500 that Honeytree borrowed from her pastor's son to record her debut album (that price included 1,000 copies of the record), the $1,800 spent on Phil Keaggy's first solo album *What a Day,* or the bargain-basement rate (and sound) of $800 for which Randy Stonehill made his *Born Twice* album—were minuscule in comparison.[105]

But in the early '70s, new developments moved Jesus music closer to the mainstream business of popular music. The true transformation of the Jesus music scene came when it established a relationship with Waco, Texas–based Word Records. Founded in 1953 by Jarrell McCracken, a recent graduate of Baylor University, Word specialized in recorded sermons, children's records, and cheaply produced sacred music and became the nation's largest religious record company during the 1960s. Although convinced upbeat youth musicals were a passing fad, McCracken had a nose for a quick payoff and bought the recording and distribution rights for *Good News* (1968), *Tell It Like It Is* (1970), and *Natural High* (1971). To oversee this new dimension of his business, McCracken hired the former Southern Baptist youth choir director, Billy Ray Hearn.[106]

In 1970, Hearn received a telephone call from young Randy Matthews of Cincinnati's Jesus House. "He told me," Hearn recalled, "that the music we were doing [the youth musicals] really wasn't connecting with the kids on the street."[107] Knowing that Matthews was right, Hearn auditioned him and subsequently signed him to a contract. Released in early 1971, *I Wish We'd All Been Ready* did feature Matthews's title version of Larry Norman's song, but the album—though contemporary within its context—was a tame affair that mixed in folk hymns and cuts from the new folk musicals. Although the album did not sell particularly well, the company survived the experiment, and Hearn was emboldened to sign other acts from the Jesus movement for a new Word-sponsored subsidiary aimed specifically at young people: Myrrh Records.[108] With production budgets in the $10,000 to $15,000 range, Hearn tagged Matthews's follow-up record, *All I Am Is What You See*, along with albums by Crimson Bridge (a Chicago-area group whose brass-dominated sound was akin to the popular secular group Blood, Sweat & Tears) and First Gear (a band made up of former members of the Thurlow Spurr troupe), as the label's first releases. By early 1973, Hearn tapped deeper into the emergent Jesus music circles and inked contracts with Barry McGuire, Honeytree, and the English duo of Malcolm (Wild) & Alwyn (Wall).[109]

While Hearn put together a growing roster of Jesus music artists, actually selling the albums he produced proved more daunting. Many Christian bookstores, which Hearn says accounted for 90% of Myrrh's sales, were mom-and-pop operations that, if they weren't governed by the particular outlooks and doctrinal perspectives of their owners, were managed with a nervous eye to the sensibilities of their customer base. Not a few stores either flat-out refused to sell the new Jesus rock or haltingly added the records to their stock. Some stores agreed to sell the albums but handled them like contraband, hiding them in the back of the store or (as Hearn recalled of the Moody Bible Institute's bookstore in downtown Chicago) keeping them under the counter out of "fear that somebody would come in and accuse them of selling that stuff."[110]

The bookstores likewise resented the fact that Word's record club offered bonus albums to loyal customers. In late 1973 to placate the bookstores, Word began placing stickers on all albums offering a "buy three—get one free" deal to retail customers (a needed come-on for the consumer of Jesus music, as albums were almost never discounted in Christian bookstores). This "terrible"—as Hearn deemed it—sticker redemption scheme soon became standard among the evangelical labels, adding a whole new layer of expense, as well as a time-consuming accounting hurdle for managing their accounts with individual bookstores.[111]

Still, Myrrh managed to turn a profit. With lower production costs and modest royalty agreements, Hearn's label could afford to come in well below the industry standard break-even point of 85,000 albums for average commercial releases in the early and mid-1970s. Thus it was good news when 1973 releases such as Barry McGuire's *Seeds*, Honeytree's first record (for which Hearn had purchased the rights), Malcolm and Alwyn's *Fool's Wisdom*, and Randy Matthews's third—and first forthright rock—album, *Son of Dust*, chalked up sales in the vicinity of 40,000 to 50,000 albums each.[112] While the results from these records confirmed Myrrh's course, what proved to be its first major Jesus music coup came the following year from a group with its roots in the Southern California Jesus movement—the 2nd Chapter of Acts.[113]

The 2nd Chapter of Acts was a sister-brother trio, made up of Annie Ward Herring, her younger sister Nellie Ward, and her brother, Matthew Ward. Hailing from a large Roman Catholic farming family in North Dakota, Annie had been the first to make the trek to Southern California in the mid-1960s, hoping to pursue a career in pop music. Her prospects looked promising, and by 1968, she felt she was on the cusp of making it as part of a musical group. But given the times, she was also sampling the wild life, as well as shopping the wares of the hippie religious market in an attempt to find herself. During this time, she received the news of her mother's death; devastated, she bumped into an old boyfriend, Buck Herring, an ex-dj who had recently been converted at a local Assemblies of God church. He told her about his experience and gave her a copy of *Good News for Modern Man*. She read the paraphrased New Testament and prayed to receive Jesus, immediately quitting her musical group. Shortly thereafter, they married and became members of Jack Hayford's Church On the Way (International Church of the Foursquare Gospel), the church home of Pat Boone and youth musical impresarios Jimmy and Carol Owens.[114] While her husband tried to learn the ropes as a recording engineer, Annie stayed at home and began a career as what she described as a "song receiver"—spending hours at an old upright piano while "the Lord taught" her to "receive songs from Him."[115]

In 1970, following her father's death from leukemia, the Herrings took in her two youngest teenage siblings—sister Nelly and brother Matthew. The two soon underwent a born-again experience and began to join Annie in singing around the old piano. Friends and fellow church members heard the group and urged them to begin singing for the public. It took some convincing, but the trio formed a group called the 2nd Chapter of Acts, which began to appear at local venues in the thriving Southern California Jesus People scene, as well as singing for some of

Owens's musicals and backing up records for Larry Norman and Barry McGuire.[116] Hearn first heard the group sing at the Salt Company in early 1973 and "almost fell out of [his] chair," immediately offering them a contract. Herring's husband and the group's manager, Buck Herring, however, had visions of an MGM contract and turned down the offer. But within several months, the group, unsuccessful in their bid for a contract with the secular label, came back to Hearn and signed with Myrrh in the fall of 1973.[117]

In late 1973, 2nd Chapter went into the studio to record their first album, *with footnotes*. One tune in particular, "Easter Song"—which songwriter Annie Herring had been tempted to discard—caught Hearn's ear, and he built a promotional campaign and single around the song. Released in the spring of 1974, "Easter Song" received some radio airplay on secular stations and, with its soaring vocals and traditional message ("Hear the bells ringing, they're singing, that we can be born again"),[118] seemed to melt the resolve of many evangelicals who were otherwise against Jesus music.[119] Recalled Hearn in 1989, "[Everybody] loved that song, loved that sound, it was so fresh. And even with the drums and guitars it still ministered to everybody, and they couldn't deny it."[120]

Within the world of sacred music, where the sales of a gospel quartet or traditional singer that topped the 60,000 mark was considered a major hit, *with footnotes* was a smash; when Hearn learned that 2nd Chapter had surpassed the sales of the latest album from Word's best-selling Southern gospel group, the Happy Goodmans, he knew that he had stumbled on something. By the end of 1974, the 2nd Chapter of Acts debut had sold 65,000 copies, and it eventually sold between 250,000 and 300,000 albums and tapes.[121] The sales of *with footnotes* and totals in the 20,000 to 50,000 range for follow-up releases by Myrrh artists like Matthews, McGuire, and Honeytree and newly signed artists such as Petra and Michael Omartian signaled that a solid evangelical market existed for Jesus music.[122]

Overall, the decision to give Jesus music a chance paid off for Word Records; by 1974, sales of Jesus music accounted for 12% of Word's total revenue (including its music publishing sales) of $14.5 million.[123] Sales of contemporary artists, according to Billy Ray Hearn, rose from nothing at the beginning of 1971 to 50% of Word's total record sales by 1975.[124] The success also seemed to make corporate America see the light—after a fashion. In late 1974, the media conglomerate ABC, in keeping with its general philosophy of buying up-and-coming smaller labels to find new talent, purchased Word Records from McCracken for ABC stock valued at $12.6 million. Recognizing its lack of corporate expertise in dealing with an evangelical audience, ABC left Word management intact and maintained a hands-off relationship to the company.[125] However, ABC's deep pockets and media strength seemed to promise a more secure base and held out the possibility of major media exposure.

The Growth of Jesus Music on the Airwaves

The mechanism that created pop superstars and filled record companies' coffers in the postwar era was constant exposure of artists' music on the nation's radio stations. The bulk of record company marketing was devoted to courting program directors and disc jockeys in the (slim) hope that a particular song might be selected and added to a station's rotation. Here was one of the major differences between the world of secular popular music and Jesus music—the latter's almost total lack of access to radio airplay.

Many secular rock stations were either disinclined to air Jesus music or, in light of the passing of the spate of religious songs from the national charts by 1973, prone to view it as just another musical fad whose time had come and gone. Evangelical-owned and -operated religious stations, on the other hand, were conservative by nature and rarely open to the new music. The majority sold large blocks of time to evangelistic and teaching ministries and often reaped much of their income from their listeners' gifts—listeners who tended to skew elderly and very conservative. Not surprisingly, neither the listeners nor the managers of these stations had much use for Jesus music.[126] However, as the 1970s progressed, the growth of the Jesus movement and the expanded sales of Jesus music were reflected in a slow growth of radio airplay.

One of the first programs to provide exposure to the music of the Jesus movement was *PowerLine*, a half-hour weekly syndicated program sponsored by the Radio Commission of the Southern Baptist Convention. Begun in the late 1960s, *PowerLine* mixed friendly, low-pressure counsel and offers for free literature with rock songs that explored philosophical or moral questions. Frequently carried on Sunday mornings or late at night on hundreds of secular rock stations, the bulk of its music was chosen from singles and albums on the secular charts; however, it did provide air time for artists like Larry Norman, Randy Matthews, and Barry McGuire.[127]

While *PowerLine* provided some airplay, other local and syndicated programs devoted their time almost totally to the new music. As early as 1968, a disc jockey named Scott Campbell began a program on KARI in Blaine, Washington, that featured the most contemporary-sounding Christian music he could find. *A Joyful Noise*, the personal project of "Paul Baker" (Frank Edmonson), a young disc jockey just out of the Air Force who collected every upbeat, modern record with spiritual themes he could lay his hands on, began on WLCY in St. Petersburg, Florida, in early 1970. Later that year, he moved to Wichita, Kansas, where he worked a variety of part-time radio gigs and continued his show, first on KEYN and later on KFH.[128]

It was during this time that he began to pitch his show to rock stations eager for something a little hipper than the local Baptist preacher to fill the

Federal Communication Commission's dictates for public service programming. Soon his show was being heard via Radio Shack reel-to-reel tapes on about twenty stations in cities such as Indianapolis, Tampa, Richmond, Tulsa, Phoenix, and Oklahoma City. His biggest problem in those early days was that contemporary gospel musical pickings were mighty lean; eking out enough good songs to fill a program often proved to be a challenge. Reminiscing years later, Edmondson recalled how he "would go several weeks doing the show and just reversing the order" of the songs because there "were that few songs that were good enough quality to play." The scattered geographic range of the stations in his network played into his favor, however, as he never had to coordinate weekly broadcasts; he would simply send out his tapes in random order to different stations as he received them back in the mail. After being hired to do some public address play-by-play and announcements at Explo '72, Edmondson/Baker was invited back to Dallas in the fall of that year and began a nightly show of Jesus music on KDTX, in addition to continuing his weekly syndicated program.[129] By that time, similar syndicated shows had cropped up elsewhere around the country, including *Jesus-Solid Rock*, based in Carbondale, Illinois, and *The Rock That Never Rolls*, a show out of Burlington, Vermont, hosted by former *Hollywood Free Paper* cartoonist Dale Yancy.[130]

The single most influential of these programs, however, was *The Scott Ross Show* originating out of the Love Inn Community in Freeville, New York. Ross had originally come to upstate New York in late 1968 to manage five FM stations for Pat Robertson's Christian Broadcasting Network but quickly became the focal point for an outreach to youth that developed into a commune. Ross convinced Robertson to let him begin a three-hour nightly show in early 1970 on a syndicated network of sixteen stations. "I had to find something I could relate to," Ross recalled years later. "I came up with a format idea, disc jockeys playing contemporary music, and talking about Jesus." Luckily for Ross, "[Robertson] bought it." And so he set about creating radio broadcasts that typically combined mainstream rock by artists such as Paul Simon, Roberta Flack, Stevie Wonder, and Eric Clapton with Jesus music artists like Larry Norman, The Way, Andrae Crouch, and "e." Ross consciously set out to create a program that had a mainstream, Top 40 sound, interspersing songs and promotional jingles ("Thisssss is the Scott Ross Showwww") between sermonettes on various topics, news about the conversions and spiritual searches of mainstream rock artists (Ross was in and out of the life of his old friend Eric Clapton, mired in alcohol, drugs, and relationship woes), and prayer requests mailed and phoned in from around the United States.[131] Eventually, Ross and his Jesus People staff managed to line up volunteer counselors manning "Love Lines" in dozens of cities to pray with, evangelize, and advise listeners in response to Ross's programs:

> You may have some personal hassles in your home, you may need a job, you might be pregnant, all sorts of those things—and those people are there to answer telephones to help you.... They're not going to try to beat you in the head with a Bible or jam Jesus down your throat, they're just gonna help you in any way they can.[32]

For anyone willing to call in and request it, Ross sent out a free copy of *Good News for Modern Man*.[33] Ross's broadcasts often produced profound results. Years later, one woman wrote to thank Ross for the impact his talks between records had made on her life:

> Scott, I'm one of those people that "just happened" to find your radio broadcast on the CBN radio network all across New York State! All you talked about was a living Jesus. I was an ex-Catholic nun, depressed and recovering from back surgery. I listened to the Word that you spoke. Thank God for your faithfulness in those early days as I became born again in my bedroom and filled with the Holy Spirit in 1969![34]

Roger McLaughlin looked back in 2002 and recalled that he "was not interested in formalized religion" and was turned off by his Methodist church, finding it "dull and uninteresting." But then he began to listen to Scott Ross:

> The show absolutely revolutionized my life. It opened my eyes to who Jesus was instead of him just being a religious figure.... I sat on my sofa and wept as I heard Jesus Music for the first time.... Second Chapter and the rest blew me away with their freshness and being real. 30 minutes a day with Scott has had an ongoing impact upon my life.[35]

Overall, Ross's formula proved highly successful. By the fall of 1972, Ross's show aired on eighty radio stations—many of them secular rock stations. By 1974, he was carried on more than 150 stations and, within another year or so, had peaked at 185 broadcast outlets in the United States, along with several others overseas.[36]

The success of syndicated programs like the *Scott Ross Show* eventually led the owners and management of a few stations to consider the plunge into an all-Jesus music approach. In early March 1975, KBHL-FM in Lincoln, Nebraska, became the first station to implement an all-Jesus music format. Managed by evangelicals but owned by a commercial entity, The Sound of the New Life operated like almost any other pop station selling commercial time to businesses in the community, distributing bumper stickers, giving away T-shirts and record albums, and sponsoring concerts—in this case by Jesus music artists such as the 2nd Chapter of Acts.[137]

A few weeks later, a second all-Jesus music station debuted, KYMS-FM, fittingly located in the Orange County heartland of the Jesus movement in Santa Ana, California. The Spirit of 106 was closely identified with nearby Calvary Chapel and occasionally broadcast its Saturday night concerts. Its success prompted the station's parent company to institute an all-Jesus music format at its station KBRN-AM in Brighton, Colorado, near Denver.[138] Later that year, KFMK-FM in Houston, Texas, part of the Crawford Broadcasting Company, implemented a format combining MOR ("middle-of-the-road") secular pop tunes with Jesus music.[139] Although these new Jesus music stations hardly constituted a sea change in the American radio industry, in tandem with syndicated programs like *The Joyful Noise* and *The Scott Ross Show*, their appearance meant that Jesus music was steadily gaining entrée to larger audiences across the country.

1975: Jesus Music in Transition

The small but growing presence of Jesus music on the nation's airwaves during 1975 was but one of the signs that the genre had secured a solid footing. For those involved in Jesus music, the year was pivotal, marking a new self-consciousness: an increased sense of professional unity and a growing identification with mainstream evangelical musicians in music ministry. In April 1975, a meeting in Fort Wayne, Indiana, led to the formation of the Fellowship of Contemporary Christian Ministries (FCCM). The charter group of twenty members included not only several Jesus musicians but also youth ministers, concert promoters, record company representatives, broadcasters, the purveyor of an evangelistic light show ("Heavy Light"), and even a Christian magician (figure 8.4). Publishing its own newsletter, FCCM sponsored a three-day retreat in 1976 and, by 1978, had grown to include more than 300 members.[140]

In addition, 1975 saw the beginning of a series of annual summertime retreats for Christian artists at a camp in the Rocky Mountain resort community of Estes Park, Colorado. Organized by Cam Floria (of Continental Singers fame), the meeting included a range of musicians, with Larry Norman and Chuck Girard representing Jesus music, along with participants from the realms of traditional sacred music, the newer contemporary evangelical music, and black and Southern gospel music. Eight hundred attended this first Christian Artists' Seminar, which, in years to come, included workshops on everything from church worship to getting started in the music business, as well as talent competitions with prize money and recording contracts.[141]

FIGURE 8.4 As shown in this flyer from 1976, the Adam's Apple coffeehouse in Fort Wayne, Indiana, was a major node on the developing Jesus People concert scene.

Courtesy of Mark Hollingsworth.

Another major development was the proliferation of Jesus festivals. Providing big venues for Christian acts, these multiday events resembled, on a smaller scale, the major outdoor concerts that dominated the secular rock scene. The first significant Jesus festivals had been held at Knott's Berry Farm and in Evansville, Indiana, in 1970.[142] A repeat festival in Evansville in 1971 brought a reported crowd of 15,000.[143] In the next few years, EXPLO '72 and festivals in California and central Pennsylvania kept up the tradition, and by 1975, the nation was covered with Jesus festivals. In addition to Jesus '75 (the third in what became a long-standing series of yearly festivals held in Lancaster County, Pennsylvania) and Knott's Berry Farm's Maranatha!/Calvary Chapel Nights at its Southern California amusement park, were the Hallelujah Jubilee at Magic Mountain amusement park in Valencia, California; Salt '75 in Howell, Michigan; Fishnet '75 in Front Royal, Virginia; Jesus '75 Midwest in St. Louis; the Sonshine Festival in Ohio; Lodestone in Vancouver, British Columbia; the Hill Country Faith Festival in Texas; and the Jesus Festival of Joy at the Joyland Amusement Park in Wichita, Kansas.[144]

The success of these festivals varied, depending on the financial backing of the organizers and the strength of the Jesus movement in the area. The Lancaster County, Pennsylvania, gathering was backed by a trio of local middle-class laymen (two Mennonites and a United Presbyterian) who made sure that organization and propriety were the event's trademark. The first festival (Jesus '73) attracted a crowd of 15,000 to a 150-acre potato farm outside Morgantown to hear local Jesus music bands and speakers like charismatic preacher Bob Mumford and Jesus People leader Scott Ross. By Jesus '75, the festival was attracting crowds in the neighborhood of 30,000 for artists such as former Love Song frontman Chuck Girard, Phil Keaggy, and Andrae Crouch and the Disciples.[145]

Of course, many secular rock festivals of the era were failures, so it was no surprise that some of the Jesus festivals flopped. Petra guitarist Bob Hartman recalled one festival in Texas organized by a twenty-something would-be Jesus music entrepreneur who—without financial backing, it turned out—booked most of the major artists "on faith." When the big day actually arrived, faith had not produced many paying customers—a crowd of maybe 1,000 to 2,000 gathered in the Lone Star heat. Looking out on the sparse assembly, Hartman estimated: "There were more Port-a-Potties than there were people." Not surprisingly, the checks the young promoter issued to everyone afterward—right before he skipped town—bounced like tennis balls.[146] Still, most of the Jesus festivals attracted several thousand participants who endured the ravages of sun, rain, mud, and mosquitoes to hear the music and preaching.[147] Whether they managed to break even or went on to become annual events, the festivals nonetheless turned out to be an important source for group solidarity and a way for Jesus People to see and support their favorite artists.

While festivals provided fans with an opportunity to hear new acts and old favorites, the publication of fanzines encouraged both fans and aspiring musicians to keep abreast of the latest doings in the Jesus music world. Frank Edmondson/Paul Baker was the author and publisher of one of the first, *Rock in Jesus*, which was briefly underwritten by a Wichita contractor in 1972.[148] A more professional attempt to cover the Jesus music scene came in the form of *Harmony* magazine. Published in Buffalo, New York, the first bimonthly issue in May 1975 offered record reviews, articles, and interviews with Jesus rockers, as well as information on concert schedules and industry news.[149] Although *Harmony* ceased publication in 1977 (its place taken by the much more solidly underwritten and slickly produced monthly *Contemporary Christian Music* in 1979), its short existence reflected the new realities and prospects of the music and the expectations of its audience.[150] Coupled with attempts to foster professional interaction among Jesus music artists and to encourage and cultivate up-and-coming music ministry, the publication of a magazine devoted to Jesus music was just part of what had become, by 1975, an increasingly self-conscious and professionalized segment of the larger music industry.

Conclusion

By 1976, Jesus music had come far from its humble beginnings. What had originally thrived as a natural outgrowth of countercultural music within communes and coffeehouses had become a firmly established subgenre of American popular music.

The evolving nature of the Christian music business meant change for all of the musicians who had emerged from the Jesus movement. Love Song broke up in 1974, with its leader, Chuck Girard, embarking on a solo career and two other members joining recently converted rock star Richie Furay's (ex-Buffalo Springfield, ex-Poco) new band.[151] Following another undermarketed and poorly selling album in 1973, *So Long Ago the Garden* (this time on MGM), Larry Norman was still able to attract start-up capital from various backers and sign a deal with Myrrh to find talent and distribute albums on his own Solid Rock label. With the decent production budgets and improved distribution to Christian bookstores that Word could guarantee, his 1976 album, *In Another Land*, sold more than 150,000 copies and helped his friend Randy Stonehill's 1977 album, *Welcome to Paradise*, sell more than 120,000 copies.[152] But other artists—including Honeytree and Barry McGuire—whose folky musical styles had fit in well with the countercultural ethos of the coffeehouse and small concert venues saw their influence beginning to wane after 1976, as new, more pop-sounding stars like Keith Green and Evie Tornquist emerged.

Meanwhile, Agape, perhaps the first self-identified hard rock Jesus band, called it quits entirely, having held their farewell concert in late 1974. The band had lasted five years, played innumerable gigs, and recorded two self-produced albums, *Gospel Hard Rock* (1971) and *Victims of Tradition* (1972), with pressings of about 2,000 copies each. It was obvious that big-time success was not in their future and that it was time to move on. Fred Caban recalled: "We were getting married and developing families, jobs and it was too hard to keep [the band] going." But other changes had really told them it was time to throw in the towel. To them, it seemed as if a lot of the music that was getting out there was, in Caban's words, "real soft-sell kinda stuff" that seemed to compromise the music and the message. Moreover, they recognized that the atmosphere around the Jesus movement itself seemed to have changed. Caban recalls they had increasingly been playing for Christian kids: "It was part of the church thing…it was just entertaining their group of people…we just couldn't set up and play anymore like we used to."[153] The Jesus movement was changing, but Jesus music had blazed the path for an evolving evangelical youth culture for which Contemporary Christian Music would be the cement in the decades ahead.

9

I Wish We'd All Been Ready

THE JESUS PEOPLE FADE FROM VIEW

THE SINISTER-LOOKING, cigarette-smoking evangelist Evan Calder sat in the camper he used as headquarters for his traveling tent revival and reprimanded his young protégé Matthew Crowe for overlooking the bonanza they were set to reap from youthful audiences:

> Do you have any idea what percentage of the people in this country are between 16 and 25—over 40%! And that's the audience we're after—why this Jesus movement is the biggest religious gag around, and we're right in the middle of it![1]

The exchange was fictional, however—a scene from a 1972 grade B film titled *The Lovin' Man*, a title that was shortly changed to *The Day the Lord Got Busted*. The movie was produced and directed by Burt Topper, an independent Hollywood producer-director-writer who previously had been involved in the 1966 stock-car-themed *Thunder Alley* and in *Wild in the Streets*, the surprise 1968 cult hit about a revolt of turned-on psychedelic youth. *The Day the Lord Got Busted/Lovin' Man* featured early '60s teen idol Fabian (with a beard and long hair in place of his pompadour) as a singing, drug-taking drifter taught the tricks of the evangelistic trade by a cynical, middle-aged revivalist (played by Tony Russel). Sharpening his preaching chops under the watchful eye of his mentor, he begins to attract a following of mostly young Jesus freaks as the white-robed, guitar-picking, "Matthew, Son of Jesus." Promoted by an unsavory SoCal media relations flack (played by famed disc jockey Casey Kasem), he hits the big time amid a continual regimen of booze, heroin, and hookers, moving from the hinterlands to the center stage. Predictably, young Matthew begins to turn himself around before he finally has his inevitable stock-'70s youth film's tragic reckoning with the Establishment.[2] The movie was released briefly in 1973 and then rereleased the next summer (under yet another new title, *The Soul Hustler*) with ad taglines like "He put one hand toward heaven—the other around a female willing to sell her soul." Perhaps not surprisingly, *The Day the Lord Got Busted/Soul Hustler* bounced ignominiously around the nation's drive-in theater circuit for a short while before being sold off for late, late-night TV showings and subsequent video sales in the late 1970s.[3]

The existence of a secular film on the Jesus People movement—even such dreck as *The Lovin' Man/The Day the Lord Got Busted/The Soul Hustler*—was a concrete indicator that the Jesus freak had become a piece of the American cultural furniture in the early and mid-1970s. And Burt Topper's drive-in fodder was not alone. There was *Walking in My Time*, a stage musical about a group of communalists called the New Time Jesus Church. Debuting in San Francisco in the spring of 1972, the play's authors had ambitious plans for the show, projecting a move to Broadway, an original cast album, and troupes in Los Angeles and London. But weighed down by reviews that blasted it for "bad" singing and dancing and a book labeled sophomoric and "ineptly written," the play closed after three months.[4]

In contrast, ABC produced a fairly well-crafted, ninety-minute, made-for-TV drama that addressed the deprogramming controversy. *Can Ellen Be Saved?* starred Leslie Nielsen, John Saxon, and young actress Katherine Cannon (later the TV mother of actress Tori Spelling on the '90s teen soap opera *Beverly Hills 90210*) and aired twice on ABC in 1974. Originally titled *Children of God* before the network's legal department thought better of it, the movie followed the story of Ellen Lindsey, a troubled teen who becomes involved with a group called the Children of Jesus and its dictatorial leader Joseph (played by Michael Parks). The movie was deemed relevant and popular enough to merit a mass-market paperback novelization based on the original screenplay.[5]

On the literary side, there was *Jesus Song*, a good-natured adolescent novel that appeared in 1973. Penned by R. R. Knudson, a lesbian poet and writer who authored a moderately successful series of girls' sports novels (the Zan series), it told the story of Joy Cheever, a chubby, fifteen-year-old girl on a spiritual quest who links up with a group called the Heavenly Children of Angel Lake. After composing a musical play titled *Jesus Song* that the group performs across northern Ontario, Joy returns to her family with a clearer understanding of "what is real and useful in religion" and a better sense of herself.[6]

For a more adult audience, there was the 1972 novel *The Jesus Freaks*, written by author Richard Hubbard, a veteran pulp novelist who had been churning out westerns, detective novels, gothic horror, and TV novelizations (*Gunsmoke*, *Adam 12*, *Then Came Bronson*) under his own name and several pseudonyms for more than two decades.[7] The cover of *The Jesus Freaks* made it amply clear that one was not picking up anything analogous to Billy Graham's best-selling *The Jesus*

Grin and Bear It

'You counsel people, you comfort them, you marry
them, dear!. . .It's too late for you to chuck
it all and become a Jesus freak!'

FIGURE 9.1 Jesus People as part of the
cultural furniture: "Grin and Bear It" for June
12, 1974.
Used with permission, North America Syndicate,
King Features.

Generation. A heavily shadowed color photo of two scantily clad couples (one in a
rather amorous embrace) was superimposed on a photo of a long-haired, bearded
man who appeared to have stepped out of a production of *King Lear*. The cover's
words shouted at prospective purchasers that *The Jesus Freaks* was:

> The big new novel about the saints who swing. FIRST SEX. THEN
> DRUGS. AND AFTER THAT THE WILDEST TRIP OF THEM ALL...
> SALVATION!

Inside, the plot centered on a Jesus freak compound called the Old Rugged
Crossroads in that most atypical of Jesus People centers—the East Seventies of
Manhattan. Led by Matt Conroy, a guilt-scarred Marine pilot and Vietnam vet, the
little band of Jesus freaks navigate their way through corrupt real estate tycoons
and snooty society reverends while trying to carve out a Jesus People oasis in the

urban desert. After 246 pages of cocktails, profanities, sex, a botched abortion, a homosexual jailhouse rape, and a funeral, the little band had managed to thwart the cynical establishment types and head off for a new start in Vermont. Published by Pyramid Books (ironically, the mass-market paperback publisher for many of evangelist David Wilkerson's books), the novel graced the bookracks of drugstores and truck stops for a short while before quickly disappearing into rummage sale obscurity.[8]

A Changing and Maturing Movement?

The existence of Jesus freak-derived pop culture artifacts was a significant sign that the hippie Christians and their evangelical supporters had entered the warp and woof of everyday American life (figure 9.1). Going into the mid-1970s, the Jesus People looked like they were here for the cultural long haul. In fact, the movement had begun to spread beyond the North American continent and looked like it might be ready for international takeoff. A nascent Jesus movement had appeared in Britain among pockets of church youth following the arrival of the Children of God, a 1971 visit by the cross-walking Arthur Blessitt, and the subsequent presence of Jim Palosaari and his Jesus Family group.[9] Pockets of counter-culturally oriented young Christians were also popping up in very nonevangelical European countries. In France, the l'Eau Vive (Living Water) missions movement had established nearly two dozen outposts by the fall of 1973, and in Denmark, a group called the Unge Kristne i København (Young Christians of Copenhagen) battled the nation's secularized culture.[10]

The Jesus People showed especial strength Down Under. In Australia, the movement surfaced as young Australian evangelicals read about, and made contact with, North American Jesus People groups. Coffeehouses like Jacob's Ladder, the Salt and Light Company, and the One-Way Inn sprang up; Jesus papers like the *Sydney Town Express*, *Dayspring*, and *Coming Home* were published; full-service ministries like House of the New World and the Glebe Zoo popped up in Australian urban centers; and American Jesus music artists such as Larry Norman and Barry McGuire toured the continent.[11] Unlike the American scene, however, the Jesus movement in Australia did not emerge from its indigenous hippies but from evangelicals who were rebelling against the values of middle-class Australian society and moribund church life.[12] Particularly key in promoting the movement was John Smith, a Methodist clergyman from Melbourne who established a relationship with Carl Parks and his Spokane-based Jesus People Army. In 1971, he began producing an Australian edition of the JPA's paper, *Truth* (later, *Truth and Liberation*).[13] In 1972, he founded the Truth and Liberation Concern and created an outreach to the continent's rugged motorcycle gangs in the form of the God's Squad Christian Motorcycle Club. In 1973, Smith journeyed to the United States "to connect with the rest of the tribe" and visited such hot spots as Calvary Chapel and the Christian World Liberation Front in Berkeley.[14] He was particularly impressed with the latter group and its leader Jack Sparks's concern about social and political issues, and he reproduced and adapted many of the CWLF's materials to the Australian context.[15]

But even as the Jesus People managed to inspire groups overseas, by the mid-1970s, the movement was clearly undergoing change. Although Duane Pederson could still round up a crowd of 5,000 Jesus People and church kids to pass out the *Hollywood Free Paper* with coffee and doughnuts at the 1974 Rose Bowl Parade, it was becoming clear that the Jesus People movement was no longer quite the exuberant, Jesus-marching, street-corner-preaching expression of the flower children gone revivalist Christian it had been just a few years earlier.[16] If anything, the growth of such things as the Jesus music industry seemed to betoken a movement that was coming of age. In terms of specific organizations, that certainly seemed to be the case in looking at the growth of a group like the Oregon-based Shiloh Youth Revival Centers.

Through the mid-1970s, Shiloh was a remarkable example of the manner in which the Jesus People movement had grown and prospered. What had started out as a wandering band of fewer than twenty bedraggled Jesus People from Southern California had become one of the largest communal groups to emerge out of the hippie counterculture, much less the Jesus movement. Thousands of people came into contact with Shiloh: The organization once counted more than 11,000 "visits" and 168 "conversions" in a five-week period in 1977 at its communes and churches.[17] A hard count of its members is probably impossible to come by, but one estimate maintains that over its span nearly 10,000 people passed through Shiloh, with about half that number being core members.[18]

By late 1977, Shiloh had thousands of full-time members in and around its headquarters near Eugene, Oregon, and within a far-flung network that in the late '70s consisted of several dozen communal houses across the United States.[19] Scattered from the Aleutian Islands (Dutch Harbor, Alaska), to Savannah, Georgia, the houses served as bases for evangelization and recruitment, as well as sites for businesses that supported the individual houses and the organization. The owner of farms, houses, apartment buildings, an office building, and other properties in their headquarters area around Eugene, Shiloh sponsored a number of traveling ministry teams, printed a monthly journal, and operated a number of businesses ranging from tree planting and beekeeping to an Alaskan crabbing operation. The group even had its own two-engine plane and operated a medical clinic and credit union. Altogether, Shiloh, according to one of its former caretakers, Joe V. Peterson, had accumulated millions of dollars in "land, equipment, businesses and investments." Its annual budget, according to scholars David T. Stewart and James Richardson, was probably running well over $3 million dollars. It was indeed, as Peterson described it, "a nearly self-sufficient coast-to-coast empire."[20]

Table 9.1 "Did you attend a local church during your involvement in the JP movement?"

Yes	84.6%
No	12.6%
Not sure	1.1%
No Answer	1.7%[26]

Despite the national success of such a large organization, the Jesus movement was not receiving much recognition outside its own boundaries. In fact, by the mid-1970s, the general absence of God's Forever Family from the national media spotlight had made it easy for casual observers to lose track of the movement. As early as the fall of 1973, articles appeared in both the secular and evangelical media to update readers on what was going on with the Jesus freaks. *Time*'s two-page article "The Jesus Evolution" appeared in the September 24 issue and was a broad survey of what was going on in the movement, checking in on groups such as Calvary Chapel and the Alamo Foundation and getting quotes from the likes of Ted Wise and Kent Philpott. They assured their readers that the Jesus movement, "unlike many aspects of the youth counterculture," had "survived the fad phase" and was "settling down for the long haul."[21]

In the evangelical monthly *Eternity*, sociologist Ronald M. Enroth, coauthor of the briskly selling book *The Jesus People: Old-Time Religion in the Age of Aquarius*, asked, "Where Have All the Jesus People Gone?" For his part, Enroth—surveying the scene on the West Coast, where he had done most of his research in the summer of 1971—also reiterated that the Jesus People were still there. However, that an article under that title was being published was plain enough evidence that the movement was starting to fall off the public's—even, it would seem, the evangelical public's—mental radar screen. "Although the TV cameras and news reporters have moved on to new assignments," Enroth reassured *Eternity* readers, "the Jesus movement is still alive, and in some places, thriving." He did have a sense, however, that the Jesus People were less given to "superficial fervor" displayed in public and were concentrating on "more committed discipleship" through Bible study and education. He noted that many Jesus People were in evidence in established evangelical churches that had, for their part, "made a definite, commendable effort to accommodate the young people." Overall, Enroth saw the signs of a movement he believed was undergoing "healthy growth" and evidencing a "more enlightened, balanced maturation."[22]

Enroth's observations were seconded over the following three years by similar articles that appeared in the *International Review of Missions* in April 1974, the evangelical periodical *Christianity Today* in late 1975, and the national newsweekly *U.S. News*

& World Report in the spring of 1976.²³ The author of the article in the *International Review of Missions* noted that the impact of the Jesus People in conservative congregations not only had added "much-needed" warmth to "emotion-starved" evangelical congregations but also was so strong that "the average hair length [had] grown by several inches."²⁴ Similarly, the piece in *U.S. News & World Report* emphasized the manner in which the Jesus People were becoming a "potent force in old-line congregations."²⁵ These comments on church participation by Jesus People were not just wishful thinking, either. Survey results of former movement members, decades later, clearly pointed to the fact that the overwhelming majority of Jesus People seem to have been involved in traditionally styled church congregations in addition to their activities as Jesus People (table 9.1).

The *Christianity Today* article was particularly insightful, coming as it did from Ed Plowman, the pastor and former Evangelical Concerns board member who had served as the evangelical mainstream's unofficial liaison and publicity agent with the Jesus People movement during 1971 and 1972. The article examined the evolution of a few of the Jesus People's more prominent figures and marveled at the growth of Chuck Smith's Calvary Chapel in Costa Mesa, California. Plowman noted that the movement itself had continued to expand after the glory days of 1971, particularly in the Midwest. Overall, however, he had the distinct impression that the ethos of the overall movement had changed from an apocalypse-driven concentration on evangelism to a quieter emphasis on personal discipleship and learning. Large segments of "the movement [had] disappeared behind closed doors," Plowman commented. The trend was "away from [the] streets and into books, away from confrontation and toward contemplation...there [was] less emphasis on outreach, more on worship and Bible study." Plowman nonetheless saw that all these positive developments carried with them a possible trade-off:

> Undeniably, the movement has made an impact for good on the lives of many individuals, and a lot of churches are stronger for it. But with all the present-day emphasis on discipleship, community, and church activity in the apparent absence of...evangelism, the current crop of teenagers might well ask: Whatever happened to the Jesus movement?²⁷

Indeed, Plowman was more prescient than he knew. Despite the general spread of the Jesus Revolution and its coffeehouses and fellowships across the country and the impressive status of organizations like Shiloh, the Jesus People movement was, by the late 1975 printing of his article, actually on its last legs. As in the decline of nearly any cultural movement, the factors were several and complex: an unfortunate mix of local personalities and case-specific circumstances interacting with larger cultural and social trends. Within the space of just a few years, these factors would spell the end of the Jesus People movement.

The "Shepherding" Movement

If any widespread internal development contributed to the passing of the Jesus People, it was the investment of a number of local groups in a movement that greatly impacted charismatic and Pentecostal churches in the 1970s—Shepherding. This movement was the brainchild of a group of charismatic ministers and evangelists—Bob Mumford, Derek Prince, Ern Baxter, Don Basham, and Charles Simpson—who had begun a group called Holy Spirit Teaching Ministries (later known as the Christian Growth Movement) in 1969 and created a magazine (*New Wine*) to flesh out their vision of shepherding the growing number of mainline Protestants and Catholics coming into independent charismatic churches toward a vigorous New Testament Christianity.[28] Based in Fort Lauderdale, Florida (the leaders were popularly known as the Fort Lauderdale Five), they quickly came to see the ranks of the burgeoning Jesus movement as in need of their guiding hand.[29]

For their part, many Jesus People leaders and their evangelical helpers had seen the need to firm up their shaky theology in the wake of their internal troubles with the Children of God, which came to the fore during 1971. A string of less dramatic but steady threats from other unorthodox groups such as Victor Paul Wierwille's The Way International and Sun Myung Moon's emerging Unification Church merely reinforced the perception that many Jesus People were spiritual babes in the woods. The Shepherding movement, with its emphasis on a prolonged period of study and discipleship coupled with strict lines of authority, offered an attractive solution.

Scott Ross, head of the Love Inn ministry in upstate New York and the man behind the microphone for the syndicated *Scott Ross Show*, was one Jesus People leader who by 1976 was looking to Shepherding as a way to make sense of his multiplying responsibilities. The growth of his radio program, a community with more than 250 people, a school, the *Free Love* Jesus paper, a new record label (NewSong), oversight of a score of house church groups, and being on the road for speaking engagements had produced a serious case of burnout. "I was very vulnerable," Ross recalled years later. "I was hanging out there [alone]," he remembered, and sensed a need for "check and balance.... I needed to find more mature men who would help mentor me and help keep me on track." Ross brought the Love Inn into the orbit of the Fort Lauderdale Five and eventually moved to Florida to work with Prince and Mumford.[30] A number of other Jesus People leaders, including influential figures such as Oliver Heath and Ray Rempt, likewise put themselves "under the covering" of the Fort Lauderdale Five or other pastors associated with the movement. Lonnie Frisbee, Calvary Chapel's "hippie evangelist," also became involved with the group. The Frisbees' motivation was divided. Lonnie was eager to pursue a ministry based more on signs and wonders under Bob Mumford's tutelage; Connie had long been deeply troubled about the state of their marriage and had received no help at Calvary Chapel. In an interview many years later, she claimed that attempts to get counseling were swatted away with the implication that—in eternal calculations—her marriage was insignificant compared to Lonnie's ministry and the number of souls being saved. With a split agenda that foreshadowed the breakup of their marriage, the Frisbees headed for Florida in 1972.[31]

Meanwhile, dozens of local Jesus People fellowships across North America— whether officially connected or merely influenced by tapes and literature—also ended up participating in the Shepherding movement to one degree or another. Although the movement spoke to the Jesus People's desire for a deeper grounding in the Christian faith, Shepherding proved to be, for the most part, a disaster. Reports of overbearing intrusion and authoritarian control in such matters as personal finances, career and job decisions, courtship, marriage, and childbearing were rampant. One couple, who had at one time been connected with Jesus People houses in Tallahassee, Florida, reported how "covering pastors" would "help" married couples select the color and style of new furniture purchases and even chose names for new babies.[32] Patrick Bowen, a member of another Jesus People fellowship in Florida, noted how he "once was corrected for moving across town without first getting the 'witness' of [his] elders."[33] At the Oak Park Fellowship in Oak Park, Illinois, Arthur Cook reported that his shepherds told him what job to take. When his wife objected, she was "told to put up and shut up. Women were basically to be seen and not heard."[34] Brian Carling depicted his experiences with a Fort Lauderdale Five–influenced faction that emerged at Nashville's Jesus People– packed Belmont Church of Christ as nothing short of "cultic control," which "humiliated [him] and a lot of others."[35] At one point, Jesus People USA (JPUSA) in Chicago—influenced by the teaching emanating from within the Shepherding movement—instituted public spankings of adult members of the community who were perceived as being out of line.[36]

But it was not only individuals and couples who suffered from the controversy. Many Jesus People groups and churches were damaged by their participation in the Shepherding movement. Besides JPUSA in Chicago, Ross's long-established Love Inn community was also badly shaken.[37] The Belmont Church of Christ, a Nashville church heavily laced with Jesus People, saw a segment of the leadership pull out to form the House of Blessing.[38] By the beginning of the 1980s, the Shepherding movement had been severely stigmatized within evangelical circles, exacerbated by concerns within the larger culture over reports of mind control and abuse by groups labeled cults, such as Jim Jones's People's Temple.[39] But by this time, Shepherding had already brought havoc to a number of Jesus People churches and groups and proved to be a contributing factor to the demise of the overall Jesus People movement.

The Jesus People: Growing Up

Although the Shepherding movement inflicted damage, its reach was nowhere deep enough to derail the entire movement by itself. Much more significant were factors that were not spawned by any personalities, theologies, or controversies within the movement. The Jesus People were simply getting older and moving into the adult phase of their lives.

If the Jesus People were getting on with life, they were in plenteous company. More and more of the Baby Boom generation were beginning to move past the troubled years of adolescence, and 1976 marked a significant demographic milestone: In that year, the oldest Baby Boomers turned thirty. The generation that had once declared, "Don't trust anyone over 30" had now, in the words of the famous *Pogo* cartoon strip, "met the enemy and it is us." Millions more of their contemporaries were hurtling toward this same realization; by that same year, a majority of their generational peers had reached that official milestone of legal American adulthood, twenty-one. Despite the fears of their elders, the mid-1970s revealed that America's youth had not utterly eschewed the normal rites of adult passage or completely dropped out of society—not by a long shot. Education, careers, marriage (despite the growth in cohabiting couples—sure evidence of the changes wrought by the 1960s), and young, growing families (although frequently delayed by a few years) were just as much the normal pattern for the Baby Boomers as they had been for previous generations.[40]

If anything, the Jesus People movement, having imbibed traditional values of hard work, responsibility, and domesticity, seemed to have done more than its part in the domestication of the Baby Boom generation, particularly its hard-core, countercultural cohort. Indeed, the requirements for faithful discipleship did much to propel many individual Jesus People back on track and steadied others as they attempted to cope with the life choices of late adolescence and early adulthood. As the '70s progressed, the Jesus People experience had, it turned out, proved to be a spiritual staging area for tens of thousands of young Americans who were making up their minds about marriage, schooling, and careers.

One of the most prominent indirect functions of the movement's coffeehouses, communes, communal houses, and churches was to serve as a gigantic Jesus People marriage bureau. "Almost every month there was a wedding," remembered one former member of a California commune who wondered when it would be her turn to find the Lord's intended man for her life: "God paired people up like socks, and there I was mate-less."[41] Joan Jallette, a 1972 University of Maryland dropout who had hitchhiked cross-country, been converted, and joined the Lighthouse Ranch commune near Eureka, California, recalled that there were probably fifteen to twenty weddings per year. There was no dating per se at the Lighthouse Ranch and, to avoid temptation, potential twosomes were discouraged from going out as couples. But there was courtship. In mid-1974, as she was working as a secretary for the commune's in-town doughnut shop, Jallette and the store's manager, Chris Pritchard, began to take a liking to each other. They began to chat about their situation, wondering if "God [was] drawing [them] together." About two months later, they went out with a group from the commune to see the movie version of *Man of La Mancha* and afterward slipped away to a local diner, where, "over burgers and fries," Pritchard proposed to her. After informing the elders of their decision, they were married a few weeks later during a Sunday morning church service, followed by a spaghetti-and-meatball reception dinner (the meatballs facilitated by $50 from Jallette's parents who had come from Philadelphia for the ceremony), replete with a de rigueur cross-shaped cake.[42]

Primary sources from the Jesus People are filled with announcements, anecdotal asides, and passing references to the matrimonial links being forged among the movement's numbers. Marriages were celebrated as signs of stability and maturity. For example, Steven Derek Preston, a member of Chicago's JPUSA group, testified of the turnaround in his life by concluding his autobiographical narrative of being rescued from drugs, meditation, and biker violence by recounting how God had brought him into maturity: "Now I'm married and serving God where He wants me....I've been a Christian for four years now."[43] The Christian World Liberation Front announced an upcoming wedding in one of its 1974 fund-raising letters: "Peggy Lee has been with us for two years and is responsible for filling literature orders," the letter noted. "In June, she will marry Gene Burkett," who had "come to us recently to be with the Street Theatre."[44] In similar fashion, the March 1971 newsletter from the Antioch Ranch in Mendocino, California, noted that they had just "had the honor of having" their "first ranch wedding." "Dan and Jeannine are cozy in the Hammer House," the letter stated, assuring their supporters that they were "working out things as carefully as possible to provide a balance of privateness [sic] and autonomy" for the couple, while ensuring that they still had the "needed fellowship and responsibility" that their Christian community provided.[45]

San Francisco Bay area Jesus People leader Kent Philpott consistently saw the inclinations toward matrimony in boy-girl relationships among the Jesus People as a sign that young people's lives were being turned around. In late 1970, he noted in his journal the progress of two of the residents of his Zion's Inn in San Rafael, California: "Two of our girls will be married soon," he happily wrote. "Linda has been here for over thirteen months....And Kathy, with us six months....They are marrying brothers, Ernie and Jimmy Ayala."[46] A year later, Philpott's newsletter informed supporters that "there had been ten people fully-involved in our immediate ministry marry, and several more marriages are coming up."[47] Four years later in 1975, the story was much the same within Philpott's communal houses around Marin and Sonoma counties. He told his supporters only half-jokingly in a monthly newsletter: "You see, we are opening houses and people are getting married. That seems to be the main thing we are doing."[48]

That people in their late adolescence and early adulthood would be developing relationships and getting married is certainly not surprising, especially within a religious movement that touted the virtues of premarital chastity in the midst of an increasingly sex-obsessed society. What was particularly meaningful about it among the Jesus People, however, were the consequences such developments held for the movement itself. Given the earlier intensity of Jesus People's evangelistic efforts and sometimes near-daily rounds of group Bible study and worship, the continual siphoning off of young couples to a more domestic, cocooning phase of life carried with it an inevitable change in the maintenance of Jesus People life as usual.

This dynamic became particularly problematic for those young married couples who were attempting to carry on within communal living arrangements. The lack of privacy, financial hardships, and the sometimes grating habits and pathologies of one's house or commune mates often proved to be a real problem for young married Jesus People couples. This need for more space—physical, financial, and psychic—is hinted at in a 1974 letter from one young wife in a communal home in Novato, California. Kris wrote the wife of her group's leader a long, breezy letter and slipped in a short but telling passage:

> You know Bobbie that I love my house an awful lot, but I decided that if you and Kent stay in England for a year then I am going to encourage Mark to find us our own place to live. It gets to be a drag for Mark.... Same people, same mistakes ... and problems.[49]

The Shiloh communes recognized the problems with privacy and elbow room married couples faced in a communal setting—to say nothing of the economic problems—and made provisions for them in the early 1970s. Shiloh began allowing married couples to rent houses and apartments from the organization, even instituting a "salary" in 1974 for about fifty of the group's leaders and staff.[50] At first Shiloh attempted to house married couples in married people's communes but that, John Higgins remembered, "went over like a lead balloon...they were fighting over kids, arguing...calling each other names," and that was scrapped in favor of separate housing. By 1977, almost all of the 200 married couples in Oregon were living noncommunally "within" the commune. Although the economic and privacy issues might have been more-or-less solved by this strategy, the overall life of the group took an unavoidable hit. Sociologists studying the group in the mid to late 1970s noted that "the two groups (married and single people) live somewhat separate lives, with there being an apparent decreasing contact between the two groups."[51] Significantly, smaller, less well-heeled communal Jesus People groups could seldom afford so sweeping an arrangement. For these more numerous and typical Jesus People groups, the impact of the marrying off of its members usually meant something much more akin to separation, if not divorce, from the group.

While marriage represented a continual coming-of-age drain on the core constituency of most, if not all, Jesus People groups, America's burgeoning opportunities for higher education provided another source of shrinkage. Despite the movement's countercultural and sometimes anti-intellectual bent, the vast majority of the Jesus People showed by life example that they more than shared the larger American belief in the powers and virtues of education. Results from the 2004 survey compilation of more than 800 former Jesus People showed that slightly more than 70% of those respondents had the equivalent of an associate's degree or two full years of college education, and a full 48% claimed to have earned a bachelor's degree (compared to 27% of the general American population in 2003).[52]

At the time, a move to acquire education was viewed as a positive. For many who had perhaps fallen behind as the result of adolescent trials and/or drug-related incapacity, an effort to undertake or resume formal education was hard-earned evidence of the way Jesus was helping them get it together. As Kent Philpott surveyed the progress of his work in late 1971, one of the sure gauges of the success of his ministry was that "in the overall Bay Area ministry 40 to 50 young people" had "enrolled in college for the Fall semester."[53]

Many Jesus People were part of the movement even as they attended college but were eventually taken out of their local scene by further educational and career choices. For example, Gordon Lewis was an engineering student at Rensselaer Polytechnic Institute in Troy, New York, and in the mid-'70s was a member of a local Jesus House and involved with a local coffeehouse. But when he moved on to graduate education at Penn State, his involvement with the movement ended.[54] Stephen Jay Briggs was a student at the University of North Carolina–Chapel Hill as a business administration student when he was converted in 1973. A member of a secular rock band, Briggs formed a Jesus band called the Forever Family Band and played in coffeehouses in Virginia and the Carolinas but then left to enroll as a student at Dallas Theological Seminary in 1976.[55]

In some cases, these sorts of life decisions proved fatal to an entire group. For example, the Avalon Jesus People group in Akron, Ohio, had a network of affiliated Christian centers in and around the Akron area, a street paper, and a Jesus Free Store.[56] However, the group's leader, Craig Yoe, encountered strong resistance from a segment of the group that opposed his desire to organize the group as a church. The Avalon group began to split apart, and with Yoe's decision to pursue his abilities as a graphic artist and cartoonist, the enterprise disbanded entirely, and the group's properties were sold.[57]

The situation in Akron was symptomatic of the age-related demographic changes that were affecting the Jesus People. Marriage, family, education, and career choices naturally began to change their time commitments and financial priorities. As tens of thousands of Jesus People moved on with their lives, they were pulled away from the movement.

Hard Times: Jesus People Close Up Shop

For the vast majority of former Jesus People, the movement's evaporation in the mid and late '70s was a gentle fading away, another change in a period of life transition marked by marriage, new families, new homes, new jobs and careers, and the hunt for a good church. In many ways, the transition was similar to that of any group of young adults who begin to leave the ethos and institutions of youth culture behind as they settle into the adult world. These sorts of changes, however, are usually easier for individuals than for institutions and organizations. Having already taken on a life of their own, Jesus People groups were forced to respond to the new life directions of their individual members.

The easiest and perhaps most natural response, of course, was simply to close up shop and call it a day. For the vast majority of small Jesus People fellowships, groups, communal houses, and coffeehouses, this was the scenario that most often played itself out. The heretofore booming American economy had run into some major problems by the mid-1970s, triggered by the costs of the Vietnam War, the beginning of a change from a manufacturing to a technology- and service-oriented economy, and the first shockwaves caused by American dependence on OPEC oil.[58] Stunned economists coined a new term, *stagflation*, to describe the combination of the usually opposite trends of recession and inflation.[59] By the end of 1974, consumer prices were increasing over 12% a year (compared with a mere 4% as late as 1969), and the unemployment rate had moved past 7% (it had been just 3.5% in 1969). By the end of 1975, the median price of American homes had climbed 50% in just three years, and mortgage rates had passed 9% (up from the standard 4% to 5% of the 1950s and 1960s).[60] Understandably, rising unemployment and inflation hit especially hard among young people, who were not only attempting to establish themselves financially but also vying with other Baby Boomers in a constricted job market.

All these factors took their toll on struggling Jesus People groups that were hardly flush to begin with. The fate of the House of Peter in Winnipeg, Manitoba, serves as a typical example of the challenges facing Jesus People due to the combined pressures of adulthood and a depressed economy. The ministry had been opened in the fall of 1970 by Russell "Cousin" Leamen, a native of New Brunswick who had gone west to California and been immersed in the drug culture before being converted. Venturing northward to begin his Jesus People outreach in Manitoba, he gathered a small group of converts and somewhat avant-garde evangelical youth about him. Remodeling a vacant storefront near the heart of downtown Winnipeg, he attempted to run a free store for the street youth of the city. The group existed pretty much hand-to-mouth, depending on what random Canadian dollars floated their way through odd jobs and the good will of fellow believers. "The Lord provides us with all we need," he told a reporter in a 1971 article. "Once, someone found it in his heart to leave $200," he exulted, and "a plumber, and then an electrician gave us free assistance....Praise the Lord!" Leamen and his fellow Jesus People carried on in their communal house and worked the streets of Winnipeg, spreading the gospel for more than two years. But by the spring of 1973, the situation had changed. Cousin was now married to Wendy, had an infant daughter, and soon would have another child on the way, and the dedicated life of ministry within a hippie Jesus People setting proved hard to pull off with a family to look after. In April 1973, the House of Peter was closed, and Leamen pursued work as a construction laborer. Others from the group also moved on—Ed was married and working at a tannery; Siggy worked at a retirement home and was considering getting married. A reporter for the *Winnipeg Free Press* summed up the change in an early-1974 update on the group's fate: "No doubt about it, an ex-Jesus Freak really can find happiness as a settled-down family man and unemployed drywall contractor."[61]

The changing times coupled with bad economic conditions undoubtedly proved to be a tough set of obstacles for many maturing Jesus People groups in the mid and late '70s. But it was not only the stand-alone coffeehouse or local Jesus House operations that suffered; even some of the movement's leading lights were being forced to close their doors. Evangelical Concerns, the San Francisco group that had overseen the establishment of the Living Room coffeehouse in Haight-Ashbury back in 1967 and provided legal and financial support that set a number of Bay Area Jesus People groups on their feet (the Christian World Liberation Front and Jews for Jesus among them), lost their market niche within the regional evangelical parachurch world as the movement waned. The organization attempted to sponsor special events and rallies in the Bay Area in the mid-'70s, but the financial drain—absent the excitement of the movement's salad days—proved too much. By 1976, with its assets under $1,000, the organization's board decided to call it quits.[62]

A similar fate befell the movement's premier Jesus paper, Duane Pederson's *Hollywood Free Paper* (*HFP*). At one point in the early '70s, it had become a national operation with an average circulation of more than 400,000 copies and had several print runs over 1 million. In early 1972, the *HFP* was ambitiously lobbying supporters like entertainer Pat Boone and Stan Mooneyham (chairman of the evangelical relief agency World Vision) to tab friends "who can contribute $1,000 to $5,000 or more."[63] In that same year, Pederson's once-homemade street paper had expenditures of nearly $220,000—the bulk of it raised through small donations from both earnest Jesus People and rank-and-file evangelical church folk.[64] But as the cultural landscape began to change and the underground newspaper as a national symbol of the counterculture faded, so, too, did the novelty of the *HFP*.[65] By the mid-70s, Pederson had been forced to trim his staff of more than twenty back to a pair of helpers, as the paper's active circulation dwindled to well under the 50,000 mark. The paper officially ceased publication in 1979, but by that time, Pederson had already shifted gears to prison ministry and shortly thereafter became the pastor of a Venice, California, congregation belonging to the Missionary Church.[66]

While the waning of the Jesus movement and attendant financial hardship brought about the demise of Evangelical Concerns and the *Hollywood Free Paper*, the recipe for financial disaster was quite different for the heretofore prospering Shiloh Youth Revival Centers. That group fell apart because of a mixture of internal personality clashes and politics, exacerbated by government-initiated legal proceedings. Shiloh's rapid growth had been marked by three major changes over the course of the decade. First had been the growing differentiation between married and single members. Another change that began to surface about 1971 was that old-time Shilohites began to notice a "second-wave" of members coming into their ranks. "We were starting to get people in who had not even experienced the hippie generation and they weren't as loose and radical," recalled one longtime member in a 1994 interview with social scientist Lynne Isaacson. Many of the new recruits were already converted or came from churched backgrounds and were looking at Shiloh as a vehicle for their Christian commitment or as a desirable Christian environment in which to immerse themselves.[67]

Although this development created some minor tensions, a more significant change came with the decision in late 1974 to move from a strictly communal setup to one whereby a number of individuals—mostly married males—began to receive small salaries. By 1976, administrators encouraged married men, if at all possible, to seek secular employment outside the organization in an effort to curb costs and make room for more salaried pastoral staff. This, along with a streamlining of Shiloh's operations in which an expanding core of middle managers oversaw operations, signaled a departure from the original communal vision that had once characterized Shiloh's internal culture.[68]

But these changes, while marking a shift in tone and direction, did not in and of themselves augur the destruction of the group. Two further developments proved more deadly: the group's overall finances and a growing power struggle between Shiloh's core leadership and the commune's founder, John Higgins. Central to the concern about finances were mounting worries over the group's relationship with the Internal Revenue Service (IRS). Although Shiloh had legal status as a nonprofit corporation, the IRS audited the group in 1977 and contended that Shiloh's business endeavors were subject to the Unrelated Business Income Tax (UBIT). Shiloh was hit with a $750,000 judgment for back UBIT—a crushing blow to a successful, property-rich but cash-poor, up-from-the-counterculture outfit. Immediately, the group secured a battery of lawyers to contest the decision.[69]

While a major concern, the IRS troubles exacerbated internal divisions and served to intensify discontent among some with Higgins's standard of living and the feeling among some leaders that there was a growing lifestyle division between the people who earned the money to keep Shiloh afloat and those who engaged in ministry. Disgruntled leaders complained about Higgins and several key administrators living in their own cabins or houses while "regular" married couples struggled to house themselves, and singles crammed into crowded houses and apartments. Many Shiloh members worked long hours, six days a week, and exercised creativity to stretch their food budgets while Shiloh installed a Jacuzzi during a bathroom remodel at John Higgins's house.[70]

Even as this was going on, these tensions were aggravated by Higgins's belief that Shiloh had outlived its usefulness. "Shiloh was just a dead horse," he remembered in an interview years later; "we had outlived the hippies." As early as 1976, Higgins reportedly wrote a letter to his elders stating his conviction that "we needed to shave, cut our hair, and blend in with middle class society so that we could take the message of Christ" to a changing American culture. He argued that it was time to "break this thing up" and urged his leaders—most of whom he claimed resisted the idea—to pick a city and start a church.[71]

Much of this sentiment was fueled by Higgins's growing conviction that the prophecy timetable was hurtling forward toward the End Times. Believing it was Shiloh's duty to reach as many people as possible with the gospel, he oversaw the development of combined musical-evangelistic strike teams, the "Persuaders," whom he often accompanied on special outreaches and tours across the country. But this also fueled internal grumbling. One house pastor recalled the discrepancy between how this elite subset lived and the lifestyles of the rank and file in the houses:

> ... we'd have to send a requisition to the Eugene office downtown for approval so that we could buy underwear for these guys who are out there working 13 hours a day.... And later on, I happened to come across some invoices for the same period, for someone in the upper circle, to buy four silk blouses and two swim suits and, you know, some nice sport clothes because he and four other people were going to Hawaii on a [Persuaders] team ... seeing these receipts for $185 worth of nice sports clothes at the

same time that we were wearing rags and trying to get some decent under-
wear for $36, and having trouble doing it, you know, that [was] just symp-
tomatic [of the divisions in Shiloh].[72]

These internal problems were intensified by Shiloh's run-in with the IRS. Some of
Shiloh's administrators lectured Higgins on the need to cut expenses to get their
financial affairs in order. Convinced an imminent Second Coming trumped these
concerns, Higgins announced he was leaving on an extended evangelistic tour
across the United States—in a new motor home. One former member of Shiloh's
Pastor's Council—actually a Higgins supporter—recalled his chagrin at what he
perceived as Higgins's decision to "go cruising around the country" to "rally the
troops" in the belief that "God [would] cover [the shortfall]" of the organization's
"deficit spending"; to his mind, that was "the final straw" for Shiloh.[73]

The problems came to a head in April 1978, when eight Shiloh board members
suddenly appeared in Savannah, Georgia, where Higgins was attending his sister's wedding. In an early morning tribunal held in the back of a passenger van,
the eight accused him of a dictatorial leadership style, mismanaging funds, and
practicing favoritism. In the face of such opposition from within his leadership
corps, Higgins was fired as the head of Shiloh, returned to Oregon, moved his
family out of their Shiloh-owned house, and set off shortly thereafter to establish
a Calvary Chapel church plant in Phoenix.[74]

News of Higgins's departure sent shock waves through the organization, especially among the rank and file who were oblivious to any problems at headquarters. Karen Castillo, a divorced mother of two who had been with the group for
several years, was typical of those surprised by the turn of events. In an interview
more than two decades later, she remembered how all the "Captains of Ten" had
suddenly been told to round up the members of their groups to come to a special
meeting at the Shiloh Church in Eugene, where, to their shock, they learned that
the ministry was in crisis and that Higgins had been shown the gate:

> I wasn't politically savvy at all, I wasn't aware of the politics, I didn't pay
> any attention to all that…[the Elders] felt that John was out of order, that
> he needed to submit himself to the authority of [Calvary Chapel leader
> and Higgins's old mentor] Chuck Smith…that the ministry was in deep
> financial straits….[75]

Overnight, Shiloh began to unravel. Heated meetings occurred all across the
country, and people began to leave in droves. Several houses split off—some of
them forming the seeds for new Calvary Chapel churches—and a number of others simply closed. By the end of 1978, there were only three houses still operating
under the Shiloh umbrella; by June 1980, Shiloh had officially ceased to exist. "The

Land," the site of the commune's once-bustling training school outside Eugene, continued to operate as a retreat center for various evangelical church groups from 1982 until 1989. However, Shiloh's lingering tax case was rejected by the IRS in 1987. In their opinion, Shiloh had been able "to grow as rapidly as it did in large part by organizing businesses which put all of its members to work earning income for [the] petitioner (Shiloh) in return for providing for…basic needs."[76] For the Feds, Shiloh's argument that their enterprise was a holistic one in which their fiscal structure could not be separated out from the spiritual and economic dimension of their organization was an invalid rationalization. With their decision, there was no choice but to sell The Land in 1989 to pay legal fees.[77]

The legal end of Shiloh was but the postponed tail end of a series of closures and moving on for the Jesus People. The financial hard times of the mid and late 1970s effectively spelled the end for scores and scores of groups already in flux. The scarcity of money was often the last straw in a series of challenges.

Changes in the Larger Youth Culture

Even with Jesus People beginning to move into mainstream adult society, the movement might very well have endured beyond the mid to late 1970s had there been a steady influx of younger believers. However, the cultural terrain had changed a great deal since the Summer of Love in 1967. Much of the style and general zeitgeist that had made the Jesus People with it and relevant no longer dominated the youth culture.

The most obvious change was that the counterculture, while it exerted a lasting influence on the society at large, had long since faded; its heyday, according to the estimation of historian Timothy Miller, having passed by the early 1970s, after a mere four to five years.[78] As the decade progressed, the emerging American youth culture(s) reflected what contemporary commentators labeled the "Me Decade," a rejection of the ethos that had characterized the hippie counterculture and formed so central a part of the Jesus People identity and style.[79] With the seedbed culture from which it had emerged undermined, its main connection to the secular youth culture had been severed.

As the 1970s progressed, the "spiritual" edge to popular culture and music that had existed in the early 1970s had also long since evaporated: On the rock charts, Jesus was no longer cool. Aside from a two-week February 1973 appearance in the Top 40 of a remake of the song "Jesus Is Just Alright" by the Doobie Brothers (hardly a Jesus People band—their name saluting a popular term for a marijuana cigarette) and the pan-Christian pop appeal of Australian nun Janet Mead's hip version of the "The Lord's Prayer" in the spring of 1974, not a single song featuring spiritual content of a Christian nature would appear on the American hit parade again until the recently born-again Bob Dylan's "Gotta Serve Somebody" rose to #24 in the autumn of 1979.[80]

FIGURE 9.2 A group from Jesus People USA in Chicago prepare for a downtown witnessing expedition in the Loop in early 1976.
Courtesy of Jesus People, USA.

The cultural factors that helped produce the Jesus movement and catapult it into the national limelight were nearly nonexistent by the mid to late '70s. What was worse, a bevy of new youth cultures arose during this period that stood in dramatic contrast to, and in rejection of, what had existed just a few years before. Backed by record companies, radio stations, and marketers eager to tap into the next big thing in a rapidly segmenting youth market, these new versions of teen culture revolved around emergent musical styles—heavy metal, disco, punk, and new wave—that represented a reaction against the cosmic idealism of the '60s flower child. Even though the new youth subcultures shared an enthusiasm for sex, drugs, and rock 'n' roll, the emerging scene was, in the words of cultural critic John Street, more about "paint your face" than "feed your head."[81] All in all, it was hardly promising cultural terrain for the Jesus People. Framed against this backdrop, the Jesus People image and style looked like an out-of-date relic of Haight-Ashbury. Evangelical young people might continue to embrace rock music, and that youthful bridge to the youth culture might still bring in some lost secular sheep, but increasingly the avenue would be evangelical youth cultures that mirrored the larger evolving scene, not through recruitment to a Jesus People movement marked by all the countercultural trappings that had once made it a powerful force. In many ways, the demise of the counterculture and the rise of a variety of new, startlingly different youth cultures was the ultimate coup de grace to the Jesus People. With all its other troubles—a maturing base, internal squabbles, and financial problems—the new terrain in American youth culture was just one problem too many. It was clear that, by the late 1970s, the Jesus People movement was over.

Jesus People Adaptations

Not all Jesus People groups were pulled under by the treacherous cultural currents of the mid to late 1970s. Jesus People USA (JPUSA) in Chicago continued on as an urban commune, growing throughout the late 1970s, with its newspaper *Cornerstone* achieving a small national readership among young evangelicals (figure 9.2). In 1978, the group merged with a small African American communal group called New Life and the next year moved into Chicago's rough, poverty-stricken Uptown neighborhood. Numbering more than 300 by this time, JPUSA began to evolve into a more activist community from the 1980s forward, involved not only in evangelization but also in local efforts to fight gentrification and work among the poor.[82]

However, most surviving Jesus People groups did not hew so close to their old hippie roots or to a conscious countercultural stance. A more common strategy was an attempt to find ways to adapt to the changing American cultural terrain by gravitating toward evangelical ministry models that were not dependent on a Jesus People orientation. One group, the Berkeley-based Christian World Liberation Front, adopted a niche strategy. By 1975, the CWLF was an established organization with dozens of full-time staff members in a number of different ministries—the *Right On!* newspaper, discipleship ministries, halfway houses working with addicts, campus ministries, a street theater troupe, a developing anticult research group called the Spiritual Counterfeits Project, and a free university, the Crucible.[83] However, its leader, former Campus Crusade staffer Jack Sparks, had become increasingly concerned with the theological problems surrounding parachurch work and the quest for a pristine, authentic Christianity. As part of his intellectual wrestling with this question, Sparks and several ex-Campus Crusade acquaintances had quietly formed a study group independent of the CWLF to dig into theology and church history.[84]

Inevitably, Sparks's intellectual and spiritual pursuits affected some of those in the CWLF. Thus, in the spring of 1975, when Sparks announced that he and his group had come to the conclusion that Eastern Orthodoxy was the end of their search, some of the CWLF who had been privy to Sparks's concerns were ready to go along with him in an attempt to create an evangelical version of Orthodoxy. However, for a large segment of the CWLF, the news came as a complete surprise: "It kind of came out of the blue for a lot of us," recalled former *Right On!* staff member Sharon Gallagher, "when these...five [former] Campus Crusade guys started saying they were apostles and linked to the 3rd-century Church—I didn't get it."[85] Ultimately, about two-thirds of the CWLF staff were unconvinced by Sparks's arguments for Orthodoxy as the living connection to ancient Christianity and enduring template for the contemporary church; recalled CWLF member Bill Squires, "It was a very big shift for most of us and we just couldn't go along with it."[86]

Sparks, for his part, respected the difference of opinion and agreed to step down from his position. He proceeded to write a cordial and supportive letter to financial contributors and the readers of *Right On!*[87] and moved on to become "Father Jack," the leader of what in 1979 became the Evangelical Orthodox Church. (The group was officially admitted into the North American Antiochian [Syrian] Orthodox Church in 1987.)[88] With Sparks's departure, the disparate arms of the CWLF lost their center and eventually separated into several different independent components: the Spiritual Counterfeits Project became an apologetics ministry with its own newsletter and journal; *Right On!* was transformed into *Radix* magazine, which probed the arts, theology, and politics from a left-of-center perspective; and the Crucible eventually became New College–Berkeley, a decade-long experiment in evangelical seminary education.[89]

Jews for Jesus: A Jesus People Group Goes Parachurch

Martin "Moishe" Rosen's Bay Area Jews for Jesus group adjusted to the changing times by moving into the mold of an evangelical parachurch organization. Jews for Jesus closely resembled any number of other Jesus People groups working with disaffected, drug-taking hippies and students, with the one distinctive that the majority of their clientele tended to be—not surprisingly—Jewish. But as the 1970s progressed, Rosen, sensing that there were bigger evangelistic opportunities available, consciously steered Jews for Jesus away from a concentration on disillusioned young Jews in the counterculture. Increasingly, the group's street witnessing campaigns, street theater, and the group's very name—splashed on tracts and worn boldly on T-shirts and the backs of jean jackets—made themselves visible in downtowns throughout the country as they targeted Jews and Gentiles across the age spectrum.[90] In the process, Jews for Jesus quickly became the subject of much discussion and concern among the leaders of the American Jewish community, even as the temperamental Rosen and his aggressive workers became victims of physical and verbal abuse in their evangelistic efforts.[91] The militant Jewish Defense League (JDL) became a particular problem, and at one point Rosen claimed the FBI had warned him that the JDL had targeted him for assassination.[92]

Capitalizing on the group's growing visibility, Rosen positioned it as a vibrant new outreach to the Jewish people—a particularly vital concern at the time within the evangelical church, given its enthusiasm for dispensational prophetic schemes that books like Hal Lindsey's *The Late, Great Planet Earth* had stirred up. Jews for Jesus speakers and its musical team(s), the Liberated Wailing Wall, regularly spoke at evangelical churches and missions conferences and developed a popular presentation titled "Christ in the Passover," all of which built a substantial donor base among rank-and-file evangelicals. By the late 1990s, the organization had become the largest of the evangelical missions to the Jews, with an annual budget of more than $14 million and more than 150 full-time workers in sixteen offices in the United States, Canada, England, France, Israel, Russia, South Africa, Argentina, and Australia.[93]

The Jesus People as Church

The manner in which the CWLF and Jews for Jesus were able to move on as the larger movement broke up around them is testimony to the fact that despite the changes in American youth culture, a number of Jesus People groups managed to weather the storm. Many of these entities were individual fellowships of Jesus People like the Gospel Outreach mission churches (from Jim Durkin's Lighthouse Ranch in Eureka, California) in Philadelphia and New York City; the Cornerstone Church in Brantford, Ontario; the Solid Rock Jesus Fellowship in Salina, Kansas; the Fellowship of Christian Believers in Anderson, Indiana; and the Koinonia Church in Potsdam, New York, which eventually assumed the identity and role of independent (and usually charismatic) local churches. However, for many of these local Jesus People fellowships, a logical course was to link up with one of the most prominent and successful manifestations of the Jesus People movement, Chuck Smith's Calvary Chapel.

With nothing like the fanfare that had surrounded it in 1971, the "Little Country Church" in Orange County continued to grow throughout the 1970s. By 1974, the church had constructed a new facility with a sanctuary seating 2,300 people—which filled three times every Sunday morning. A new fellowship hall with a closed-circuit TV connection to the recently built auditorium was soon erected, adding seating for another 700 per service. In addition to the church itself, Calvary Chapel's musical arm, Maranatha! Records and Music, was going strong, and through the efforts of an entrepreneurial forty-something couple who had begun attending, the church acquired a local radio station and established Maranatha Village, a Christian strip mall with bookstore and office space.[94]

Reflecting his own success, Smith decided that he would encourage several of the Jesus People converts he had mentored—whom sociologist Donald Miller called Smith's "sons" in his book *Reinventing American Protestantism*—to begin new Calvary Chapels.[95] With little or no financial support (Smith reasoned that if God's anointing was on an individual, he would soon have a congregation that could support him), these protégés, Mike McIntosh, Greg Laurie, Raul Ries, Kenn Gullicksen, Jeff Johnson, Tom Stipe, Oden Fong, and others—ordained by filling out a form and handing it in to Smith[96]—created new Calvary Chapels in Riverside, Downey, San Diego, and other cities that maintained the emphasis on simple, upbeat worship music, come-as-you-are informality, and expository Bible teaching. Each church remained self-supporting, and ties with the home church in Costa Mesa were associational and relational—usually consisting of telephone conversations with Smith.[97] Many of these churches proved stunningly successful: For example, Mike McIntosh's Horizon Christian Fellowship in San Diego, which began in January 1975, was by the early '80s attracting 5,000 people per week, had more than 100 home fellowship groups meeting, published a magazine, and maintained radio and TV broadcast ministries.[98]

The story was similar in several other cases, and the pastors of these new congregations in turn sent out their protégés (now often trained at a new Calvary Chapel Bible College in Costa Mesa) to plant new churches. But given the group's informal nature and the phenomenal growth it was experiencing, problems were inevitable. The most serious began to develop among several Calvary Chapel churches that placed a more overt emphasis on charismatic worship and healing—in particular, the 1,800-member Calvary Chapel in Yorba Linda led by former rock band musician and manager John Wimber and eight churches that had originated under one of Smith's "sons," Kenn Gullicksen.[99] In 1982, Smith gave his blessing for the more charismatic churches to go their own way, and the Vineyard Fellowship was born. Soon another thirty Calvary Chapels joined the new movement, and it was off and running.[100]

By the end of the twentieth century, both Calvary Chapel and its offspring, the Vineyard, had become major forces within American evangelicalism. Although these nondenominational denominations had lost their overt identification as Jesus People churches, like many other aspects of contemporary American evangelicalism, they owed much of their style to the Jesus movement. The Jesus movement faded during the mid and late 1970s, but it continued to influence American evangelicalism long after it passed out of the public eye.

10

God's Forever Family

THE LONG-TERM IMPACT OF THE
JESUS PEOPLE MOVEMENT

THE ISSUE OF *Newsweek* magazine for October 25, 1976, had a cover featuring a longish-haired man around thirty years old, wearing one of the era's trademark open-collared polyester shirts and a sports coat, kneeling at the front of a church. Next to him stood a middle-aged preacher, one hand placed on the younger man's head, his other hand with a raised index finger pointing skyward. In bright yellow letters, the headline said, "Born Again!" Inside, *Newsweek*'s religion editor, Ken Woodward, declared that 1976 was "The Year of the Evangelical." The article's genesis lay in the imminent national election in which, for the first time in modern American history, two born-again candidates—the Southern Baptist Democrat Jimmy Carter and the Episcopalian Republican Gerald Ford—vied for the nation's highest office. And while the article's focus was the political and social implications of America's sprawling evangelical population, the story outlined the basic history, beliefs, and contemporary demographic contours of the movement for the presumably nonevangelicals who constituted *Newsweek*'s readership.[1]

But a veteran 1970s news junkie might have noticed one dimension in the recent history of these evangelicals that was glaringly absent in the *Newsweek* article: Despite all the publicity it had received just a few years earlier, there was not a solitary mention of the Jesus People movement in the entire story. And although the story mentioned "younger evangelicals" and students on evangelical college campuses, there was nary a word about the Jesus People coffeehouses or communes that were still operating in a number of American cities or the Jesus music festivals that had become a regular part of summer across the land for many conservative Protestant youth.[2] But although the Jesus movement was not dead by any means, the *Newsweek* piece in its silence grasped the truth that by late 1976 the movement's influence was on the wane.

Although the Jesus People movement had ceased to be a major force within American evangelicalism by the late 1970s, God's Forever Family had not been a mere cultural flash in the pan. The Jesus movement's impact would continue to be felt far beyond the end of the decade in the local, regional, and national footprint it left in its wake. The influence of the Jesus People, however, was felt well beyond any ongoing remnants of the movement itself; the trends and forces it loosed had a lasting impact on the internal life and direction of a resurgent evangelical subculture increasingly noted for its size and growing activism. The influence of the Jesus People on American evangelicalism can be broadly grouped into three categories: music, youth and popular culture, and church life (or, perhaps more aptly, "doing church").

The Contemporary Christian Music Industry

The most visible outgrowth of the Jesus People movement was the Contemporary Christian Music (CCM) industry. From its humble beginnings in the movement's coffeehouses and communes, Jesus music was, by the mid-'70s, becoming a sanctified version of the larger music and recording industries. Unlike its parent, however, Jesus music did not fade away in the mid and late 1970s. Instead, the newly defined genre of CCM continued to expand its sales, record labels, radio airplay, and—in step with a rapidly segmenting pop music scene—the styles and genres of its stable of Christian rock artists. By the end of the '70s, artists from the latter days of the Jesus music years, such as the 2nd Chapter of Acts and Keith Green, and new CCM stars, such as pert Norwegian American songstress Evie (pronounced "Eh-vee") Tornquist, combined with a fresh round of secular music converts, such as country pop crooner B. J. Thomas, to push CCM's numbers ever higher, frequently garnering sales of more than 100,000 copies for the genre's better-selling albums.[3] Almost inevitably, given the early success of Myrrh Records and the existing infrastructure of the Southern gospel music world (to say nothing of the stronger evangelical demographics of the Southern United States), the CCM industry quickly came to revolve around Music City—Nashville, Tennessee.

In the 1980s, CCM's maturation was best evidenced in the skyrocketing career of the young Nashville-bred pop singer, Amy Grant. A wealthy radiologist's daughter, Grant was influenced by the tail end of the Jesus movement through her high school youth group and local coffeehouse hangouts. Grant released her first album while still in high school in 1977 and gradually moved from occasional teenage coffeehouse singer to bona fide CCM superstar with her 1982 album, *Age to Age*, which became the first CCM album to reach first Gold (the sale of 500,000 copies) and then Platinum (sale of 1 million copies) album status. The release of her next Platinum album, *Unguarded*, in the summer of 1985 made her the first CCM artist to land a song ("Find a Way") in the Billboard Top 40 charts (peaking at #29).[4]

Amy Grant was, of course, a spectacular individual success story. However, her popularity and sales trajectory was emblematic of what was going on in the larger world of CCM. By 1984, CCM was chalking up sales of about $75 million, a figure that increased by over 15% the next year.[5] A little more than a decade later (1996), "gospel" music sales (the largest component of which was CCM) had jumped to over $550 million, and when ticket sales and merchandising were added in, made perhaps $900 million in total revenue. By that point, CCM had eclipsed both classical and jazz music in the U.S. marketplace.[6] Overall, during the 1990s, gospel music experienced an average yearly jump in sales of about 22%, compared to an annual 5% increase for other musical formats.[7] By 2000, there were $750 million in gospel music sales, representing 7% of total American music sales—double the revenue of Latin music and more than the sales in the jazz, classical, and New Age genres combined.[8] Changes wrought by the inroads of music downloading, as well as the economic downturn in the latter half of the twenty-first century's first decade meant hard times for CCM, as well as the entire music industry. Yet sales for 2008 still ranked at nearly half a billion dollars, and downloaded sales of digital albums and individual tracks climbed nearly 40% from the previous year.[9]

Praise Music

The Jesus People were also the major force behind a musical revolution that made its way straight into the heart of American church life. Whether known as contemporary worship music, praise and worship music, or, more simply, praise music, thousands and thousands of church congregations across North America adopted musical styles in their congregational worship that had originated in the Jesus People movement. Cutting straight to the heart of Sunday morning, praise music proved to be an even more prolific—and controversial—bequest of the Jesus People than was CCM.

The use of simple, self-composed songs, largely influenced by folk music, had been a ubiquitous feature of the Jesus movement from its earliest communal houses and coffeehouses. As we have seen, the single most important source was the original Calvary Chapel in Costa Mesa, California, where pastor Chuck Smith bankrolled a recording of the church's chapel's groups and subsequently founded Maranatha! Music. Maranatha!'s first album, *The Everlastin' Living Jesus Concert*—later simply *Maranatha! 1* (1971)—blurred the boundaries between Jesus music as entertainment and Jesus music intended for worship; the record sold more than 160,000 copies and spread the Calvary Chapel praise sound beyond Southern California.[10]

As evangelical church teens identified with the Jesus movement, praise music began to make inroads into many established evangelical congregations—and not just in the Spirit-filled churches of the Pentecostals and Charismatics. It was apparent that a majority of evangelicals instinctively realized that keeping the Jesus generation in church meant a willingness to put up with, in the words of one evangelical church music doyen writing in 1977: "guitar-plucking kids who play three bad chords but smile a lot."[11] Whereas Jesus rock was tolerated for teens' personal listening but viewed as unacceptable in church services, praise songs like "Father, I Adore You" (1972), "Seek Ye First" (1972), and "Humble Thyself in the Sight of the Lord" (1978) found favor—or at least, forbearance—within worship services, even among older churchgoers.

By the late '70s, the spread of praise music into American church life was so successful that the leaders of Maranatha! Music were beginning to notice that their roster of solo artists and bands was being steadily outperformed by recordings and sheet music devoted strictly to worship songs. In 1980, Maranatha! pulled the plug on all their artists, releasing them from their contractual obligations to refocus their efforts on the development and distribution of praise music.[12] To supplement their recordings, Maranatha! published a comprehensive *Maranatha! Music Praise Chorus Book* in 1983 that quickly became a leading resource for chorus-singing congregations.[13]

During the 1980s and into the 1990s, praise music continued to make steady advances into the nation's churches. A range of new companies joined with Maranatha! in publishing praise and worship music, including the Vineyard International's Mercy Publishing (1983) and Integrity/Hosanna! Music (1987). Praise music's impact was undoubtedly helped by the expansion of its musical cousin CCM and the work of artists such as John Michael Talbot and Michael Card, whose music tended toward the softer, reflective, and devotional side of the musical spectrum.[14] Additionally, occasional worship anthems by mainstream CCM artists such as Michael W. Smith's "Great Is the Lord" (1983) and Rich Mullins's "Awesome God" (1990) went straight from popularity on the radio to a featured place in congregational worship.[15] The trend toward praise music was also intensified by the rise of the so-called seeker-sensitive churches (see later) that leaned toward pop-sounding contemporary choruses to attract otherwise nonchurchgoing Baby Boomers and their generational successors.

Although praise music made tremendous inroads into the life of thousands of American congregations from the 1970s forward, its acceptance was by no means universal. Many older, more traditionally minded churchgoers, along with musical and theological elites within the church and seminaries—particularly on the Reformed side of the evangelical spectrum—fought the new music tooth and nail, resulting in a struggle that by the 1990s had come to be dubbed the "worship wars."[16] The critics not only did not like the praise music style but also cited a number of major shortcomings they believed were endemic to the overall genre. To the antipraise music critics, the new worship tunes were too subjective and self-centered, emphasizing worshippers and their feelings, rather than God and the gospel. Moreover, they regarded praise music as too consumerist and pragmatic in its service of church growth—an attempt to appeal to people's "felt needs" and entertainment tastes, as opposed to the preaching of the hard-won truths of Scripture and theology. Worst of all, many of them felt it was just plain anti-intellectual—a dumbing down of worship that was at best "milk for babes," a style of music that aimed for the lowest common denominator and by its mere existence drove out high-quality music and worship.[17]

In spite of the critics, however, there was no perceptible rolling back of the praise music tide in the nation's evangelical churches. If anything, compromise seemed to be the answer to most local skirmishes in the worship wars in the form of blended worship services or separate traditional and contemporary services. On all other fronts, the progress of praise music seemed to move forward, strengthened by the influx of imported praise music from Britain (the music of Graham Kendrick and the band Delirious) and Australia (the very popular Hillsongs oeuvre from Hillsong Church in the Sydney suburbs).[18] Perhaps most indicative of the genre's appeal was the increasing domination of praise cds and worship songs on the CCM charts and Christian radio stations in the early years of the twenty-first century. By 2007, praise and worship as a distinct category accounted for nearly 10% of all gospel music sales.[19] Increasingly, the songs that evangelicals listened to on their personal stereos, radios, or MP3 players at home, at work, and in their cars were often the same ones they might end up singing in their Sunday morning church services. Praise music, the often controversial offspring of the Jesus People movement, had truly worked its way into the very warp and woof of American evangelical life within a period of less than thirty years.

Youth Culture

One of the most startling impacts of the Jesus People was on American evangelicalism's handling of its young people's relationship to the larger youth culture. Prior to the advent of the Jesus People, evangelicals had been extremely suspicious of youth culture and attempted to isolate their children from its styles, fads, and music. The evangelical embrace of the Jesus People movement in the early to mid-'70s, however, forever changed that dynamic.

The major element of this new evangelical relationship to youth culture was the peace many evangelicals had established with the world of rock 'n' roll. Although there was still plenty of evangelical resistance to the content of rock music and the lifestyles of contemporary secular rock artists during the 1980s and thereafter,[20] the acceptance or tolerance of Jesus rock had fundamentally altered the stakes of the game. Now in the wake of the passing of the hippie youth culture, the controlling assumption within most evangelical circles was that rock 'n' roll and the trappings of youth culture were essentially neutral. Thomas E. Trask, the general superintendent of the Assemblies of God denomination, when asked about contemporary youth ministry methods in a 2005 interview, specifically looked back to the Jesus People movement as casting the mold for youth evangelization:

> I remember when people from the Jesus Movement... began pouring into our churches. The churches that said, "These people don't fit our mold and style" missed a tremendous opportunity for evangelism and discipleship. Churches that welcomed the Jesus people had the joy of seeing a great harvest.... It isn't a matter of style, it's the content. We don't compromise the message—that is sacred. Churches need to make adjustments—as long as they don't water down the gospel—to reach young people.[21]

From the late 1970s onward, multiple evangelical youth cultures flourished in North America, all of them supported by bands and artists that provided a musical subtext. For instance, an evangelical youth subculture mimicked the electronic music, exotic hairdos, and fashions of the mainstream New Wave style until the music's popularity waned in the late 1980s.[22] Down through the years, a Christian heavy metal subculture supported different metal subvarieties—glam, thrash, speed metal, even a Christian version of so-called death metal.[23] For those youth who were into reggae music and Rastafarian styles, there were gospel reggae bands like Christafari, Imisi, and God and I and Temple Yard, sans ganja (marijuana) but replete with dreadlocks and West Indian patter.[24] For the black-on-black-garbed Christian Goths who arrived on the scene in the 1990s and afterward, there were study groups and Web sites like "The Church of the Living Dead" and bands such as The Groaning, Beauty for Ashes, and Crimson Moonlight.[25] Christian rap—pioneered by popular groups like DC Talk in the late '80s—and then hip-hop became an ever-larger draw for both urban black teens and suburban white fans, who by the twenty-first century could follow favorite artists like Souljahz, Praya P, and Gospel Gangstaz with Web sites like Rapzilla.com and Christian-hiphop.net.[26]

Perhaps the ultimate sign that evangelical youth culture had come of age was the development of the Christian hipster scene of the early twenty-first century. Tracing their roots back musically and culturally to the Christian alternative music scene of the late 1980s and 1990s (represented by artists such as Charlie Peacock, The Choir, Relient K, and Starflyer 59), Christian hipsters tended to disavow the Contemporary Christian Music industry except in a decidedly ironic celebration of nostalgia or kitsch. The new Christian hipsters openly embraced the larger popular culture and secular music, although less over-the-top Christian artists in the mainstream music industry, such as quirky singer-songwriter Sufjan Stevens found great favor. Web sites such as *Relevant* magazine (Its motto: "God. Life. Progressive Culture") and pitchfork.com provided a cyber foundation for the subculture.[27]

The Broader Popular Culture

Another aftereffect of the Jesus People movement was the way the larger world of popular culture had become more friendly terrain for evangelical Christians. This was a huge change from attitudes most conservative Protestants had traditionally held against worldly entertainments and amusements right down into the postwar period. The Jesus People, with their penchant for rock music, posters, bumper stickers, buttons, cartoons, jewelry, and various types of Jesus clothing and merchandise, signaled a massive break with these old evangelical taboos that expanded and intensified in the 1980s and beyond.

One of the major beneficiaries of this new evangelical interest in music and other pop culture-related products was the Christian bookstore industry. Colleen McDannell in her 1996 book *Material Christianity* discussed how Christian bookstores met the Jesus People's desire for a totally enveloping Christian lifestyle.[28] McDannell argued that the new Jesus People–driven merchandise revolution, combined with a new surge in evangelical publishing, played a major role in the near-tripling of Christian bookstores in the period between 1965 and 1975.[29] Even after the Jesus People faded away, the Christian bookstore industry, fueled by the growing sales of music, greeting cards, videos, toys, witness-wear, and curios, continued its tremendous growth. In recent years, the impact of the Internet and the sale of Christian merchandise in big-box stores like Wal-Mart were a major blow to the industry. But this is the reflection of a changing marketplace, not a sign that the thirst for Christian merchandise has eased. As of 2009, the Association for Christian Retail (formerly the Christian Booksellers Association) estimated that the sales of Christian merchandise through all distribution channels had surpassed $4.6 billion.[30]

From the 1970s onward, evangelicals created an entire parallel universe of baptized entertainment options.[31] Religious television reflected this reality and increasingly brought a wide variety of entertainment options into evangelical homes. Recorded video entertainment—particularly for children—produced such best-selling series as Focus on the Family's mixed live-action/animation *McGee and Me*, and Thomas Nelson Publishing's *Bibleman* video series. The most successful franchise was the computer-animated *Veggie Tales* series, which debuted in 1993, sold more than 22 million videos by 2001, and in 2002 produced *Jonah*, a general-release, feature-length cartoon that pulled in over $25 million in ticket sales at the nation's movie theaters.[32]

The growth of evangelical entertainment options during this period highlights a larger reality—the fact that evangelicals had also greatly relaxed their general resistance to secular entertainment. Nowhere was this more apparent than in the realm of moviegoing and video watching. As late as 1957, a prominent evangelical leader such as Youth for Christ's Robert A. Cook could assume that no professing

Christian would consider darkening the door of a movie theater.[33] By the late-1980s, conservative psychologist and radio host James Dobson could invite Ted Baehr, evangelical publisher of the biweekly newsletter *Movieguide*, to provide his vast *Focus on the Family* radio audience with tips on new film releases.[34] In fact, by 2004, a study cited in *Time* magazine showed that evangelical Christians were among the most frequent movie attendees in the American population.[35] Since the 1980s, Hollywood producers and marketers have increasingly seized on this new reality, targeting evangelical audiences for films as diverse as *Chariots of Fire*, *The Mission*, *The Passion of the Christ*, and *The Blindside*.[36]

Obviously, such a major shift in attitudes toward popular culture among American evangelicals was the result of a combination of cultural and social forces. However, the Jesus People were the first sizable group of evangelicals to disregard traditional conservative Protestant strictures against popular culture. The approval the Jesus People received from the bulk of the evangelical establishment may well have provided the entire subculture with a pop culture emancipation proclamation.

Calvary Chapel and the Vineyard: "New Paradigm Churches"

The influence of the Jesus People movement was hardly limited to the nonecclesiastical elements of the evangelical subculture. One of the results of the movement was a new crop of earnest young men who were convinced that God was calling them into the ministry or other positions in the institutional church. Many pastors who came into the nation's evangelical pulpits beginning in the '70s—from megachurch pastors like Greg Laurie to legions of unknown preachers laboring in small congregations across the country—had spent time in the Jesus People movement. Others trained to become full-time Christian workers, serving with various evangelical parachurch media, evangelistic, social service, and missions organizations. The extent to which individual Jesus People took up full-time positions in the institutional church is hinted at in the Web-based survey of 812 movement participants. Overall, slightly more than 16% of those who responded claimed to be involved in some sort of church-oriented career (see Appendix).

But the Jesus People were also responsible for institutional developments with an impact on the larger ecclesiastical picture in North America. Among the most important was the emergence from within its midst of a group of successful evangelical churches and denominations that, while no longer associated in the public mind with the Jesus Revolution, continued to reflect its style and values. Unhindered by the fading of the Jesus movement, Calvary Chapel and the Vineyard Fellowship adapted their old formulae for success—an emphasis on Bible-centered teaching, the gifts of the Spirit, contemporary music, and a relaxed, come-as-you-are atmosphere—from a countercultural constituency toward middle-class suburbanites and experienced tremendous growth from the mid-1970s onward. By the late 1980s, these churches had established themselves as an important part of the American evangelical scene.

Calvary Chapel, from its beginnings as a small, independent, charismatic church in Costa Mesa, California, began planting new churches in Southern California in the early 1970s that paralleled the success of the parent church. Through starting new church plants and voluntary affiliations by independent charismatic churches (about 13% of all Calvary Chapels in a 1997 survey),[37] Calvary Chapels soon began to sprout up outside California and then beyond the West Coast and Southwest. By the mid-1990s, there were more than 600 Calvary Chapels in the United States and about 100 abroad.[38] By 2010, Calvary Chapel had expanded to nearly 1,100 affiliated congregations in the United States and over 300 churches overseas, half of them in Europe.[39] Because most Calvary Chapel churches do not offer formal membership and there is no denominational structure as such, the size of the group is hard to gauge. However, a reasonable estimate of weekly attendance in the United States in the latter parts of the first decade of the twenty-first century would have been in the neighborhood of 180,000 to 220,000.[40]

Calvary Chapel's stepchild, the Vineyard Fellowship, originated within Calvary Chapel and formally separated as a group of about forty churches in the early 1980s over the Vineyard's heavier concentration on the gifts of the Spirit. From that beginning, the Vineyard, helped by its leader John Wimber's increasing role in the "signs and wonders" movement and the spreading influence of its music, grew steadily. Among the Vineyard's most notable member congregations was the Toronto Airport Vineyard (joined 1991), the source of the Toronto Blessing movement that began shaking charismatic circles worldwide in 1994.[41] By the mid-1990s, there were 400 Vineyard churches in the United States (about 35% of them "adopted" from other denominations) and another 200 outside the country.[42] By 2010, there were nearly 600 Vineyard churches in the country with a total membership placed at 140,000, and another estimated 800 churches overseas. To put this in perspective, in a little over twenty years, the U.S. membership of the Vineyard had surpassed long-standing evangelical denominations like the Cumberland Presbyterian Church, the Wesleyan Church, the Christian Reformed Church, and the Baptist General Conference.[43]

In his important 1997 book, *Reinventing American Protestantism*, University of Southern California sociologist Donald E. Miller identified Calvary Chapel and the Vineyard as the cutting edge of a movement of New Paradigm churches in the United States. In Miller's estimation, these New Paradigm churches achieved a unique balance, incorporating aspects of the therapeutic, individualistic, and antiestablishment values of the counterculture while rejecting its inherent narcissistic tendencies.[44] Although Miller (a self-described liberal Episcopalian)[45] largely painted the new churches' success over and against the increasingly ossified congregations of mainline Protestant churches, he also pointed out that Calvary Chapel and the Vineyard were a step beyond business as usual in America's evangelical churches. Whereas he believed that their theology "might even be described as fundamentalist," Miller contended that because of their desire to be "culturally relevant in their music and organizational style," they distanced themselves from "formalized worship patterns" found "in most evangelical denominations." As such, in Miller's opinion, they represented a "new paradigm."[46]

Although Miller's analysis was stimulating, he failed to grasp that the new paradigm he described had in fact been the Jesus People movement. The members of God's Forever Family had set the template for Calvary Chapel, the Vineyard, and all who followed, with the combination of very conservative, even fundamentalist, theology with a style that was "culturally relevant in their music and organizational style," even as they distanced themselves from "formalized worship patterns of churches in most evangelical denominations." Calvary Chapel and the Vineyard, amid all their success in the late twentieth and early twenty-first centuries, were the ecclesiastical legacy of the new paradigm, not its fount.

Willow Creek and the "Seeker-Sensitive" Movement

Another component of the New Paradigm churches that Miller lumps in with Calvary Chapel and the Vineyard—although he does not directly study them in *Reinventing American Protestantism*[47]—are the proliferating "seeker-sensitive" megachurches that sprang up all across the United States during the 1980s and 1990s. In many ways similar to Calvary Chapel or the Vineyard, these explicitly user-friendly churches such as Saddleback Community Church (Lake Forest, California), Wooddale Church (Eden Prairie, Minnesota), and Calvary Church (Grand Rapids, Michigan) featured upbeat praise music and a casual atmosphere. While tending to target middle-class and up white suburbanites, there were certainly many similarities to their Jesus People–rooted, Southern Californian cousins.

Interestingly, the roots of the most famous and influential of these seeker-sensitive churches—Willow Creek Community Church in South Barrington, Illinois, in Chicago's northwestern suburbs—go back to a burgeoning youth ministry called Son City that was created during the height of the "second phase" Jesus People movement, when evangelical teenagers were adapting elements of the countercultural Jesus People persona as their own.[48] From the beginning, Son City's leaders Dave Holmbo and Bill Hybels were awash in the new music of the Jesus movement, which served as the catalyst for their attempts to find a relevant way to reach high school youth. The music of the group Love Song was particularly influential: "Their 8-track—we actually wore that thing out" recalled Scott Pederson, who served on the Son City staff and shared an apartment with Hybels and two other leaders. "The music, the lyrics had a profound effect...it was something that we were all really hungry for, for a lot of us who had grown up in the church...trying to find how...we personally [could] establish our own relationship with Christ."⁴⁹ Other Jesus music artists such as Phil Keaggy, Larry Norman, Michael Omartian, and the JC Power Outlet were also big favorites with the Son City leadership, and they often took groups of their young followers to local Chicago-area Jesus music concerts. As Lynne Hybels recalled about the impact of these Jesus People musicians in the Hybels' 1995 history of the Willow Creek movement:

> Their songs echoed the longings and beliefs of the kids' hearts but set the lyrics to music they loved.... Kids like my own, who have grown up with Christian contemporary music, can't appreciate what this meant to a generation of Christian kids who had grown up without a music to call their own. It was exciting. It was emotional.⁵⁰

In September of 1975, Hybels began a new church at the Willow Creek movie theater in nearby Palatine that sought to offer this innovative type of service to an adult audience.⁵¹ There, according to historian Fred W. Beuttler, "the youth group formed a church in its own image and structure."⁵² Continuing its emphasis on upbeat music, drama, a casual atmosphere, and a general nonthreatening ambience, with Sunday services aimed at a posited "Unchurched Harry" and "Unchurched Mary" and weekday services for more intensive Bible study and discipleship, Willow Creek was attracting over 2,000 in weekly attendance by 1978. In 1981, the church christened a new auditorium on ninety acres of farmland it had purchased in South Barrington. As the '80s progressed Willow Creek became nothing short of a phenomenon: weekly attendance went over 10,000, new services were added, facilities were enlarged, and the number of ministries and special concerns groups grew.⁵³

By 2005, Willow Creek was averaging 21,000 in attendance each week, sponsoring 100 separate ministries, employing more than 400 full- and part-time employees, and taking in over $48 million dollars in annual revenue. To share its successful techniques through literature, conferences, and workshops, the church incorporated the Willow Creek Association in 1992; by 2010, more than 10,000 churches in North America and around the world from ninety different denominations were members.⁵⁴

The Generational Impact of the Jesus People Movement

The cumulative effect of these ongoing cultural and institutional legacies would be enough to establish the Jesus People movement's role in the shaping of American evangelicalism and the larger American cultural landscape in the early twenty-first century. However, these lingering influences should not be allowed to eclipse the significance of the movement in its historic, generational context. The Jesus People movement arose amid the chaos and tumult of 1960s America. It is no exaggeration to state that the direction and allegiance of a whole generation of American youth was up for grabs during this period with no sure outcome in sight. Even as the combination of events, countercultural rebellion, and radical politics caused many young people to reject their parents' values, morality, and religion, the Jesus People movement became something of a bridge back to the American mainstream for thousands and thousands of the era's youth.

Louis Berry, a Vietnam veteran, was one such example. Looking back in 2000, Berry recalled returning to the States in May 1969 as "a mental mess from the drugs and death and all that. Anti-military would be putting it mildly!" Berry came into contact with people in the Jesus movement in Seattle while awaiting discharge from the army in 1970 and, upon returning to his home in Vallejo, California, ran into more street Christians from a local coffeehouse:

> I noticed how they loved one another.... I told them what ever you have I want it. So they told me about the Lord Jesus.... Well, I got saved...the day I got saved Jesus set me free from the drugs. My whole attitude about everything changed. My hatred and rebellion left me.[55]

Milton Resh, a Michigan pastor, reminisced in 2001 about how he became involved with the "God's Thing" ministry as a teenage hippie in Detroit.

> The year was 1969. I started dating a girl who went to the home meetings that were held nightly at this couple's home. I went one night and it was as though my whole life was in the light. I freaked and ran out to my car to escape....A good friend of mine followed me out to the car and asked me to pray with [him] about asking Jesus into my life. I did and it was like a ton of bricks was lifted off my shoulders. I lost every desire to get high. Before you know it, I had moved...along with about 25 others into this Jesus Freak commune.[56]

Peggy Hillick had a similar story. An eighteen-year-old girl living on her own in New York City, she was involved through friends in radical politics and "had attempted suicide and was regularly sniffing glue" when she came to a coffeehouse in the West Village. Given a copy of *Good News for Modern Man*, she read it and gave her "life to the Lord." The decision changed her life:

> I began to realize that the problems facing our country and society were not solely caused by the government...that the root of so much pain and

suffering was basically our separation from God. We were steeped in a lot of anger and revolt primarily because of our sin and self-centeredness. It slowly became apparent that I could no longer justify serious radical protests of behavior or even the ongoing hatred for authority and deep-seated mistrust. My whole focus changed from how unfair my life was to how incredible was the love of God. It pretty much turned my world topsy-turvy (and a better topsy-turvy!!!).[57]

These experiences were echoed by many thousands during the course of the movement. The results of the survey of former participants in the Jesus People movement provide an indication as to how many had at one point numbered themselves among the Woodstock Nation (table 10.1).

Table 10.1 Did you consider yourself a hippie prior to involvement with the Jesus People?

Yes	38.9%
No	39.3%
Not sure	9.5%
No answer	12.3%[58]

Clearly, a substantial slice of those who were involved with the Jesus People had been either full-fledged hippies or fellow travelers with the counterculture.

However, just as the Jesus People movement was a life-changing, worldview-altering experience for many former hippies, it proved perhaps only slightly less earthshaking to many evangelical teenagers who became involved in the movement. For these straight youth, caught between the allures of popular culture and the counterculture on the one hand, and their loyalties to their families and the strictures of their evangelical upbringing on the other, the Jesus Revolution appeared as a literal Godsend. At a time when the culture was all about relevance and authenticity, the Jesus People offered both in spades. For many evangelical teenagers, the Jesus People movement provided a safe—or safer—path through the adolescent minefields of culture, faith, and identity.

Looking back years later, these teenage evangelical converts to the Jesus People movement singled out different aspects of the movement's attraction. To some it was clearly a matter of relevance to the times and youth culture. Reminiscing in 1998, Dan Brady, an early attendee at Calvary Chapel in Costa Mesa, recalled, "I was a Christian before the Jesus movement…[however] I was thrilled to find that there was music that I could listen to and enjoy."[59] Susie Melkus of the Agape Fellowship in San Anselmo, California, remembered in 1999 how "thrilled I was

that 'rock' music became such an integral part of church," replacing "the old fashioned hymns and organ 'boring' music."[60] Similarly, Mitch Bright, raised in the
United Pentecostal Church in the Midwest, looked back and recalled, "I fell in love
with [Phil] Keaggy and [the] 2nd Chapter [of Acts'] music along with many of the
others. [I] liked the idea of keeping my hair long!"[61] The opportunity to include
familiar aspects of youth culture within their spiritual experience was a definite
attraction for many church youth who joined the Jesus movement.

For some evangelical teenagers the sense of unity and purpose that the Jesus
People movement seemed to offer was its most striking feature. Doug McCleary
was involved with the Jesus People during his high school days in Oregon in the
mid-1970s. Writing in 1998 from his vantage point as a Presbyterian minister in
Washington state, he recalled that "there was an electricity in the air. . . . I was excited.
I remember running into other young Christians in school and other places, and
there being a tangible sense of unity of allegiance and purpose."[62] Carolyn Barta,
who grew up in Conley, Georgia, recollected how the Jesus People movement
served to unite her friends from different denominational backgrounds. Raised
in a strict Southern church setting, her fellow Jesus People were instrumental
in her attempts to "open [her] mind and not be so narrow-minded . . . we were all
from different churches, yet when we all got together doctrine wasn't important."[63]
This grassroots ecumenism they found in the Jesus People was another appealing
feature of the movement for many straight churched kids.

For other church-raised teens, however, it was the fervor and transparency
of the Jesus People, combined with their relevance, that made the movement so
attractive. Bill Overpeck, who was involved with the Jesus People in his hometown of Terre Haute, Indiana, recalled being invited to one of their meetings by
a friend:

> The group [Jesus People of Terre Haute] had rented the second floor of
> a downtown building and held meetings several times a week. I was dis-
> satisfied with my church (mainline Christian fundamentalist) and wanted
> something more. On April 7, 1972 I walked into a roomful of scraggly kids
> and immediately realized two things: they had something REAL and I
> wanted it.[64]

Joe Stephen McNair, a Texas teenager raised in the Church of Christ, had a similar reaction. Becoming involved at The Well coffeehouse in Austin, he found the
Jesus People very different. "These folks at The Well really believed in God and
Jesus and were not into the whole 'church thing,'" he wrote in 2000. "I wanted to
know their Jesus and not the safe Jesus I had been taught in church."[65] McNair's
experience mirrored that of Paul Basden in Virginia. Growing up the son of a pastor who worked for the Southern Baptist Foreign Missions Board in Richmond,

he recalled in 2003 how his "life was unalterably changed" when as a high school sophomore in 1971 a group of Jesus People from the University of North Carolina visited the First Baptist Church of Richmond. "They talked unabashedly about Jesus," Basden recalled. "I had never heard such a thing—and my parents were devout believers."[66] To these teens and many others from churched backgrounds, the Jesus People represented a fervent, vital expression of Christian faith they did not find in their parents' lives or traditional church settings.

All in all, the coming together of hippie freak and straight church youth in the Jesus People movement left a deep imprint on a major segment of the Baby Boomer generation. Survey results from former participants in the Jesus People movement suggest several ways in which this may have been the case. One major impact of the movement for those who took the survey seems to have been a clear rejection of countercultural attitudes about drug use. When asked if they had been users of marijuana before their involvement with the Jesus People, just under 30% reported themselves to have been "regular" users and a little over 17% had been "occasional" users of the drug. When asked about prior use of LSD, 10.5% claimed to have been "regular" users and 16.3% said that they had been "occasional" "trippers." But after involvement with the Jesus People, attitudes toward drug use changed dramatically among the more than 800 former Jesus People who took the survey (table 10.2).

Table 10.2 Did the Jesus People movement alter your attitude toward drug use?

Yes	61.8%
Not sure	3%
No	29.4%
No answer	5.8%[67]

Given the fact that the majority of evangelical teens involved in the movement had been against drug use before their involvement with the Jesus People (hence, 29.4% "No"), these numbers probably reflect changes wrought among the converts from the counterculture. In fact, the more conservative post–Jesus People attitudes toward drugs among survey participants mirrors the thrust of findings about growing resistance to the legalization of marijuana within the American population in the years between 1977 and 1985.[68] The rise of the Jesus People movement constituted a significant obstacle to the spread of recreational drug use among American youth.

Another major impact of the Jesus People movement may have been in decelerating the otherwise runaway social locomotive that was the sexual revolution. Over 45% of the survey respondents noted that they had been involved in sexual activity either "regularly" or "occasionally" prior to their involvement in the Jesus People. Remembering that many of these respondents were in fact evangelical teenagers reared in the church made their response to a follow-up question about the impact of the movement on their attitudes toward premarital sex particularly surprising (Table 10.3).

Table 10.3 Did the Jesus People movement alter your attitude toward premarital sex?

Yes	62.8%
Not sure	3.8%
No	28.6%
No answer	4.8%[69]

These numbers, in light of the strong teachings against sexual immorality within the evangelical subculture, suggest that a sizable number of youth raised as evangelicals—lured by adolescent urges and the siren song of the counterculture's free and easy ethic of sexual pleasure—may have perceived themselves as having been more open to the possibility of sexual activity *before* their involvement with the Jesus People movement. It is enough, in fact, to raise the question of just how utterly complete the triumph of the sexual revolution might have been, had it not been for the Jesus Revolution. A 1977 general study of changes in the attitudes of young adults under the age of twenty-five, for example, showed that 41% of those surveyed had actually become more liberal since they were teens.[70] Given that sort of change in the larger culture, the survey numbers here suggest the possibility of just how much greater the loosening in attitudes toward traditional sexual morality might have been in the 1970s and thereafter, had it not been for the impact of the Jesus People movement.

Another one of the fascinating implications of the survey was the impact that the Jesus People movement might have had on the political leanings of those who became involved. Robert Ellwood in his 1973 study of the Jesus People, *One Way,* noted that the possibility of the Jesus movement producing more conservative voters was one of the concerns of "politicians."[71] The survey results suggest that there may have been merit in this speculation. When asked how they would have perceived their individual political identity before they became involved with the Jesus People, respondents as a group definitely skewed toward the left (table 10.4).

When asked to describe their political orientation at the time of taking the survey, however, the consensus of the participants had swung far to the right (table 10.5).

Table 10.4 What was your political identity prior to involvement
with the Jesus People movement?

Liberal	42%
Moderate	27.2%
Conservative	22.4%
No answer	8.4%[72]

Table 10.5 What is your political identity today?

Liberal	10.3%
Moderate	25.2%
Conservative	57%
No answer	7.5% [73]

Granted that these definitions were certainly in the "eye of the [self-] beholder," they nonetheless provide an indicator of the respondents' perceptions of where they stood at two points of time in light of the commonly used categorizations of American politics. It suggests that the Jesus People movement—particularly in the incorporation of its hard-core countercultural element into the larger evangelical community—may have played an important role in moving many young people into the conservative ranks. Historian Preston Shires argues in his book *Hippies of the Religious Right* that the activism and fervor that the Jesus freaks brought to their evangelistic efforts and Christian commitment may well have been key ingredients in the nascent evangelical prolife movement that first developed in the late 1970s and the rise of the Religious Right in 1980 and beyond. "The Christian Right," he argues, must not simply be viewed "as a reactionary movement fomented by enraged fundamentalists who had finally come round to rebelling against the Sixties . . . [it] also was an extension of the Sixties counterculture."[74] But it was not an inherently political movement that steamed out of the '60s ready for culture wars in the '70s and '80s—God's Forever Family was anything but a political dynamo during its heyday. Certainly, its apocalyptic orientation went a long way toward defusing sustained concentration on political solutions: Why spend your time on registering voters for the coming primary when Jesus was coming back at any moment?[75] But the Jesus People undoubtedly served as a training ground that prepared its constituency to eventually begin to think more seriously about the nation's political direction.

Conclusion

Far from being an ephemeral blip or a religious fad, the Jesus People movement was a major episode in American religious history. It was not merely a Californian phenomenon, a by-product of pop culture that was around just long enough to flash across the cover of *Time* magazine before it became little more than a fading memory of the 1960s. Instead, the Jesus People movement was from its beginnings a unique combination of the counterculture and American evangelical religion that eventually had a national impact during a life span that lasted almost a decade.

For many Baby Boomers who were involved in the movement, their experiences as part of God's Forever Family continued decades later to be the benchmark by which they measured their own spirituality and the health of the American church (figure 10.1). In 2000, Freddie Rodriguez was a pastor in Ohio, but he looked back to his involvement with Sonlight Ministries in Youngstown, Ohio, as "the most spiritual time in my life. I will never forget the Jesus movement."[76]

FIGURE 10.1 Quiet time: A member of a communal home in Berkeley, California, gets into some heavy personal Bible study, ca. 1971.

Courtesy of Archives, Hubbard Library, Fuller Theological Seminary.

Grace Mullen Cook, who was part of Lamb's Chapel in Charlotte, North Carolina, wistfully recalled in 2003 her involvement there: "The worship was so awesome. I think I am still trying to go there.... And I find if I connect with anyone who was there at that time our connection goes beyond time and space."[77] Mark Weston, who had been involved with a Jesus People fellowship in Connecticut, echoed her sentiments: "I miss those days so much. So much has happened. I've become lukewarm, even unbelieving in some areas. But how can I ever deny such an experience?"[78] Paul Reilly, who had been involved with the Jesus People in northeastern New Jersey in the early to mid-'70s, put it well in 2002 when he reminisced about the meaning of the movement:

> We all know that events we live in our "coming of age" experience will always hold a great sway in our lives. Combine this with an encounter with the Living God, and the memories can never be eclipsed. Even with a family and exciting church home, I realize that I often dream very fondly of my time in the Jesus movement. It was the defining experience of my life.[79]

For many who were involved with the movement, the feeling of nostalgia blends with a sense of sorrow that their offspring had missed out on such a tremendous rite of passage. Many, like Jeanne Clark, who was a regular at Calvary Chapel in the '70s, admitted that they "miss it all. I would love...my children to experience the power of God and the joy of the time."[80] Others, like Sharon Hanson, formerly involved at the Fish House in San Diego, looked to the future with anticipation of a renewal along the lines of the Jesus Revolution. "I believe we're on the brink of another Jesus Movement," she wrote. "Something similar, but even more sweeping. I think we are coming into a time that has been unequaled in the history of the Church in America."[81] The memory of the movement, or the movement's template, still lingers within the evangelical subculture, and an enduring hope abides that a new revival might spring up among future generations coming of age within a culture that many believers feel has turned its back on God. This possibility was reflected in a survey completed in 2000 by a then fifteen-year-old girl named Summer living in Glenpool, Oklahoma. She noted that she had seen a video about the movement and had heard her "friend's parents talk about [the Jesus People]." She closed with a short note:

> This survey probably wasn't for me.... Just note this, I'm fifteen and I want the Jesus Movement again. I want it in my family. I want it in the halls of my high school. My generation is crying out for more...we need it here stronger than before, so strong, to be moved by Jesus; moved out of complacency, pride, religion, out of darkness. Don't once think the Jesus Movement is completely gone.... [82]

Jesus People Survey

Tabulations and Comments

The information here, originally compiled in May 2004, represents a statistical breakdown of 812 surveys completed by people who considered themselves a part of the Jesus People movement of the 1960s and 1970s. With the technical assistance of webmaster Dave Hollandsworth, the survey, a joint collaboration between David Di Sabatino (author of *The Jesus People Movement: An Annotated Bibliography and General Resource*) and me, was hosted on the Web site "Remembering the Jesus Movement" (www://oneway.org/jesusmmovement/index.html) from November 1997 through the end of April 2004. The site drew people who surfed in via search engines and through a direct link with a site catering to fans of the beginnings of Contemporary Christian Music, "A Decade of Jesus Music, 1969–1979" (www://oneway.org/jesusmusic.index.html). I have assembled the statistical information here; percentile breakdowns are provided (in a few cases, a raw number count), and in many instances, I have provided explanatory and interpretive notes. Although the following does not pretend to be a final word as a statistical picture of the Jesus People movement, it nonetheless provides the first major retro statistical tool for interpreting the characteristics, beliefs, scope, and nature of the movement.

Basic Statistical Information

Three of the surveys tabulated represent "shared" husband-wife surveys. One thing that is immediately striking about this survey's data is—given the traditional proclivity for female religious involvement—the large percentage of male respondents. This could be the result of a combination of factors—perhaps a product of a male predisposition to be more computer-savvy, a higher likelihood of males to have access to job-related computer equipment and Internet connections, or perhaps the simple fact that males may have more free time on their hands. However, its thrust also reflects a general recollection and perception about the Jesus People movement in that it seemed that male participation in the movement was particularly strong in overall terms of percentage as compared with many traditional Christian settings.

Gender

Males	68.1%
Females	30.2%
Undetermined	1.7%

Educational Level of Jesus People Survey Respondents

Of the 812 surveys tabulated, the educational attainment of these former members of the Jesus People were, on the whole, at or slightly above national levels in terms of those who have earned at least an associate's degree, technical school degree, or two full years of higher education. In all, 70.2% of respondents claimed to have achieved an associate's degree or the equivalent of at least two full years of college education, and 48% of respondents claimed to have earned a bachelor's degree. Meanwhile, 11.3% claimed to have earned a graduate degree.

Christian Vocation

As would be expected, a movement such as the Jesus People inspired a fair portion of its number to undertake pastoral, evangelistic, or other church-oriented work as their chosen career path. Among the respondents of this survey, a total of 16.1% indicated that they had indeed become pastors, missionaries, or evangelists or were employed in full-time church or parachurch-related careers.

Geographic Distribution of Jesus People Movement Involvement

The responses in table A.1 reflect the area in which people lived when they were involved in the Jesus People movement–*not* where they resided at the time they completed the survey. In a few cases, the respondents were involved in one or more states, provinces, or countries (especially true of those involved in the Shiloh Youth Centers, an organization that not only became national in scope by the late '70s but also had a policy of shifting members from one location to another—the legendary or infamous "Shiloh Shuffle"). In these sorts of cases, geographical location was split between the two major locations their responses indicated most time had been spent, hence the appearance of a few 0.5 designations in the list. (In the case of the Shiloh people, location was assigned on the basis of where they first became involved in the movement and/or where they seemed to have spent the bulk of their time.)

Table A.1 Geographic Distribution of Jesus People Movement Involvement
(812 responses)

California	255	[31.4% of North American respondents]
Pacific Northwest	(50)	[6.2%]
	British Columbia	4.5
	Oregon	21
	Washington	24.5
Southwestern U.S.	(79.5)	[9.8%]
	Arizona	12
	New Mexico	2.5
	Oklahoma	10
	Texas	55
Great Lakes Region	(130.5)	[16.1%]
	Illinois	27.5
	Indiana	18.5
	Michigan	18
	Minnesota	10.5
	Ohio	30.5
	Ontario	14
	Wisconsin	11.5
Great Interior/Rocky Mtn. Region	(48.5)	[6%]
	Colorado	9
	Idaho	2
	Iowa	6.5
	Kansas	10
	Missouri	9.5
	Montana	1
	Nebraska	6
	Nevada	2.5
	South Dakota	2
Southeastern U.S.	(97)	[11.9%]
	Alabama	4
	Arkansas	1.5
	Florida	25.5
	Georgia	9
	Kentucky	5

Table A.1 Continued

	Louisiana	6
	Mississippi	2
	North Carolina	10.5
	South Carolina	4
	Tennessee	9
	Virginia	20.5
Mid-Atlantic States	**(68)**	**[8.4%]**
	Delaware	1
	District of Columbia	2
	Maryland	7.5
	New Jersey	20.5
	New York	14
	Pennsylvania	21.5
	West Virginia	1.5
New England	**(12)**	**[1.5%]**
	Connecticut	1
	Maine	1
	Massachusetts	6
	Vermont	4
Other U.S.	**(18)**	**[2.2%]**
	Alaska	3
	Hawaii	3.5
	U.S. Military Overseas	9
	Puerto Rico	2
	Panama Canal Zone	0.5
Other Canada	**(5)**	**[0.6% of all respondents]**
	Alberta	3
	Nova Scotia	1
	Saskatchewan	1
International	**(17.5)**	**[2.1% of all respondents]**
	Australia	(6)
	New South Wales	2
	Queensland	4
	England	4
	Israel	1
	Italy	1
	Mexico	5
	New Zealand	2
	South Africa	2
	Sweden	1
Unknown/Unclear	**31**	**[3.8% of all respondents]**

The geographic segment of the responses indicate that the Jesus People movement was certainly a national movement—forty-six of fifty states are represented (those with no respondents: North Dakota, Rhode Island, Utah, Wyoming), as well as the District of Columbia, Puerto Rico, and the Panama Canal Zone. The survey data also reveal that the impact of the movement did not end at the borders of the United States—survey takers also represented five Canadian provinces and seven other foreign countries.

The survey data clearly indicate the major role that California played as the cradle of the Jesus People movement and the unique way it fit in with the overall California ethos: Nearly a third of those from North America taking the survey indicated that all or a portion of their direct experience with the Jesus movement had taken place in California. It must be noted, however, that overstressing the indigenous Californianess of the movement is problematic: California was at that time the second most populous state in the Union—it is now the first—and was always receiving influxes of new arrivals and, particularly during this period, attracting numbers of young runaways and fortune seekers from other states. The problem this creates for any kind of California paradigm is this: What does one do with a runaway from Arkansas who went to Huntington Beach and became involved with Calvary Chapel in Costa Mesa? Or does an eighteen-year-old who moved in from Michigan at age fifteen count as Californian? Not counting the responses that did not answer that portion of the survey, over 65% of the respondents were involved with the movement outside the state of California.

The survey also confirms various contemporary observations about the regional strengths of the movement in the early and mid-1970s. First of all, the survey echoed the relatively light presence the movement exerted in the Northeastern part of the United States (defined here as New England, New York, and New Jersey), which has been traditionally true about evangelical forms of religion for the last century. Altogether, a little under 6% of the responses came from that area of the country (a region that accounted for nearly 20% of the overall U.S. population in 1970), with only 1.5% of all responses showing Jesus People involvement from New England.

Second, the survey reaffirms an observation Billy Graham made at the height of the publicity explosion surrounding the Jesus People in 1971: The movement seemed to have less of an impact in the South, traditionally the most religious and overwhelmingly evangelical section of the country. Respondents to the survey whose participation in the Jesus People movement occurred in the Southeastern United States represented only 11.9% of all North American survey respondents.

A third regional observation that this survey appears to affirm is that the Jesus People movement did seem to resonate in the Southwest, which, while having much in common with their culturally Southern cousins in the Southeast, also tends to be more culturally diverse, as well as a bit more on the flexible and innovative side— more like their counterparts in Southern California. The respondents to the survey representing Texas, Oklahoma, New Mexico, and Arizona made up 10.4% of those North American respondents who reported the location of their experiences with the Jesus People.

Fourth, the survey seems to confirm that the movement seemed to make significant inroads in the Midwestern United States and in Ontario, Canada. Indeed, a Great Lakes region of Illinois, Indiana, Michigan, Minnesota, Ohio, and Wisconsin plus Ontario accounts for more than 16% of North American respondents. One factor in this development might have been that the counterculture had a fairly strong presence in many of the major cities of the region.

Note that the surveys indicating non-North American involvement and identification with the movement were included for statistical purposes because the content of their answers demonstrated a conscious awareness of the larger movement and its American context and origins.

General Questions

1. Considered themselves a hippie prior to involvement with JP

Yes	38.9%
No	39.3%
Not sure	9.5%
No answer	12.3%

The responses here and to the next four questions seem to support the fact that participation and self-identification with the Jesus People was divided between youth who came from two larger camps—the counterculture and the evangelical subculture.

2. Use of alcohol prior to involvement with JP

Regular	24.8%
Occasional	29.6%
Rarely/Never	43.2%
No answer	2.4%

3. Use of marijuana prior to involvement with JP

Regular	29.8%
Occasional	17.2%
Rarely/Never	50%
No answer	3%

4. Use of LSD prior to involvement with JP

Regular	10.5%
Occasional	16.3%
Rarely/Never	67.6%
No answer	5.6%

5. Sexual activity prior to involvement with JP

Regular	19.7%
Occasional	25.5%
Rarely/Never	50%
No answer	4.8%

6. Listener to rock music prior to involvement with JP

Regular	78.2%
Occasional	12.9%
Rarely/Never	6.4%
No answer	2.5%

While the previous five questions sketched out two divergent camps of "pre–Jesus People" individuals associated with either the counterculture or the traditional taboos of the evangelical subculture, the responses to this question highlight the near-universal importance of the medium of rock 'n' roll music within the larger youth culture, and bespeak the key role that Jesus music must have played as a common denominator within the movement.

7. Interest in other religion prior to involvement with JP

Yes (Christian)	11%
Yes (non-Christian)	32.4%
No	33.4%
No Answer	23.2%

This question very broadly addressed the disposition of the individual toward an unspecified "other religion" and could have been construed by some respondents to refer to an openness to their own evangelical background or to their Roman Catholic and mainline Protestant backgrounds—"other" manifestations of Christianity that, by contrast, seemed foreign to the teaching and ethos of the JP movement and evangelicalism. Whatever the case, the response makes it clear that many of the respondents had *no* particular interest in religion of *any* kind prior to their involvement with the JP.

8. Political identity prior to involvement with J P

Liberal	42%
Moderate	27.2%
Conservative	22.4%
No answer	8.4%

Granted that this and the next question are largely in the realm of the eye of the (self) beholder, nonetheless, the responses seem to be an interesting indicator of the respondents' perceptions of where they stood—and stand—in light of the commonly bandied-about political categorizations of recent American politics. The possible importance of the Jesus People movement in moving many young people into the ranks of conservative American politics looms as an important dimension of the rise of the so-called Religious Right.

9. Political identity today

Liberal	10.3%
Moderate	25.2%
Conservative	57%
No answer	7.5%

10. Did drugs contribute to your conversion experience?

Yes	14.3%
Not sure	4.9%
No	79.2%
No answer	1.6%

This question was intended to gauge whether drug taking had been directly related to the spiritual state leading to the respondent's conversion. In retrospect, it is clear that the question may have been construed as whether drug abuse had led to such personal turmoil and problems that it had set the person on a quest for help. In either case, it is clear that drugs and drug-related problems were a not unusual but hardly overwhelming scenario in the personal routes that led people into the J P.

11. Did the J P movement alter your attitude toward premarital sex?

Yes	62.8%
Not sure	3.8%
No	28.6%
No answer	4.8%

In light of the fact that a fair number of respondents' profiles indicate a background within the larger evangelical subculture and its concomitant teachings against sexual immorality, the numbers here are surprising—they seem to indicate that perhaps a sizable number of evangelical young people perceived themselves as having been more open to the possibility of sexual activity before their involvement with the Jesus People movement. In that regard, it is highly reasonable to suspect that the Jesus movement was a significant factor in combating the spread of the free-and-easy ethic of sexual pleasure from the counterculture to the larger American youth culture. Indeed, one wonders how complete the triumph of the sexual revolution may have been in the 1970s had it not been for the rise of the Jesus People.

12. Did the JP movement alter your attitude toward drug use?

Yes	61.8%
Not sure	3%
No	29.4%
No answer	5.8%

13. Did you attend a local church during your involvement in the JP movement?

Yes	84.6%
No	12.6%
Not sure	1.1%
No answer	1.7%

The responses to this question pose a major challenge to the dominant image of the nature and structure of the Jesus People as they were portrayed in the popular and academic literature associated with the 1971–1972 publicity explosion surrounding the movement. Rather than isolated within communes and counterculture-oriented fellowships, this response suggests that for the vast majority of JP—and not just the kids from evangelical backgrounds who were adopting the Jesus People style—it was a natural reflex to become involved in the larger mix of church and community by their attendance and involvement with the services and programs of local churches. It would also seem to explain how the movement could have seemed to disappear in the late '70s—many of the Jesus People were by then well integrated within the larger evangelical culture by virtue of their primary involvement with local congregations.

14. Did you participate in, or see, the "Baptism of the Holy Spirit" in your JP involvement?

Participated	76.6%
Saw	17.2%
No answer	6.2%

This and the next eight questions explore the presence and extent of Pentecostal-style manifestations of the gifts of the Spirit in the life of the Jesus People. The answers show the degree to which an emotional and demonstrative style were a major characteristic of the movement; the manner in which it easily fed into, and related with, the burgeoning charismatic movement; and the broadening experience the Jesus People movement must have been for many of the church kids who became involved with God's Forever Family.

15. Did you participate in, or see, "Speaking in Tongues" in your JP involvement?

Participated	72.2%
Saw	23.2%
No answer	4.6%

16. Did you participate in, or see, "Slaying in the Spirit" in your JP involvement?

Participated	38.3%
Saw	46.3%
No answer	15.4%

17. Did you participate in, or see, "Prophecy" in your JP involvement?

Participated	42.5%
Saw	45.3%
No answer	12.2%

Prophecy, as understood here, would be perceived as a pronouncement or message from the Lord, given through an individual with future ramifications that could be meant for an individual, the group, or occasionally even larger, universal applications.

18. Did you participate in, or see, a "Word of Knowledge" in your JP involvement?

Participated	45.3%
Saw	40.9%
No answer	13.8%

A "Word of Knowledge" was a Spirit-led pronouncement that usually was perceived as providing specific guidance or discernment concerning present decisions and circumstances and could apply to either an individual or a larger group. The technical differentiation between a "Word of Knowledge" and "Prophecy" was always something of a fuzzy matter.

19. Did you participate in, or see, "Healing" in your JP involvement?

Participated	49.5%
Saw	32.5%
No answer	18%

20. Did you participate in, or see, "Other Miracles" in your JP involvement?

Participated	36.1%
Saw	32.5%
No answer	31.4%

"Other miracles" include anything perceived to have been extraordinary or of supernatural origin not covered by any of the previous questions. Probably the major miracle that most Jesus People would have been familiar with would be the unexpected and seemingly miraculous supplying of some physical, financial, or circumstantial need.

21. Did you participate in, or see, "Demon Possession/Exorcisms" in your JP involvement?

Participated	30.4%
Saw	30.6%
No answer	39%

The Jesus People had a very real sense of supernatural warfare. Their penchant for utilizing exorcism was the result of both Pentecostal influences and the concurrent impact of the era's upsurge in occult interest. It may have also been affected by the prominence in popular culture at the time of films like *Rosemary's Baby* and *The Exorcist*.

22. Did you participate in, or see, "Singing in the Spirit" in your JP involvement?

Participated	59.9%
Saw	22.1%
No answer	18%

23. Did you have contact with the Children of God group during your JP involvement?

Yes	40.1%
No	47%
Not sure	9.5%
No answer	3.4%

The Children of God (COG), led by the charismatic recluse David "Moses" Berg, was one of the most publicized groups associated with the Jesus People movement. While at the peak there were only a few thousand members, they traveled in bands and targeted other Jesus People groups for takeovers—something that proved increasingly difficult as the movement matured and the COG were marked as cultic by the evangelical mainstream. The data here demonstrate the broad awareness of the group in the larger movement and the fact that they did, indeed, get around.

24. Were there other groups that you considered cults during your JP involvement?

Yes	58.7%
No	17.2%
Not sure	12.8%
No answer	11.3%

The rise of new religions and competing sects made for a dynamic 1970s religious marketplace, with young people being the dominant target group. The resultant sense of competition and need to engage rival truth claims and maintain boundaries against theological error was a prominent component of life in the Jesus People movement. Among the most frequently mentioned groups respondents viewed as cults during their Jesus People years were Sun Young Moon's Unification Church ("Moonies"), devotees of transcendental meditation, and the International Society for Krishna Consciousness (ISKCON). Also frequently mentioned were groups long considered cults within the evangelical community, such as Jehovah's Witnesses and Mormons. Being similar to the Jesus People in style and culture did not make other groups immune to cult charges. Many respondents pointed to groups that were often perceived as Jesus People groups in the media but developed a reputation as cults, such as the Way International, the Local Church, and the Alamo Foundation. Even more mainstream Jesus People groups generally accepted by the evangelical community—Shiloh, Jesus People USA, Scott Ross's Love Inn group—were occasionally targeted by some respondents as having been perceived as cultlike at the time.

25. Did you attend any Jesus Music Festivals during your JP involvement?

Yes	56.4%
No	32.6%
Not sure	7.3%
No answer	3.7%

26. Were women given positions of authority during your JP involvement?

Yes	42.3%
No	23.2%
Not sure	29.3%
No answer	5.2%

This question represents another of those "eye of the beholder" questions, which is complicated further by the mists of time. Unfortunately, in most conventional approaches to North American Christianity, the role of women's participation is often reduced to a one-dimensional obsession with the ordination of women and the appointment of female pastors. This slant, of course, underplays and/ or discounts other ways women can participate, wield power, and be perceived as holding positions of authority. The Jesus People were known as patriarchal for their adherence to conservative evangelical interpretations of biblical guidelines for male-female, husband-wife relationships. The data here seem to indicate that in many cases these guidelines were not necessarily followed down the line or that women were at least perceived to have authority and influence, despite what might be construed from a flat reading of biblical texts or group policies and pronouncements.

27. Were minorities included in your experience during the JP movement?

Yes	69.6%
No	14.6%
No answer	15.8%

The Jesus People movement was, overwhelmingly, a movement made up of North Americans of European descent. However, there was some participation by African Americans, Hispanics, Native Americans, and Asian Americans (and on a "minority" level, the movement was conspicuous in its inclusion of Messianic Jews). This question attempted to get a better handle on attitudes toward minorities, as well as their inclusion and participation in the movement. Overwhelmingly, it would seem to indicate—coming at the tail end of the civil rights movement and during a time of heightened racial tension and expanding ethnic consciousness—that a number of Jesus People groups did prove attractive to minorities, who must have felt a sense of welcome therein. Overall, the data point to a very open and progressive outlook in this regard as compared with many of their older Establishment evangelical counterparts during this time. Many of those who answered no went out of their way to indicate that they thought there would have been no problem with minority participation in their groups or made a point to note that they lived in areas (rural Ohio, Minnesota, Pennsylvania, for example) where minorities were relatively nonexistent.

28. Were you convinced that Jesus' return was imminent during your involvement with the JP movement?

Yes	79.2%
No	9.8%
Not sure	7%
No answer	4%

The apocalyptic nature of the Jesus People movement and the influence of books like Hal Lindsey's *The Late, Great Planet Earth* were well documented. The data here reflect this and also demonstrate that they indeed believed that Christ's return was a matter of "any day now."

29. Did you believe in the "Rapture" during your involvement in the JP movement?

Yes	89.9%
No	4.2%
Not sure	2.6%
No answer	3.3%

30. Do you still believe in the "Rapture"?

Yes	66.3%
No	16.3%
Not sure	14%
No answer	3.4%

Over the years, there has been slippage in the overwhelming belief in the Rapture and dispensational interpretations of the Bible among former Jesus People. Still, the number who retain a belief in this interpretation of the Scriptures is quite high—some respondents indicated that they now believe that the Second Coming is all the more at hand.

31. Did you believe that spiritual gifts are for today?

Yes	86.1%
No	2.9%
Not sure	6.4%
No answer	4.6%

This question indicates that one key element of dispensational thinking had been thrown out the window by the Jesus People—the teaching that "spiritual gifts" (e.g., speaking in tongues) had only been meant for the early church and that for the "present dispensation" such gifts had ceased.

32. Did you believe that the creation of Israel in 1948 was prophetically significant during your involvement in the JP?

Yes	86.1%
No	4.4%
Not sure	5.7%
No answer	3.8%

This and the next question also represent keys in dispensational interpretations of Bible prophecy and are also indicative of larger evangelical support for Israel.

33. Did you believe that the '67 Arab-Israeli War was prophetically significant during your involvement in the JP?

Yes	61.1%
No	13.7%
Not sure	20.7%
No answer	4.5%

Perhaps surprisingly, given that it was rather recent history at the time and involved Israel's achieving control over the entire city of Jerusalem, not as many were sure that this event had prophetic significance. Nonetheless, it does demonstrate a high degree of potential political support for future Israeli claims to a "Greater Israel," occupation of Palestinian and other Arab lands, and pro-Israeli policies of the American government.

34. Did you believe that "tongues" were the initial evidence of the "Baptism of the Holy Spirit" during your JP involvement?

Yes	52.8%
No	37.2%
Not sure	6.3%
No answer	3.7%

A formal tenet of most brands of traditional Pentecostal theology, the responses to this question probably indicate the perspective that many youth from non-Pentecostal evangelical backgrounds brought with them into the movement and perhaps a greater degree of flexibility in the Jesus People than in most old-line Pentecostal groups.

35. Do you still believe that "tongues" are the initial evidence of the "Baptism of the Holy Spirit"?

Yes	24.1%t
No	50%
Not sure	10.7%
No answer	15.2%

It would appear that the years brought a significant change in this regard, indicative of involvement and interaction with a wider variety of Christian groups.

36. Do you still consider yourself a Christian?

Yes	94.1%
No	1.5%
Not sure	0.6%
No answer	3.8%

Although participation in this survey would seem to skew toward those who still felt that Christian faith was important to them, the numbers nonetheless provide important evidence that involvement with the Jesus People movement had a major impact and that it apparently tended to strengthen adherence to Christianity. By contrast, it would also seem to discredit any notion that involvement eventually led to a mass exodus of disillusioned youth who subsequently discarded their faith, therefore accounting for the movement's ultimate disappearance. If such had been the case, one might suppose that many more embittered ex-Jesus People might have found their way to the survey.

37. What is your current religious affiliation (choose as many as apply from list, or "other")?

[number of responses out of 812]	
"Christian" as 1st choice	509 (62.7%)
"Evangelical" as 1st or 2nd choice	328 (40.4%)
"Pentecostal," "Charismatic," or Pentecostal Denomination as 1st or 2nd choice	191 (23.5%)

This question tried to give some shape to where the Jesus People were in terms of their affiliation thirty to forty years after their involvement in the movement. Overwhelmingly, most simply saw "Christian" as their baseline, first sense of identification. This is in keeping with general evangelical self-identification but also may indicate a lingering reductionist roots consciousness. Perhaps the surprising element of this response—given the troubles many scholars have in trying to pin down and estimate the "evangelical" population because of the lack of popular awareness of that label among evangelicals—is that many of the respondents actually saw the term *evangelical* as a major self-identifier. Additionally, given that so many of the respondents had Pentecostal and Charismatic experiences, it is perhaps surprising that a specifically Pentecostal or Charismatic involvement and self-identification had not arisen among a large number of the respondents in the intervening years.

38. Do you still listen to "Jesus Music" that was current during your involvement in the JP movement?

Yes	66.1%
No	27%
Not sure	0.9%
No answer	6%

Although old dogs are known not to learn new tricks, it is rather surprising, given the rise of new technologies (much of the old music is still available only in

LP record and cassette form) and a flood of music created since the days of the Jesus People (the rise of Contemporary Christian Music), that many of the people answering the survey were still inclined—either out of actual enthusiasm for the music or the artists or out of nostalgia—to pull out their Jesus music. Again, this accents the important role that music played as a bonding agent in the movement.

Addendum: Survey Respondents' "Favorites" and "Most Influentials"

As part of our survey, we asked those who had taken part in the Jesus People movement to name those they considered most influential or their personal favorites in five specific categories: (1) most influential/favorite artists/musical groups, (2) most influential/favorite songs, (3) most influential/favorite albums, (4) most influential leaders/speakers, and (5) most influential/favorite authors or books. We encouraged respondents to follow their hearts in these questions and not to think just in national terms, but to honestly name local leaders, speakers, or bands if they had been most influential in their lives or if they had been their favorites. The responses to these questions were both very interesting and very complex to tabulate. A fair percentage of our respondents either did not answer these questions at all or simply remarked "too many to list" for such things as favorite song or author. Others listed one or two responses to these questions, while some people took the time to list five, ten, or twenty favorite Jesus music bands, authors, or speakers. Like the question about people's current denominational affiliation, I thought it probable in the case of multiple responses that the first responses were more likely to be the most influential or their absolute favorites. So I accepted up to three responses for each question and kept running tabs of who and what garnered how many votes. In the end, we had a wide variety of responses; many leaders and bands, for example, received only one, two, or three mentions. Many were mentioned time and time again but were listed at various spots outside the top three criteria we were using to gauge "most influential" and "favorite." Overall, when all was said and done, however, I believe we ended up with fairly clear indications of those artists, songs, albums, leaders, and authors who were broadly influential for the Jesus People movement. Table A.2 shows the results for the most influential musicians and groups.

Table A.2 Most Influential/Favorite "Jesus Music" Musicians, Groups

1. Love Song (340)
2. Larry Norman (226)
3. 2nd Chapter of Acts (153)
4. Keith Green (108)
5. Barry McGuire (96)
6. Phil Keaggy (81)

Table A.2 Continued

7. Randy Stonehill (75)
8. Chuck Girard (70)
9. Andrae Crouch (53)
10. Children of the Day (52)
11. The Way (51)
12. Mustard Seed Faith (49)
13. Honeytree (48)
14. Resurrection/Rez Band (29)
15. Randy Matthews (27)
16. Daniel Amos (20)
17. Debby Kerner/Ernie Rettino (19)
18. Petra (17)
19. The Road Home (13)
20. tie—Pat Terry (12)
Paul Clark (12)

Other artists with eight to eleven "first three" mentions were John Fischer, John Michael Talbot, Don Francisco, Karen Lafferty, Lamb, Dallas Holm, Country Faith, Sweet Comfort Band, and Evie.

Artists with five to seven "first three" mentions were Oden Fong, Parable, Darrell Mansfield, Malcolm & Alwyn, the Imperials, the Archers, Michael Omartian, the Talbot Brothers, Terry Talbot, Blessed Hope, Hope, and Glass Harp.

Note that within this segment of the survey, there was a decided Calvary Chapel effect that is not surprising, given the size and importance of Calvary Chapel in Costa Mesa in the early movement and the important role that Southern California played within the larger movement. In this particular category, there was a resulting tendency for the major groups at Calvary Chapel (#1, #10, #11, #12, #17, #19) to show up as a cluster in the survey responses from those who had been a part of the Calvary Chapel scene or those whose Jesus People experience had taken place in Southern California. In terms of overall voting, #2 vote getter Larry Norman seemed to have a more broadly national following. However, Love Song won its convincing show in the #1 spot by virtue of both an overwhelming regard among those in the Calvary Chapel–Southern California orbit and by having a strong national impact and following.

Table A.3 shows the favorite Jesus music songs.

Table A.3 Favorite "Jesus Music" Songs

1. "I Wish We'd All Been Ready"—Larry Norman (55)
2. "Little Country Church"—Love Song (35)
3. "Come to the Water (For Those Tears I Died)"—Children of the Day (31)

4. "Easter Song"—2nd Chapter (23)

5. "Love Song"—Love Song (22)

6. "Welcome Back"—Love Song (20)

7. tie—"Two Hands"—Love Song (17)

"Why Should the Devil Have All the Good Music?"—Larry Norman (17)

9. tie—"We Are One in the Spirit" (14)

"Little Pilgrim"—Love Song (14)

11. tie—"Your Love Broke Through"—Phil Keaggy/Keith Green (13)

"Sometimes Alleluia"—Chuck Girard (13)

13. "I Am a Servant"—Larry Norman/Honeytree (10)

14. "Why Don't You Look into Jesus?"—Larry Norman (9)

15. tie—"Front Seat, Back Seat"—Love Song (8)

"The Outlaw"—Larry Norman (8)

"Pass It On" (8)

18. "One Way"—Larry Norman (7)

19. tie—"Which Way the Wind Blows"—2nd Chapter (6)

"Seek Ye First"—Karen Lafferty (6)

Songs just out of the running were "Alleluia," "Amazing Grace," "Asleep in the Light" by Keith Green, "Lay Your Burden Down" by Chuck Girard, "Sweet, Sweet Song of Salvation" by Larry Norman, "Clean before My Lord" by Honeytree, "Hand to the Plow" by Paul Clark, "What a Day" by Phil Keaggy, "Keep Me Running" by Randy Stonehill, and "Sail on Sailor" by Mustard Seed Faith.

Note that this particular question received the most widely varied set of responses, including the most instances of responses like "too many to mention" and "all of it."

Table A.4 shows the most influential Jesus music albums.

Albums just out of the running were *Bootleg* by Larry Norman, *Seeds* by Barry McGuire, *Shotgun Angel* by Daniel Amos, *Jesus Christ Superstar, Live at Carnegie Hall* by Andrae Crouch & the Disciples, and *Welcome to Paradise* by Randy Stonehill.

Table A.4 Most Influential "Jesus Music" Albums

1. *Love Song*—Love Song (152)

2. tie—*The Everlastin' Living Jesus Music Concert/Maranatha # 1* (41)

Only Visiting This Planet—Larry Norman (41)

4. *Upon This Rock*—Larry Norman (27)

5. **with footnotes*—2nd Chapter of Acts (22)

6. *No Compromise*—Keith Green (19)

7. "All Maranatha albums"—(18)

Table A.5 Continued

8. "All Keith Green's albums"—(16)

9. tie—*What a Day*—Phil Keaggy (14)

Sail on Sailor—Mustard Seed Faith (14)

11. "All Larry Norman albums"—(12)

12. "All Love Song albums"—(11)

13. *Final Touch*—Love Song (10)

14. tie—*Chuck Girard*—Chuck Girard (9)

How the West Was One—2nd Chapter/Keaggy (9)

"All 2nd Chapter albums"—(9)

To the Bride—McGuire/2nd Chapter (9)

18. tie—*Street Level*—Larry Norman (8)

For Him Who Has Ears to Hear—Keith Green (8)

20. *In Another Land*—Larry Norman (7)

Table A.5 shows the most influential speakers and leaders.

Table A.5 Most Influential Speakers/Leaders

1. Chuck Smith (219)
2. David Wilkerson (51)
3. Lonnie Frisbee (44)
4. Billy Graham (43)
5. Greg Laurie (36)
6. tie—Derek Prince (29)

Keith Green (29)

8. Bob Mumford (27)
9. Tom Stipe (26)
10. Larry Norman (22)
11. Winkey Pratney (19)
12. Josh McDowell (18)
13. tie—Arthur Blessitt (17)

John Higgins (17)

Hal Lindsey (17)

16. tie—Kathryn Kuhlman (13)

Mike McIntosh (13)

18. tie—Bill Bright (11)

Glenn Kaiser (11)

Walter Martin (11)

Mario Murillo (11)

Duane Pederson (11)

Other speakers or leaders with eight to ten "first three" mentions are Nicky Cruz, Ken Gulliksen, Scott Ross, L. E. Romaine, and Mike Warnke. Speakers or leaders with five to seven mentions are Loren Cunningham, Bill Gothard, Kenneth Hagin, Jack Hayford, Roy Hicks Jr., Dawson McAllister, Pat Robertson, Larry Tomczak, Corrie Ten Boom, and Ralph Wilkerson.

Note that the Calvary Chapel effect is also fairly obvious in this particular category (Calvary Chapel figures at #1, #3, #5, #9, and tied for #16, along with two others with eight to ten mentions). Nonetheless, the ministry and impact of #1, Calvary Chapel founder Chuck Smith, went beyond a mere clustering of regional votes. Smith was obviously an important figure in the Jesus People movement not only in Orange County, California, but also throughout North America via widely distributed cassette tapes of his sermons and Bible studies and—to a lesser extent—his writings.

Most Influential Authors and Books

Not surprisingly, the Bible was overwhelmingly the first response of the people who took our survey, but this was expected. Tables A.6 and A.7 take into account the authors and other titles (including various new paraphrases or formats of the Bible that appeared in the '70s) that were mentioned most frequently among initial responses.

Table A.6 Most Influential Authors

1. Hal Lindsey (136)
2. David Wilkerson (78)
3. C. S. Lewis (75)
4. Watchman Nee (46)
5. Francis Schaeffer (43)
6. Josh McDowell (41)
7. Chuck Smith (23)
8. tie—Bob Mumford (18)

The Living Bible (18)
10. Billy Graham (16)
11. tie—Nicky Cruz (13)
Derek Prince (13)
John L. Sherrill (13)
Corrie Ten Boom (13)
15. tie—Dennis and Rita Bennett (11)
Hannah Hurnard (11)
A. W. Tozer (11)
18. tie—Arthur Blessitt (10)
Merlin Carrothers (10)
20. Pat Boone (8)

Other authors or titles with five or more "first three" mentions were Brother Andrew, Dietrich Bonhoeffer, Bill Bright, John Bunyan, Charles G. Finney, *The Good News Bible*, Tim LaHaye, *Letters to Street Christians*, Andrew Murray, Pat Robertson, Ray Steadman, John Stott, Mel Tari, and Winkey Pratney.

Table A.7 Top Ten Most Frequently Mentioned Titles

1. *The Late, Great Planet Earth*—Hal Lindsey (Hands-down winner)
2. *The Cross and the Switchblade*—David Wilkerson
3. *Mere Christianity*—C. S. Lewis
4. *Evidence That Demands a Verdict*—Josh McDowell
5. *The Living Bible*
6. *The God Who Is There*—Francis Schaeffer
7. tie—*Run, Baby, Run*—Nicky Cruz
They Speak with Other Tongues—John L. Sherrill
The Hiding Place—Corrie Ten Boom
10. tie—*Nine O'Clock in the Morning*—Dennis and Rita Bennett
Hinds' Feet on High Places—Hannah Hurnard

Notes

INTRODUCTION

1. "The New Rebel Cry: Jesus Is Coming!" *Time*, June 21, 1971, pp. 56–63; quotes found on p. 56.
2. Martin E. Marty, *Pilgrims in Their Own Land: 500 Years of Religion in America* (Boston: Little, Brown, 1984), p. 469; see also "Top '71 Religious News—World Revival," *Christianity Today*, January 1, 1971, pp. 26–27; and "Religion in Review, 1971," *Moody Monthly*, February 1972, p. 8.
3. For practical purposes, it would be imprudent to list all of them here. See David Di Sabatino, *The Jesus People Movement: An Annotated Bibliography and General Resource. Bibliographies and Indexes in Religious Studies, No. 49*, G. E. Gorman, Advisory Editor (Westport, CT: Greenwood, 1999), chapter 2, "Historical Resources" (pp. 24–80) for the books published by, on, or related to the Jesus movement in 1971 and 1972.
4. The major contemporary academic books about the Jesus movement were Lowell Streiker, *The Jesus Trip: Advent of the Jesus Freaks* (Nashville, TN: Abingdon, 1971); Ronald M. Enroth, Edward E. Ericson Jr., and C. Breckinridge Peters, *The Jesus People: Old Time Religion in the Age of Aquarius* (Grand Rapids, MI: Eerdmans, 1972); Jorling Erstad, *That New Time Religion* (Minneapolis, MN: Augsburg, 1972); Robert S. Ellwood Sr., *One Way: The Jesus Movement and Its Meaning* (Englewood Cliffs, NJ: Prentice-Hall, 1973); and James T. Richardson, Mary White Stewart, and Robert B. Simmonds, *Organized Miracles: A Study of a Contemporary Youth, Communal Fundamentalist Organization* (Brunswick, NJ: Transaction, 1979).
5. Billy Graham, *The Jesus Generation* (Grand Rapids, MI: Zondervan, 1971), pp. 11, 21–22.

6. Everett Hullum Jr. and Dallas Lee in Walker L. Knight, compiler, *Jesus People Come Alive* (Wheaton, IL: Tyndale, 1971), pp. 9, 12. For insight into how the hope for a national revival played into the very warp and woof of the postwar evangelical movement, see Joel Carpenter's excellent history *Revive Us Again: The Reawakening of American Fundamentalism* (New York: Oxford University Press, 1997).

7. Ronald Enroth, "Where Have All the Jesus People Gone?" *Eternity*, October 1973, pp. 14–17, 28.

8. Ellwood, *One Way*, p. x.

9. To their credit, sociologists are much more inclined to treat adolescent interests and pastimes as something to be taken seriously—even in the realm of religion. See, for example, Christian Smith with Melinda Lundquist Denton, *Soul Searching: The Religious and Spiritual Lives of American Teenagers* (New York: Oxford University Press, 2005).

10. Nick Bromell, *Tomorrow Never Knows: Rock and Psychedelics in the 1960s* (Chicago: University of Chicago Press, 2000), p. 24.

11. Ibid., pp. 24–25.

12. Oral histories and interviews have played an important part in the research for this project. Obviously, the opportunity to interview people who were directly involved in, or who observed, historical events and eras is a great boon to the historian. Even so, it is a resource that is not without limitations: "Participant-observers" possess their own individual perspectives and biases, they have a sometimes limited grasp of the larger picture, and they have often developed a long-rehearsed and oft-repeated narrative regarding their particular experience. Add to this the all too human universal experience of failing and blurred memory, and it becomes clear that oral histories are hardly a foolproof source. With these potential pitfalls in mind, I have made every attempt to be judicious in my use of interviews, cross-checking general impressions and particular facts with print sources, as well as against other interviews and the overall knowledge I have gained of the larger topic. I believe the end result of this process has made for a more balanced and accurate understanding of the Jesus People movement.

13. The "Worship Wars" are well laid out from the traditionalist point of view in Marva Dawn, *Reaching Out without Dumbing Down: A Theology of Worship for the Turn-of-the-Century Culture* (Grand Rapids, MI: Eerdmans, 1995). A good defense of the contemporary position can be found in John Frame, *Contemporary Worship Music: A Biblical Defense* (Phillipsburg, NJ: Presbyterian & Reformed, 1997). Periodic salvoes in the conflict can be tracked in the periodicals *The Hymn* (from the traditionalist bastion of the Hymn Society) and *Worship Leader Magazine* (an outgrowth of Maranatha! Music).

14. Sydney Ahlstrom, *A Religious History of the American People* (New Haven, CT: Yale University Press, 1972), n. 1086.

CHAPTER 1

1. *Youth for Christ*, September 1961, p.4.
2. Ibid.; see also "TAMI Talks to Teenagers," *Youth for Christ*, April 1961, pp. 24–25.
3. George Gallup and Evan Hill, "Youth: The Cool Generation," *Saturday Evening Post*, December 20–23, 1961, p. 64.
4. Ibid.
5. Ibid., p. 70.
6. Talcott Parsons, "Youth in the Context of American Society," *Daedalus*, Winter 1962, pp. 97–123; quote from pp. 122–123.
7. Michael Brake, *Comparative Youth Culture: The Sociology of Youth Culture and Youth Subcultures in America, Britain and Canada* (London: Routledge, 1985), p. 40.
8. Clark Kerr quoted in Jay Stevens, *Storming Heaven: LSD and the American Dream* (New York: Grove, 1987), p. ix.
9. John MacDonald, Taped Reminiscence, November 1998, in possession of author; John A. MacDonald interview, May 7, 1993, Collection 489-T1, Billy Graham Center Archives, Wheaton College, Wheaton, IL.
10. MacDonald, Taped Reminiscence.
11. Ted Wise telephone interview with author, October 27, 2010; John MacDonald, *House of Acts* (Carol Stream, IL: Creation House, 1970), p. 26; Edward Plowman, *The Jesus Movement in America* (Elgin, IL: David C. Cook, 1971), p. 43.
12. For a look at the early development of San Francisco's Haight-Ashbury counter-cultural community see Charles Perry, *The Haight-Ashbury* (New York: Random House, 1984), pp. 3–86. See also Edward P. Morgan, *The 60s Experience: Hard Lessons about Modern America* (Philadelphia: Temple University Press, 1991); Joel Selvin, *Summer of Love: The Inside Story of LSD, Rock and Roll, Free Love and High Times in the West* (New York: Cooper Square, 1994); and Paul Perry, Michael Schwartz, and Neil Ortenberg, eds., *On the Bus: The Complete Guide to the Legendary Trip of Ken Kesey and the Merry Pranksters and the Birth of the Counterculture* (New York: Thunder's Mouth, 1997).
13. Wise interview.
14. Ted Wise, "Jason Questions a Jesus Freak," September 13, 1997, Peninsula Bible Church, www.pbc.org/dp/wise/jason.html; Wise interview.
15. Ted Wise, comment on "Santo Daime" Yahoo! chat group, comment posted on February 22, 2001; http://groups.yahoo.com/group/daime/message/222; MacDonald, *House of Acts*, pp. 22–26; Wise, "Jason Questions a Jesus Freak"; Wise interview.
16. Wise interview; Wise, "Jason Questions a Jesus Freak"; MacDonald, *House of Acts*, pp. 22–26.
17. MacDonald, *House of Acts*, p. 27.
18. Maurice Allan, "God's Thing in Hippieville," *Christian Life*, January 1968, p. 21.
19. Plowman, *The Jesus Movement in America*, p. 43.

20. Wise interview; Wise, "Jason Questions a Jesus Freak."
21. Ibid.
22. Wise interview; MacDonald, *House of Acts*, pp. 29–30.
23. Jimmy E. Dopp, "When the Hippies Found Jesus: A True Story of the Sixties" (unpublished mss., ca. 1990), copy in possession of author, pp. 72–73; Wise interview.
24. Wise interview; Wise, "Jason Questions a Jesus Freak."
25. Allan, "God's Thing," p. 35; MacDonald, *House of Acts*, pp. 31, 35–39, 42–46, 51–57; MacDonald interview, 1993, BGC Archives; Wise, "Jason Questions a Jesus Freak."
26. MacDonald, *House of Acts*, p. 62.
27. Ibid., pp. 62–63.
28. Wise interview.
29. MacDonald interview, 1993, BGC Archives.
30. MacDonald, *House of Acts*, p. 63.
31. Ibid.
32. Wise, "Jason Questions a Jesus Freak."
33. Judy Doop Marshall telephone interview with author, August 16, 2007; David Di Sabatino, "History of the Jesus Movement" (master's thesis: McMaster University, 1994), pp. 32–33; Dopp, "When the Hippies Found Jesus," pp. 16–31.
34. Judy Doop Marshall interview.
35. Dopp, "When the Hippies Found Jesus," pp. 2, 4, 6, 8–9.
36. Ibid., pp. 53–54, 79.
37. Judy Doop Marshall interview; Dopp, "When the Hippies Found Jesus," pp. 56–57.
38. Steve and Sandi Heefner telephone interview with author, August 2, 2007, and September 21, 2007; Oral Roberts meeting cited in Dopp, "When the Hippies Found Jesus," p. 49.
39. Heefner interview.
40. Heefner interview; "Hippie Evangelist Explains Mission," *Daily Review* (Hayward, CA), January 27, 1968, p. 6; Bill Rose, "Hippies Find Christianity 'Groovy,'" *Oakland Tribune*, June 5, 1968, p. 37-A.
41. Heefner interview, August 2, 2007; Dopp, "When the Hippies Found Jesus," pp. 37–42.
42. Steve Heefner conversion anecdote featured in *Frisbee: Life and Death of a Hippie Preacher*, DVD, produced and directed by David Di Sabatino (Seal Beach, CA: Jester Media, 2005); Heefner telephone interview with author, August 26, 2010; Wise interview; Dopp, "When the Hippies Found Jesus," pp. 40–42.
43. Wise interview; Doop, "When the Hippies Found Jesus," pp. 83–90.
44. Sandy Sands Kinder, e-mail message to author, September 20, 2010; Dopp, "When the Hippies Found Jesus," pp. 83–90.

45. Sandy Sands Kinder, e-mail message to author, September 15, 2010; Wise interview; Doop, "When the Hippies Found Jesus," pp. 93, 114–118, 131.

46. Dopp, "When the Hippies Found Jesus," pp. 97–98.

47. Ibid., p. 100.

48. Acts 2: 44–45 (KJV); Heefner telephone interview with author, August 2, 2007; Dopp, "When the Hippies Found Jesus," p. 121.

49. Wise, "Jason Questions a Jesus Freak."

50. Wise interview; MacDonald, *House of Acts*, p. 55; Dopp, "When the Hippies Found Jesus," p. 121; Heefner interview.

51. Ronald Enroth, Edward E. Ericson Jr., and C. Breckinridge Peters, *The Jesus People* (Grand Rapids: Eerdmans, 1972), p. 13; Wise interview; Dopp, "When the Hippies Found Jesus," pp. 121, 124–125.

52. Wise interview.

53. Part of Evangelical Concerns, Inc.'s early promotional publicity for their "missionary to the hippie," Ted Wise revolved around this understanding of persecution: "He lost his job because his employer felt that [his] enthusiastic witness was inimical to the business!" (promotional bulletin from Evangelical Concerns, Inc., ca. 1967 in author's possession).

54. MacDonald, *House of Acts*, pp. 63–64; Wise interview.

55. Dopp, "When the Hippies Found Jesus," pp. 126, 130; MacDonald, *House of Acts*, p. 64.

56. Doop, "When the Hippies Found Jesus," pp. 131–132.

57. Heefner interview; Dopp, "When the Hippies Found Jesus," pp. 134–137.

58. Heefner interview.

59. Dopp, "When the Hippies Found Jesus," pp. 137–138.

60. Heefner interview; Dopp, "When the Hippies Found Jesus," pp. 139–141.

61. Heefner interview.

62. Helen Swick Perry, *The Human Be-In* (New York: Basic Books, 1970), pp. 22–23; Perry, *The Haight-Ashbury*, pp. 165–169; MacDonald, *House of Acts*, p. 65.

63. Notes in e-mail from Elizabeth Wise, October 30, 2010; Dopp, "When the Hippies Found Jesus," pp. 106–109, quote from pp. 107–108.

64. MacDonald interview, BGC Archives; Doop, "When the Hippies Found Jesus," pp. 104–109; MacDonald, *House of Acts*, pp. 68–69.

65. MacDonald interview, BGC Archives; Wise, "Jason Questions a Jesus Freak"; MacDonald, *House of Acts*, pp. 67–69.

66. MacDonald, *House of Acts*, p. 69; Wise interview.

67. State of California nonprofit incorporation charter for Evangelical Concerns, Inc., May 1967; "Evangelical Concerns, Inc." flyer, ca. fall 1967; Rick and Megan Sacks telephone interview with author, April 21, 2010; MacDonald, *House of Acts*, pp. 69–71; MacDonald interview, 1993, BGC Archives; Dopp, "When the Hippies Found Jesus," pp. 145, 151.

CHAPTER 2

1. John MacDonald, *House of Acts* (Carol Stream, IL: Creation House, 1970), pp. 71–72; Rick and Megan Sacks telephone interview with author, April 21, 2010.

2. Kent Philpott, interview with author, Mill Valley, CA, August 7, 2002; John MacDonald, taped reminiscence, ca. November 1998, in possession of author; Steve and Sandi Heefner telephone interview with author, August 2, 2007; David Di Sabatino, "A History of the Jesus Movement," master's thesis: McMaster Divinity College, 1994, pp. 30–31; MacDonald, *House of Acts*, p. 71.

3. Charles Perry, *The Haight-Ashbury: A History* (New York: Random House, 1984), p. 99.

4. Nicholas von Hoffman, *We Are the People Our Parents Warned Us Against* (Chicago: Quadrangle, 1968), p. 67; Charles Perry, *The Haight-Ashbury*, pp. 99, 212.

5. Terry Anderson, *The Movement and the Sixties: Protest in America from Greensboro to Wounded Knee* (New York: Oxford University Press, 1995), p. 175.

6. Timothy Miller, *The Hippies and American Values* (Knoxville: University of Tennessee Press, 1991), p. 63; Edward P. Morgan, *The 60s Experience: Hard Lessons about Modern America* (Philadelphia: Temple University Press, 1991), p. 182. The Haight-Ashbury Free Medical Clinic had thirty doctors donating their services part-time during the Summer of Love (Perry, *The Haight-Ashbury*, p. 201).

7. Kent Philpott and David Hoyt, "Two Brothers in Haight" (unpublished mss., ca. 1971), p. 74.

8. Flyer from the "Communications Company," April 16, 1967, quoted in Perry, *The Haight-Ashbury*, p. 181.

9. Quote found in Morgan, *The 60s Experience*, p. 184. For a contemporary account of the devolution of the Haight, see "Trouble in Hippieland," *Newsweek*, October 30, 1967, pp. 84–90.

10. Steve Heefner quoted in Karl Kahler, *The Cult That Snapped: A Journey into the Way International* (Los Gatos, CA: Karl Kahler, 1999), p. 60.

11. Heefner interview; quote from Rick Sacks (Sacks interview).

12. The Digger Archives guestbook, www.diggers.org/guestbook/guestbook_03_sep.htm, posting by Mickey Stevens, September 9, 2003.

13. Ted Wise telephone interview with author, October 27, 2010; Jimmy E. Dopp, "When the Hippies Found Jesus" (unpublished mss., ca. 1990), pp. 173, 184; Heefner interview.

14. Heefner interview; Di Sabatino, "A History of the Jesus Movement," p. 31.

15. Bill Rose, "Hippies Find Christianity 'Groovy,'" *Oakland Tribune*, June 5, 1968, p. 37-A.

16. In their book *The Jesus People* (Grand Rapids, MI: Eerdmans, 1972), Ronald M. Enroth, Edward E. Ericson Jr., and C. Breckinridge Peters estimated that the

Living Room made contact with between 30,000 and 50,000 young people (p. 13). In a 1993 interview with David Di Sabatino, group member Danny Sands believed this number to be an exaggeration and put forth an estimate of daily contact with fifty to seventy-five people. However, even using the lower estimate of fifty per day, six days a week, for only eighteen months, one comes up with more than 20,000 people—significantly higher than the number Sands estimated ("A History of the Jesus Movement," p. 32, n. 18).

17. Sacks interview; MacDonald, *House of Acts*, pp. 101–104.

18. Sacks interview; MacDonald, *House of Acts*, pp. 101–108.

19. David Di Sabatino, "Lonnie Frisbee: A Modern Samson," in Di Sabatino, *The Jesus People Movement: An Annotated Bibliography and General Resource*, 2nd ed. (Lake Forest, CA: Jester Media, 2004), pp. 206–207; Enroth, Ericson, and Peters, *The Jesus People*, p. 13; Wise interview.

20. Lonnie Frisbee testimony (Anaheim, CA: Vineyard Ministry International, ca. 1980), Tape 003, audiocassette.

21. Michael McFadden, *The Jesus Revolution* (New York: Harrow, 1972), pp. 23–24; Di Sabatino, "Lonnie Frisbee," p. 207.

22. Telephone interview with Connie Bremer-Murray, January 7, 2013; *Frisbee: The Life and Death of a Hippie Preacher* (Jester Media, 2006); Enroth, Ericson, and Peters, *The Jesus People*, pp. 13–14.

23. Philpott and Hoyt, "Two Brothers in Haight," pp. 42–52; Philpott interview.

24. Philpott and Hoyt, "Two Brothers in Haight," p. 54.

25. Quote found in Philpott and Hoyt, "Two Brothers in Haight," p. 55; Philpott interview.

26. David Hoyt telephone interview with author, July 11, 2008; Philpott interview.

27. Philpott and Hoyt, "Two Brothers in Haight," pp. 8–26; Hoyt interview.

28. Philpott and Hoyt, "Two Brothers in Haight" p. 27.

29. David Hoyt, "Only One Way? How Narrow Minded!" *Right On!* February 1, 1970, p. 3; Philpott interview.

30. Philpott interview; Hoyt interview; Hoyt and Philpott, "Two Brothers in Haight," pp. 28–29.

31. Philpott interview; Philpott and Hoyt, "Two Brothers in Haight," pp. 29–31.

32. Philpott and Hoyt, "Two Brothers in Haight," pp. 31–33.

33. Hoyt interview.

34. Hoyt, "Only One Way?"; Philpott and Hoyt, "Two Brothers in Haight," pp. 34–36.

35. Philpott and Hoyt, "Two Brothers in Haight," p. 36.

36. *The Jesus Movement*, DVD (Mill Valley, CA: Miller Avenue Baptist Church, ca. 2007); Philpott interview; Hoyt interview; Philpott and Hoyt, "Two Brothers in Haight," p. 37.

37. Sandy Sands Kinder e-mail to author, September 15, 2010; Dopp, "When the Hippies Found Jesus," pp. 149–150.

38. Dopp, "When the Hippies Found Jesus," pp. 157–160; Sandy Sands Kinder e-mail; Heefner interview.

39. Dopp, "When the Hippies Found Jesus," p. 159.

40. Bremer-Murray interview; Heefner interview; MacDonald, *House of Acts*, p. 46.

41. Judy Doop Marshall telephone interview with author, August 16, 2007; Bremer-Murray interview; Heefner interview.

42. Heefner interview; Sandy Sands Kinder e-mail.

43. Heefner interview; MacDonald, *House of Acts*, pp. 89–90.

44. "Hippie Evangelist Explains Mission," *Daily Review* (Hayward, CA), January 27, 1968, p. 6.

45. Heefner interview.

46. Ed Plowman telephone interview with author, June 25, 2004.

47. Maurice Allan, "God's Thing in Hippieville," *Christian Life*, January 1968, pp. 20–23, 34–38.

48. MacDonald, tape reminiscence, 1998; Dopp, "When the Hippies Found Jesus," pp. 141–142, 145–147.

49. Allan, "God's Thing in Hippieville," p. 37.

50. Ibid., pp. 37–38.

51. Dopp, "When the Hippies Found Jesus," p. 147.

52. Letter to the editor from Ted Wise, *Christian Life*, May 1968, p. 10.

53. MacDonald, *House of Acts*, p. 114.

54. MacDonald, taped reminiscence.

55. Robert Walker, "From the Editor," *Christian Life*, April 1968, pp. 6–8; "Storm over Hippieville," p. 9.

56. "Storm over Hippieville," p. 9.

57. 2 Corinthians 6:17 (KJV); "Storm over Hippieville," p. 9.

58. "Storm over Hippieville," p. 9.

59. "Postscript on the Hippies," *Christian Life*, May 1968, p. 10.

60. "Addenda on the Hippies," *Christian Life*, June 1968, p. 6.

61. Heefner interview; see also Dopp, "When the Hippies Met Jesus," pp. 155–156, 182–183.

62. David Wilkerson, *The Cross and the Switchblade* (New York: Pyramid, 1963).

63. Heefner interview.

64. Dopp, "When the Hippies Found Jesus," pp. 187–188.

65. Dopp, "When the Hippies Found Jesus," pp. 188–189; Heefner interview; Sacks interview.

66. Walker, "From the Editor"; Heefner interview. For his part, *Christian Life* editor Walker was reassured by a letter from Maurice Allan and communications with Evangelical Concerns that the group were "babes in Christ" who were maturing and making progress and concluded: "Somehow or other, I do not believe this is the last we shall hear of the 'hippie Christians'" (p. 8).

67. David Wilkerson, *Purple Violet Squish* (Grand Rapids, MI: Zondervan, 1969; New York: Pyramid, 1970), p. 22.

68. MacDonald, *House of Acts*, pp. 83–84.

69. Wise interview; Doop, "When the Hippies Found Jesus," pp. 189–190.

70. Dopp, "When the Hippies Found Jesus," pp. 189–190.

71. Sacks interview.

72. Dopp, "When the Hippies Found Jesus," pp. 189–190; Wise interview; Walker, "From the Editor," p. 7.

73. Philpott interview; Hoyt interview; *The Jesus Movement*, DVD. Philpott also had become something of a grade B celebrity in Southern Baptist circles for his work with youth and spent some of his time speaking to SBC youth groups and retreats (see Letter from John Courtland Shepard to Kent Philpott, November 22, 1968; Letter from Crawford Howell to Kent Philpott, September 2, 1969, photocopies in possession of author). Philpott's role is also alluded to in Charles Marsh's biographical reminiscence of his father—a pastor from Laurel, MS—and a 1968 retreat in the California mountains in his book, *The Last Days: A Son's Story of Sin and Segregation at the Dawn of the New South* (New York: Basic Books, 2001), pp. 198–202.

74. Philpott and Hoyt, "Two Brothers in Haight," p. 62.

75. Ibid., pp. 64–65.

76. Ibid., p. 72.

77. Ibid., p. 74.

78. Ibid., p. 75.

79. Philpott interview.

80. Heefner interview; Wise interview; see, for example, Philpott and Hoyt, "Two Brothers in Haight," pp. 61–62, 68, 77, 84–86.

81. Kent Philpott, "Jesus People Christian Houses," unpublished mss, ca. 1970, pp. 3–4, Kent Philpott collection; Kent Philpott telephone interview with author, September 23, 2003; Philpott interview, August 7, 2002; Hoyt interview.

82. Heefner interview.

83. Judy Doop Marshall interview; Heefner interview.

84. MacDonald tape reminiscence, 1998.

85. S.v., "The Way International," in J. Gordon Melton, *Encyclopedic Handbook of Cults in America*, 2nd ed. (New York: Garland, 1992), pp. 315–322. For an in-house history of The Way into the mid-1970s, see Elena S. Whiteside, *The Way: Living in Love*, 2nd ed. (New Knoxville, OH: American Christian Press, 1974). For a more detailed overview of The Way from its beginnings into the mid-1990s by an ex-member, see Karl Kahler, *The Cult That Snapped: A Journey into the Way International* (Los Gatos, CA: Karl Kahler, 1999), pp. 33–55.

86. Kahler, *The Cult That Snapped*, pp. 61–62; Heefner interview; Wise interview; Dopp, "When the Hippies Found Jesus," pp. 213–218.

87. Steve Heefner quoted in Kahler, *The Cult That Snapped*, p. 62.

88. Heefner interview.

89. Heefner interview; Kahler, *The Cult That Snapped*, p. 63.

90. Kahler, *The Cult That Snapped*, p. 63.

91. Heefner interview; Sacks interview.

92. Heefner interview; MacDonald, *House of Acts*, pp. 110–111.

93. Dopp, "When the Hippies Found Jesus," pp. 231–245; Heefner interview.

94. MacDonald, taped reminiscence; Wise interview; Elizabeth Wise e-mail; MacDonald, *House of Acts*, pp. 111–112; for an example of Wise's travels to college campuses, see note about his trip to Malone College in Ohio in minutes of Evangelical Concerns, Inc., March 19, 1970 (from Kent Philpott collection).

95. See minutes of Evangelical Concerns, Inc., September 26, 1969, Kent Philpott collection. Individual churches also provided support—see letter from Phillip T. McGallian, pastor of Placer Hills Community Church (United Methodist) in Meadow Vista, CA, to Kent Philpott, February 17, 1969, Kent Philpott collection.

96. United Youth Ministries, report for May 9, 1969; United Youth Ministries, report for June 1, 1969 (both from Kent Philpott collection); MacDonald, *House of Acts*, p. 120.

97. United Youth Ministries newsletter, ca. summer 1969; United Youth Ministries/ Evangelical Concerns Budget for 1970.

CHAPTER 3

1. Ronald Enroth, Edward E. Ericson, and C. Breckinridge Peters, *The Jesus People: Old-Time Religion in the Age of Aquarius* (Grand Rapids, MI: Eerdmans, 1972), p. 73.

2. Arthur Blessitt with Walter Wagner, *Turned On to Jesus* (New York: Hawthorn, 1971), see pp. 26–102; quotes on p. 74.

3. Peter Michelmore, *Back to Jesus* (Greenwich, CT: Fawcett, 1973), pp. 18–22; Walter Wagner, "A Trip to His Place," *Christian Life*, March 1970, pp. 75–78; Enroth, Ericson, and Peters, *The Jesus People*, p. 69.

4. Blessitt with Wagner, *Turned On to Jesus*, p. 110.

5. Arthur Blessitt, *Life's Greatest Trip* (Waco, TX: Word, 1970), p. 26; Enroth, Ericson, and Peters, *The Jesus People*, p. 73.

6. Glenn D. Kittler, *The Jesus Kids and Their Leaders* (New York: Warner, 1972), pp. 41–43; Blessitt, *Life's Greatest Trip*, pp. 13–16; Blessitt with Wagner, *Turned On to Jesus*, pp. 111–113, 131–137.

7. Back cover notes, *Soul Session at His Place*, Arthur Blessitt, Creative Sound, CSS-1530, ca. 1970, Frank Edmondson Contemporary Christian Music Collection, Judson College, Elgin, IL; Rita Klein, "God, Blessitt and 'His Place,'" *Eternity*, January 1971, pp. 34, 46–47; Blessitt, *Life's Greatest Trip*, pp. 19–23.

8. Edward Plowman, *The Jesus Movement in America* (Elgin, IL: David C. Cook, 1971), p. 97.

9. Blessitt, *Life's Greatest Trip*, pp. 40–41.

10. Kittler, *The Jesus Kids and Their Leaders*, p. 43.

11. Edmond E. Plowman, "Witnessing to Hippies," *Christianity Today*, June 7, 1968, p. 41; *Santa Ana (CA) Register*, April 27, 1968, p. A5; August, 17, 1968, p. A5.

12. Michael McFadden, *The Jesus Revolution* (New York: Harrow, 1971), pp. 28–29.

13. Blessitt with Wagner, *Turned On to Jesus*, pp. 209–234; Kittler, *The Jesus Kids and Their Leaders*, pp. 43–44.

14. Blessitt with Wagner, *Turned On to Jesus*, pp. 235–239.

15. For example, see photo of Sacramento March for Jesus, February 1971, in Lowell D. Streiker, *The Jesus Trip: Advent of the Jesus Freaks* (Nashville, TN: Abingdon, 1971), pp. 16–17; and *Hollywood Free Paper* vol. 2, issue 22, ca. early 1971, p. 7.

16. For an example of the nationwide publicity Blessitt received, see the AP wire photo in the *Joplin* (MO) *Globe*, July 20, 1969, p. 2D. For details on Blessitt's cross-walking adventures, see Arthur Blessitt, *The Cross: 38,102 miles. 38 years. 1 Mission* (Colorado Springs, CO: Authentic, 2009).

17. Don Williams interview with author, La Jolla, CA, August 1, 2002.

18. Ibid.

19. Don Williams, *Call to the Streets* (Minneapolis, MN: Augsburg, 1972), p. 23.

20. Williams interview.

21. Williams, *Call to the Streets*, pp. 27–28; Williams interview.

22. Williams, *Call to the Streets*, pp. 28–32; Williams interview.

23. Williams, *Call to the Streets*, pp. 29–34.

24. Williams interview.

25. Williams, *Call to the Streets*, pp. 59–72; Williams interview.

26. *Jesus Style* (Hollywood Presbyterian Church, 1970) Family Films Collection (Collection 307, F143), Billy Graham Center Archives, Wheaton College; Enroth, Ericson, and Peters, *The Jesus People*, p. 145.

27. Williams interview.

28. Chet Flippo, "Siege of the Alamos," *People*, June 13, 1983, pp. 28–33; McFadden, *The Jesus Revolution*, pp. 60–66; Enroth, Erickson, and Peters, *The Jesus People*, pp. 60–61.

29. Southern Poverty Law Center, Susy Buchanan, "The Daughter's Tale: Anti-Catholic Cult Leaders' Child Recounts Abuse," *Intelligence Report*, Spring 2008, www.splcenter.org/intel/intelreport/article.jsp?aid=881; Flippo, "Siege of the Alamos," pp. 28–33.

30. Tony Alamo, "Signs of the Time," www.alamoministries.com/content/english/testimonytracts/signsofthetimes.html; Kittler, *The Jesus Kids and Their Leaders*, pp. 65–66.

31. State of California, nonprofit articles of incorporation, Tony and Susan Alamo Foundation, #561933, Hollywood, CA (December 16, 1968); McFadden, *The Jesus Revolution*, pp. 66–67.

32. Tim Cahill, "Infiltrating the Jesus Army," *Rolling Stone*, June 21, 1973, p. 56; Alamo Ministries, "How This Mighty Work Started," ca. 1988, www.alamoministries.com/content/english/newsreleases/history.html; Craig Ott interview with author, Deerfield, IL, September 29, 2010.

33. Enroth, Ericson, and Peters, *The Jesus People*, p. 62: Kittler, *The Jesus Kids and Their Leaders*, p. 118.

34. Tim Cahill, *A Wolverine Is Eating My Leg* (New York: Vintage, 1989), pp. 47–53; Lowell Streiker, *The Jesus Trip* (Nashville, TN: Abingdon, 1971), pp. 20–34; Enroth, Ericson, and Peters, *The Jesus People*, pp. 54–60.

35. Tim Cahill, "True Believers and the Guise of the Weasel," *Rolling Stone*, June 7, 1973, p. 46.

36. Enroth, Ericson, and Peters, *The Jesus People*, pp. 73–74.

37. Flippo, "Siege of the Alamos"; McFadden, *The Jesus Revolution*, pp. 70–71.

38. J. Gordon Melton, *Encyclopedic Handbook of Cults* (New York: Garland, rev. ed., 1992), pp. 183–188; Guy Lancaster, "Tony Alamo," entry in *The Encyclopedia of Arkansas History & Culture*, updated September 9, 2008, www.encyclopediaofarkansas.net/encyclopedia/entry-detail.aspx?search=1&entryID=4224.

39. David Berg, "Survival!" Mo Letter, No. 172—GP, June 1972, sec. 70–71, 86; Deborah Davis, *The Children of God: The Inside Story* (Grand Rapids, MI: Zondervan, 1984), pp. 23–24.

40. David E. Van Zandt, *Living in the Children of God* (Princeton, NJ: Princeton University Press, 1991), pp. 31–32; Walter Martin, *The New Cults* (Ventura, CA: Vision House, 1980), pp. 143–144; Berg, "Survival!" sec. 86.

41. David Berg, "Dad's Own Story of the Revolution for Jesus," a booklet distributed to members of The Family International, 1982, pp. 79–93, www.xfamily.org/index.php/Oldie_Goldies; Berg, "Millions of Miles of Miracles!" Mo Letter, DO897, sec. 170–181.

42. Martin, *The New Cults*, p. 144; Berg, "Survival!" sec. 103.

43. Berg, "Millions of Miles of Miracles!" sec. 188.

44. Davis, *The Children of God*, p. 36.

45. Van Zandt, *Living in the Children of God*, pp. 33–34; Enroth, Ericson, and Peters, *The Jesus People*, p. 23.

46. Kent Philpott interview with author, Mill Valley, CA, August 7, 2002; David Hoyt telephone interview with author, July 11, 2008.

47. Berg, "Millions of Miles of Miracles!"

48. David Berg, "Reformation or Revolution?" section 8, MO Letter, No. I-GP, June 19, 1970.

49. David Berg, "Other Sheep," sections 6–7, MO Letter, No. 167 GP, June 1, 1972.

50. Ibid., sections 13–14.

51. Van Zandt, *Living in the Children of God*, pp. 33–34; Enroth, Ericson, and Peters, *The Jesus People*, p. 23; quote from Berg, "Other Sheep," sec. 14.

52. Berg, "Millions of Miles of Miracles!" sec. 191.

53. Berg, "Survival!" sections 109–115; Enroth, Ericson, and Peters, *The Jesus People*, p. 24; McFadden, *The Jesus Revolution*, pp. 89–90.

54. James McNabb Jr., "6 Church Hopping Teens Held after GWC Incident," *Orange Coast Daily Pilot* (Newport Beach, CA), ca. February 1969, clipping copied in Berg, "Dad's Own Story," pp. 114–115; Berg, "Survival!" sections 110–111.

55. "Hippies Eye New Church," "'Teens for Christ' Invited to Meeting," "Teens for Christ Challenge Churches," miscellaneous newspaper clippings copied in Berg, "Dad's Own Story," pp. 112–113; Berg, "Survival!" sections 111–113.

56. "Six Members of the Flock Remain in Jail," *Santa Ana Register*, ca. February 1969; "Six Arrested in Religious Tract Dispute," "Teens for Christ Trial Set Jan 9"; McNabb, "6 Church-Hopping Teens," copied in Berg, "Dad's Own Story," pp. 114–115; Berg, "Millions of Miles of Miracles!" section 195.

57. Berg, "Survival!" section 118–119.

58. Berg, "Survival!" sections 120–132; Berg, "Millions of Miles of Miracles!" sections 209–216; Van Zandt, *Living in the Children of God*, pp. 34–35.

59. Robert Ellwood Jr., *One Way: The Jesus Movement and Its Meaning* (Englewood Cliffs, NJ: Prentice-Hall, 1973), p. 107.

60. McFadden, *The Jesus Revolution*, p. 95.

61. Van Zandt, *Living in the Children of God*, p. 37.

62. Enroth, Erickson, and Peters, *The Jesus People*, pp. 26–28.

63. Donald E. Miller, *Reinventing American Protestantism: Inside Calvary, Vineyard, & Hope Chapel* (Berkeley: University of California Press, 1997), p. 33; Chuck Smith with Hugh Steven, *The Reproducers: New Life for Thousands* (Glendale, CA: Regal, 1972), pp. 13–36.

64. Chuck Smith interview with author, Costa Mesa, CA, February 9, 2000.

65. Chuck Smith in *A Venture in Faith: The History and Philosophy of the Calvary Chapel Movement*, VHS (Diamond Bar Ranch, CA: Logos Media Group, 1992); Smith interview.

66. David Di Sabatino, "A History of the Jesus People Movement" (master's thesis: McMaster University, 1994), pp. 46–47; telephone interview with Connie Bremer-Murray, January 7, 2013; Smith, *The Reproducers*, pp. 37–38.

67. Enroth, Ericson, and Peters, *The Jesus People*, p. 93; Smith, *The Reproducers*, pp. 55–59.

68. Telephone interview with John Higgins, February 18, 2013; transcript of John Higgins interview with Chuck Fromm, March 14, 2000, Tape 1; John Higgins podcast, "The Beginnings of the Jesus People Movement," ca. 2005, www.radiofreechurch.com/john-higgins/#more-8; Joe V. Peterson, "Jesus People: Christ, Communes, and the Counterculture of the Late Twentieth Century in the Pacific Northwest" (master's thesis, Northwest Christian College, 1990), pp. 44–45.

69. Transcript of John Higgins interview with Chuck Fromm, March 14, 2000, Tape 1; Higgins interview.

70. James T. Richardson, Mary W. Stewart, and Robert B. Simmonds, *Organized Miracles: A Study of a Contemporary Youth, Communal, Fundamentalist Organization* (New Brunswick, NJ: Transaction, 1979), pp. 7–8; Bremer-Murray interview; Smith, *The Reproducers*, pp. 43–47.

71. Richardson, Stewart, and Simmonds, *Organized Miracles*, p. 7; Smith, *The Reproducers*, pp. 46–47.

72. Philpott interview. Later, after Calvary Chapel began to really take off in the spring of 1969, Evangelical Concerns discussed whether the Orange County group might be interested in becoming "an organic part" of their organization; Ted Wise was authorized to approach Lonnie Frisbee to see if there was any interest on Calvary Chapel's part (see "Minutes for Evangelical Concerns Board of Directors," May 30, 1969, Kent Philpott collection).

73. Richardson, Stewart, and Simmonds, *Organized Miracles*, pp. 8–9; Smith, *The Reproducers*, pp. 48–53; Higgins interview; Smith interview.

74. Enroth, Ericson, and Peters, *The Jesus People*, p. 90; Richardson, Stewart, and Simmonds, *Organized Miracles*, pp. 8–9; Higgins interview.

75. Transcript of John Higgins interview.

76. Greg Laurie with Ellen Vaughn, *Lost Boy: My Story* (Ventura, CA: Regal, 2008), pp. 87–88.

77. Paul Baker, *Contemporary Christian Music: Where It Came from, What It Is, Where It's Going* (Westchester, IL: Crossway, 1985), pp. 35–41; Higgins interview transcript.

78. Kittler, *The Jesus Kids and Their Leaders*, pp. 100–106; Enroth, Ericson, and Peters, *The Jesus People*, pp. 85–89.

79. Chuck Smith interview. "There was no question that Chuck, in those days, spoke a lot on Bible prophecy and a lot from the Book of Revelation, I wouldn't say predominantly...but when you [ask that question] that comes to my mind immediately" (Greg Laurie telephone interview with author, June 30, 2010).

80. Survey submitted by David Rosales, Chino, CA, January 27, 2001 to Jesus People survey webpage linked to "Remembering the Jesus Movement" at http://oneway.org/jesusmovement/; surveys in possession of author.

81. Philpott interview.

82. Oden Fong interview with author, Huntington Beach, CA, July 31, 2002.

83. Williams interview.

84. Laurie with Vaughn, *Lost Boy*, pp. 106–107.

85. Donald E. Miller, *Reinventing American Protestantism: Inside Calvary, Vineyard, & Hope Chapel* (Berkeley: University of California Press, 1997), pp. 94–95; Smith, *The Reproducers*, pp. 75–76; quote found in Kittler, *The Jesus Kids*, pp. 98–99. Description of Frisbee as being "kept in line" by Chuck Smith: Enroth, Ericson, and Peters, *The Jesus People*, p. 93. Former Calvary Chapel singer Debby Kerner Retino recounted that young leaders amid the congregation during Frisbee-led meetings would go so far as to hold up youth "slain in the spirit" to keep them from falling in an attempt to keep Frisbee out of "trouble" with Smith (*Frisbee: Life and Death of a Hippie Preacher* DVD). For Frisbee's perceptions, see Lonnie Frisbee with Roger Sachs, *Not by Might nor by Power* (Santa Maria, CA: Freedom, 2012), pp. 116–117, 138–139.

86. Peter Michelmore, *Back to Jesus* (Greenwich, CT: Fawcett, 1973), pp. 142–143; Smith, *The Reproducers*, pp. 55–61.

87. Smith interview.

88. Survey submitted by Noel Holly, Costa Mesa, CA, January 23, 2004; quote from survey submitted by "Elizabeth" of Morrison, CO, February 13, 2004.

89. Miller, *Reinventing American Protestantism*, pp. 33–34; Smith, *The Reproducers*, pp. 62–63.

90. Smith, *The Reproducers*, pp. 91–97, discusses the role and symbolism of these events in the life of Calvary Chapel.

91. See Enroth, Ericson, and Peters, *The Jesus People*, p. 137–140.

92. See Brian Vachon, "The Jesus Movement Is upon Us," *Look*, February 9, 1971, pp. 16–21; see also Enroth, Ericson, and Peters, *The Jesus People*, pp. 94–98.

93. Williams interview.

94. See Plowman, *The Jesus Movement in America*, 57–58; Enroth, Ericson, and Peters, *The Jesus People*, pp. 148–149; Lutheran Youth Alive published its own toned-down version of a street paper, *Speak Out*.

95. Andy Smith interview with author, Nashville, TN, July 11, 2002.

96. For further information on the paper's history and Pederson, see the Duane Pederson Collection in the Special Collections and Archives at the David Allan Hubbard Library at Fuller Theological Seminary, Pasadena, CA. See also Duane Pederson with Bob Owen, *Jesus People* (Pasadena, CA: Compass, 1971).

97. See D. W. Bebbington, *Evangelicalism in Modern Britain: A History from the 1730s to the 1980s* (London: Unwin-Hyman, 1989), pp. 2–17.

98. Ellwood, *One Way*, p. ix.

99. Hiley H. Ward, *The Far-Out Saints of the Jesus Communes: A Firsthand Report and Interpretation of the Jesus People Movement* (New York: Association, 1972), pp. 122–126.

100. John H. Sherrill, *They Speak with Other Tongues* (New York: McGraw-Hill, 1964); David Wilkerson, *The Cross and the Switchblade* (Old Tappan, NJ: Fleming H. Revell, 1963).

101. See, for example, Kent Philpott and David Hoyt, "Two Brothers in Haight," unpublished ms, ca. 1970, p. 87.

102. Philpott's embrace of Pentecostalism caused troubles between him and his seminary mentor; see the letter from Francis M. Dubose to Kent Philpott, July 11, 1969, Kent Philpott Collection; Philpott interview.

103. Quoted in Kittler, *The Jesus Kids*, p. 95.

104. See Appendix.

105. Ibid.

106. Scott Ross with John and Elizabeth Sherrill, *Scott Free* (Old Tappan, NJ: Chosen, 1976), pp. 115–118, 137–138; Scott Ross interview with author, Virginia Beach, VA, August 14, 2002.

107. Craig Yoe telephone interview with author, July 13, 2004.

108. Newsletter from John Higgins, January 30, 1971, quoted in Lynne M. Isaacson, "Delicate Balances: Rearticulating Gender Ideology and Rules for Sexuality in a Jesus People Communal Movement" (PhD diss., University of Oregon, 1996), p. 35.

109. Mark MacDonald, one of the leaders of a Jesus People group in Duluth, MN, and Superior, WI (and who became the Episcopal bishop of Alaska in 1998), remembered these sorts of instances as happening "all the time." (Mark MacDonald telephone interview with author, July 29, 2004); Philpott interview.

110. Survey response submitted by Marlon Finley of Mableton, GA, December 10, 1998.

111. Survey response submitted by Brad Davis of Clovis, CA, March 24, 1999.

112. Philpott interview.

113. "Shiloh History," *Shiloh Magazine*, 3, vol. 2 (1977), p. 14.

114. Survey response submitted by James K. Foley of Bradford, VT, April 29, 1999.

115. Survey response submitted by Mary Anne Miller of Sweet Home, OR, December 1, 1997.

116. "Religious Festival Marked by Healings," article reprint from the *Sunday Patriot News* (Harrisburg, PA) in *Jesus '73* (August 9–11, 1973), p. 1.

117. Ross, *Scott Free*, pp. 115–118, 137–138; Ross interview.

118. Mary Ganz, "These Kids Call Themselves 'Christians,' Not Jesus Freaks," AP wire story in the *Burlington* [NC] *Times-News*, September 10, 1971, p. 15.

119. Survey response submitted by Peter Romanowsky of Sausalito, CA, April 1, 1998.

120. Survey submitted by Dennis Knotts of Moreno Valley, CA, December 25, 2001.

121. Survey submitted by Keith Swaine of Leonard, MO, December 5, 2003.

122. Survey submitted by Kevin Newman of Chesterfield, VA, February 27, 2003.

123. "Lighthouse Victim 'Blessed Brother' to Former Comrades," *Eureka Times-Standard* (Eureka, CA), May 17, 1973, p. 5; "Eureka Detectives Figure in Nabbing Hit-Run Suspect in Redding Wednesday," *Eureka Times-Standard*, May 17, 1973, p. 5.

124. Survey response submitted by "anonymous," who was affiliated with coffeehouses in Harrisonburg, VA, May 17, 2003.

125. Survey response submitted by Jackie Alden of Fife, WA, August 5, 2003.

126. Survey response submitted by Scott Jacobsen of Hamilton, ON, June 20, 1998.

127. Survey response submitted by Doreen Laughlin of Tigard, OR, November 23, 2002.

128. Survey response submitted by David Ruffino of Sacramento, CA, May 3, 2003.

129. "Hard to Take," *Cincinnati Jesus Paper*, vol. 1, no. 3, ca. July 1971, p. 3. The story is very similar to the urban legend of "The Vanishing Hitchhiker"; see Jan Harold Brunvand, *The Vanishing Hitchhiker: American Urban Legends & Their Meaning* (New York: W. W. Norton, 1989). Craig Ott, a college student in Southern California in the early '70s, recalls the story of the mysterious vanishing evangelist as an oft-told story in the Jesus People circles in which he traveled (Craig Ott interview).

130. Alden survey.

131. Survey response submitted by Dale R. Yancy of Merrimack, NH, June 27, 2000, in possession of author.

132. Steve and Sandi Heefner telephone interview with author, August 26, 2010.

133. See Appendix.

134. Ibid.

135. For example, see Terry H. Anderson, *The Movement and the Sixties: Protest in America from Greensboro to Wounded Knee* (New York: Oxford University Press, 1995), pp. 279–289; Ellwood, *One Way*, pp. 17–18.

136. Ellwood, *One Way*, p. 89.

137. See Appendix.

138. "Let's Get Ready!" *Hollywood Free Paper*, vol. 3, issue 12 (ca. June 1971), p. 2; "Daniel's Seventy Weeks," *Right On!* no. 9, January 15, 1970, p. 3.

139. For example, see the ads: "Emporium," *Logos*, vol. 1, no. 3 (ca. September 1971), p. 7, and "Witness Items," in the *Hollywood Free Paper*, vol. 4, issue 5 (ca. 1972), p. 9.

140. "I Wish We'd All Be Ready," by Larry Norman, 1969, Strawbed Music, appeared on his album *Upon This Rock*; "The Cossack Song," 1973, by Tommy Coomes and Tom Stipe, Dunamis Music, 1972, appeared on Love Song's 1973 album *Final Touch*; "Evacuation Day," by Randy Matthews, Music, appeared on his 1973 album *Son of Dust*.

141. Survey response submitted by Pat Cordial of Lawton, OK, March 29, 1999.

142. Survey response submitted by David Bielby of Normal, IL, July 31, 2003.

143. Survey response submitted by Nancy Vander Schaaf of London, ON, March 20, 1998.

144. Paul S. Boyer, *When Time Shall Be No More: Prophecy Belief in Modern American Culture* (Cambridge, MA: Belknap, 1992), p. 80.

145. Acts 2: 44–46 (KJV).

146. Ted Wise, "Jason Questions a Jesus Freak," September 13, 1997, Peninsula Bible Church, www.pbc.org/dp/wise/jason.html.

147. Ward, *The Far-Out Saints*, p. 174.

148. Timothy Miller, *The 60s Communes: Hippies and Beyond* (Syracuse, NY: Syracuse University Press, 1999), p. 94.

149. For an account of the Love Inn commune in Freeville, NY, see Ross, *Scott Free*. For a history of the Jesus People USA in Chicago, see Jon Trott, "Life's Lessons," *Cornerstone*, 22:102 (1993), pp. 11–21; 23:104 (1994), pp. 18–23; 23:105 (1994), pp. 36–39.

150. The most complete examination of the Shiloh communal network is found in Richardson, Stewart, and Simmonds, *Organized Miracles*.

151. See Timothy Miller, *The Hippies and American Values* (Knoxville: University of Tennessee Press, 1991), pp. 59–62; Anderson, *The Movement and the Sixties*, p. 261.

152. Survey response submitted by Dan Brookshire of Charlottesville, VA, January 16, 2001.

153. Survey response submitted by Barb Link of St. Louis Park, MN, December 3, 2003.

154. Survey response submitted by Denise Peca of Westland, MI, March 14, 2002.

155. For example, see Colleen McDannell, *Material Christianity: Religion and Popular Culture in America* (New Haven, CT: Yale University Press, 1995), pp. 250–260.

156. See Christopher D., "Notes from the Editor," *The Oracle* (San Francisco, CA), 1:1, ca. April 1971, p. 3.

157. For a contemporary look at JPUSA's Holy Ghost Players in action, see "Resurrection Band & the H.G. Players: Some Like It Hot," *Cornerstone*, 5:31 (1976), p. 23; CWLF's Street Theater troupe had at least five full-time workers, led by a graduate of the University of South Florida and Dallas Theological Seminary (CWLF Newsletter, ca. 1973, pp. 1–3); Akron, Ohio, passion parade anecdote supplied in survey response submitted by John White of Kent, OH, January 28, 2002.

158. For insights into the history of Toronto's Catacombs, see Bruce Douville, "'And We've Got to Get Ourselves Back to the Garden': The Jesus People Movement in Toronto," in Brian Gobbett, Bruce L. Guenther, and Robynne R. Healey, eds., *Historical Papers 2006* (Waterloo, ON: Canadian Society of Church History, 2006); and "The Son-Worshipers: Toronto's Jesus Movement in a Transnational Context," paper presented at the American Society of Church History meeting in Montreal, QB, April 16–20, 2009; see also Vander Schaaf survey.

159. Ward, *The Far-Out Saints*, p. 26; see within an included quote from a letter by John R. Sampey III published in "Jesus Explosion" (Part II), *Home Missions 22*, vol. 8 (August 1971).

160. See Charles E. Fromm, "Textual Communities and New Song in the Multimedia Age: The Routinization of Charisma in the Jesus Movement" (PhD, Fuller Theological Seminary, 2006).

CHAPTER 4

1. Minutes of Evangelical Concerns, January 16, 1970 (Kent Philpott collection). The leaders of Evangelical Concerns were dreaming big in early 1970—at their meeting, they approved an ambitious plan that called for monthly financial support to the tune of $500+ for communal houses, as well as combined salaries, housing, and auto allowances for people like Kent Philpott that clocked in at over $800 a month. The dream budget hoped to funnel $160,000 a year alone into the recently adopted Christian World Liberation Front (CWLF).

Overall, the dream budget for the entire organization in 1970 totaled more than $477,000. Although some significant money did flow into Evangelical Concerns from individuals and churches, such evidence as remains indicates that at even the height of publicity for the Jesus People movement in 1971, Evangelical Concerns' total finances never reached the level of support envisioned for just the CWLF (see Minutes of Evangelical Concerns for July, August, September, and November 1971—Kent Philpott Collection).

2. For example, see the Minutes of Evangelical Concerns, January 16, 1970: The board hoped to raise $1,000 per month to help Antioch Ranch, as well as $820 per month salary and expenses for Jerry and Pat Westfall. It is doubtful if the group ever saw more than occasional expense money, however; see, for instance, the Financial Report for Evangelical Concerns, April 1972 (Kent Philpott collection). For a glimpse into the history of Antioch Ranch and its involvement in the local evangelical scene in and around Mendocino, see R. Stephen Warner, *New Wine in Old Wineskins: Evangelicals and Liberals in a Small-Town Church* (Berkeley: University of California Press, 1988), pp. 108–135, 214–255.

3. Ronald M. Enroth, Edward E. Ericson Jr., and C. Breckinridge Peters, *The Jesus People: Old-Time Religion in the Age of Aquarius* (Grand Rapids. MI: Eerdmans, 1972), pp. 107–108; Kevin John Smith, "The Origins, Nature, and Significance of the Jesus Movement as a Revitalization Movement" (PhD diss., Asbury Theological Seminary, 2002), p. 244; "How to Start Something: Jack Sparks," *Newsletter of the American Scientific Affiliation*, vol. 17, no. 1 (February 1975).

4. For a good look at the "Berkeley Blitz," see John G. Turner, *Bill Bright & Campus Crusade for Christ: The Renewal of Evangelicalism in Postwar America* (Chapel Hill: University of North Carolina Press), 2008, pp. 121–126.

5. Ibid., p. 129.

6. Jack Sparks, *God's Forever Family* (Grand Rapids, MI: Zondervan, 1974), pp. 19–26.

7. David R. Swartz, *Moral Minority: The Evangelical Left in an Age of Conservatism* (Philadelphia: University of Pennsylvania Press, 2012), pp. 94–95; Edward E. Plowman, *The Jesus Movement in America* (Elgin, IL: David C. Cook, 1971), pp. 73–75; Sparks, *God's Forever Family*, p. 32; Enroth, Erickson, and Peters, *The Jesus People*, pp. 107–109.

8. Sparks, *God's Forever Family*, pp. 33–34; Enroth, Erickson, and Peters, *The Jesus People*, p. 108.

9. Enroth, Erickson, and Peters, *The Jesus People*, p. 106. For further detail on the development of the CWLF's various ministries, see Sparks, *God's Forever Family*.

10. The minutes for the January 16, 1970, meeting of Evangelical Concerns, Inc., show that by this time CWLF had been integrated into the organization; the Evangelical Concerns financial reports for July and August 1971 showed

contributions to CWLF of over $2,700 and $4,500, respectively, and the reports for September and November of that year came in at over $11,000 and almost $9,000, respectively (Kent Philpot Collection).

11. Quote in Sparks, *God's Forever Family*, p. 86; see pp. 86–102 for a more in-depth look at the CWLF's Rising Son Ranch.

12. Sharon Gallagher interview with author, Berkeley, CA, August 6, 2002; Swartz, *Moral Minority*, pp. 89–90, 98.

13. James T. Richardson, Mary W. Stewart, and Robert B. Simmonds, *Organized Miracles: A Study of a Contemporary Youth, Communal, Fundamentalist Organization* (New Brunswick, NJ: Transaction, 1979), pp. 8–11.

14. Telephone interview with John Higgins, February 18, 2013; Chuck Smith interview with author, Costa Mesa, CA, February 9, 2000.

15. John Higgins, "Ministry History," *Cold Waters* (February–March 1974), p. 34; Higgins interview.

16. "Shiloh," from Shiloh Shuffle Web site, www.shiloh-shuffle.com/shiloh.htm (accessed November 20, 2000), photocopy in author's possession; Higgins interview; Richardson, Stewart, and Simmonds, *Organized Miracles*, pp. 11–13.

17. Richardson, Stewart, and Simmonds, *Organized Miracles*, pp. 13–15; Higgins interview.

18. Richardson, Stewart, and Simmonds, *Organized Miracles*, pp. 15–16; Higgins interview.

19. Richardson, Stewart, and Simmonds, *Organized Miracles*, pp. 46–48.

20. Ibid., pp. 57–64.

21. Mary Ganz, "These Kids Call Themselves 'Christians,' Not Jesus Freaks," AP wire story in *Burlington* (NC) *Times-News*, September 10, 1971, p. 15.

22. Lynne M. Isaacson, "Delicate Balances: Rearticulating Gender Ideology and Rules for Sexuality in a Jesus People Communal Movement" (PhD, University of Oregon, 1996), p. 44; "Shiloh"; Richardson, Stewart, and Simmonds, *Organized Miracles*, pp. 22–38, 49–51, 57–62, 85–87.

23. Di Sabatino, "A History of the Jesus People," p. 39.

24. Richardson, Stewart, and Simmonds, *Organized Miracles*, pp. 22–35, 85–87; Higgins interview.

25. For his part, historian Timothy Miller firmly believes Shiloh was among the largest communes the counterculture produced, with perhaps as many as 175 communal houses in existence at one time or another; see Miller, *The 60s Communes: Hippies and Beyond* (Syracuse, NY: Syracuse University Press, 1999), pp. 95–96.

26. John Breithaupt telephone interview with author, July 14, 2004; Pat King, *The Jesus People Are Coming* (Plainfield, NJ: Logos International, 1971), pp. 11–12.

27. Breithaupt interview.

28. King, *The Jesus People Are Coming*, pp. 11–12; Breithaupt interview.

29. Linda Gebaroff interview with author, October 21, 2002, Monroe, WA.

30. Ibid.

31. Linda Meissner, *The Voice* (Seattle, WA: Gloriana, 2012), pp. 27–52; Glenn D. Kittler, *The Jesus People and Their Leaders* (New York: Warner, 1972), pp. 140–141; Breithaupt interview.

32. Transcript of David Di Sabatino interview with Linda Meissner (ca. January 1994); Meissner, *The Voice*, pp. 57–64; Enroth, Ericson, and Peters, *The Jesus People*, p. 118; Kittler, *The Jesus People and Their Leaders*, pp. 140–141.

33. Di Sabatino, Meissner interview transcript; Meissner, *The Voice*, pp. 77–78.

34. King, *The Jesus People Are Coming*, p. 10; for an account of Meissner speaking engagements, see "Youth Worker to Speak at Local Church," *Walla-Walla* [WA] *Union-Bulletin*, August 29, 1969, p. 5.

35. Jim Palosaari interview with author, Brentwood, TN, July 12, 2002; Sue Cowper Palosaari telephone interview with author, October 24, 2004; Meissner, *The Voice*, pp. 77–78; King, *The Jesus People Are Coming*, p. 13.

36. Meissner, *The Voice*, pp. 79–82; King, *The Jesus People Are Coming*, p. 13; Enroth, Ericson, and Peters, *The Jesus People*, pp. 119–121.

37. Robert S. Ellwood Jr., *One Way: The Jesus People Movement and Its Meaning* (Englewood Cliffs, NJ: Prentice-Hall, 1973), p. 62; Meissner, *The Voice*, pp 101–102; Sue Palosaari Cowper interview.

38. Meissner, *The Voice*, pp. 102–103; King, *The Jesus People Are Coming*, p. 21; Enroth, Ericson, and Peters, *The Jesus People*, p. 121.

39. Di Sabatino, Meissner interview transcript; Meissner, *The Voice*, pp. 123–126.

40. Meissner, *The Voice*, pp. 113–121; Kittler, *The Jesus People and Their Leaders*, pp. 177–180; Enroth, Ericson, and Peters, *The Jesus People*, p. 126.

41. Kittler, *The Jesus People and Their Leaders*, p. 181; Plowman, *The Jesus People Movement*, pp. 106–107. For an example of Wilson-McKinley's role in Parks's ministry, see the ad for an August 1971 concert in *Truth*, vol. 2:7A, n.d., ca. June 1971, p. 16.

42. For various glimpses into the size and scope of Parks's branch of the Jesus People Army, see Edward Plowman, "Revival in the Underground," *Christianity Today*, January 29, 1971, pp. 34–35; Mark Owen, "Grand Opening Huge Success" [Jesus Free Store], *Truth*, vol. 4:2, issue 28, April 1973, pp. 46–47.

43. Scott Ross with John and Elizabeth Sherrill, *Scott Free* (Old Tappan, NJ: Chosen, 1976), pp. 82–86.

44. Scott Ross interview with author, Virginia Beach, VA, August 20, 2002; Scott Ross with Bob Combs, "Scott on the Rocks," *Campus Life*, October 1973, p. 30; Ross, *Scott Free*, pp. 12–36; the Lost Souls band featured Jackie Lomax, one of the first artists the Beatles would sign to their new Apple label in 1968.

45. Ross, *Scott Free*, pp. 36–69; Ross, "Scott on the Rocks," pp. 30–31.

46. Ross interview; Ross, *Scott Free*, p. 74.

47. Bob Combs, "Genuine Natural-Grown, Electronic Music Man," *Campus Life*, December 1972, pp. 61–66; Ross interview; Ross, *Scott Free*, pp. 86–106.

48. Ross interview; Ross, *Scott Free*, pp. 94–100; Kittler, *The Jesus People and Their Leaders*, pp. 207–209.

49. Ross, *Scott Free*, pp. 103–129; Combs, "Genuine Natural-Grown," pp. 61–62.

50. Edward B. Fiske, "'Jesus People' Are Happy with Their Life in Love Inn," *New York Times*, June 15, 1971, pp. 1, 4; Michael McFadden, *The Jesus Revolution* (New York: Harrow, 1972), pp. 172–174; Ross, *Scott Free*, pp. 130–146, 155.

51. Karl Kahler, *The Cult That Snapped: A Journey into The Way International* (Los Gatos, CA: Karl Kahler, 1999), p. 64.

52. Victor Paul Wierwille, quoted in Elena S. Whiteside, *The Way: Living in Love*, 2nd ed. (New Knoxville, OH: American Christian Press, 1974), p. 234.

53. Steve and Sandi Heefner telephone interview with author, July 29, 2007.

54. Judy Doop Marshall telephone interview with author, August 16, 2007; Kahler, *The Cult That Snapped*, p.66.

55. Steve and Sandi Heefner interview; Kahler, *The Cult That Snapped*, p. 66.

56. Jane Howard, "The Groovy Christians of Rye, NY," *Life*, May 14, 1971, pp. 78–86; Steve and Sandi Heefner interview; Kahler, *The Cult That Snapped*, pp. 66–67.

57. Steve and Sandi Heefner interview; Kahler, *The Cult That Snapped*, p. 74.

58. Jimmy E. Dopp, "When the Hippies Found Jesus: A True Story of the Sixties" (unpublished mss., ca. 1990), pp. 271–275; Judy Doop Marshall interview; Kahler, *The Cult That Snapped*, p. 75.

59. Kahler, *The Cult That Snapped*, p. 75; Judy Doop Marshall interview; Dopp, "When the Hippies Found Jesus," pp. 280–297; Steve and Sandi Heefner interview.

60. Victor Paul Wierwille, *Jesus Christ Is Not God* (New Knoxville, OH: American Christian Press, 1975). For examples of evangelical critiques of The Way, see Joel A. McCollam, *The Way of Victor Paul Wierwille* (Downers Grove, IL: InterVarsity Press, 1978); and Robert L. Sumner, *Jesus Christ Is God! An Examination of Victor Paul Wierwille and His "The Way International," a Rapidly Growing Unitarian Cult* (Murfreesboro, TN: Biblical Evangelism, 1983).

61. Figures cited in Zay N. Smith, "The Way—40,000 and Still Growing," *Chicago Sun-Times* (August 17, 1980); and Kahler, *The Cult That Snapped*, pp. 8, 110–111.

62. Ruth A. Tucker, *Another Gospel: Alternative Religions and the New Age Movement* (Grand Rapids, MI: Zondervan, 1989), pp. 229–230; Howard Goodman, "Critics Contend The Way Points Its Followers in Wrong Direction," *Kansas City Times*, February 5, 1983, p. A10; Kahler, *The Cult That Snapped*, pp. 117–150, 167–184, 203–210, 240–242, 246–250.

63. David Hoyt, "Journal of Trip South," unpublished mss., October–November, 1969, Kent Philpott Collection; David Hoyt telephone interview with author, April 15, 2009; David Hoyt, "Lonesome Stone," unpublished mss., ca. 2009, pp. 153–160; Letter from David Hoyt, Walnut Creek, CA, to supporters, n.d., ca. early 1970, Kent Philpott collection.

64. Kent Philpott interview with author, Mill Valley, CA, August 7, 2002; Atlanta Discipleship Training Center newsletter, ca. Fall 1970, p. 1.

65. Philpott interview; Atlanta Discipleship Training Center newsletter, p. 1; David Hoyt, "Lonesome Stone," p. 163.

66. Ken Pitts interview with author, Nashville, TN, July 9, 2002; Hoyt, "Lonesome Stone," pp. 163–166.

67. Atlanta Discipleship Training Center newsletter, p. 1; Hoyt, "Lonesome Stone," p. 166.

68. Atlanta Discipleship Training Center newsletter, pp. 2–3.

69. Ibid., p. 5.

70. Interview with Roger Allen, Nashville, TN, July 13, 2002; Pitts interview; Philpott interview; Atlanta Discipleship Training Center newsletter, pp. 8, 11.

71. "New Property—New Milford, New Jersey," *Ink-Links*, New York District of the Church of the Nazarene (February 1968), p. 1; Frank Cook and Al Truesdale, *The New Milford Story* (Kansas City, MO: Beacon Hill, 1983), pp. 20–21; Paul Moore and Joe Musser, *The Shepherd of Times Square* (Nashville, TN: Thomas Nelson, 1979), pp. 15–16, 18, 22–23.

72. Charlie Rizzo telephone interview with author, March 6, 2003.

73. Cook and Truesdale, *The New Milford Story*, pp. 20–23; Rizzo interview.

74. Cook and Truesdale, *The New Milford Story*, pp. 22–24; Moore and Musser, *The Shepherd of Times Square*, pp. 28–29; Rizzo interview.

75. Jack White quoted in Moore and Musser, *The Shepherd of Times Square*, pp. 16–17.

76. For example, see "Jesus Places," *Good News of Jesus*, 1, no. 6, September 1972, p. 16.

77. "Make a Joyful Noise unto the Lord," *Good News of Jesus*, 1, no. 4, June 1972, p. 1; "'Jesus Joy' Festival Pulls 3,000 in Madison Square Garden Forum," AP wire story in the *Register* (Danville, VA), September 5, 1972, p. 2B; William Reel, "Jesus People Claim Madison Square Garden," *New York Daily News*, reprinted in *Good News of Jesus*, 1, no. 6, September 1972, pp. 1, 6; Bob Chuvala, "Connecticut Jesus Festival," *Good News of Jesus*, September 1972, p. 15; Moore and Musser, *Shepherd of Times Square*, p. 34.

78. Cook and Truesdale, *The New Milford Story*, pp. 26–28; Rizzo interview.

79. John Lloyd telephone interview with author, February 26, 2010.

80. Nancy "Honeytree" Henigbaum Miller telephone interview with author, June 26, 2007; Lloyd interview.

81. Michael Hawfield, "City Was Home of Many Inventions," *Fort Wayne Sentinel*, December 13, 1993, http://fwnextweb1.fortwayne.com/ns/projects/history/haw16.php; Roy M. Bates and Kenneth G. Keller, *The Columbia Street Story* (Fort Wayne, IN: Fort Wayne Bicentennial Commission, 1975), p. 126; "Fort Wayne's Famed Landing, Seemingly Doomed to Decay, Undergoes Massive Facelifting," AP wire story in *The Anderson* [IN] *Herald*, October 8, 1970, p. 8.

82. Lloyd interview.

83. Ibid.

84. Palosaari interview; Kittler, *The Jesus Kids and Their Leaders*, pp. 199–200.

85. Sue Cowper Palosaari interview.

86. Sue Cowper Palosaari interview; Jim Palosaari interview; Kittler, *The Jesus Kids and Their Leaders*, pp. 200–204.

87. Jim Palosaari interview.

88. Enroth, Ericson, and Peters, *The Jesus People*, p. 128; Kittler, *The Jesus Kids and Their Leaders*, p. 204.

89. Jim Palosaari interview; Kittler, *The Jesus Kids and Their Leaders*, pp. 204–205.

90. "Heat's On in Duluth," *Christianity Today*, March 3, 1972, pp. 529–530; Enroth, Ericson, and Peters, *The Jesus People*, pp. 128–129; Jim Palosaari interview. For an example of the Milwaukee Jesus People's excursions into northern Wisconsin, see "Eagle River Story, Part 1," *Street Level*, vol. 1:6, August 1971, pp. 7–9, 12.

91. Enroth, Ericson, and Peters, *The Jesus People*, p. 129; Kittler, *The Jesus Kids and Their Leaders*, p. 205.

92. Ibid.

93. Di Sabatino, "A History of the Jesus People Movement," pp. 37–38; "The Heat's On in Duluth," pp. 529–530.

94. Ron Rendleman interview with author, Chadwick, IL, May 9, 2002.

95. David F. Gordon, "A Comparison of the Effects of Urban and Suburban Location on Structure and Identity in Two Jesus People Groups" (PhD diss., University of Chicago, 1974), pp. 3, 72–74; Ron Rendleman, *The Making of a Prophet* (Sterling, IL: Sterling, 2003), pp. 1–27; Rendleman interview.

96. Rendleman, *The Making of a Prophet*, p. 30.

97. Rendleman interview; Rendleman, *Making of a Prophet*, pp. 42, 64.

98. See letter from Rev. Henry John Naparla, O.F.M., to whom it may concern, June 30, 1973; miscellaneous flyers from Jesus Is Lord rock concerts and festivals ca. 1970–1972; tape of Jesus Is Lord concert featuring Ron Rendleman and "e" at the University of Illinois, Urbana, ca. fall 1971, all from Ron Rendleman collection, copies in author's possession; Rendleman, *Making of a Prophet*, pp. 40–42.

99. Sherry Lang, "Jesus Movement Rocks Its Way through Aurora Saturday Night," *Beacon-News* (Aurora, IL), June 1, 1971, p. 9.

100. Jim Palosaari interview; Rendleman interview.

101. Ward, *The Far-Out Saints*, p. 87.

102. Peter Michelmore, *Back to Jesus* (Greenwich, CT: Fawcett, 1973), pp. 70–78. For a contemporary glimpse at the Lighthouse Ranch, see *Lighthouse at Loleta*, a PBS-produced film in the Religious America series (Boston: WGBH, 1971).

103. Kittler, *The Jesus Kids and Their Leaders*, pp. 188–194; Enroth, Erickson, and Peters, *The Jesus People*, p. 133.

104. Don Williams, *Call to the Streets* (St. Paul, MN: Augsburg, 1972), pp. 72–77; Kittler, *The Jesus Kids and Their Leaders*, pp. 182–188; quote found on p. 187.

105. Ward, *The Far-Out Saints*, pp. 37, 80, 94–95, 103–104.

106. The most extensive source on the history of the Church of the Risen Christ is the autobiographical reminiscence by ex-member and All-Saved Freak Band cofounder, Joe Markko. "When Someday Comes: Memoirs of a Survivor," www.allsavedfreakband.com/toc.htm.

107. Gordon Walker interview with author, Franklin, TN, July 10, 2002; Joan Brown, "Ranch Tries to 'Save' Lost Youths," *News-Journal* (Mansfield, OH), September 13, 1970, p. 1F; Enroth, Ericson, and Peters, *The Jesus People*, pp. 140–142.

108. Gary Sweeten telephone interview with author, May 28, 2003; Paul Baker, *Contemporary Christian Music: Where It Came from, What It Is, Where It's Going* (Westchester, IL: Crossway, 1985), p. 58.

109. James C. Hefley, *The New Jews* (Wheaton, IL: Tyndale House, 1974), pp. 33–42; Plowman, *The Jesus People Movement*, pp. 19–20.

110. See, for example, *Together*, vol. 2:3 (n.d., ca. July 1971); Plowman, *The Jesus People Movement*, p. 63.

111. Frank Tuci, "Religious Coffeehouse Draws Youths," wire story in *News-Journal* (Mansfield, OH), September 20, 1970, p. 6.

112. Jerry Halliday, *Spaced Out and Gathered In: A Sort of an Autobiography of a Jesus Freak* (Old Tappan, NJ: Fleming H. Revell, 1972), pp. 23–32.

113. Julia Duin, *Days of Fire and Glory: The Rise and Fall of a Charismatic Community* (Baltimore: Crossland, 2009), pp. 3–4, 70–73, 76, 96–97.

114. Richard Hogue telephone interview with author, March 5, 2003; Baptist Press news release, Southern Baptist News Service, February 15, 1971; William S. Cannon, *The Jesus Revolution: New Inspiration for Evangelicals* (Nashville, TN: Broadman, 1971), pp. 13–21. See also Richard Hogue, *The Jesus Touch* (Nashville, TN: Broadman, 1972).

CHAPTER 5

1. Maurice Allan, "Doing God's Thing in Hippieville," *Christian Life*, January 1968, pp. 20–23, 34–38.

2. For examples of the light coverage during 1968 and 1969 on developing aspects of what would become known as the Jesus movement, see Edward E. Plowman, "Witnessing to Hippies," *Christianity Today*, June 7, 1968, pp. 41–43; Dallas Lee, "Take a 'Trip' with God, Evangelist Tells Hippies," Baptist Press Release, June 16, 1968, p. 7; Dallas Lee, "Gut-Level Witnessing Urged among the Hippies," Baptist Press Release, October 14, 1968, p. 4.

3. *Santa Ana Register*, August 17, 1968, p. A5.

4. Arthur Blessitt, *Life's Greatest Trip* (Waco, TX: Word, 1970); John A. MacDonald, *House of Acts* (Carol Stream, IL: Creation House, 1970).

5. David Wilkerson with John and Elizabeth Sherrill, *The Cross and the Switchblade* (New York: Random House, 1963); Nicky Cruz, *Run, Baby, Run* (Plainfield, NJ: Logos, 1968); Bob Harrington with Walter Wagner, *The Chaplain of Bourbon Street* (New York: Doubleday, 1969).

6. For examples of more in-depth coverage during 1970 of what was now beginning to be perceived as an actual Jesus movement within the evangelical press, see Brian Bastien, "Hollywood Boulevard—One Way," *Christianity Today*, January 2, 1970, p. 328; Rick Joslin, "Love in the Park," *Decision*, May 1970, p. 7; Carl F. H. Henry, "Evangelical Pathbreaking," *Christianity Today*, May 8, 1970, p. 746; L. F. Backmann, "Linda's Revolutionary Army," *World Vision Magazine*, July–August 1970, p. 14.

7. Rita Klein, "Spiritual Revolution—West Coast Youth," *Christianity Today*, June 19, 1970, p. 876.

8. Langdon Winner, "Let It Be," *Rolling Stone*, April 16, 1970, p. 48.

9. "TV Key Previews," *Victoria* [TX] *Advocate*, June 28, 1970, p. 48.

10. "Street Christians: Jesus as the Ultimate Trip," *Time*, August 3, 1970, p. 31; Ed Plowman telephone interview with author, June 25, 2004.

11. For a discussion of the impact of Southern black and white gospel music on the musical mechanics and performing styles of rock 'n' roll, see Philip H. Ennis, *The Seventh Stream: The Emergence of Rocknroll in American Popular Music* (Hanover, NH: University Press of New England, 1992), pp. 72–79, 95–97; see also the entry on "Gospel Music" in Donald Clarke, ed., *The Penguin Encyclopedia of Popular Music* (London: Penguin, 1989).

12. Joel Whitburn, *The Billboard Book of Top 40 Hits* (New York: Billboard Publications, 1989), pp. 197, 350, 462; Paul Baker, *Contemporary Christian Music: Where It Came from, What It Is, Where It's Going* (Westchester, IL: Crossway, 1985), pp. 20–21.

13. *Hit Parader*, January 1971, p. 27. Despite the fact that Greenbaum lived at the time in Mill Valley, California—the home of the first Jesus People like Ted and Liz Wise—he claims to have had no direct contact with them and no idea that there was such a thing as a Jesus Freak before he wrote the song (Norman Greenbaum e-mail to author, April 30, 2002).

14. Whitburn, *The Billboard Book*, p. 188.

15. Ibid., pp. 204, 382. The title of "He Ain't Heavy, He's My Brother" was adapted by songwriters Bobby Russell and Bobby Scott from a signature phrase ("He Ain't Heavy, Father, He's My Brother") associated with Father Flanagan's famous Boys' Town orphanage in Omaha, Nebraska. While it had no intrinsic Christian themes or subject matter, the concept of "Bridge over Troubled Water," borrowed from Simon and Garfunkel's hit song, would become the theme of numerous Jesus People tracts, buttons, posters, and bumper stickers during the early and mid-1970s.

16. Whitburn, *The Billboard Book*, pp. 195, 317, 402, 415; Baker, *Contemporary Christian Music*, pp. 22–23. The 45 rpm single version of the Byrds' "Jesus Is Just Alright" did not climb into the U.S. Top 40 but did receive extensive exposure via the film *Easy Rider* and subsequent play on underground and progressive FM stations; PG&E's "Are You Ready?" reached #14 on the charts. Taylor's ballad had brief reference to Christian themes in the lyrics "Won't ya look down upon

me Jesus? You got to help me make a stand; I won't make it any other way." In his 1980 reminiscence, *I, Me, Mine* (Guildford, England: Genesis, 1980; San Francisco: Chronicle, 2002), Harrison cited the Edwin Hawkins Singers' 1969 hit "O Happy Day" as the inspiration for "My Sweet Lord." Moreover, he admitted that he wanted to draw in Westerners familiar with the Hebrew "Hallelujah" to singing the praises of Krishna: "I wanted to show people that 'Halleluja' [*sic*] and 'Hare Krishna' are quite the same thing. So I did the voices singing 'Halleluja' first and then the change to 'Hare Krishna' so that people would be chanting the Maha mantra—before they knew what was going on!" (p. 176).

17. Ellis Nassour and Richard Broderick, *Rock Opera: The Creation of "Jesus Christ Superstar" from Record Album to Broadway Show and Motion Picture* (New York: Hawthorn, 1973), pp. 6, 12–14, 24–25, 32–35.

18. Jack Shadoian, "Jesus Christ Superstar," *Rolling Stone*, March 4, 1971, p. 52.

19. Quote found in Nassour and Broderick, *Rock Opera*, pp. 80–81.

20. Hubert Saal, "Pop Testament," *Newsweek*, November 16, 1970, pp. 96–97.

21. Louis Cassels, "Religion in America," in the *Lebanon* (PA) *Daily News*, January 23, 1971, p. 18.

22. Saal, "Pop Testament."

23. Cheryl A. Forbes, "'Superstar': Haunting Questions," *Christianity Today*, December 9, 1970, pp. 38–39. The hope that an evangelical Christian "answer" to *Jesus Christ Superstar* might emerge from the huge number of new "youth musicals" being written within conservative Christian circles during this period was echoed in news notices that appeared in *Moody Monthly* in February (p. 12) and March (pp. 8–9) 1972.

24. Joel Whitburn, *The Billboard Book of Top 40 Albums* (New York: Billboard, 1987), p. 296; Nassour and Broderick, *Rock Opera*, pp. 82, 192. Beyond the $15 million in sales in North America, *Superstar* was a blockbuster hit throughout most of Europe, South America, Australia, and South Africa. Through bootleg albums brought in from Finland, *Jesus Christ Superstar* also played a seminal role in the underground rock culture of the Soviet Union during the 1970s. By the end of the decade, the theme song from the rock opera had become the signature music for the nightly state-run news program *Vremya*; see Timothy W. Ryback, *Rock around the Bloc: A History of Rock Music in Eastern Europe and the Soviet Union* (New York: Oxford University Press, 1990), pp. 149, 153, 241, 243.

25. Nassour and Broderick, *Rock Opera*, p. 73. The author recalls the rock opera being played in its entirety on WFMT, Chicago's longtime fine arts station on Good Friday, 1971—paired with Bach's *St. Matthew Passion*.

26. "'Superstar' Rock Opera Closes Gap," *Boston Globe*, July 29, 1971, p. 1; "Two Views of Superstar," *Charlotte Observer*, August 24, 1971, p. 1C; Robert C. Marsh, "'Superstar' Rings with Glory," *Chicago Sun-Times*, August 8, 1971.

27. Nassour and Broderick, *Rock Opera*, pp. 95–98, 128–175.

28. See entry for "Godspell," in Peter Gammond, *Oxford Companion to Popular Music* (New York: Oxford University Press, 1991), p. 230.

29. Billy Graham, *The Jesus Generation* (Grand Rapids, MI: Zondervan, 1971), p. 13; "1,300,000 Greet New Year at 'Biggest' Rose Parade," *Van Nuys Valley News and Green Sheet*, January 3, 1971, in Collection 360: BGEA-Scrapbooks, Reel #33 (June 1970–December 1971); Graham Press Conference, February 28, 1971, Greenville, SC, Collection 24: BGEA-Billy Graham Press Conferences, Tape T9, Archives of the Billy Graham Center, Wheaton College, Wheaton, IL; "U.S. Journal: Pasadena—Waiting for the Roses," *New Yorker*, January 16, 1971, pp. 85–88; Graham, *The Jesus Generation*, pp. 13–14.

30. For example, see Toby Druin, "Graham Challenges N.C. to Be State of Destiny," *Biblical Recorder*, February 27, 1971, p. 4; "Moving toward Revival," *United Evangelical Action*, Summer 1971, p. 15; "The NAE: New Marching Orders," *Christianity Today*, May 7, 1971, p. 37.

31. Plowman, *The Jesus Movement*, p. 61. The generally positive spin of the original documentary was retracted in a 1972 update on *Chronolog* after NBC learned of extensive criticism of COG among converts' family members and mainstream church leaders; see Deborah Berg-Davis, *The Children of God: The Inside Story* (Grand Rapids, MI: Zondervan, 1984), pp. 95, 112–113.

32. Brian Vachon, "The Jesus Movement Is upon Us," *Look*, February 9, 1971, pp. 15–21; quote on pp. 16, 19.

33. Patrick Corman, "Freaking Out on Jesus," *Rolling Stone*, June 24, 1971, p. 24; "California Youth March, Urge 'Spiritual Revolution Now,'" Baptist Press press release (February 23, 1971).

34. Earl C. Gottschalk Jr., "Hip Culture Discovers a New Trip: Fervent, Foot-Stompin' Religion," *Wall Street Journal*, March 2, 1971, p. 1; "The Jesus People," *Newsweek*, March 22, 1971, p. 97; Jane Howard, "The Groovy Christians of Rye, NY," *Life*, May 14, 1971, pp. 78–86.

35. "The New Rebel Cry: Jesus Is Coming!" *Time*, June 21, 1971, pp. 56–63.

36. Ibid., p. 59.

37. Edward Plowman, "Shore to Shore Wave of Witness," *Christianity Today*, May 17, 1971, p. 34; "Jesus Festival Hosts Rock Gospel Groups," *Yuma* (AZ) *Daily Sun*, January 19, 1973, p. 30; NBC *Today Show*, July 8, 1971, NBC News Archives.

38. The AP wire story by Jay Sharbutt appeared under various headlines, including "Jesus People's Theories Appear to Be Billy Graham Explained by Timothy Leary," *Anderson* (IN) *Daily Bulletin*, February 14, 1971, p. 12; "Jesus Movement in Calif. Is Like 'Billy Graham Explained by Dr. Leary" and "Sin Is 'No, No,'" *Gettysburg* (PA) *Times*, February 5, 1971, p. 14.

39. See, for example, David Poling, "Church, 'Jesus Freaks' Run Collision Course," *Reno* (NV) *Evening Gazette*, February 12, 1971, p. 14; Paul Harvey, "Jesus Freaks: A Fad or a Trend," *Ruston* (LA) *Daily Leader*, April 30, 1971, p. 2; George Cornell, "'Jesus Freaks' Spread the Word," *Billings* (MT) *Gazette*, June 4, 1971, p. 1.

40. "Jeane Dixon Sees a Dark Plot in Pentagon Papers Publication," *Salina* (KS) *Journal*, July 8, 1971, p. 14.

41. See Joan Laliberte Maupin, "Shiloh House: Direction of Our Modern Faith?" *Idaho State Journal* (Pocatello), May 14, 1971, pp. 8–9; Norma Skamenca, "Youths Find Peace in Jesus," *Edwardsville* (IL) *Intelligencer*, February 12, 1971, p. 7; "Eye Witness Account of Jesus Festival," *Rock Valley* (IA) *Bee*, September 9, 1971, p. 2; "Youth Coffeehouse to Open," *Post-Tribune* (Jefferson City, MO), August 12, 1971, p. 8; Gene Hahn, "A Revolution with Jesus for a Leader," *Post* (Frederick, MD), September 18, 1971, p. 23.

42. Ray Renner telephone interview with author, August 10, 2007.

43. Compare the minor citation of the "Jesus Freaks" in *Christianity Today*'s review of religious news in 1970, "Religion on the Big Board" (January 1, 1971, pp. 26–27) with its prominence in the comparable article for 1971, "Top '71 Religious News—World Revival" (January 7, 1972, pp. 40–41). The Evangelical Press Association voted the Jesus movement its top story for 1971 ("Religion in Review, 1971," *Moody Monthly*, February 1972, p. 8).

44. For an example of articles on the Jesus movement that appeared in *Christianity Today* during 1971, see "Blessitt Trail," January 21, 1971, p. 35; "Followers of the Way," March 26, 1971, pp. 618–619; "The Cross Bearers," August 27, 1971, pp. 32–34; Anne Eggerbrotten, "Jesus Festivals," August 6, 1971, pp. 38–40; Donald M. Williams, "Close-Up of the Jesus People," August 27, 1971, pp. 5–7; "From Freaks to Followers," October 22, 1971, pp. 33–34.

45. Plowman interview; for some of Plowman's reporting on the Jesus movement for *Christianity Today*, see "Pacific Northwest: Revival in the Underground," January 29, 1971, pp. 34–35; "Jesus Freaks Move Right On," March 12, 1971, p. 53; "Jesus Presses Are Rolling," April 19, 1971, pp. 38–39; "Shore to Shore Wave of Witness," May 7, 1971, pp. 34–35; "The Jesus Movement: Now It's in the Hamlets," June 18, 1971, 35–36.

46. Harold Lindsell, "The New Christians," *Christianity Today*, July 16, 1971, pp. 20–21.

47. June–July 1971 *Campus Life*—see such features in this issue as "Middle America Meets the Jesus Freaks," pp. 12–17; Donna Day and Thomas Diggs, "Travelin' with Jesus," pp. 18–20.

48. For 1971 articles in *Eternity*, see, for example, Rita Klein, "God, Blessitt, and 'His Place,'" January 1971, pp. 34, 46–47; "God's Gentle Irony: The Jesus People," August 1971, pp. 6–7; Edward Plowman, "Jesus Saves: Our Alienated Youth," August 1971, pp. 8–11, 31.

49. For examples of April 1971 articles on the Jesus Movement in *Christian Life*, see Donald Hughes, "Underground Papers Go Christian," pp. 25–26, 56–58; Martin Meyer (Moishe) Rosen, "Jesus' Kids Turn on Others," pp. 22–25, 59–63.

50. For examples of coverage of the Jesus movement during 1971 in *Moody Monthly*, see "Reporter Converted to Jesus Movement," April 1971, p. 11; Robert Flood,

"What Is Shaking California?" May 1971, pp. 36–37, 60; "Blessitt Leads 'Jesus' March in Chicago," July–August 1971, p. 8.

51. K. Murray, "1,000 Jesus People Baptized in Ocean off California," *Pentecostal Evangel*, June 13, 1971, p. 23.

52. For examples of the extensive coverage of the Jesus movement and youth stirrings within Baptist circles in various Baptist periodicals and newspapers during 1971, see James Lee Young, "Jesus March Attracts 7,000 to State Capital," *California Southern Baptist*, February 26, 1971, pp. 5, 12; "Billy Graham Has a 'Plus' View of the Jesus People Movement," *Alabama Baptist*, June 17, 1971, p. 1; Jack Park, "10,000 Attend Festival for Christ near Muncie," *Indiana Baptist*, October 27, 1971, p. 3.

53. J. Furman Miller, "The Jesus Movement and Joel," *Alliance Witness*, May 26, 1971, pp. 5–6.

54. Rev. Father I. J. Mikulski, "Jesus People Sound Groovy," *Catholic Weekly*, May 7, 1971, p. 4; Herb W. David, "1,300 Cheers for Jesus," *Lutheran Standard*, October 5, 1971, pp. 29–31. For other examples of what were generally upbeat looks at the Jesus movement from religious periodicals outside the evangelical community in 1971, see R. Croskery, "The Jesus Revolution Is On," *Congregationalist*, November 1971, p. 8; Earl C. Gottschalk Jr., "The Jesus People Are Coming," *Lutheran*, May 5, 1971, p. 12.

55. *I Believe in Miracles*, programs 258–260 (Pittsburgh, PA: Kathryn Kuhlman Foundation, 1971); photo captions in *Logos* (San Diego, CA), ca. July 1971, p. 4.

56. Norman Vincent Peale, "Young Now Finding Substance in Life," *Kokomo* (IN) *Tribune*, March 26, 1972, p. 4.

57. "'Jesus People' Boosted by Bishop of Canterbury," *Bridgeport* (CT) *Post*, January 28, 1972, pp. 1, 6; Archbishop of Canterbury Michael Ramsey, quoted in Peter Michelmore, *Back to Jesus* (Greenwich, CT: Fawcett, 1973), p. 6.

58. "Chief Bishop Raps Priest in Congress," *Oakland Tribune*, January 10, 1972, p. 77.

59. Bishop Fulton J. Sheen, "Love Expels Bad Habits," *Syracuse* (NY) *Herald-American*, December 5, 1971, p. 102. Sheen's superior, Pope Paul VI, seemed to be rather mystified by his first remote encounter with the Jesus People phenomenon. A *New York Times* wire story reported in December 1971 that he had told pilgrims to St. Peter's that "he had seen pictures of hippies in 'I Love Jesus' t-shirts. 'Why, is not explained,'" he reportedly said, adding "'but, then, many attitudes of these paradoxical young people are unexplained'" ("'Jesus People' Puzzle the Pope," *Salina* (KS) *Journal*, December 16, 1971, p. 3).

60. Graham's and Nixon's copopularity is attested to in "Nixon Again Leads the List, Graham Second," *Boston Evening Globe*, January 2, 1972, Collection 360: BGEA-Scrapbooks, Reel #34 (March–October 1972). For the best analysis of this period of Graham's life and his relationship with Richard Nixon, see William Martin, *A Prophet with Honor: The Billy Graham Story* (New York: William

Morrow, 1991), pp. 269–283, 350–371, 391–399, 420–435. For Graham's interpretation of these years and his friendship with Nixon, see Graham, *Just as I Am: The Autobiography* (San Francisco: HarperCollins, 1997), pp. 440–465.

61. For example, local fundamentalists used Graham's support of the Jesus People as prime reasons for boycotting Graham's crusades in Chicago (1971) and Atlanta (1973). See Philip E. Bennett, "Billy Graham's 1971 Chicago Crusade—Beware!" *Christian Militant*, May–June 1971, pp. 2–3 (Collection 360: BGEA—Scrapbooks, Reel #102, 1971).

62. "Billy Graham's Crusade Draws Record Throngs to Kentucky U. Coliseum," Religious News Service press release, April 29, 1971, Collection 345: BGEA—Media Office, Box 30, Folder 13.

63. "Jesus People Movement Is Growing Fast," *Herald* (Arlington Heights, IL), June 10, 1971, p. 24; "24,000 at Billy's 'Youth Night,'" *Chicago Today*, June 8, 1971, p. 16; "Billy's Crusade Here Attended by 325,000," *Chicago Daily News*, June 14, 1971, p. 9; "Wonderful Chicago," *Decision*, September 1971, pp. 8–9, 14; Greater Chicago Crusade (1971), Collection 113: BGEA—Films and Videos, F#252 & F#255. Orders of service and excerpts from Graham's sermons are contained in Collection 345: BGEA—Media Office, Box 30, Folders 24, 26–27, 29–31.

64. Ron Rendleman interview with the author, Chadwick, IL, May 9, 2002; Ron Rendleman, *The Making of a Prophet*, Sterling, IL: Sterling, 2003, p. 28; Sutton Kinter III e-mail to author, October 6, 2010.

65. Ingrid Spellnes Faro e-mail to author, November 4, 2008; "Hecklers Routed by Billy Backers," *Chicago Daily News*, June 9, 1971, in Collection 345: BGEA—Media Office, Box 31, Folder 8.

66. "Hecklers Routed by Billy Backers" and BGEA press release "Greater Chicago Graham Crusade Becomes Tri-State Affair," June 13, 1971, in Collection 345: BGEA—Media Office, Box 31, Folder 8; Rendelman interview; Martin, *A Prophet with Honor*, pp. 376–377; Faro e-mail.

67. Faro e-mail; Pollock, *Billy Graham*, pp. 124–125; "Hecklers Routed by Billy Backers"; BGEA press release "Greater Chicago Graham Crusade Becomes Tri-State Affair"; Rendelman interview; Martin, *A Prophet with Honor*, pp. 376–377.

68. Kinter e-mail; Rendleman interview; "Hecklers Routed by Billy Backers."

69. "Graham Urges Governor to Trust 'Jesus Power,'" *San Bernardino Sun*, June 30, 1971, Collection 360: BGEA—Scrapbooks, Reel #33 (June 1970–December 1971).

70. "Graham Attracts 44,500," *Oakland Tribune*, July 30, 1971, p. 21; "One Way in Oakland," *Decision*, October 1971, pp. 8–9; Northern California Crusade—Oakland, CA (1971), Collection 113: BGEA—Films & Videos, F#261.

71. Northern California Crusade—Oakland, CA (1971), Collection 113: BGEA—Films and Videos, F#261.

72. Ibid.; Billy Graham, "The Jesus Revolution," July 29, 1971, sermon excerpt in Collection 345: BGEA—Media Office, Box 32, Folder 3.

73. BGEA Team Office, press release, August 1, 1971, Collection 345: BGEA—Media Office, Box 32, Folder 7; "Decisive Hour for 21,000," *Christianity Today*, August 27, 1971, p. 30; Billy Graham, sermon, "The Jesus Revolution."

74. Billy Graham, *The Jesus Generation* (Grand Rapids, MI: Zondervan, 1971).

75. Arthur Blessitt with Walter Wagner, *Turned On to Jesus* (New York: Hawthorne, 1971); Duane Pederson with Bob Owen, *Jesus People* (Pasadena, CA: Compass, 1971).

76. Two Brothers from Berkeley, *Letters to Street Christians* (Grand Rapids, MI: Zondervan, 1971).

77. Ibid., p. 56.

78. So claimed the banner on the cover of the book's November 1971 3rd edition.

79. Edward Plowman, *The Jesus Movement in America* (Elgin, IL: David C. Cook, 1971).

80. Ibid. Plowman provides a good—especially for that time—thumbnail summary of the movement's origins, leading figures, and characteristics on pp. 43–55. Sales figures cited in "Jesus People to Be Described," *Bucks County Courier* (Levittown, PA), February 18, 1972, p. 15.

81. Jess Moody, *The Jesus Freaks* (Waco, TX: Word, 1971).

82. See Graham, *The Jesus Generation*, pp. 13–22.

83. William S. Cannon, *The Jesus Revolution* (Nashville, TN: Broadman, 1971); Dick Eastman, *Up with Jesus* (Grand Rapids, MI: Baker, 1971); Pat King, *The Jesus People Are Coming* (Plainfield, NJ: Logos International, 1971); Roger C. Palms, *The Jesus Kids* (Valley Forge, PA: Judson, 1971).

84. Walker L. Knight, compiler, *Jesus People Come Alive* (Wheaton, IL: Tyndale House, 1971).

85. Ibid., p. 12.

86. Lowell D. Streiker, *The Jesus Trip: Advent of the Jesus Freaks* (Nashville, TN: Abingdon, 1971).

87. Ibid., pp. 14–15.

88. Ibid., p. 120.

89. Martin E. Marty, "Theological Table-Talk," "Jesus: The Media and the Message," *Theology Today*, January 1972, pp. 471, 476.

90. Elwood Hensley, "I'm a 'Jesus People'" article from the *Baptist Banner* reprinted in *Sword of the Lord*, October 13, 1972, p. 4.

91. Bud Lyles, "Teen Talks—Hair and Tongues and Jesus People," *Sword of the Lord*, August 25, 1972, p. 4; see also "Hair Again," *Sword of the Lord*, July 27, 1973, p. 4.

92. Bob Jones III, *Look Again at the Jesus People* (Greenville, SC: Bob Jones University Press, 1972), quotes found on pp. 13 and 14.

93. Ad, "To Whom It May Concern," *Evening Sentinel* (Holland, MI), July 2, 1971, p. 7; ad, "He That Hath Ears to Hear, Let Him Hear," *Evening Sentinel* (Holland, MI), May 11, 1973, p. 7.

94. See "Letters to the Editor," *Frederick* (MD) *News-Post*, May 15, 1971, p. A4; May 26, 1971, p. A4; May 29, 1971, p. A4; June 7, 1971, p. A4; June 16, 1971, p. A4.

CHAPTER 6

1. Among the people I interviewed, a surprising number claimed to have been utterly unaware of the Jesus movement before their actual conversion and subsequent involvement. This impression is given contemporary support in the study of Jesus People in Rockford, Illinois, conducted by California–Berkeley anthropology grad student Sally Dobson Bookman during 1972 and 1973. She noted that of 85 individuals she surveyed, 51 had at some point in time seen the Jesus movement portrayed in magazines and television reports or had seen photos of the mass baptisms in Southern California. Stunningly, however, she noted that "practically all" of these individuals "recalled reading or hearing about the Jesus Movement only *after* they had already committed themselves" (author's italics). (Bookman, "Jesus People: A Religious Movement in a Midwestern City," PhD diss.: California–Berkeley, 1974, p. 313).

2. As part of my research I have attempted—attempted—to compile a comprehensive list of all the Jesus People communal homes, rural communes, coffeehouses, ministries, churches, and fellowships that I have come across either in the printed sources or in interviews. At this point, that list has about 1,200 entries, and I am convinced that it probably accounts for much less than half of the Jesus People groups and gathering spots that actually existed in the years between 1969 and 1977. There are great swaths of various states where I am convinced Jesus People groups existed for which I have, unfortunately, not readily been able to find sources. Even in my native Chicago area, there are large suburbs and cities where I am sure there must have been Jesus People groups—I just have not run across them yet.

3. Edward E. Plowman, "Whatever Happened to the Jesus Movement?" *Christianity Today*, October 24, 1975, p. 46; Billy Ray Hearn telephone interview with author, February 9, 2005.

4. Jack Hovelson, "A Look into Hearts of Jesus Freaks," *Des Moines* (IA) *Register*, October 17, 1971, pp. 1C, 5C.

5. Marti Little, "Jesus People Find 'Sign' in New Movement," *El Paso* (TX) *Herald-Post*, February 24, 1972, p. 13.

6. "Youth Coffeehouse to Open," *Post-Tribune* (Jefferson City, MO), August 12, 1971, p. 8.

7. Bookman, "Jesus People," pp. 259–264.

8. Craig Yoe telephone interview with author, July 13, 2004.

9. Nancy "Honeytree" Henigbaum Miller telephone interview with author, June 26, 2007; John White, Kent, OH, survey submitted January 28, 2002; Yoe interview.

10. Yoe interview.

11. Denny Keitzman interview with author, Franklin, TN, July 9, 2002.

12. "The Heat's On in Duluth," *Christianity Today*, March 3, 1972, p. 38; Glenn Kaiser telephone interview May 23, 2005; Jon Trott, "Life's Lessons: A History of Jesus People USA Covenant Church, Part One," *Cornerstone*, 22: 12 (1993), pp. 11–12.

13. Jim Palosaari interview with author, Brentwood, TN, July 12, 2002; Trott, "Life's Lessons...Part One," p. 12.

14. John M. Bozeman, "Jesus People USA: An Investigation of an Urban Communitarian Religious Group," Master's thesis: Florida State University, 1990, http://faraday.clas.virginia.edu/~jmb5b/jp.html (accessed February 10, 1997), pp. 13–14, copy in possession of author; Shawn David Young, "Jesus People USA, The Christian Woodstock and Conflicting Worlds: Political, Theological, and Musical Evolution, 1972–2010," (PhD diss., Michigan State University, 2011), pp. 32–33; Jim Palosaari interview; Trott, "Life's Lessons...Part One," p. 12.

15. *Milwaukee Journal*, November 11, 1972, p. 4; "'Jesus People' Settle in U.K.," Religious News Service wire story, *Winnipeg* (MB) *Free Press*, January 27, 1973, p. 17; unidentified former member of Milwaukee Jesus People quoted in Bozeman, "An Investigation," pp. 14–15; Jim Palosaari interview.

16. Bozeman, "An Investigation," p. 15; Trott, "Life's Lessons...Part One," pp. 12–13.

17. Trott, "Life's Lessons...Part One," pp. 12–13.

18. Bozeman, "An Investigation," p. 16; Trott, "Life's Lessons...Part One," p. 13; Young, "Jesus People USA," pp. 34–36.

19. Kirsten Scharnberg, "Commune's Iron Grip Tests Faith of Converts," *Chicago Tribune*, April 1, 2001, p. 14; Bozeman, "An Investigation," p. 16; Trott, "Life's Lessons...Part One," pp. 13–14.

20. Glenn Kaiser, telephone interview with author, May 23, 2005; Bozeman, "An Investigation," p. 17; Trott, "Life's Lessons...Part One," pp. 15–16; Young, "Jesus People USA," p. 41.

21. Bozeman, "An Investigation," pp. 16–17; Trott, "Life's Lessons, Part Two," *Cornerstone* 23:104, 1994, pp. 18–19.

22. See, for example, letter to the editor from Mrs. Tauno Maki detailing JPUSA's run-ins and arrests by the Chicago Police while the Krishnas continued to ply their wares at O'Hare ("Christians Jailed for Witnessing," *Ironwood* [MI] *Daily Globe*, July 6, 1974, p. 4). See also "Aggressive Religious Panhandlers Are Stirring Anger," *New York Times* Wire Service story in the *Freeport* (IL) *Journal-Herald*, December 24, 1976, p. 26.

23. Bill Lowery telephone interviews with author, December 2, 2009; July 29, 2010.

24. Lowery interview, July 29, 2010.

25. Dave and Diana Fogderud interview, Beloit, WI, May 22, 2002; Lowery interview, July 29, 2010.

26. Sam Negri, "City Youth Hear the Word," *Tucson* (AZ) *Daily Citizen*, January 10, 1975, p. 1; Lowery interview, July 29, 2010.

27. John M. Bozeman, "Christ Is the Answer: An Examination of a Religious Group Influenced by the Jesus Movement," academic paper, December 1990, www.geocities.ws/jmb5b/cita1990.html, p. 5; Lowery interview, July 29, 2010.

28. Mark Hollingsworth interview, Nashville, TN, July 12, 2002.

29. See for example John M. Bozeman, "Christ is the Answer: An Examination of a Religious Group Influenced by the Jesus Movement," p. 4, http://www.geocities.com/jmb5b/cita1990.html (accessed May 11, 2005); Lowery interview, July 29, 2010.

30. Edward E. Plowman, "The Jesus Movement: Now It's in the Hamlets," *Christianity Today*, June 18, 1971, pp. 35–36.

31. Edward E. Plowman, *The Jesus Movement in America* (Elgin, IL: David C. Cook, 1971), p. 124; Bob Durham telephone interview with author, August 29, 2007; Plowman, "The Jesus Movement: Now It's in the Hamlets."

32. Plowman, *The Jesus Movement in America*, p. 124; Plowman, "The Jesus Movement: Now It's in the Hamlets."

33. In her study of Jesus People in Rockford, Illinois, in the early and mid-1970s, anthropology doctoral student Sally Dobson Bookman came up with "peer-oriented" as another good way to describe the younger kids from more of a hippie orientation who were attracted to the Jesus movement (Bookman, "Jesus People," pp. 219–221).

34. Survey response by Lee Ann Powers, Globe, AZ, submitted January 11, 1998.

35. Ingrid Spellness Faro e-mail to author, November 4, 2008.

36. Survey response by William (Bill) G. Radcliffe, El Paso, TX, submitted November 22, 1998; see also, for example, Gary Spelts, "Ferris High School Revival," *Truth*, vol. 5:1, issue 32, April 1974, pp, 24–28.

37. Survey response by Steve Church, Blountville, TN, submitted December 6, 1998.

38. Survey response by Jeff Lough, Englewood, OH, submitted June 25, 1999.

39. Survey response by Thomas C. Medley, Vinton, VA, submitted September 22, 1998.

40. Letter to the editor from Chris Brunson, *Rockford* (IL) *Star*, February 28, 1972, Collection 360: Billy Graham Evangelistic Association (BGEA)-Scrapbooks, reel #34 [March-October 1972], Billy Graham Center Archives, Wheaton College, Wheaton, IL.

41. Survey response by Jim Sterling, College Station, TX, submitted June 9, 1998.

42. Survey response by Phil Spence, Aspley, Queensland, Australia, submitted March 15, 1998.

43. Survey response by Twila Beaubien, Rio Linda, CA, submitted December 14, 1997.

44. Survey response by Gary Seals, Garland, TX, submitted January 12, 1998.

45. Survey response by Tim Harris, Albemarle, NC, submitted July 19, 1999.

46. Randy Rohn, "God, Satan, Drugs Face Teens," *Anderson (IN) Daily Bulletin*, February 8, 1972, p. 16.

47. Bookman, "Jesus People," pp. 173–174.

48. Kerry Moore, "On the Merry-Go-Round," *Zoa Free Paper*, vol. 2, no. 4, October–November 1974, pp. 1, 5.

49. Rick Peterson, "Rebirth," *Truth*, 4:3, issue 29, May–June 1973, p. 32.

50. For a contemporary observation on the new popularity of crosses and religious jewelry, see Anne Eggebrotten, "The Cross-Bearers," *Christianity Today*, August 27, 1971, pp. 32–34. See also Colleen McDannell, *Material Christianity: Religion and Popular Culture in America* (New Haven, CT: Yale University Press, 1995), pp. 248–256.

51. See, for example, the illustration section in Timothy Miller, *The Hippies and American Values* (Knoxville: University of Tennessee Press, 1991).

52. Ronald Enroth, Edward E. Ericson Jr., and Breckinridge C. Peters, *The Jesus People: The Old-Time Religion in the Age of Aquarius* (Grand Rapids, MI: Eerdmans, 1972), p. 73.

53. Randy Mathews, "Oh My," Paragon Music, 1975.

54. Enroth, Ericson, and Peters, *The Jesus People*, p. 78.

55. See, for example, *Hollywood Free Paper*, 3:5, March 2, 1971, p. 15; Enroth, Ericson, and Peters, *The Jesus People*, p. 78.

56. There is no real work on this subject—ads and photographs are, at the moment, the best source of information. McDannell's *Material Christianity*, although it treats the rise of Jesus merchandise, uses mostly sources from 1972 and after and does not attempt to track its origins (see notes, pp. 303–304).

57. "Bible Bumper Stickers, Buttons, Bangles Being Sold to Millions," *New York Times* Wire Service story, *Salina (KS) Journal*, February 16, 1973, p. 10. By 1973, Ferm Publishing Company was grossing $250,000 in annual sales and projecting double that by 1976.

58. "The New Rebel Cry: Jesus Is Coming!" *Time*, June 21, 1971, p. 59; Enroth, Ericson, and Peters, *The Jesus People*, pp. 154–155; "Melodyland Drug Prevention Center Sells Jesus Watches," *Santa Ana Register*, August 7, 1971, p. A11.

59. Ad, *Campus Life*, October 1971.

60. Grason: ad, *Christian Life*, June 1972, pp. 107–110; ad, *Campus Life*, March 1973, pp. 27–28; Christian Lettering: Ad, *Campus Life*, October 1972, p. 13; Harold's Signs: *Campus Life*, November 1972, p. 19.

61. See, for example, the ad in *Campus Life* (September 1972), p. 63, as well as Peter Lundstrom, "New Products for Kids," *Christian Life*, June 1973, p. 56.

62. McDannell, *Material Christianity*, p. 251.

63. See John P. Ferre, "Searching for the Great Commission: Evangelical Book Publishing since the 1970s," in Quentin J. Schultze, ed., *American Evangelicals*

and the Mass Media (Grand Rapids, MI: Zondervan, 1990), pp. 99–117; Bruce Bickel and Stan Javitz, *His Time, His Way: The CBA Story, 1950–1999* (Colorado Springs, CO: Christian Booksellers Association, 1999), pp. 59–65; McDannell, *Material Christianity*, pp. 247–256.

64. Mark Clutter, "Briefly... ," *Long Beach* (CA) *Independent Press Telegram*, August 7, 1971, pp. B3–B4.

65. Gordon R. Brown, "Comics Go Fast at Religious Bookstores," *Tucson* (AZ) *Daily Citizen*, July 14, 1973, p. 4.

66. *Winona* (MN) *Daily News*, April 30, 1972, p. 12.

67. Twila Beaubien survey.

68. "Action Line: Gets Things Done," *Pasadena* (CA) *Star-News*, December 1, 1972, p. 1.

69. Lundstrom, "New Products for Kids," p. 56.

70. See, for example, Hiley Ward's comments about the instability of Jesus People communes in *The Far-Out Saints of the Jesus Communes: A Firsthand Report and Interpretation of the Jesus Movement* (New York: Association Press, 1972), p. 36.

71. Survey response by Rebecca Kelly, of unknown, submitted February 24, 2002.

72. Bookman, "Jesus People," pp. 186–187.

73. Survey response by Bill Kaffen, unknown Virginia, response submitted March 24, 1999.

74. Survey response by Elizabeth T. Knuth, Rockville, MN, submitted December 1, 1997.

75. Barry Mankowitz, "The Warehouse: A Place to Rap," *Blytheville* (AR) *Courier-News*, July 15, 1973, p. 1. The young evangelists prevailed on the local Kiwanis Club to jump-start their coffeehouse.

76. "His Place: A Christian Coffeehouse," *Chillicothe* (MO) *Constitution-Tribune*, October 5, 1971, p. 1; "Movement Is under Way for an Area Youth Crusade," January 27, 1972, p. 16.

77. Edward P. Morgan, *The 60s Experience: Hard Lessons about Modern America* (Philadelphia: Temple University Press, 1991), p. 172; Terry H. Anderson, *The Movement and the Sixties: Protest in America from Greensboro to Wounded Knee* (New York: Oxford University Press, 1995), pp. 35–36, 170.

78. Many of these sorts of ministries are cataloged in an appendix to Jess Moody's *The Jesus Freaks* (Waco, TX: Word, 1971), pp. 86–127, in a mistaken assumption that they comprised the Jesus movement.

79. Classic models of these sorts of ministries can be found in the stories presented in David Wilkerson, *The Cross and the Switchblade* (New York: B. Geis, 1963) and Bob Harrington, *The Chaplain of Bourbon Street* (New York: Doubleday, 1969). Of course, these also have their roots, ultimately, in the long work of gospel missions.

80. Enroth, Ericson, and Peters, *The Jesus People*, pp. 144–145.

81. See, for example, Mary Anne Berry, "Coffeehouse," *Campus Life*, November 1969, pp. 56–60. However, as was the case until late 1970, there was no understanding of these coffeehouses being part of any sort of a Jesus movement.

82. Don and Ann Wilkerson, *A Coffee House Manual* (Minneapolis, MN: Bethany Fellowship, 1972).

83. Survey response by Jo Ellen Brown, Alvord, TX, submitted December 31, 1997; survey response by Dallas Hewett, Kennewick, WA, submitted October 1, 1998; survey response by Karl Kerr, Nacogdoches, TX, submitted February 7, 2000: Monica B. Williams, "Carpenter's Shop Theme Is Holy Spirit in '76," *Chronicle-Telegram* (Elyria, OH), September 20, 1975, p. 50.

84. Larry Cheek, "Stout Church to Begin Cedar Falls Coffeehouse," *Waterloo* (IA) *Daily Courier*, December 27, 1971, p. 16.

85. Paul Baker, *Contemporary Christian Music: Where It Came from, What It Is, Where It's Going* (Westchester, IL: Crossway, 1985), p. 69. For an account of Belmont Church of Christ's troubles with its denomination, see Richard T. Hughes, *Reviving the Ancient Faith: The Story of Churches of Christ in America* (Grand Rapids, MI: Eerdmans, 1996), pp. 340–341.

86. Probably the worst moniker for any of the Jesus People coffeehouses that I came across was the appallingly named For Christ's Sake Coffeehouse in Frederick, Maryland. See Tom Ferraro, "Jesus Freaks," *Tri-State News* (Hagerstown, MD), April 8, 1972, p. 1.

87. Baker, *Contemporary Christian Music*, p. 65.

88. "Church-Coffee House Opens Today on Water Street," *Kennebec* (ME) *Journal*, Augusta edition, April 18, 1972, p. 14.

89. "Coffeehouse Seeks Operating Funds and Materials," *News-Palladium* (Benton Harbor, MI), June 23, 1973, p. 4.

90. Author's recollection; this initial cash outlay painted, repaired, and equipped a combination coffeehouse and small bookstore that lasted eighteen months until expenses—including loan repayments—made it impossible to keep the doors open any longer, The loan was repaid in full by ex-coffeehouse members within two years after the doors were closed.

91. Baker, *Contemporary Christian Music*, pp. 67–70.

92. See, for example, *Hard Core*, no. 5, October 1971, and *Adam's Apple Juicy News*, issue 2, February 1975; Baker, *Contemporary Christian Music*, p. 68.

93. See ad in the *Indianapolis Jesus Press*, vol. 1, no. 6, ca. 1971, p. 7.

94. David Hoyt telephone interview with author, April 15, 2009; Atlanta Discipleship Training Center newsletter, ca. Fall 1970, p. 5.

95. Gary Byers telephone interview with author, October 9, 2007; survey response by Ronda Caton, Allen, TX, submitted November 1, 1999; "You Can't Beat the Prices at This Restaurant," AP wire story, *Abilene Reporter-News* (TX), May 1, 1978, p. 1. Due to an internal rift and financial difficulties, the Fatted Calf shut down in 1979; see Tom Tiede, "Fate Deals 'Fatted Calf' Cruel Blow," *Paris* [TX] *News*, December 5, 1979, p. 53.

96. Edward B. Fiske, "A 'Religious Woodstock' Draws 75,000," *New York Times*, June 16, 1972, pp. 1, 19; "The Christian Woodstock," *Newsweek*, June 26, 1972, p. 52.

97. Paul Eshleman, *The EXPLO Story: A Plan to Change the World* (Glendale, CA: Regal, 1972), pp. 95–96.

98. "EXPLO '72 Fact Sheet," ca. 1972, EXPLO '72 Director's Notebook, Jesus Film Project Offices, San Clemente, CA.

99. "1972 Congress—With Training: What It Would Look Like," ca. 1970, Series: EXPLO '72, box 2, folder 4, Campus Crusade for Christ Archives, Orlando, FL.

100. "Profile: Paul A. Eshleman," ca. May 1971, EXPLO '72 Director's Notebook; details on the planning for EXPLO can be found in Eshleman, *The EXPLO Story*, pp. 95–107; John G. Turner, *Bill Bright and Campus Crusade for Christ: The Renewal of Evangelicalism in Postwar America* (Chapel Hill: University of North Carolina Press, 2008), p. 140.

101. "1972 Congress—With Training"; Eshleman, *The EXPLO Story*, pp. 97–98.

102. "Proposed Budget for International Student Congress on Evangelism," ca. 1970, Series: EXPLO '72, box 1, folder 34; "June 30, 1972 Budget Report," box 1, folder 30; Campus Crusade for Christ Archives; Turner, *Bill Bright & Campus Crusade for Christ*, p. 140.

103. "EXPLO '72 News Statement," Series: EXPLO '72, box 2, folder 4, Campus Crusade for Christ Archives.

104. "EXPLO '72 News Statement"; "1972 Congress—With Training." See also William Martin, *A Prophet with Honor: The Billy Graham Story* (New York: William Morrow, 1991), pp. 368–369.

105. "EXPLO '72" promotional film, 1971, Arrowhead Productions, San Bernardino, CA; Eshleman, *The EXPLO Story*, p. 102.

106. "EXPLO '72 Fact Sheet—Short Presentation," ca. 1971, EXPLO Director's notebook, Jesus Film Project Office.

107. "Jesus Music Festival—Final Format," ca. June 1972, EXPLO Director's notebook, Jesus Film Project Office.

108. Eshleman, *The EXPLO Story*, pp. 16–19; in Campus Crusade's "1972 Congress—With Training: What It Would Look Like" initial planning document, it was estimated that the meeting would attract 60,000 college students and about 16,000 high school students.

109. Colson quoted in Turner, *Bill Bright & Campus Crusade*, p. 141; Martin, *A Prophet with Honor*, p. 395.

110. Eshleman, *The EXPLO Story*, pp. 1–8.

111. Edward E. Plowman, "'Godstock' in Big D," *Christianity Today*, July 7, 1972, pp. 31–32; Fiske, "A Religious Woodstock"; Eshleman, *The EXPLO Story*, p. 8.

112. "EXPLO '72, Show #1," 1972, Arrowhead Productions International, San Bernardino, CA; Eshleman, *The EXPLO Story*, pp. 59–65.

113. Fiske, "A Religious Woodstock," p. 19.

114. Plowman, "'Godstock' in Big D," p. 32; Eshleman, *The EXPLO Story*, pp. 80–82.

115. "EXPLO '72, Show #3," 1972, Arrowhead Productions, San Bernardino, CA; Eshleman, *The EXPLO Story*, pp. 85–89.

116. "EXPLO '72, Show 3"; Eshleman, *The EXPLO Story*, pp. 86–88.

117. *Jesus Sound Explosion*, Campus Crusade for Christ, 1972, Frank Edmondson Contemporary Christian Music Collection, Judson College, Elgin, IL; "EXPLO '72, Show #3."

118. "EXPLO '72, Show #3."

119. Ibid.

120. Ibid.

121. "Christians Urged to Go to Miami," *Chronicle-Telegram* (Elyria, OH), July 6, 1972, p. 27.

122. The most publicized, and likely the largest, attempt to do something of this nature was the Spiritual Revolution Day march in California, where 8,000 Jesus People came together on February 13, 1971, for a Jesus march on the state capitol in Sacramento (see "California Youth March, Urge 'Spiritual Revolution Now,'" Baptist Press press release, February 23, 1971). But the Jesus march was hardly limited to the West Coast. For other examples, see Les Rodney, "Jesus Movement Growth," *Independent Pilot-Telegram* (Long Beach, CA), January 1, 1972, p. B6; "Jesus People on Parade," *Northwest Arkansas Times* (Fayetteville), April 10, 1972, p. 1; telephone interview with Gary Sweeten, May 28, 2003.

123. See Larry Eckholt, "'Jesus People' Displace Protestors on Pentacrest," *Des Moines Register*, May 4, 1972, p. 1.

124. This particular incident occurred on a Saturday in December 1971 at the Northwest Plaza Shopping Center in St. Ann, Missouri, just outside St. Louis. A group of Jesus People from the Alton Jesus Center across the river in Illinois was in the mall passing out tracts and faced off with a band of militants from a St. Louis–based group called ACTION that specialized in street theater. On this day, ACTION evacuated the center, leaving the disputed space in the possession of the shoppers and the Jesus People, two of whom remained "kneeling and praying with their eyes uplifted" (Andy Yakstis, "Jesus Freaks Warn of Christmas Commercialism," *Alton* [IL] *Telegraph*, December 12, 1971, p. 9; information on ACTION found in Thomas Morris Spencer, *The St. Louis Veiled Prophet Celebration: Power on Parade, 1877–1995* [Columbia: University of Missouri Press, 2000], pp. 117–119).

125. Preston Shires, *Hippies of the Religious Right* (Waco, TX: Baylor University Press, 2007), p. 150; Adon Taft, "The World at Miami," *Christianity Today*, August 11, 1972, p. 13; Jeffrey Hart, "No Repeat of Chicago," *Cumberland* [MD] *News*, July 14, 1972, p. 15.

126. See Jack Sparks, *God's Forever Family* (Grand Rapids, MI: Zondervan, 1974), pp. 135–148.

127. See, for example, "EXPLO '72: A Gospel of Affirmation from America's Youth," *Newsday*, June 20, 1972, Collection 360, BGEA—Scrapbooks, Reel 34: March–October 1972, Billy Graham Center Archives; Fiske, "A Religious Woodstock."

128. Letter from Robert E. Mead Jr., Director of Sales, Dallas Hilton, to Paul Eshleman, June 21, 1972, Paul Eshleman EXPLO '72 Files.

129. Letter from Mrs. James W. Gee to EXPLO '72 Directors, June 16, 1972, Paul Eshleman EXPLO '72 files.

130. Letter from A. Kerekes, Mesquite, TX, to EXPLO '72 staff, ca. June 1972, Paul Eshleman EXPLO '72 files.

131. John F. Taylor, "A Word with Alumni," clipping from first page of *Wheaton Alumni* ca. late 1972, attached to letter from John F. Taylor, executive director of the Wheaton College Alumni Association, Paul Eshleman EXPLO '72 files.

132. Letter from Clyde W. Taylor, general director of the National Association for Evangelicals, Washington, D.C., to Bill Bright, June 20, 1972, Paul Eshleman EXPLO '72 files.

133. Letter from Dr. Robert A. Cook, president of the King's College, Briarcliff Manor, NY, to Bill Bright, July 24, 1972, Paul Eshleman EXPLO '72 files.

134. Letter from Harm A. Weber, president of Judson College, Elgin, IL, to Bill Bright, August 4, 1972, Paul Eshleman, EXPLO '72 files.

135. Letter from Wendell G. Collins, vice president for development, Gospel Films, Inc., Muskegon, MI, to Paul Eshleman, June 26, 1972, Paul Eshleman EXPLO '72 files.

136. Letter from Paul E. Little, Campus Crusade for Christ assistant to the president, to Bill Bright, July 20, 1972, Paul Eshleman EXPLO '72 files.

137. Letter from LeRoy Eims, vice president of Navigators, Int'l, Colorado Springs, CO, to Bill Bright, June 24, 1972, Paul Eshleman EXPLO '72 files.

138. Letter from Lucy Kalijian, Pasadena, CA, to Paul Eshleman, June 26, 1972, Paul Eshleman EXPLO '72 files.

139. Letter from Dean C. Olson, Medford, WI, to Paul Eshleman, June 21, 1972, Paul Eshleman EXPLO '72 files.

140. Beverly Walker, "Mini-Explo Ready to Go," *Advocate* (Newark, OH), August 25, 1972, p. 9.

141. The *Methodist Messenger* (First Methodist Church, Crossett, AR), vol. 4, no. 9, June 29, 1972, pp. 1–6, Paul Eshleman EXPLO '72 files.

142. "EXPLO '72, Shows 1, 2 & 3"; Eshleman, *The EXPLO Story*, p. 89.

143. "EXPLO '72: A Gospel of Affirmation."

CHAPTER 7

1. Ray Ruppert, "Opponents Break In, Order Children of God to Leave," *Seattle Times*, December 3, 1971, p. A1; John Salvesen telephone interview with author, November 19, 2002.

2. See, for example, Ruben Ortega, *The Jesus People Speak Out!* (Elgin, IL: David C. Cook, 1972), pp. 11, 14, 28, 45, 85, 90.

3. Walker L. Knight, compiler, *Jesus People Come Alive* (Wheaton, IL: Tyndale House, 1971), pp. 41–49; quotes on pp. 43–44, 46.

4. Ronald M. Enroth, Edward E. Ericson Jr., and C. Breckinridge Peters, *The Jesus People: The Old-Time Religion in the Age of Aquarius* (Grand Rapids, MI: Eerdmans, 1972), pp. 30–31.

5. Ibid., pp. 21–54; anecdote on p. 36.

6. This is borne out in the tone of Berg's MO Letters during this period, wherein he coached and advised his Stateside inner circle but, for security's sake, still kept very much to the background; for example, see "General Epistle to Leaders," *MO Letter* 24, December 13, 1970.

7. Jay Sharbutt, "Jesus People's Theories Appear to Be Billy Graham Explained by Timothy Leary," AP wire story carried in the *Anderson* [IN] *Daily Bulletin,* February 5, 1971, p. 12; Lowell D. Streiker, *The Jesus Trip: Advent of the Jesus Freaks* (Nashville, TN: Abingdon, 1971), p. 50.

8. Enroth, Erickson, and Peters, *The Jesus People,* p. 25.

9. James D. Chancellor, *Life in the Family: An Oral History of the Children of God* (Syracuse, NY: Syracuse University Press, 2000), pp. 2–3; Deborah (Linda Berg) Davis, *The Children of God: The Inside Story* (Grand Rapids, MI: Zondervan, 1984), pp. 52–59; David E. Van Zandt, *Living in the Children of God* (Princeton, NJ: Princeton University Press, 1991), p. 35; Don Lattin, *Jesus Freaks: A True Story of Murder and Madness on the Evangelical Edge* (New York: Harper One, 2007), pp. 44–46.

10. Davis, *The Children of God,* p. 12; for a statement of "Faithy" Berg's comments on her father's visits and her endorsement of adults' sexual involvement with their children, see the section "My Childhood Sex—June 1977" within the British legal document by Lord Justice Alan Ward, "The Judgment of Lord Justice Ward on the 26th May 1995" (October 19, 1995), stemming from a 1992 suit. For a contemporary summary of the case and Ward's judgment, see Emma Wilkins, "Judge Condemns Cult's Founder as Perverted and Malign Influence," *London Times,* November 25, 1995.

11. Lattin, *Jesus Freaks,* pp. 55–56, quoting Sarah Glassford from New York State Attorney General Herbert J. Wallenstein's *Final Report on the Activities of the Children of God* (1974).

12. Lattin, *Jesus Freaks,* pp. 56–58; Berg notes that the 1971 conferences took place at the Dalrich Motel (David Berg, MO Letter DO2778, "Now It Can Be Told!—Chapter 14: Oklahoma to London" [April 1991], sec. 2).

13. Rodney Stark and Roger Finke, *The Churching of America, 1776–1990* (New Brunswick, NJ: Rutgers University Press, 1993) is the classic analysis of how the American religious market operates. For an example of evangelical disapproval

of, and concern over, sheep stealing, see William Chadwick, *Stealing Sheep: The Church's Hidden Problems of Transfer Growth* (Downers Grove, IL: InterVarsity Press, 2001).

14. "ORU Gets Heavy Sample," *New Nation News*, Ch. 29, vol. 2, ca. Spring 1971, pp. 1, 8.

15. "Open Letter from Inter-Varsity Christian Fellowship, Southwestern College," *Hollywood Free Paper*, vol. 3, issue 12, ca. June 1971, p. 2.

16. Information on circulation of the *Hollywood Free Paper* from Duane Pederson interview with author, Lake Los Angeles, CA, August 2, 2002, tape 1; *Hollywood Free Paper*, vol. 3, issue 15, ca. summer 1971, p. 3.

17. Letter from Fred Jordan and the Children of God, *Hollywood Free Paper*, vol. 3, issue 13, ca. June 15, 1971, p. 3; photographic proofs of pictures snapped at the meeting between Pederson and COG leaders are contained in the Duane Pederson Collection, Box 14, Folder 11, Archives and Special Collections, David Allan Hubbard Library, Fuller Theological Seminary, Pasadena, CA.

18. This allegation was made a year later by Berg himself, who claimed that the COG had sent their lawyers after both the *Hollywood Free Paper* and Inter-Varsity Christian Fellowship (IVCF) and that the latter's lawyers had branded it a "fraud" "written by a girl student at one of the colleges where [IVCF] operate, but a student who was not even a member of Inter-Varsity!" See David Berg, "Survival!" MO Letter 172, GP—June 1972, sections 206–209.

19. Letter from Kent Philpott printed in *Hollywood Free Paper*, ca. summer 1971, quoted in Enroth, Erickson, and Peters, *The Jesus People*, p. 42.

20. Ibid.

21. Minutes of the General Board Meeting, Evangelical Concerns, July 17, 1971 (Kent Philpott collection).

22. David Hoyt telephone interview with author, April 15, 2009.

23. David Hoyt, "Lonesome Stone," unpublished mss. in possession of author, pp. 161–164; Hoyt interview.

24. Ibid.

25. Hoyt, "Lonesome Stone," pp. 166–168; Hoyt interview.

26. Hoyt interview.

27. Hoyt, "Lonesome Stone," p. 168.

28. Hoyt interview; Hoyt, "Lonesome Stone," pp. 168–169.

29. Hoyt, "Lonesome Stone," pp. 169–173.

30. Ibid., pp. 173–174.

31. Hoyt interview.

32. Hoyt, "Lonesome Stone," pp. 168, 172; Hoyt interview.

33. Kent Philpott interview with author, Mill Valley, CA, August 7, 2002; *The Jesus Movement* DVD (Mill Valley, CA: Miller Avenue Baptist Church, ca. 2007).

34. Philpott interview.

35. Ibid.

36. Ken Pitts interview with author, Nashville, TN, July 9, 2002; Roger Allen interview with author, Nashville, TN, July 13, 2002; Philpott interview; Hoyt, "Lonesome Stone," pp. 172–173.

37. Pitts interview.

38. Allen interview; Pitts interview.

39. Glenn D. Kittler, *The Jesus Kids and Their Leaders* (New York: Warner, 1972), pp. 141, 144; Ruth Wangerin, *The Children of God: A Make-Believe Revolution?* (Westport, CT: Greenwood, 1993), p. 36; Salvesen interview.

40. Russell Griggs, quoted in Ray Ruppert, "Issue of the Church Splits Jesus People Army," *Seattle Times*, October 17, 1971, p. B10.

41. Ibid.

42. Transcript of Linda Meissner taped interview with David Di Sabatino, ca. 1995.

43. Linda Meissner, *The Voice* (Seattle, WA: Gloriana, 2012), p. 140; Salvesen interview; Meissner interview transcript.

44. Michael McFadden, *The Jesus Revolution* (New York: Harrow, 1972), pp. 80–81.

45. Ruppert, "Issue of the Church."

46. "Parents Call Jesus Movement Subversive," AP wire story in the *Galveston* [TX] *Daily News*, October 16, 1971, p. 13; "Michael James Rambur, 1946–1968," www. chulavistaca.gov/vet/Vietnam/Rambur,%20Michael.pdf.

47. Merrill Sheils, "Children of God Reject Everything in Modern Society," Newsweek Feature Service wire story in *Mansfield* [OH] *News Journal*, December 10, 1971, p. 5.

48. McFadden, *The Jesus Revolution*, p. 102.

49. "Parents Call Jesus Movement Subversive," AP wire story in *Galveston Daily News*, October 16, 1971, p. 13.

50. Quoted in McFadden, *The Jesus Revolution*, p. 102.

51. Ted Patrick with Tom Dulack, *Let Our Children Go!* (New York: E. P. Dutton, 1976; Ballantine Books edition, 1977), pp. 28–52. Patrick often claimed or implied he was the founder of FREECOG (see Patrick, p. 55, for example), but he was one of several who founded the group.

52. Ibid., pp. 59–68.

53. Enroth, Ericson, and Peters, *The Jesus People*, pp. 25–28; Martha Hand "'Children of God' Evicted from Ranch," AP wire story in *Odessa* [TX] *American*, October 1, 1971, p. 5B.

54. Meissner interview transcript; Salvesen interview.

55. Meissner interview transcript.

56. Meissner, *The Voice*, pp. 140–141.

57. McFadden, *The Jesus Revolution*, pp. 81–82.

58. Wangerin, *The Children of God*, pp. 35–36; Ruppert, "Issue of the Church."

59. Kent Philpott interview in *The Jesus Movement*, DVD.

60. Hoyt interview.

61. David Berg, "To the Northwest Brethren—And Sisters!" MO Letter 109—LTA, September, 1971, secs. 15–16; see also sections 17–20.

62. Hoyt interview; Hoyt, "Lonesome Stone," pp. 173–174.

63. Richard Vicknair interview with author, Seattle, WA, October 19, 2002.

64. Jim Palosaari interview with author, Brentwood, TN, July 12, 2002.

65. Palosaari interview; Vicknair interview; Meissner, *The Voice*, p. 142.

66. John Salvesen quoting Linda Meissner in David Di Sabatino, "History of the Jesus Movement" (master's thesis: McMaster Divinity School, 1994), p. 76; Salvesen interview.

67. Vicknair interview; Palosaari interview; Salvesen interview; quote found in Meissner, *The Voice*, p. 142.

68. Ray Ruppert, "Sect Has Pied-Piper Effect," *Seattle Times*, October 17, 1971, p. B1; "The Children of God," p. B6; "Who Are the Children of God?" p. B6; "Some of the People at Northwest Headquarters," p. B6; Salvesen interview.

69. David Berg, "Dear Deb and Jeth," MO Letter 110—LTA, September 27, 1971, section 28.

70. David Berg, "General Letter on Various Business," MO Letter 112—LTA, October 1, 1971, sections 36–37; see also sections 38–40.

71. Salvesen interview; Palosaari interview; Vicknair interview. For examples of some of the negative press the COG began to receive in Washington state press, see Ray Ruppert, "Prominent Minister Warns against 'Children of God,'" *Seattle Times*, November 9, 1971, p. 1; and "Children of God: Christian Crusaders or Fanatics?" *Daily Chronicle* (Centralia, WA), November 19, 1971, p. 16.

72. "Jesus People Army Meet with Children of God," *Seattle Times*, November 1, 1971, p. A3; Patrick, *Let Our Children Go!* p. 56; Salvesen interview.

73. Ed Stover, "Moses' Fears Push Sect Too Hard," *Seattle Post-Intelligencer*, November 9, 1971, p. A6: see also Berg, "General Letter on Various Business," MO Letter 112–LTA, October 1, 1971, sections 36–40.

74. David Berg, "A Shepherd-Time Story," MO Letter 113–GP, February 10, 1971, Section 17; Stover, "Moses' Fears."

75. David Hoyt quoted in Stover, "Moses' Fears."

76. Sheils, "Children of God Reject Everything."

77. "'Children of God' Sect Surrounded by Controversy," *Denton* [TX] *Record-Chronicle*, November 5, 1971, p. 8A; Ruth Gordon, *Children of Darkness* (Wheaton, IL: Tyndale House, 1988), p. 135; Sheils, "Children of God Reject."

78. David Berg, "Emergency Call Home," MO Letter 144A, November 21, 1971, Section 5.

79. David Berg, "Statistics," MO Letter 141–LTA, November 23, 1971, Section 2.

80. See, for example, Carroll Mills, "Jesus Group in Mass Exodus," *Daily Review* (Hayward, CA), November 23, 1971, pp. 1, 8; James T. Wooten, "Children of God Accept Parents' Challenge," New York Times wire story in *Independent Press-Telegram* (Long Beach, CA), November 30, 1971, p. A18.

81. Duston Harvey, "'Children of God' Get a Reminder," UPI wire story in the *Times* (San Mateo, CA), December 21, 1971, p. 14.

82. Salvesen interview; Meissner, *The Voice*, pp. 143–145.

83. Davis, *The Children of God*, pp. 112–114; Berg, "Now It Can Be Told!" Sections 20–34; Hoyt, "Lonesome Stone," pp. 184–185.

84. David Berg, "Let the Dead Bury the Dead," MO Letter 153–GP, January 31, 1972; "802 South," MO Letter 187–GP, October 23, 1972; Van Zandt, *Living in the Children of God*, pp. 38, 40–41.

85. Berg, "Now It Can Be Told," Section 29.

86. Davis, *Children of God*, pp. 5–6; Berg, "Now It Can Be Told," Sections 35–36.

87. Geoffrey Corry, *Jesus Bubble or Jesus Revolution* (London: British Council of Churches Youth Department, 1973), pp. 18–19; Wangerin, *Children of God*, pp. 37–38.

88. Hoyt interview; Hoyt, "Lonesome Stone," pp. 174–176.

89. David Berg, "The Laws of Moses," MO Letter 155–LTA, February 21, 1972, Section 30.

90. Ibid., Sections 30–32.

91. Berg, "The Laws of Moses," Sections 33–38. For Wilkerson's take on the COG, see David Wilkerson, *Purple Violet Squish* (Grand Rapids, MI: Zondervan, 1969), pp. 53–62.

92. See statistics in Van Zandt, *Living in the Children of God*, pp. 41–43.

93. Hoyt, "Lonesome Stone," pp. 179–180.

94. David Berg, "Baalzebub Lord of the Flies," Mo Letter 168–LTA, June 12, 1972, Sections 1–4; Hoyt interview; Hoyt, "Lonesome Stone," pp. 180–182.

95. David Berg, "Emergency Notice to All Leaders of All Colonies!" MO Letter 168a–LTA, June 12, 1972; Hoyt, "Lonesome Stone," pp. 179, 183.

96. Hoyt, "Lonesome Stone," pp. 183–184; Corry, *Jesus Bubble or Jesus Revolution?* p. 24. For Berg's claims of Hoyt's physical abuse of his family, see David Berg, "Christmas Eve Massacre!" MO Letter, DO 856, December 25, 1979, Sections 103–106.

97. Gordon Landreth, "The Dangers of the Children of God," *Church of England Newspaper*, November 10, 1972.

98. Corry, *Jesus Bubble or Jesus Revolution*, pp. 24–25, 28; Palosaari interview.

99. Palosaari interview; Corry, *Jesus Bubble or Jesus Revolution*, p. 28.

100. The Sheep, *Jeesus-Rock!* (Finnlevy Records, SFLP-8520, 1972).

101. Palosaari interview.

102. Ibid.

103. Corry, *Jesus Bubble or Jesus Revolution*, pp. 28–29.

104. Tony Jasper, *Jesus in a Pop Culture* (Glasgow: William Collins Sons, 1975), p. 62; Palosaari interview; Corry, *Jesus Bubble or Jesus Revolution*, p. 29.

105. Palosaari interview.

106. Steve Grant, *Time Out*, July 20, 1973.

107. Jasper, *Jesus in a Pop Culture*, pp. 64–65.

108. Michael Jacob, "Lonesome Stone" (review), *Church of England Newspaper*, July 20, 1973, p. 2.

109. Tony Jasper, *Jesus in a Pop Culture*, pp. 63, 127, 135.

110. Newspaper clipping from *The Star* (Sheffield, UK) quoted in (Kevin) John Smith, "The Origins, Nature and Significance of the Jesus Movement as a Revitalization Movement" (PhD diss., Asbury Theological Seminary, 2002), p. 143.

111. Graham Moore, "A Not-So-Lonesome Response to Enthusiastic Cast of 'Multi-Media' Rock Musical," *Wythenshawe Express* (Manchester, UK), November 15, 1973; Palosaari interview.

112. Corry, *Jesus Bubble or Jesus Revolution*, p. 25.

113. Ibid.

114. Hoyt, "Lonesome Stone," pp. 184–185; Corry, *Jesus Bubble or Jesus Revolution*, p. 25; Davis, *The Children of God*, pp. 112–114.

115. Letter from Mark Carlisle of the British Home Office to John Hunt, M.P., November 30, 1972, quoted in Corry, *Jesus Bubble or Jesus Revolution*, p. 25.

116. Corry, *Jesus Bubble or Jesus Revolution*, pp. 32–34.

117. See, for example, Jasper, *Jesus in a Pop Culture*, pp. 112–119. Palosaari and his crew came back to the United States in 1974 and tried to take *Lonesome Stone* on the road in the United States, playing towns like Davenport, Iowa; Oconomowoc, Wisconsin; and Lancaster, Pennsylvania. But the rock musical failed to ignite the passions of either secular or Jesus People audiences, causing Kenneth Frampton to apparently pull the plug on his financial support and forcing the touring cast to call it a wrap (see, for example, "English Rock Opera Opens in Davenport," *Muscatine* [IA] *Journal*, October 31, 1974, p. 15; Jack Swanson, *Farewell to Fences* [Oconomowoc, WI: Living Waters, 1996], pp. 213–221; Palosaari interview).

118. John Bisagno, "Foreword," in William S. Cannon, *The Jesus Revolution: New Inspiration for Evangelicals* (Nashville, TN: Broadman Press, 1971), p. 13.

119. For the best examination of the rise and fall of the Shepherding movement's vision and the network it spawned, see S. David Moore, *The Shepherding Movement: Controversy and Charismatic Ecclesiology* (London: T & T Clark, 2003); for Jesus People involvement, see pp. 50–51; see also Ronald M. Enroth, "Where Have All the Jesus People Gone?" *Eternity*, October 1973, p. 28.

120. See, for example, "TM behind Closed Doors," *Right On!* November 1975, pp. 8–13; Bill Remine, "Who Is Guru Maharaj Ji?" *End Times*, November 1973, p. 8; "The T.M. Deception," *Free Love* (Summer 1976); ad offering tracts for sale of past *Cornerstone* features on the COG, the Unification Church, the Way International, the Local Church, TM, Baha'I, and Scientology, *Cornerstone*, vol. 5, no. 34, 1977, p. 5.

121. See ad for SCP literature in *Right On!* 7:4, November 1975, p. 14.

122. See, for example, Walter Martin, *Kingdom of the Cults* (Grand Rapids, MI: Zondervan, 1965; Minneapolis: Bethany revised and expanded ed., 1985) and Josh McDowell, *Understanding the Cults* (San Bernardino, CA: Campus Crusade for Christ, 1982).

123. For examples of the burgeoning 1970s flood of evangelical literature concerned with various dimensions of the occult, see, for example, Josh McDowell, *Understanding the Occult* (San Bernardino, CA: Campus Crusade for Christ, 1982); Richard W. DeHaan, *Satan, Satanism, and Witchcraft* (Grand Rapids, MI: Zondervan, 1972); Nicky Cruz, *Satan on the Loose* (Old Tappan, NJ: Fleming H. Revell, 1973); and Edmund C. Gross, *The Ouija Board: Doorway to the Occult* (Chicago: Moody, 1975).

124. For a good summary of the anticult movement in the United States, see Philip Jenkins, *Mystics and Messiahs: Cults and New Religions in American History* (New York: Oxford University Press, 2000).

125. Ibid., pp. 205–207.

126. Ibid., pp. 193–205.

127. See, for example, such lurid exposés of the COG's sexual doings and child-rearing practices as Miriam Williams, *Heaven's Harlots: My Fifteen Years in a Sex Cult* (New York: Harper Perennial, 1999); Kristina Jones, Celeste Jones, and Juliana Buhring, *Not without My Sister: The True Story of Three Girls Violated and Betrayed* (London: Harper UK, 2007); Davis, *The Children of God*; and Lattin, *Jesus Freaks*.

128. See, for example, James R. Lewis and J. Gordon Melton, eds., *Sex, Slander, and Salvation: Investigating The Family/Children of God* (Stanford, CA: Center for Academic Press, 1994); Steven A. Kent, "Misattribution and Social Control in the Children of God," *Journal of Religion and Health*, vol. 33. no. 1 (Spring 1994), pp. 29–43; William Sims Bainbridge, *The Endtime Family: The Children of God* (Albany: State University of New York Press, 2002); and Gary Shepherd and Gordon Shepherd, "Accommodation and Reformation in the Family/Children of God," *Nova Religio*, vol. 9, no. 1 (August 2005), pp. 67–92.

CHAPTER 8

1. "The New Rebel Cry: Jesus Is Coming!" *Time*, June 21, 1971, p. 61.

2. Hiley H. Ward, *The Far-Out Saints of the Jesus Communes: A Firsthand Report and Interpretation of the Jesus People Movement* (New York: Association, 1972), p. 26; see also excerpt contained on that page from a letter by John Sampey III published in "Jesus Explosion" (Part II), *Home Missions*, 22, vol. 8, August 1971.

3. "Pastor Says Christianity Should Have Room for Jesus Freaks," *Delaware County* [PA] *Daily Times*, November 13, 1972, pp. 13, 18.

4. Marlin "Butch" Hardman, "The Real Scoop on Rock n' Roll," *Youth for Christ*, October 1959, p. 10; see also William Ward Ayer, "Jungle Madness in American Music," *Youth for Christ*, November 1956, pp. 19–21.

5. Billy Graham, *Billy Graham Talks to Teenagers* (Grand Rapids, MI: Zondervan, 1960), p. 16.

6. See Ralph Carmichael, *He's Everything to Me* (Waco, TX: Word, 1986). Carmichael was the composer of the 1966 hit song "Born Free" and the arranger for Nat King Cole's classic 1960 rerecording of "The Christmas Song (Chestnuts Roasting on an Open Fire)."

7. For example, see Wendell P. Loveless, "Records for a Musical Christmas," *Christian Life*, December 1951, p. 65.

8. *The Restless Ones*, Worldwide Pictures, 1965. Ironically, Carmichael's score was originally too "with it" for the tastes of those in charge of Worldwide Pictures, but due to budget constraints, the score was retained for the film. See Thomas E. Bergler, "I Found My Thrill: Youth for Christ and American Congregational Singing, 1940–1970," in Richard J. Mouw and Mark A. Noll, eds., *Wonderful Words of Life: Hymns in American Protestant History and Theology* (Grand Rapids, MI: Eerdmans, 2004), p. 126.

9. Paul Baker, *Contemporary Christian Music: Where It Came from, What It Is, Where It's Going* (Westchester, IL: Crossway, 1985), pp. 11–12.

10. Billy Ray Hearn telephone interview with author, February 9, 2005; Baker, *Contemporary Christian Music*, pp. 14–15; *Good News*, Word Records, 1968. Many of the recordings cited in this chapter from the early days of Jesus music are exceedingly rare and can be found only through contacts with individual fans and collectors. For researchers, there is, thankfully, an excellent collection of Jesus music and Contemporary Christian Music (ca. 1969–1988) in the Frank Edmondson Contemporary Christian Music Collection at the Benjamin P. Browne Library of Judson College in Elgin, IL. For those interested in a comprehensive guide to the body of either Jesus music or CCM, their first resource should be Mark Allan Powell, *Encyclopedia of Contemporary Christian Music* (Peabody, MA: Hendrickson, 2002).

11. William David Romanowski, "Rock 'n' Religion: A Socio-Cultural Analysis of the Contemporary Christian Music Industry" (PhD diss., Bowling Green State University, 1990), pp. 129–130. Carmichael, *He's Everything to Me*, pp. 144–149; Hearn interview. For an example of contemporary comment, see Nina M. Ball, "Musicals Come to Church," *Christian Life*, November 1971, p. 46.

12. Baker, *Contemporary Christian Music*, pp. 15–16.

13. See, for example, Campus Crusade's *Collegiate Challenge*, Winter 1966, p. 24;

14. Lowell Lytle telephone interview with author, September 7, 2007.

15. Gene Cotton interview with author, Leiper's Fork, TN, July 11, 2002; Lytle interview.

16. Cotton interview.

17. Cotton interview; Lytle interview.

18. Lytle interview; Cotton interview. Ray Renner, a member of a band called the Fishermen out of Anderson, Indiana, pointed out: "You know at that time if you would say 'Thumbs down to drugs'—which was easy for us to do since a couple of us had really felt the Lord had delivered us from drugs—they'd let you say 'Thumbs up to Jesus' and do altar calls in schools and everything and we did 'em all over that

part of the country [in the mid-Atlantic states] in high schools and campuses of every kind" (Ray Renner telephone interview with author, August 10, 2007).

19. Lytle interview; Cotton interview.

20. John Ankerberg telephone interview with author, July 31, 2007.

21. Ibid.

22. Ibid.

23. Mike Johnson, unpublished autobiographical ms., ca. 2001, in possession of author, pp. 56–62; Mike Johnson interview with author, Nashville, TN, July 9, 2002.

24. Johnson, unpublished ms., p. 61.

25. Ibid., pp. 62–67, 75–76; Johnson interview. The Exkursions' role in the 1969 New York City Billy Graham Crusade coffeehouse is noted in William Martin, *A Prophet with Honor: The Billy Graham Story* (New York: William Morrow, 1991), p. 376.

26. Fred Caban telephone interview with author, June 4, 2010; David Di Sabatino, "A History of the Jesus People Movement" (MA thesis: McMaster University, 1994), pp. 94–95.

27. Caban interview.

28. Ibid.

29. Caban interview; Di Sabatino, "A History of the Jesus People," p. 106.

30. Fred Caban, "The King Is Christ," 1972, Agape Communications, copyright 1994.

31. Don Williams interview with author, La Jolla, CA, August 1, 2002; Don Williams, *Call to the Streets* (St. Paul, MN: Augsburg, 1972), pp. 32–34, 62–63.

32. Williams interview.

33. Duane Pederson interview with author, Lake Los Angeles, CA, July 31, 2002; Betty Price and Everett L. Hullum Jr., "The Jesus Explosion," in Walker L. Knight, *Jesus People Come Alive* (Wheaton, IL: Tyndale House, 1971), p. 40; Ronald M. Enroth, Edward E. Ericson Jr., and C. Breckinridge Peters, *The Jesus People: Old-Time Religion in the Age of Aquarius* (Grand Rapids, MI: Eerdmans, 1972), p. 83.

34. John Higgins interview with Chuck Fromm, March 14, 2000, transcript, pp. 4–5.

35. Interview with John Higgins, quoted in Chuck Fromm, "New Song to Contemporary Christian Music Entertainment" (Master's thesis, Fuller Theological Seminary, 1996), p. 67.

36. Higgins interview transcript, p. 4.

37. Perucci Ferraiuolo, "Love Song: Jesus Music for the '90s," *CCM*, May 1995, p. 83. "Little Honda," penned by Girard's friend, Brian Wilson of the Beach Boys, reached #9 on the Billboard music charts in late 1964 (Joel Whitburn, *The Billboard Book of Top 40 Hits*, 4th ed. [New York: Billboard, 1989], p. 206).

38. Chuck Girard telephone interview with author, August 18, 2010; Baker, *Contemporary Christian Music*, pp. 36–37.

39. Girard interview; Jay Truax, quoted in Baker, *Contemporary Christian Music*, p. 37.

40. Edward E. Plowman, *The Jesus Movement in America* (Elgin, IL: David C. Cook, 1971), pp. 104–105; Chuck Girard quoted in Baker, *Contemporary Christian Music*, p. 37; Girard interview.

41. Tommy Coomes quoted in Steve Rabey, "Maranatha! Music Comes of Age," *Christianity Today*, April 29, 1991, pp. 44–45.

42. Girard interview; Rabey, "Maranatha! Music Comes of Age," pp. 44–45.

43. Fromm, "New Song," p. 69.

44. Girard interview; Fromm, "New Song," p. 68.

45. Price and Hullum, "The Jesus Explosion," p. 31; Rabey, "Maranatha! Music," p. 45.

46. Baker, *Contemporary Christian Music*, p. 39.

47. Plowman, *The Jesus Movement in America*, p. 105.

48. John Sherrill, *They Speak with Other Tongues* (New York: Pyramid, 1964), p. 118. Grant Wacker offers some information on this phenomenon among the first generation of American Pentecostals in *Heaven Below: Early Pentecostals and American Culture* (Cambridge, MA: Harvard University Press, 2001), pp. 39–40, 110.

49. Tommy Coomes, quoted in Baker, *Contemporary Christian Music*, p. 40.

50. *The Everlastin' Living Jesus Music Concert*, Maranatha! Records, 1971; Rabey, "Maranatha! Music," p. 45; see also Oden Fong interview with author, Huntington Beach, CA, July 31, 2002.

51. "Wilson-McKinley: They're Playing for Jesus Now," *Truth*, vol. 1, no. 1, October 1, 1970, p. 3; Timothy Smith, "The Wilson McKinley Story," www.tanignak.com/WilsonMcKinleyArticle.htm; Plowman, *The Jesus Movement*, pp. 106–107.

52. See, for example, Baker, *Contemporary Christian Music*, pp. 56, 83, 92; Johnson, unpublished ms., pp. 81–89.

53. Moses Chase, "Dill Pickle Blues," *Campus Life*, June–July 1974, pp. 43–45; Steve Rabey, "Rewind: Randy Matthews: Unplugged, But Still Rockin'," *CCM*, May 1997, p. 100; Baker, *Contemporary Christian Music*, pp. 57–59.

54. Devlin Donaldson, "Rewind: Pat Terry: Evolution of a Songwriter," *CCM*, July 1997, p. 54; Baker, *Contemporary Christian Music*, p. 39.

55. See Baker, *Contemporary Christian Music*, pp. 87, 104; and the entries "Hope of Glory" (pp. 422–423) and "Liberation Suite" (pp. 528–529) in Powell, *Encyclopedia of Contemporary Christian Music*.

56. Hope was good enough to be signed by the secular label A&M Records in 1972 and serve as the opening act for Alice Cooper during that same year; see David Di Sabatino, *The Jesus People Movement; An Annotated Bibliography and General Resource*, 2nd ed. (Lake Forest, CA: Jester, 2004), p. 153.

57. Philip Yancey, "A Year in the Life of 'E' [sic]," *Eternity*, May 1972, pp. 22–25; Devlin Donaldson, "Rewind: Greg X. Volz," *CCM*, August 1996, p. 60. "e" recorded an album, produced by Scott Ross for his Love Inn's NewSong label, but after completion, the band's keyboard player "backslid," causing the band

to believe the Lord was "not in" their recording; the record was never released (Mark Hollingsworth interview with author, Nashville, TN, July 12, 2002).

58. Enroth, Ericson, and Peters, *The Jesus People*, p. 128. Because of Palosaari's Finnish heritage, the group was received as conquering hippie heroes on their visit to that land (Di Sabatino, "History of the Jesus Movement," pp. 44, 89, n. 34).

59. "Rez Band," in Steve Rabey, *The Heart of Rock and Roll* (Old Tappan, NJ: Fleming H. Revell, 1986), pp. 22–31; Rabey, "A Long Strange Trip: Resurrection Band, a Cornerstone in Christian Rock, Celebrates Its Silver Anniversary," *CCM*, October 1997, pp. 46–48.

60. Bob Hartman interview with author, Franklin, TN, July 10, 2002; Baker, *Contemporary Christian Music*, pp. 68, 76. For a look at Petra's later career, see "Petra," in Rabey, *The Heart of Rock and Roll*, pp. 80–89; and "Petra," in Powell, *Encyclopedia of Contemporary Christian Music*, pp. 692–699.

61. Nancy "Honeytree" Henigbaum Miller telephone interview with author, June 26, 2007; John Lloyd telephone interview with author, February 26, 2010; Devlin Donaldson, "Nancy Honeytree: The Life of a Pioneer," *CCM*, October 1997, p. 56.

62. Interview with Chuck Girard, July 1998, p. 2, hosted on One Way Jesus Music Web site, www.one-way.org/jesusmusic/interviews/girard/girard.htm.

63. Ferraiuolo, "Love Song," p. 83.

64. *Love Song*, Good News Records, 1972.

65. Chuck Girard and Fred Field, "Little Country Church," Dunamis Music, 1971.

66. Bob Cotterell telephone interview with author, February 18, 2005.

67. Chuck Girard, "Chuck Shares about the Songs—A Love Song," on the One-Way.org Web site, http://one-way.org/lovesong/chuksong.htm; Girard interview.

68. S.v. "Love Song" in Powell, *Encyclopedia of Contemporary Christian Music*, p. 545; the Wichita anecdote comes from syndicated Jesus Rock music show host, Frank Baker/Paul Edmondson (telephone interview with author, July 2, 2007).

69. S.v. "Love Song," in Powell, *Encyclopedia of Contemporary Christian Music*; see pp. 543–547.

70. Larry Norman e-mail to author, June 6, 2005; Tim Stafford, "Stranger in a Strange Land," *Campus Life*, March 1977, pp. 44–48, 122–126; "Didn't You Used to Be Larry Norman?" *Campus Life*, April 1977, pp. 30–33, 72–80; "Larry Norman," in Powell, *Encyclopedia of Contemporary Christian Music*, pp. 632–641.

71. Philip Yancey, "The Norman Sound," *Campus Life*, August–September 1971, p. 60; Plowman, *The Jesus Movement*, p. 108.

72. People! *I Love You*, Capitol Records, ST-2924, 1968; Yancey, "The Norman Sound," p. 60.

73. Williams interview; Pederson interview; Enroth, Ericson, and Peters, *The Jesus People*, p. 80.

74. Larry Norman, *Upon This Rock*, Capitol Records, ST-446, 1969; Impact Records, HWS-3121, 1970.

75. "Sweet, Sweet Song of Salvation," by Larry Norman. J.C. Love Publishing, 1969.

76. "I Wish We'd All Been Ready," by Larry Norman. J.C. Love Publishing, 1969.

77. Larry Norman interview, cited in Romanowski, "Rock 'n' Religion," pp. 115–116.

78. Gene Cotton, *Power to Be*, Impact Records, HWS-1984, 1969 (RE-0379); Cotton interview.

79. Larry Norman interview, cited in Romanowski, Rock 'n' Religion, p. 116.

80. For an example, see Larry Norman, "As I See It," *Hollywood Free Paper*, 3, vol. 1, March 16, 1971, p. 4.

81. Larry Norman interview, cited in Romanowski, "Rock 'n' Religion," pp. 117–118.

82. Ibid. The "guesstimate" for sales rings true, given the recollections of one of Norman's largest distributors, Bob Cotterell of Creative Sound, Inc (Bob Cotterell telephone interview with author, February 18, 2005).

83. Norman is mentioned prominently in the *Time* cover story ("The New Rebel Cry: Jesus Is Coming!" June 21, 1971) on pp. 56 and 61. Norman was interviewed at "Faith Festival '71" in Evansville, Indiana by a CBS News crew for the *Roger Mudd Show* (Philip Yancey, "The Norman Sound," *Campus Life*, August–September 1971, pp. 60–61). Much of this interview—sounding as if it was taped live off a television set—can be heard on Norman's album *Bootleg* (One-Way Records, JC-4847, 1972).

84. Larry Norman, "Why Don't You Look into Jesus?" Strawbed Music, 1972.

85. Larry Norman, "Why Should the Devil Have All the Good Music?" Strawbed Music, 1972.

86. Norman was once quoted to the effect that *Only Visiting* had sold about 30,000 copies in total (Larry Norman interview, cited in Romanowski, "Rock 'n' Religion," p. 119).

87. For information on Jeremy Spencer, Mylon LeFevre, Glenn Schwartz, and just about every Jesus music and CCM artist from the 1960s into the early twenty-first century, see Mark Allen Powell's stunningly comprehensive *Encyclopedia of Contemporary Christian Music* (Peabody, MA: Hendrickson, 2002).

88. "Peter, Me, and Mary" (Noel Paul Stookey interview), *Campus Life*, May 1972, pp. 52–58; Bob Combs, "Paul Stookey on ...," *Campus Life*, June 1972, pp. 44–47, 114, 116; Bob Combs, "Paul Stookey: Dylan Told Him about the Bible," *Campus Life*, June–July 1975, pp. 28–29.

89. The song went as high as #24 on the Billboard music charts in the fall of 1971 (Whitburn, *Billboard Book*, p. 405) and became a staple of American wedding ceremonies—particularly within the evangelical world—into the 1990s. For Stookey's later Christian releases, see, for example, *Real to Reel*, Neworld Records, MWS-090477, 1977; Billy Ray Hearn interview.

90. Devlin Donaldson, "Rewind; Barry McGuire," *CCM*, April 1996, p. 55.

91. Whitburn, *Billboard Book*, p. 281.

92. Barry McGuire with Bob Combs, "Eve of Destruction," *Campus Life*, October 1974, pp. 44–47, 70–71; Baker, *Contemporary Christian Music*, pp. 71–73; Donaldson, "Rewind," p. 55.

93. Steve Rabey, "Age to Age," *CCM*, July 1998, p. 19; Baker, *Contemporary Christian Music*, p. 93; *Glass Harp*, Decca Records, DL-75261, 1971.

94. Scott Ross with John and Elizabeth Sherrill, *Scott Free* (Old Tappan, NJ: Chosen, 1976), pp. 145–146; Baker, *Contemporary Christian Music*, pp. 93–94. Phil Keaggy, *What a Day*, New Song, NS-001, 1974.

95. *How the West Was One*, Myrrh Records, MSY-6598, 1977.

96. For a good analysis of both the cultural and economic forces that have shaped the popular music business in the United States, see Philip H. Ennis, *The Seventh Stream: The Emergence of Rock "n" Roll in American Popular Music* (Hanover, NH: Wesleyan University Press, 1992). For insight into the role of technology in this process, see Andre Millard, *America on Record: A History of Recorded Sound* (New York: Cambridge University Press, 1995).

97. Russell A. Sanjek, *American Popular Music and Its Business: The First Four Hundred Years, Volume 3 from 1900 to 1984* (New York: Oxford University Press, 1988), p. 507; "Stan Moser: Direction for the '80s," *Contemporary Christian Music*, January 1981, p. W-22: As of 1973, Word's sales—after the creation of Myrrh Records—stood at under $12 million (see "Religious Disk Gave Publisher a Start," *New York Times*, September 9, 1973, p. 26).

98. See Romanowski, "Rock 'n' Religion," pp. 106–109. For an example of Word Records' marketing in evangelical periodicals, see the ad on the back cover of the August 1968 issue of *Christian Life*.

99. See Colleen McDannell, *Material Christianity* (New Haven, CT: Yale University Press, 1995), pp. 246–247; see also John P. Ferre, "Searching for the Great Commission: Evangelical Book Publishing since the 1970s," in Quentin J. Schultze, ed., *American Evangelicals and the Mass Media* (Grand Rapids, MI: Zondervan, 1990), pp. 99–116.

100. Ad for Creative Sound Records, *Campus Life*, September 1972, p. 13; "Know Your Publishers," *Bookstore Journal*, October 1971, pp. 56–57; Bob Cotterell interview.

101. Cotterell interview; ad for Creative Sound, *Campus Life*, September 1972, p. 13.

102. Cotterell interview.

103. Sanjek, *American Popular Music*, Vol. 3, p. 367.

104. Ibid., pp. 367, 585.

105. "Honeytree" interview; Romanowski, "Rock 'n' Religion," pp. 117, 124.

106. Romanowski, "Rock 'n' Religion," pp. 127–128.

107. Hearn interview.

108. Hearn interview; Randy Matthews, *I Wish We'd All Been Ready*, Word Records, 1971, WST-8547.

109. Hearn interview. Randy Matthews, *All I Am Is What You See*, Myrrh Records, MST-6502, 1972; *Crimson Bridge*, Myrrh Records, MST-6503, 1972; *First Gear*, Myrrh Records, MST-6505, 1972; Barry McGuire, *Seeds*, Myrrh Records, MST-6519, 1973; *Honeytree*, Myrrh Records, MST-6523, 1973; Malcolm & Alwyn, *Fool's Wisdom*, Myrrh Records, MST-6518, 1973; Randy Matthews, *Son of Dust*, Myrrh Records, MST-6515, 1973.

110. Hearn interview.

111. Ibid.; the sticker practice remained a standard marketing ploy of the evangelical record industry into the mid-1980s.

112. Hearn interview; Break-even figure cited in Steve Chapple and Reebee Garofalo, *Rock 'n' Roll Is Here to Pay: The History and Politics of the Music Industry* (Chicago: Nelson-Hall, 1977), p. 174.

113. 2nd Chapter of Acts … *with footnotes*, Myrrh Records, MST-6526, 1974.

114. Devlin Donaldson, "Rewind: 2nd Chapter of Acts," *CCM*, January 1996, p. 65; Baker, *Contemporary Christian Music*, pp. 70–71.

115. "Annie Herring" s.v., in Powell, *Encyclopedia of Contemporary Christian Music*, pp. 411–412; Devlin Donaldson, "Rewind: 2nd Chapter of Acts." The term *song receiving* was used in a bio on Herring's Web site, www.annieherring.com/.

116. Donaldson, "Rewind"; Baker, *Contemporary Christian Music*, pp. 70–71.

117. Hearn interview.

118. Annie Herring, "Easter Song," Latter Rain Music and Word Music, Inc., 1974.

119. Hearn interview; Romanowski, "Rock 'n' Religion," pp. 135–136.

120. Hearn quoted in Romanowski, "Rock 'n' Religion," p. 136.

121. Hearn interview; Romanowski, "Rock 'n' Religion," p. 136.

122. Benchmark sales figures cited in Romanowski, "Contemporary Christian Music," in Schultze, ed., *American Evangelicals and the Mass Media*, p. 153; Hearn interview. Barry McGuire, *Lighten Up*, Myrrh Records, MST-6531, 1975; Honeytree, *The Way I Feel*, Myrrh Records, MST-6530, 1974; Michael Omartian, *White Horse*, ABC-Dunhill/Myrrh, MSA-6564, 1974; *Petra*, Myrrh Records, MST-6527, 1974.

123. Romanowski, "Rock 'n' Religion," pp. 134–135.

124. Hearn interview.

125. Sanjek, *American Popular Music, Volume 3*, p. 561; Hearn interview.

126. Ronald L. Johnstone, "Who Listens to Religious Radio Broadcasts Anymore?" *Journal of Broadcasting*, 16, no. 1, Winter 1971–1972, pp. 93, 97–98; Jim Palosaari, "The Christian Radio-Record Connection: Will the Circle Be Unbroken?" *Contemporary Christian Music*, May 1981, pp. 42, 46, 48.

127. S.v. "Radio and Television Commission," in *Encyclopedia of Southern Baptists*, vol. 3, p. 1933.

128. Edmondson interview; Baker, *Contemporary Christian Music*, pp. 46–48.

129. Ibid.

130. See letter to editor from Dale R. Yancy, *Cornerstone*, 3, no. 2, 1975, p. 6; Baker, *Contemporary Christian Music*, p. 109.

131. Scott Ross interview with author, Virginia Beach, VA, August 20, 2002. Uncataloged tape recordings—most of them still on the original reel-to-reel tapes—are contained in the Scott Ross Cultural Collection in Regent University's library, Virginia Beach, Virginia. For typical examples of the Ross program from which examples in this paragraph are taken, see SRS#164, Tape ENT 275 (ca. spring 1973); SRS#165, Tape ENT 279 (spring 1973); SRS #201 "C," Tape ENT 376 (ca. Nov./Dec. 1973); SRS# 272 "B," Tape ENT 629 (ca. late 1974/early 1975); for additional insights into Ross's relationship with Eric Clapton, see the Ross interview and Christopher Sandford, *Clapton: Edge of Darkness*, updated edition (New York: Da Capo, 1999), pp. 110, 117, 130.

132. "Scott Ross Show," SRS#189 "A," Tape ENT 312 (ca. fall 1973).

133. "Scott Ross Show," Tape 287 "F" (audio cassette), side B (ca. August 1975).

134. Found on Ross's CBN Web site, www.cbn.com/700club/scottross/feedback/Looking_Back.aspx.

135. Survey response by Roger McGlaughlin, West Chester, OH, submitted December 23, 2002.

136. Scott Ross interview; Ross with Sherrill and Sherrill, *Scott Free*, pp. 139, 145–146, 155.

137. Baker, *Contemporary Christian Music*, p. 90.

138. "KYMS: Flagship of a New Movement," *Contemporary Christian Music*, June 1979, p. 17; Baker, *Contemporary Christian Music*, pp. 89–90.

139. Baker, *Contemporary Christian Music*, p. 92. By the end of 1976, several other stations had adopted at least a partial Jesus music format, including WQLH in San Bernardino, CA; WYFC in Ann Arbor, MI; WINQ in Tampa–St. Petersburg, FL; KBIQ in Seattle, WA; WYCA in Hammond, IN; KSON in San Diego, CA; and, WZZD in Philadelphia, PA (Romanowski, "Rock 'n' Religion," n. 62, p. 214).

140. Sam Smith interview with author, Aurora, IL, May 23, 2002; Dave Bunker interview with author, East Dundee, IL, July 2, 2002; Baker, *Contemporary Christian Music*, p. 94. The FCCM would splinter in the late '70s over the growing tensions between "ministry-oriented" and "industry-oriented" factions within the organization.

141. Ad for first "Christian Artists Music Seminar & Camp," *Christian Life*, April 1975, p. 13.

142. Plowman, *The Jesus Movement*, pp. 110–111; Baker, *Contemporary Christian Music*, p. 83.

143. Edward E. Plowman, "Shore to Shore Wave of Witness," *Christianity Today*, May 7, 1971, p. 34.

144. See, for example, "The Great Camp Meeting in 1973," *Christianity Today*, July 6, 1973, p. 48; and "Farm Fellowship," *Christianity Today*, August 30, 1974, pp. 36–38; Baker, *Contemporary Christian Music*, pp. 85–87.

145. "Jesus People Gather in Paradise to Praise Him," *Bucks County* [PA] *Courier Times*, August 19, 1973, p. 12; "Jesus '75: The Spirit Lives On," *Christianity Today*, September 12, 1975, pp. 54–55.

146. Hartman interview.

147. See, for example, "Jesus '75: The Spirit Lives On"; "Kentucky Weekend," *Christianity Today*, May 23, 1975, p. 58; Baker, *Contemporary Christian Music*, pp. 86–87.

148. Frank Edmondson telephone interview with author, October 5, 2007; Edmondson interview, July 2, 2007.

149. *Harmony* 1, no. 1, May 1975.

150. Romanowski, "Rock 'n' Religion," pp. 197–198. For a history of *Contemporary Christian Magazine* (now *CCM*) from 1979 through early 1998, see Doug Threaten, "Cover to Cover," *CCM*, April 1998, pp. 48–50.

151. S.v. "Chuck Girard," Powell, *Encyclopedia of Contemporary Christian Music*, pp. 362–363; s.v. "Richie Furay," p. 348.

152. Larry Norman, *So Long Ago the Garden*, MGM Records, SE-4942, 1973; *In Another Land*, Solid Rock Records, 1976; Randy Stonehill, *Welcome to Paradise*, Solid Rock Records, 1977; Hearn interview; Romanowski, "Rock 'n' Religion," p. 166.

153. Caban interview.

CHAPTER 9

1. *The Soul Hustler*, a Burt Topper Production, American Films, 1973.

2. Ibid.

3. Dick Kleiner, "Hard Work Marks the Independents," *Kokomo* [IN] *Tribune*, March 26, 1972, p. 4; ad in the *Clovis* [NM] *News-Journal*, July 17, 1974, p. 20; "The Soul Hustler," Internet Movie Database, www.imdb.com/title/tt0074377/.

4. "New Musical to Open in S.F. May 23," *Times* (San Mateo, CA), April 26, 1972, p. 25; Robert Taylor, "Jesus Freak Musical," *Oakland Tribune*, May 25, 1972, p. 21; Barbara Bladen, "The Marquee," *Times* (San Mateo, CA), May 25, 1972, p. 17; Chris Curcio, "Musical Lacks Polish," *Hayward* [CA] *Daily Review*, May 30, 1972, p. 21.

5. *Can Ellen Be Saved?* ABC Circle Films, 1974; "Today's TV Highlites," *Gastonia* [NC] *Gazette*, June 8, 1974, p. 10; Internet Movie Database, www.imdb.com/title/tt0071272/.

6. R. Rozeanne Knudson, *Jesus Song* (New York: Delacorte, 1973).

7. See, for example, Chris Stratton, *Gunsmoke* (New York: Popular Library, 1970); *Adam-12: Dead on Arrival* (New York: Award, 1972).

8. Richard Hubbard, *The Jesus Freaks* (New York: Pyramid, 1972).

9. For a contemporary look at the Jesus People movement in Britain, see Geoffrey Corey, *Jesus Bubble or Jesus Revolution: The Growth of Jesus Communes in Britain and Ireland* (London: British Council of Churches Youth Department, 1973).

10. "The Jesus Evolution," *Time*, September 24, 1973, p. 80.

11. (Kevin) John Smith, "The Origins, Nature, and Significance of the Jesus Movement as Revitalization Movement" (PhD diss., Asbury Theological Seminary, 2002), pp. 323, 344; for the One-Way Inn, see the *Adelaide Jesus Paper*, vol. 1, no. 1, September 1973.

12. Smith, "The Origins, Nature," p. 345.

13. Ibid., p. 109.

14. David Di Sabatino, "John Smith and the God Squad Down Under," in Di Sabatino, *The Jesus People Movement: An Annotated Bibliography and General Resource*, 2nd ed. (Lake Forest, CA: Jester, 2004), pp. 215–217; Smith, "The Origins, Nature," p. 304, quote on p. 163.

15. See Smith, "The Origins, Nature," particularly pp. 310–399.

16. "Hot Coffee, Donuts Free for Parade," *Pasadena* [CA] *Star-News*, December 21, 1973, p. D1.

17. Shiloh statistics cited in David Tabb Stewart and James T. Richardson, "Mundane Materialism: How Tax Policies and Other Governmental Regulation Affected Beliefs and Practices of Jesus Movement Organizations," *Journal of the American Academy of Religion*, December 1999, p. 827.

18. Marion S. Goldman, "Continuity in Collapse: Departures from Shiloh," *Journal for the Scientific Study of Religion*, 34, 1995, p. 342.

19. Joe V. Peterson, "Jesus People: Christ, Communes, and the Counterculture of the Late Twentieth Century in the Pacific Northwest" (Master's thesis: Northwest Christian College, 1990), p. 48; Timothy Miller, *The 60s Communes: Hippies and Beyond* (Syracuse, NY: Syracuse University Press, 1999), p. 95.

20. James T. Richardson, Mary W. Stewart, and Robert B. Simmonds, eds., *Organized Miracles: A Study of a Contemporary, Youth, Communal, Fundamentalist Organization* (New Brunswick, NJ: Transaction, 1979), pp. 44–45; Joe V. Peterson, "The Rise and Fall of Shiloh," *Communities: Journal of Cooperative Living*, Fall 1996, p. 61; Stewart and Richardson, "Mundane Materialism," p. 831; Peterson, "Jesus People," p. 56.

21. "The Jesus Evolution," *Time*, pp. 80, 85.

22. Ronald M. Enroth, "Where Have All the Jesus People Gone?" *Eternity*, October 1973, pp. 14–17, 28.

23. Richard N. Ostling, "The Jesus People Revisited," *International Review of Missions*, 63, April 1974, pp. 232–237; Ed Plowman, "Whatever Happened to the Jesus Movement?" *Christianity Today*, October 24, 1975, p. 46. "Whatever Happened

to...Young 'Jesus People' Moving On," *U.S. News & World Report,* March 29, 1976, p. 49.

24. Ostling, "The Jesus People Revisited"; quotes found on pp. 234 and 232, respectively.

25. "Whatever Happened to...Young Jesus People," p. 49.

26. See Appendix.

27. Ed Plowman, "Whatever Happened," p. 46.

28. For the best examination of the rise and fall of the Shepherding movement's vision and the theological network it spawned, see S. David Moore, *The Shepherding Movement: Controversy and Charismatic Ecclesiology* (London: T & T Clark, 2003).

29. Ibid., p. 50.

30. Scott Ross interview with author, Virginia Beach, VA, August 20, 2002; Moore, *The Shepherding Movement,* pp. 89–90.

31. David Di Sabatino, "Lonnie Frisbee: A Modern Day Samson," in Di Sabatino, *The Jesus People Movement,* p. 209; Connie Bremer-Murray telephone interview January 7, 2013; for Lonnie Frisbee's take on the Shepherding experience see Lonnie Frisbee with Roger Sachs, *Not by Might nor by Power* (Santa Maria, CA: Freedom, 2012), pp. 137–145; Moore, *The Shepherding Movement,* pp. 51, 88.

32. Ron and Vicki Burks, *Damaged Disciples: Casualties of Authoritarian Churches and the Shepherding Movement* (Grand Rapids, MI: Zondervan, 1992), p. 91.

33. Survey response by Patrick Bowen, submitted July 9, 1998.

34. Survey response by Arthur Cook, Chicago, IL, submitted April 20, 2004.

35. Survey response by Brian Carling, Gaithersburg, MD, submitted August 5, 1998.

36. Kirsten Scharnberg, "Commune's Iron Grip Tests Faith of Converts," *Chicago Tribune,* April 1, 2001, p. 15; see also Ronald M. Enroth, *Recovering from Churches That Abuse* (Grand Rapids, MI: Zondervan, 1994), pp. 121–136, 142–145, 150–153.

37. Scott Ross interview; survey response by Barbara Pilato Haschmann, Rochester, NY, submitted May 7, 2002.

38. Carling survey response.

39. Robert Digitale, "An Idea Whose Time Has Gone?" *Christianity Today,* March 19, 1990, pp. 38, 40, 42; Randy Frame, "Maranatha Disbands as Federation of Churches," *Christianity Today,* 34:5, March 19, 1990, pp. 40–42; S.v. S. David Moore, "Shepherding Movement," in Stanley M. Burgess and Eduard M. Van Der Maas, eds., *The New International Dictionary of Pentecostal and Charismatic Christianity* (Grand Rapids, MI: Zondervan, 2002).

40. By the mid-1970s, the number of first marriages for those ages 18 to 24 had dropped by nearly 40% since the immediate postwar years (*Statistical Abstract of the United States, 1976,* table no. 97, p. 68). However, this was more reflective of a growing trend toward the postponement of marriage than the erosion

of the institution itself. See Arlene Skolnick, *Embattled Paradise: The American Family in an Age of Uncertainty* (New York: Basic Books, 1991), pp. 90–91, 168.

41. D'Arcy Fallon, *So Late, So Soon: A Memoir* (Portland, OR: Hawthorne, 2004), p. 113.

42. Joan Jallette Pritchard telephone interview with author, June 26, 2008.

43. Steven Derek Preston, "Who's Ever Heard of a Hindu Biker?" *Cornerstone*, 4:22, 1975, 10.

44. CWLF fund-raising letter, pp. 1–2, ca. 1974; Kent Philpott Collection.

45. *Antioch Ranch News Sheet*, March 1971, pp. 1, 3.

46. Kent Philpott, Journal, ca. late 1970, p. 102; Kent Philpott Collection.

47. Kent Philpott, newsletter, November 18, 1971, p. 1; Kent Philpott collection.

48. Kent Philpott, newsletter, ca. May 1975, p. 2; Kent Philpott collection.

49. "Kris" to Bobbie Philpott, July 14, 1974, p. 5; Kent Philpott collection. For an account of the strains that communal life put on married Jesus People couples, see the account of D'Arcy Fallon, a former member of the Lighthouse Ranch who eventually left the fold and evangelical Christianity, in *So Late, So Soon.*

50. Telephone interview with John Higgins, February 18, 2013; Richardson, Stewart, and Simmonds, *Organized Miracles*, pp. 35, 62–68, 84–85.

51. Richardson, Stewart, and Simmonds, *Organized Miracles*, p. 133; Higgins interview.

52. Of respondents to a survey, 11.3% claimed to have earned a graduate degree at some point (see Appendix). National figures of U.S. population holding bachelor's degrees found in *Educational Attainment in the United States: 2003* (Washington, DC: U.S. Census Bureau, 2004), p. 1.

53. Kent Philpott newsletter, November 18, 1971, p. 1.

54. Gordon Lewis interview with author, Cerritos, CA, August 3, 2002.

55. Survey response by Stephen Jay Briggs, Hendersonville, NC, submitted May 29, 2002.

56. "What the Jesus People Say about Themselves," article from *Falls News* (Cuyahoga Falls, OH), reprinted in *Jesus Loves You*, ca. 1973, pp. 6–7; "Jesus Free Store," *Jesus Loves You*, no. 18, ca. 1974, p. 10.

57. Craig Yoe telephone interview with author, July 13, 2004; survey response by John White, Kent, OH, submitted January 28, 2002.

58. James T. Patterson, *Great Expectations: The United States, 1954–1974* (New York: Oxford University Press, 1996), pp. 785–786.

59. Carroll, *It Seemed Like Nothing Happened* (New Brunswick, NJ: Rutgers University Press, 1982), pp. 127–132.

60. David Frum, *How We Got Here: The 70's: The Decade That Brought You Modern Life—For Better or Worse* (New York: Basic Books, 2000), pp. 291, 294.

61. Murph Lloy, "Like Man, It's So Beautiful," *Winnipeg* [MB] *Free Press*, June 5, 1971, p. 11; Ron Campbell, "Ex-Jesus Freak Seeks New Life," *Winnipeg* [MB] *Free Press*, January 25, 1974, p. 8.

62. Minutes of the Meeting of the Board of Directors of Evangelical Concerns, Inc., March 14, 1974; May 1, 1975; financial statement, Evangelical Concerns, Inc., December 10, 1976.

63. "Fulfilling a Financial Need," fund-raising memo from Duane Pederson to board members of the *Hollywood Free Paper*, February 10, 1972, Hollywood Free Paper Collection, Box 7, Folder 7, Archives and Special Collections, Hubbard Library, Fuller Theological Seminary, Pasadena, CA.

64. *Hollywood Free Paper*, 3:15, ca. Summer 1971, p. 3; Duane Pederson interview with author, Lake Los Angeles, CA, August 2, 2002; "Jesus People International–Distribution of Expenditures–1972," spreadsheet, Hollywood Free Paper Collection, Box 7, Folder 8, Archives and Special Collections, Hubbard Library, Fuller Theological Seminary.

65. For a good look at the general rise and fall of the underground newspaper, see Abe Peck, *Uncovering the Sixties: The Life and Times of the Underground Press* (New York: Pantheon, 1985).

66. Pederson interview.

67. Lynne M. Isaacson, "Delicate Balances: Rearticulating Gender Ideology and Rules for Sexuality in a Jesus People Communal Movement" (PhD diss., University of Oregon, 1996), pp. 50–51.

68. Ibid., pp. 44–45.

69. Stewart and Richardson, "Mundane Materialism," p. 831.

70. Isaacson, "Delicate Balances," pp. 46–48.

71. Higgins interview.

72. Isaacson, "Delicate Balances," pp. 46, 48.

73. Goldman, "Continuity in Collapse," p. 343; Peterson, "Jesus People," p. 57; quote found in Isaacson, "Delicate Balances," p. 54.

74. Web article "Shiloh," http://www.shiloh-shuffle.com/shiloh.htm (accessed November 20, 2000), photocopy of article in possession of author; Stewart and Richardson, "Mundane Materialism," p. 828; Higgins interview.

75. Karen Castillo interview with author, Olympia, WA, October 18, 2002.

76. The Internal Revenue Service, quoted in Peterson, "Jesus People," pp. 49–50.

77. Timothy Miller, *The 60s Communes: Hippies and Beyond* (Syracuse, NY: Syracuse University Press, 1999), pp. 95–96; Stewart and Richardson, "Mundane Materialism," pp. 828–833; "Shiloh" article.

78. Timothy Miller, *The Hippies and American Values* (Knoxville, TN: University of Tennessee Press, 1991), p. 3; for a good thumbnail sketch of the counterculture's enduring legacy, see pp. 125–144.

79. A contemporary view of the changing nature of American youth culture in the early 1970s and its more self-absorbed attitude is provided in Daniel Yankelovich, *The New Morality: A Profile of American Youth in the 1970s* (New York: McGraw Hill, 1974).

80. Joel Whitburn, *The Billboard Book of Top 40 Hits*, 8th ed. (New York: Billboard, 2004), pp. 189, 197, 417. Mead's "Lord's Prayer"—which one imagines by dint of

her being a nun probably sold quite well to Catholic youth—reached as high as #4 on the Billboard charts.

81. John Street, *Rebel Rock: The Politics of Popular Music* (London: Blackwell, 1986), pp. 172–174.

82. Jon Trott, "Life's Lessons: Part Three," *Cornerstone*, 23:105, 1994; Shawn David Young, "Jesus People USA, the Christian Woodstock, and Conflicting Worlds: Political, Theological, and Musical Evolution, 1972–2010" (PhD diss.: Michigan State University, 2011), pp. 44–50; Young's dissertation provides a good look at the changes and developments within JPUSA into the first decade of the twenty-first century.

83. Bill Squires telephone interview with author, October 3, 2002; CWLF fund-raising newsletter, ca. late 1973. See various issues of *Right On!* for insights into the CWLF operation.

84. Fr. Gordon Walker interview with author, Franklin, TN, July 10, 2002; Fr. Peter Gillquist interview with author, Warrenville, IL, March 23, 2002. Gillquist's book, *Becoming Orthodox: A Journey to the Ancient Christian Faith* (Ben Lomond, CA: Concilar, 1992, rev. ed. 2002), is a good guide to the history of Sparks's and friends' search for the true Christian church and their ultimate decision to go Orthodox.

85. Sharon Gallagher interview with author, Berkeley, CA, August 6, 2002; Squires interview.

86. Gallagher interview; Squires interview.

87. Jack Sparks, "Androloclean Outlook," *Right On!* September 1975, p. 4; Jack Sparks letter to CWLF supporters, ca. September 1975.

88. See Gillquist, *Becoming Orthodox*.

89. David Gill interview with author, Oakland, CA, August 6, 2002; Squires interview. *Right On!* became *Radix* in the fall of 1976. The Berkeley-based Spiritual Counterfeits Project began publishing its *Spiritual Counterfeits Journal* in 1977.

90. Martin Meyer "Moishe" Rosen interview, San Francisco, CA, August 7, 2002; Ruth A. Tucker, *Not Ashamed: The Story of Jews for Jesus* (Sisters, OR: Multnomah, 1999), pp. 84–92.

91. For an example of the concern and analysis that Jews for Jesus triggered within the Jewish community, see Moshe Adler, "Alienation and Jewish Jesus Freaks," *Judaism* 23, Summer 1974, 287–297; Samuel Z. Fishman, ed., *Jewish Students and the Jesus Movement: A Campus Perspective* (Washington, DC: B'nai B'rith Hillel Foundations, 1973); and Robert A. Cohen, "Infiltrating the Jews for Jesus," *Jewish Digest*, February 1979, pp. 8–12.

92. Tucker, *Not Ashamed*, p. 100; Rosen interview.

93. Tucker, *Not Ashamed*, p. 193.

94. Donald E. Miller, *Reinventing American Protestantism: Christianity in the New Millennium* (Berkeley: University of California Press, 1997), p. 34; survey response by Jim and Betty Willems, CA, submitted November 13, 2002.

95. Miller, *Reinventing American Protestantism*, p. 34.
96. Brought out in Sherwood Eliot Wirt, *For the Love of Mike: The Michael McIntosh Story* (Nashville, TN: Thomas Nelson, 1984), pp. 127–128.
97. Miller, *Reinventing American Protestantism*, pp. 34–37.
98. Wirt, *For the Love of Mike*, pp. 154–155.
99. Miller, *Reinventing American Protestantism*, pp. 46–48. Interestingly, the hyper-charismatic tendency toward "signs and wonders" among these churches had begun at a series of meetings in 1980 led by Smith's irrepressibly charismatic ex-colleague, the "hippie preacher" Lonnie Frisbee, who by that time had extri-cated himself from the shepherding movement and made a brief return to Calvary Chapel (Di Sabatino, "Lonnie Frisbee," pp. 209–211; see also Di Sabatino's docu-mentary video, *Frisbee: The Life and Death of a Hippie Preacher*, Jester, 2005).
100. Miller, *Reinventing American Protestantism*, pp. 48–50.

CHAPTER 10

1. Kenneth L. Woodward, "Born Again! The Year of the Evangelicals," *Newsweek*, October 25, 1976, 68–78.
2. Ibid.
3. Sales figures ca. 1978 cited in Don Cusic, *The Sound of Light: A History of Gospel and Christian Music* (Milwaukee: Hal Leonard, 2002), p. 295.
4. Jay R. Howard and John M. Streck, *Apostles of Rock: The Splintered World of Contemporary Christian Music* (Lexington: University Press of Kentucky, 1999), pp. 75–77; Steve Rabey, "Amy Grant," in *The Heart of Rock and Roll* (Old Tappan, NJ: Fleming H. Revell, 1986), pp. 100–107; S.v. "Amy Grant" in Mark Allen Powell, *Encyclopedia of Contemporary Christian Music* (Peabody, MA: Hendrickson, 2000), pp. 373–379.
5. William Romanowski, "Rock 'n' Religion: A Socio-Cultural Analysis of the Contemporary Christian Music Industry," PhD diss., Bowling Green University, 1990, p. 231.
6. Howard and Streck, *Apostles of Rock*, p. 44.
7. Ibid.
8. Lorraine Ali, "The Glorious Rise of Christian Pop," *Newsweek*, July 16, 2001, p. 41.
9. Gospel Music Association Industry Overview 2009, http://www.gospelmusic. org/images/uploads/factsForms/2009_Industry_Overview.pdf (accessed June 17, 2010), copy in possession of the author.
10. Mark Joseph, *The Rock & Roll Rebellion* (Nashville, TN: Broadman & Holman, 1999), p. 14.
11. Carlton Young, "Church Music, American Style: What's Ahead?" *Christian Ministry*, March 1977, p. 8; see also Emil Bailet, "Sing a New Song," *Pentecostal Evangel*, January 30, 1972, pp. 18–19.

12. Chuck Fromm, "New Song to Contemporary Christian Music Entertainment," Master's thesis, Fuller Theological Seminary, 1996, p. 74.

13. *Maranatha! Music Praise Chorus Book*, 1st ed. (Costa Mesa, CA: Maranatha! Music, 1983); the book's most recent edition, its fourth, was published in 1997.

14. John Michael Talbot was a product of the Jesus People movement who became a lay Franciscan brother in the late '70s and who has churned out a number of devotional and often sacramental-themed albums over the years. S.v. "John Michael Talbot" in Powell, *Encyclopedia of Contemporary Christian Music*, pp. 919–923. Michael Card was a Nashville native whose "El Shaddai" was recorded by Amy Grant in 1982 and won Card a Dove award for Songwriter of the Year. In the 1980s, his serious, biblical-based songs won a large following among age twenty-five and older evangelicals. S.v. "Michael Card" in Powell, *Encyclopedia of Contemporary Christian Music*, pp.137–139. In 1996, Talbot and Card teamed up for a best-selling album, *Brother to Brother*.

15. The story behind "Great Is the Lord" can be found in Lindsay Terry, *The Sacrifice of Praise: Stories behind the Greatest Praise and Worship Songs of All Time* (Brentwood, TN: Integrity, 2002), pp. 23–26.

16. An excellent overview of the development of the "worship wars" can be found in Michael S. Hamilton, "The Triumph of the Praise Songs: How Guitars Beat Out the Organ in the Worship Wars," *Christianity Today*, July 12, 1999, pp. 28–35.

17. The most influential blast against praise music is perhaps Marva Dawn, *Reaching Out without Dumbing Down* (Grand Rapids, MI: Eerdmans, 1995). The best counterblast from the other side thus far has been John M. Frame, *Contemporary Christian Music: A Biblical Defense* (Phillipsburg, NJ: Presbyterian & Reformed, 1997).

18. *King of Fools* (Sparrow, 1998) is one of Delirious's more popular U.S. releases; *Hosanna! Shout to the Lord (Live)* (Sony, 1998) is representative of the HillSongs "school" of praise and worship music.

19. For a look into the growing move toward praise music releases in the CCM world, see, for example, Melissa Riddle, "O for a Thousand Tongues!" *CCM*, March 1998, pp. 34–36, 38, 40, 42, 44. See also the the Gospel Music Association Industry Overview 2008.

20. See, for example, Jeff Godwin, *Devil's Disciples: The Truth about Rock Music* (Ontario, CA: Chick, 1986).

21. "Ask the Superintendent—Ministering to Today's Youth," *Enrichment Journal*, http://enrichmentjournal.ag.org/200101/0101_006_superintendent.cfm.

22. See any *CCM* magazine during the early to mid-1980s—much of mainstream CCM was oriented toward the New Wave music of the period.

23. For an early look into the rise of Christian metal, see the article on the band Stryper by Steve Rabey, "A Christian 'Heavy Metal' Band Makes Its Mark on the

Secular Music Industry," *Christianity Today*, February 15, 1985, pp. 45–47. *HM* magazine's Web site is located at www.hmmagazine.com/.

24. See, for example, Debra Akins, "Christafari: Reggae Music for Searching Masses," *CCM*, February 1995, p. 26; see also Christifari's Web site at www.christafari.com/.

25. For insight into the Christian Goth movement, see the Web site of the Decatur, Illinois, Church of the Living Dead, www.thefirstchurchofthelivingdead.com.

26. For a look at the world of Christian rap, see http://www.rapzilla.com/ and the Internet radio station www.christian-hiphop.net/.

27. For a guide to all things evangelical hipster, as well as a theological and cultural discussion of the phenomenon from an evangelical viewpoint, see Brett McCracken, *Hipster Christianity: When Church and Cool Collide* (Grand Rapids, MI: Baker, 2010).

28. Colleen McDannell, *Material Christianity: Religion and Popular Culture in America* (New Haven, CT: Yale University Press, 1995), p. 247.

29. Ibid., p. 246.

30. Heather Hendershot, *Shaking the World for Jesus: Media and Conservative Evangelical Culture* (Chicago: University of Chicago Press, 2004), p. 21; McDannell, *Material Christianity*, p. 259. See also the website for CBA, the Association for Christian Retail at www.cbaonline.org/nm/media.htm.

31. Hendershot, *Shaking the World for Jesus*, p. 21. Populist gadfly Jeremy Rifkin was one of the first to notice and write about the parallel evangelical culture in his book (with Ted Howard), *The Emerging Order: God in the Age of Scarcity* (New York: Ballantine, 1983). A perceptive, in-depth examination of the phenomenon that came out the next year was Carol Flake, *Redemptorama: Culture, Politics, and the New Evangelicalism* (New York: Doubleday, 1984).

32. Daniel Radosh, *Rapture Ready! Adventures in the Parallel Universe of Christian Pop Culture* (New York: Soft Skull, 2010), pp. 118–132; Marc Peyser, "God, Mammon and 'Bibleman,'" *Newsweek*, July 16, 2001, p. 47; Hendershot, *Shaking the World for Jesus*, pp. 40–45; box office figures for *Jonah* found at www.boxofficemojo.com/movies/?id=veggietales.htm. See also the book by Veggie Tales creator, Phil Vischer, *Me, Myself, and Bob: A True Story about Dreams, God, and Talking Vegetables* (Nashville, TN: Thomas Nelson, 2008).

33. Robert A. Cook, "What about Hollywood Movies?" *Youth for Christ Magazine*, April 1957, pp. 15–16.

34. Ted Baehr, the son of cowboy film star "Cowboy Bob Allen" (Ted Baehr Sr.), began publishing his *Movieguide* newsletter in 1985.

35. A Barna Group research study cited in "The Gospel According to Spider-Man," *Time*, August 16, 2004, p. 72.

36. See, for example, James Y. Trammel, "Who Does God Want Me to Invite to See 'The Passion of the Christ'? Marketing Movies to Evangelicals," *Journal of Religion and Media*, 9:1, January 2010, pp. 19–29.

37. Figure cited in Donald E. Miller, *Reinventing American Protestantism: Christianity in the New Millennium* (Berkeley: University of California Press, 1997), p. 50.

38. Figure cited in Miller, *Reinventing American Protestantism*, p. 19.

39. Figures taken from listing of congregations cited on Calvary Chapel's official Web site, http://calvarychapel.com/.

40. According to Miller, *Reinventing American Protestantism* (p. 35), the median attendance of Calvary Chapel in the mid-1990s was 138 per congregation, although six of the churches—not counting Calvary Chapel–Costa Mesa, for which Miller, curiously, never gives an attendance estimate (the church's Web site estimated weekly attendance at 25,000 in 2010)—had a combined weekly attendance of almost 48,000. Counting Calvary Chapel–Costa Mesa at, say, 15,000, adding the figures for the next six largest congregations, and then counting the rest of the 1,100 Calvary Chapels of 2010 at the mid-'90s level produces a conservative guesstimate well over 200,000 Calvary Chapel attendees.

41. For a look at the phenomenon of the Toronto blessing as it evolved at the Toronto Airport Vineyard and the clash that eventually came with the denomination, see Margaret Paloma, *Main Street Mystics: The Toronto Blessing and Reviving Pentecostalism* (Lanham, MD: AltaMira, 2003).

42. Miller, *Reinventing American Protestantism*, pp. 19, 50.

43. Compare this to the figures cited in Eileen W. Lindner, ed., *Yearbook of American & Canadian Churches: 2005* (Nashville, TN: Abingdon, 2005), pp. 366–377, for the Baptist General Conference (145,000), Christian Reformed Church (136,000), Cumberland Presbyterian Church (83,000), and the Wesleyan Church (114,000). Statistics on current international Vineyard churches are found on the Vineyard's Web site www.vineyardusa.org/site/about/vineyard-history.

44. Miller, *Reinventing American Protestantism*, pp. 21–22.

45. Ibid., pp. 6–9.

46. Ibid., pp. 21–22.

47. Ibid., see pp. 1–2.

48. Fred W. Beuttler, "Revivalism in Suburbia: 'Son City' and the Origins of Willow Creek Community Church, 1972–1980," in Michael J. McClymond, ed., *Embodying the Spirit: New Perspectives on North American Revivalism* (Baltimore: Johns Hopkins University Press, 2004), pp. 170–175.

49. Scott Pederson telephone interview with author, May 24, 2005.

50. Lynne and Bill Hybels, *Rediscovering Church: The Story and Vision of Willow Creek Community Church* (Grand Rapids, MI: Zondervan, 1995), p. 27.

51. Beuttler, "Revivalism in Suburbia," p. 175; see also Hybels and Hybels, *Rediscovering Church*, pp. 43–72.

52. Beuttler, "Revivalism in Suburbia," p. 194.

53. See Hybels and Hybels, *Rediscovering Church*, pp. 91–146 for basic historical information on Willow Creek up until the mid-90s.

54. The 2005 statistics are cited in "One Church's Way," *Business Week*, May 23, 2005, p. 84.

55. Survey response by Louis Berry, Vallejo, CA, submitted May 12, 2000.

56. Survey response by Milton Resh, Taylor, MI, submitted November 12, 2001.

57. Survey response by Peggy Hillick, Robbinsville, NY, submitted May 21, 2002.

58. See Appendix.

59. Survey response by Dan Brady, Flagstaff, AZ, submitted March 6, 1998.

60. Survey response by Susie Melkus, Omaha, NE, submitted November 27, 1999.

61. Survey response by Mitch Bright, Hobart, IN, submitted July 5, 2002.

62. Survey response by Doug McCleary, Sunnyside, WA, submitted March 20, 1998.

63. Survey response by Carolyn Barta, Jasper, GA, submitted June 8, 1998.

64. Survey response by Bill Overpeck, Terre Haute, IN, submitted May 14, 1998.

65. Survey response by Joe Stephen McNair, Kyle, TX, submitted January 28, 2000.

66. Survey response by Paul Basden, Frisco, TX, submitted February 2, 2003.

67. See Appendix.

68. Gallup Poll data cited in Timothy Miller, *The Hippies and American Values* (Knoxville: University of Tennessee Press, 1991), p. 134.

69. See Appendix.

70. Study cited in "The New Morality," *Time*, November 21, 1977, pp. 111–116.

71. Robert S. Ellwood Jr., *One Way: The Jesus Movement and Its Meaning* (Englewood Cliffs, NJ: Prentice-Hall, 1973), p. 132. For an example of popular press speculation in this regard, see the article about what is apparently an influx of registrations from Tony and Susan Alamo's Christian Foundation in Saugus, California: "Youth in Sects on Coast Registering Republican," *New York Times*, April 16, 1972, p. 36.

72. See Appendix.

73. Ibid.

74. Preston Shires, *Hippies of the Religious Right* (Waco, TX: Baylor University Press, 2010); see especially pp. 180–201; quote found on p. 209.

75. Sociologist Lynne Isaacson makes exactly this point in her study of the Shiloh communal network's attitudes, stating that its members believed that "social activism seemed irrelevant in light of Christ's imminent return" ("Delicate Balances: Rearticulating Gender Ideology and Rules for Sexuality in a Jesus People Communal Movement," PhD diss., University of Oregon, 1996, p. 40). This same observation could have undoubtedly been applied across almost the entire Jesus People movement.

76. Survey response by Freddie Rodriguez, Salem, OH, submitted June 1, 2000.

77. Survey response by Grace Mullen Cook, Johnson City, TN, submitted June 26, 2003.

78. Survey response by Mark R. Weston, Gainesville, FL, submitted April 4, 1999.

79. Survey response by Paul Reilly, Lawrenceville, NJ, submitted July 21, 2002.

80. Survey response by Jeanne Clark, Renton, WA, submitted January 20, 2001.

81. Survey response by Sharon Hanson, Puyallup, WA, submitted January 24, 2001.

82. Survey response by "Summer," Glenpool, OK, submitted May 27, 2000. As she was obviously too young to have actually taken part in the movement during the 1960s and 1970s, Summer's answers were not counted as part of the statistical sample used in the Jesus People survey (see Appendix).

Index

Made in the USA
Monee, IL
23 March 2023

30354757R10233